Czechoslovak Academy of Sciences

PLAN AND MARKET UNDER SOCIALISM

T0300079

Scientific Editor
George Shaw Wheeler

Reviewer
Bedřich Levčík

PLAN AND MARKET UNDER SOCIALISM
Ota Šik

Routledge
Taylor & Francis Group

LONDON AND NEW YORK

First published 1967 by International Arts and Sciencs Press, Inc.

Reissued 2018 by Routledge
2 Park Square, Milton Park, Abingdon, Oxon OX14 4RN
711 Third Avenue, New York, NY 10017, USA

Routledge is an imprint of the Taylor & Francis Group, an informa business

A Library of Congress record exists under LC control number: 66023896

ISBN 13: 978-1-138-03795-3 (hbk)
ISBN 13: 978-1-138-03791-5 (pbk)
ISBN 13: 978-1-315-17758-8 (ebk)

CONTENTS

5

PREFACE The main ideas in this book originated some time in 1957–1958 — the period when the first reorganization of planning and management in Czechoslovakia was being prepared. Even at that time, the deeper analyses of the growing economic contradictions and the disclosure of their causes were leading me to recognize the fact that the maturing socialist economy and the advanced social division of labour, following on the industrially developed capitalist economy in this country, would inevitably require a thorough-going use of socialist market relationships. It became more and more clear that insufficient use of market relationships and limitations on the economic functions of prices resulted in one-sided, immediate production stimuli in the enterprises, and were also bound up with the over-simplified, mainly quantitative, approach to planning social production, an approach which neglected questions of efficiency.

But at that time views concerning the necessity for a new concept of socialist market relationships and their relation to socialist planning could not yet be applied. The notion that planning under socialism must absolutely exclude any influence of the market on production was still much too strongly entrenched. Proposals about a broader use of instruments such as profit, prices, etc., were only very timidly advanced, without managing to expose the harmfulness of the one-sided system of planning indicators, orienting production chiefly on volume and not getting the real effect of using the market. Moreover, the growing economic contradictions were not yet so evident that the theoretical conclusions derived from an analysis of them could refute the over-simplified economic concepts in a convincing way. Under such conditions, it was inevitable that insufficiently balanced proposals for changing methods of planning were put forward, although they contained some progressive suggestions for broader use of economic instruments in management. The compromises made in linking these progressive elements with the old administrative methods in planning and management, which — as was later seen — proved to be very persistent, choked off the new elements.

Although there are much more favourable conditions today for the acceptance of quite new and progressive economic views in theory and practice, it still would be a mistake to underestimate the resistance of old, rigid ideas and deep-rooted habits in the management. Some might doubt whether it is possible to assure successful development of a socialist economy with completely different methods from those we have become accustomed to in the years of extensive economic development, when it was usual to judge the quality of planning and management according to whether the planned rates of growth were carried out or exceeded, and not by the internal harmony of the real economic development. Merely making critical remarks about the directive methods of the past system of management is sometimes taken as an attack on the fundamentals of socialist management.

Actually, "directive and administrative system of management" was used to denote a type of management of production (either direct or indirect) that takes too little account of the essential economic relationships, tries to do away with the different superficial negative phenomena by giving direct orders, without uncovering and overcoming the deeper and recurring causes. It overlooks the possibilities of arousing initiative by recognizing people's fundamental interests. These administrative elements in management themselves weakened, in fact, the advantages of a socialist economy — it was not scientific criticism that did it harm.

Naturally, criticizing the shortcomings in an administrative type of management by directives is not to deny the success of past development of a socialist economy. Only a metaphysician insists on having phenomena either black or white, and wants every judgment to be unambiguously "good" or "bad". In reality, every phenomenon has its internal contradictions and not even the progressive development of a socialist economy can be free from some internal contradictions.

The stage of socialist economic management that we have just passed through was necessarily affected by the times and could not get ahead of itself. In it were seen both the new, immensely progressive and vital forces of the oncoming socialist society, and also the inevitable weaknesses of a process that was just beginning and which lacked experience as well as theoretical knowledge. Furthermore, the methods of the "cult" had deleterious effect. The completely new social system developing under these conditions had in it much that was positive in this process which, as never before, erased all private barriers and class divisions, but at the same time could not help but be an over-simplified, one-sided process with more revolutionary will than new economic findings.

This type of management assured a mighty and rapidly growing socialist production and, with it, increasing consumption and a rising standard of living. This in itself demonstrated the vitality and progressive nature of the socialist economy. But it could not prevent the rise and growth of certain economic contradictions, just because of the one-sided directive forms and the fact that not enough attention was given to various essential economic relationships. Any increase in contradictions must at a certain moment become a brake on further rapid economic development, and this is what happened. Disclosing these shortcomings in management and criticizing them does not mean criticizing the fundamentals of a socialist system, but the negative aspects and features of the process of management. Unless these are purposefully and determinedly eradicated, we cannot rapidly overcome the serious economic contradictions or develop the economy successfully.

This study of socialist market relationship cannot give an exposition of the economic activity which would smoothly bring about these relationships. Instead it is designed to present — proceeding from the knowledge of the necessary forms of solving some fundamental economic contradictions — the necessary, although not yet applied, forms of economic activity which would really make use of market relationships. This is not a discussion of the relations that are consciously observed in the planned management of a socialist economy, but a theoretical exposition of the necessary changes in this planned system which would make it possible to put these relations in effect and help to solve the growing economic contradictions.

Only if there is a critical approach to socialist economic practice, can a Marxist economy maintain its scientific nature. But we cannot make a theoretical exposition depend on whether it will be put in practice immediately or not. Not even under socialism can we assume that every new theoretical finding, even the most correct, will be put immediately in practice, without opposition. Completely new theoretical views will become common property only by degrees. But each scientifically justified study stimulates Marxist theoretical thinking and, in one way or another, contributes to the cognition of our reality.

This work, *Plan and Market Under Socialism*, is not simply a translation of the book which appeared in Czech in 1964 under the title, *On the Problems of Socialist Commodity Relations*,[1] but has been revised and supplemented. The two years that have elapsed since the Czech edition have made possible not only further theoretical work, but also intensive collective work on the actual preparation of a new system of economic management in Czechoslovakia. Participating in this work of application — if we may call it that — where we had to think through the economic relationships in great detail, and also draw up quantitative models, and go through a continual clash of ideas and discussion, inspired me to make more precise some of my original views and to arrive at new theoretical findings.

Particularly in the chapters on planning, on the special features of socialist market relationships and on prices, I have made a number of important changes and additions which deepen or clarify my original ideas. The chapter on money is completely new; these problems were presented in over-simplified form in the Czech edition, and were influenced by the previous theoretical concepts that prevailed in socialist countries. Another new section is the analysis of the foregoing economic development in Czechoslovakia, without which the reader

---

[1] O. Šik, *K problematice socialistických zbožních vztahů*, Prague 1965.

abroad would fail to understand many theoretical approaches and conclusions.

I deliberately devoted considerable attention to somewhat philosophical problems of the relation between the general and the individual, as well as the long-term and the short-term in planning, because in my opinion one cannot understand the role of central economic planning without understanding these relationships. We must understand that a central governing body can successfully guide only the *long-term* development of *aggregated* and *generally conceived* economic phenomena in order to free ourselves from the administrative concept of planning by detailed directives. But even those who deny the significance of any economic planning, because they are influenced by the negative aspects of the previous forms of administrative planning in socialist countries, can be helped by this exposition to recognize the compatibility of central macroeconomic planning with independent specific management of production in the enterprises — with market relationships.

It seems that even in the sphere of prices there is a possibility for, and an advantage in, linking the free movement of *individual* specific prices with a planned orientation of aggregated, general price groups. In brief, it is again found that a philosophical expression of such abstract relationships as the relation between the general and the individual, between the essential and the specific phenomenon, between the necessary and the random, etc., is not just a philosophical toying with ideas as an end in itself, but something of great significance methodologically, serving to bring deeper comprehension and mastering of even such rational economic problems, seemingly unrelated to philosophy, as the problems of the optimum price trend, production programs, production capacities, market demand, etc.

An enormous amount of theoretical literature has been devoted to questions of economic planning, the market, prices, financing, etc. To avoid a complete splintering of the already quite complex positive exposition of my own ideas, it was necessary to refrain as far as possible from polemics with other theoretical standpoints within the text, or even to take up a position on them. I have therefore attempted in the introductory chapter to summarize some theories which I think have played the greatest role in solving the problems of the plan and the market under socialism, either in the negative or the positive sense. I am aware that I must have overlooked at the same time one or another idea that some will consider just as important and fundamental. But it was not my purpose to write a historical treatise on the development of these economic theories. If this study will contribute toward a deeper understanding of the need for specifically new forms of planning and for using market relationships under socialism, and if it makes for theoretical certainty in putting these new forms into effect and in their practical application, it will have served its purpose.

OTA ŠIK

I DEVELOPMENT OF A SOCIALIST MARKET THEORY AND ITS PRACTICAL APPLICATION IN CZECHOSLOVAKIA

Socialist economic theory is of extraordinary importance for the socialist economy, more so than any theory has ever been for any society in history. Actually, it is the first time that an economy is being formed purposefully from its very foundations, according to certain — although abstract — theoretical ideas. Naturally, these theories, further enriched and developed by practical experience, help again to improve practice itself. But some basic concepts of Marxist economic theories, among which is the idea that socialist planning and the market mechanism are mutually exclusive, have so far remained untouched by socialist economic experience.

As long as the socialist economy in which this theory was consistently applied was developing more or less smoothly and successfully, as long as there were no important obstacles to its development, there was no impulse to replace or invalidate this theory; even more — there was no doubting of its correctness. Not until important economic problems began to pile up in recent years in the Czechoslovak socialist economy — and to a greater or lesser degree in other socialist states — together with numerous analyses of these problems, did doubts as to the correctness of this theoretical concept begin to emerge, along with broader theoretical studies criticizing or rejecting it.

In order really to refute such a basic theoretical idea as was one of the pillars of socialist economic theory, and as has almost become an axiom in the minds of whole generations of Marxists and of the socialist public in general throughout many years of socialist economic practice, it is not enough just to make superficial criticism. There must be an attempt at deeper analysis and a well-integrated approach to show that this theory and its practical application are among the main reasons for the economic difficulties that have been generally arising. We must attempt to disclose their erroneous or oversimplified premises and replace this theory with another, one that is more true to life.

But before one can proceed to criticize the previous theoretical concepts of the mutual relationship of socialist planning and the market mechanism, and to concretize this by giving examples of experiences in the development of a socialist economy, we must show, at least briefly, how this theory has developed, what are the main specific views that have crystallized and predominated and why these are incorrect or inadequate. In doing so, we shall not make a historical study or trace all the ideas and opinions that have been expressed on the given problem, but only sketch the origin of those theories that have had a decisive influence on socialist economic practice up to the present day. Many theories that formerly prevailed were erroneous, as we shall try to show, more from a purely logical point of view or from the standpoint of the shortcomings that today are perfectly obvious at first glance. We shall try to bring out the deeper refutation in the course of the whole work, both in the analysis of former practical experience and in the positive exposition of our own theoretical views.

We should like to remind the readers that we have already attempted to disclose the most fundamental methodological errors and incorrect theoretical roots of the Stalin market concept under socialism in *Economics, Interests, Politics*[1] to which this work is, in a certain sense, a sequel. The experience we had in first publishing articles about socialist market relations in 1958 proved that Stalin's conception of commodity-money relationships, based on a specific concept of abstract categories of "production relations" and "ownership", is strongly entrenched. This is because he was able to build up an integrated and closed theoretical system, based on an oversimplified and erroneous treatment of these two categories — very

[1] O. Šik, *Ekonomika, zájmy, politika*, Prague 1958.

fundamental and important in Marxism — by a purely deductive method of formal logic. In this system his commodity-money theses form a strong link, difficult to refute. Whole generations of Marxists have completely accepted this simplified idea of "production relationships" and "ownership" and, together with this, accepted Stalin's views on commodity-money relations as the most logical and correct. For this reason, it was necessary, before starting to present our views on socialist market relationships, to make a deeper analysis of the above-mentioned most fundamental and generally accepted Marxist economic categories and thus challenge Stalin's erroneous methodology. Even though we were not yet able to shake off some dogmatic sediment when we wrote *Economics, Interests, Politics*, and were decidedly affected by the political atmosphere that prevailed when the book was written and published, still the general analysis and criticism of these two categories, "production (economic) relationships" and "ownership", was correct.

The present book, in which we shall try to show concretely the errors of Stalin's commodity-money views, proceeds as follows: first, a brief survey of the development of the most widespread Marxist ideas about commodity-money problems under socialism, then their practical application and the consequences of Stalin's views, using the Czechoslovak socialist economy as an example (and realizing that these experiences have more general validity). We shall also try to refute the former over-simplified concept of socialist planning which was logically connected with the strict rejection of the market mechanism under socialism. And, finally, we shall explain our concept of the reasons for the existence and the essence of socialist commodity-money (market) relations, and some general principles for practical application of these new views.

1 Prevalent Marxist Views on Market Relationships under Socialism

Marx and Engels, the founders of Marxist economic theory, were the first to express their views on the fate of commodity-money relationships in a future socialist society, foreseeing that socialism would logically come into being. They thought that commodity-money relationships would disappear together with the private ownership of means of production, and that they would no longer exist in a new socialist society.

Of course, in their time, the only way they could arrive at their conclusions was by deduction from findings in regard to private commodity production. They knew of only two forms of commodity production in history: the simple (production by small craftsmen or the market production by farmers, prevailing up to the time of capitalist production), and the capitalist commodity production, the substance and general characteristics of which they analysed and interpreted in great detail. In doing so, they recognized a certain economic contradiction between private and social labour which lay at the base of the two historical forms of commodity production, and in this they perceived the reason for the existence of these two forms. This economic contradiction appeared to them to be inseparably linked with private ownership which was also the common essence of both simple and capitalist commodity production. Therefore, they arrived at the logical conclusion that, when private ownership would disappear and thence the contradiction between private and social labour, commodity production would then also disappear.

Let us recall very briefly the Marxist analysis of the general substance and the main characteristics of simple and capitalist commodity production, not just to revive these basic theoretical ideas, but also for a better understanding of the universal principles of commodity production when we come later to a description of socialist problems.

Characteristic of both forms of private commodity production is the existence of separate, relatively independent, partial cooperation in production which arose through a spontaneous social division of labour. The labour is not expended purposefully as a part of social labour. Producers have no precise information about the amount and character of the work done by the others, about the finished products, the needs of the others, etc. None of the producers manufacture all the necessary material things (nor all the necessary means of production, nor the objects of consumption) for themselves alone. They can exist as people, consume and produce, only because they produce for one another.

They do, it is true, work directly as independent, private producers, but, in actual fact, they produce for society and are dependent on society. In this sense, their labour is of a social nature. But it is not expended as part of social labour, purposefully determined in advance. Whether their products are or are not socially useful, is not decided until they reach the market and are sold or left unsold. Therefore Marx called this labour indirect social labour.

Work is done under conditions where it is not in and of itself a vital necessity to human beings; it is performed only to gain the necessary use values in exchange and therefore is the most essential part of exchange. Under the given conditions, everyone is willing to expend labour for others or produce material things for others only if he obtains in exchange the products he himself needs. Each can obtain the material things from others only in an amount to which the labour that was socially necessary for their production corresponds to the socially necessary amount of labour he himself had to expend on the production of material things for others. These exchanged material goods are commodities.

If we express the socially necessary amount of labour for the production of a certain type of commodity (certain use values) as *value*, we may briefly express the substance of this law of exchange as follows: Each obtains, on the average, from other commodity producers commodities of a value corresponding to the value of the goods he produces for others. That is a very general formulation of the law of value, or the essence of commodity exchange.

Here there exists, of course, a mutual dialectical relationship between value and use value that appears in the concrete forms of exchange conditions, i.e. prices (where there is money exchange) and in their deviations from the value basis. We are not here elaborating all price theory and the Marxist interpretation of the market mechanism in private commodity production, but merely recall Marx's interpretation of the general basis for private commodity production.

Marx, of course, also clarified the differences between simple and capitalist commodity production.

In the first place, there is only a slight partial cooperation in simple commodity production. It would be more precise, perhaps, to speak of independently and separately producing individuals whose specific production is the result only of the basic development of social division of labour. Not even such individuals, of course, produce entirely alone, but at least with the cooperation of some members of the family. In this sense, one may speak here also of partial cooperation.

At first these cooperative units in handicrafts themselves produced the necessary means of production. Gradually, however, social division of labour proceeded far enough even in this primitive initial mode of commodity production that the craftsmen ceased to manufacture the necessary means of production themselves and began to exchange their own commodities for them, in addition to the necessary consumer goods. In this way, not only the specific production of means of production originated, but also the spontaneous distribution among the different spheres of production through the medium of commodity exchange.

Capitalist commodity production differs from simple commodity production in that it has large working cooperative units. These cooperative units, in which large numbers of producers worked together, arose because a large volume of means of production accumulated, by means of commodity exchange, in the hands of individuals. On the other hand, there came into being a great number of people who had no means of production and few consumer goods. A part of the people, therefore, had the possibility of buying up, in return for their products, not only the necessary consumer goods and means of production, but also the labour power of the expropriated people. They were able to gather these people under their supervision, with the means of production they had purchased and, first, simple cooperation, then a developing and detailed division of labour (within the cooperation) and, with the aid of more and more modern machine technique, evolve highly productive large-scale industry. By selling goods for their value, the owners of these new factories gained the possibility of continually appropriating part of this value that exceeded the value of the labour power they had paid for, or surplus value.

Under simple commodity production, the producer is himself the seller of the goods and the immediate stimulus for this production work and sales is the obtaining of the necessary use values for his continued production, i.e., personal and production consumption.

Under capitalist commodity production, the one who sells the goods (the legal owner) is not, at the same time, the immediate worker, and the stimulus for his entrepreneurial activity is no longer the obtaining of the necessary use values from others, but the process of expanding (constantly getting more and more surplus value). From this specific fact there comes the necessity to transform the value of goods (as the basis of exchange relations) to a capitalist production price, which does not essentially contradict the law of value. It continues to be constantly materialized *labour* that makes up the actual essence of exchange relations of commodities and which, for every change in its productive forces, brings corresponding changes in production prices.

While simple and capitalist commodity production have their own particularities, which I have attempted to recall briefly, their common characteristics, which also have common reasons for being, can be summed up as follows: the production is made up of separate, independent, partially cooperative units, producing indirectly, independent of one another, specific products (on the basis of a social division of labour) for a relatively unknown social demand. There is a contradiction, therefore, between the hidden fact that they are all producing as links in a single social work for one another, and that they must produce in proportions determined by the necessity to satisfy, by total social labour, the over-all social needs that always appear in certain proportions, that they must produce with a productive force that is always determined by the prevailing production conditions in society, etc., and the fact immediately emerging on the surface that they are producing privately, without knowledge of these hidden social inter-relationships, without full knowledge of others' production, without complete knowledge of social needs. But, while this is not only without knowledge of all these social conditions, it is also with the predominant private interest of making use of all contradictions in production and in the market for themselves, for their own profit and with an attempt to cause their competitors' failure. This is the economic contradiction that was discovered by Marx, which lies at the base of private commodity production, which makes necessary commodity relations and the law of value as the historical form of its solution, a contradiction that can be briefly characterized as the contradiction between social and private labour.

Under capitalism it appears as the contradiction between social labour and private appropriation.

From the intensification of this capitalist contradiction, which also, of course, has its social and political reflection, Marx derived the necessity to go over from capitalism to socialism, which would definitively overcome this contradiction. Here social appropriation would correspond to social labour — as Marx foresaw it — so that social labour would cease to be indirect, covertly social labour and would become direct, conscious, planned social labour. It was quite logical that, from this deduction, the conclusion would be drawn that commodity production would also be done away with, as an expression of private labour, as an expression of the inability to expend labour directly and in a planned way on a scale that covered all of society. At the same time that would be the necessary form of solving the contradiction between social and private labour.

It was a logical conclusion under conditions where socialism was only a theoretical idea, necessarily very abstract and general. The founders of scientific socialism could not, in their time, foresee in every detail the profound and complex inter-relationships within a socialist economy, nor did they set this as their task. They knew no other commodity production than private, and could not — as we can today — proceed from the reality of socialism and arrive, by generalization and comparison, at the conclusion that it is not the contradiction between private and social labour that is the most fundamental reason for the existence of commodity production, but necessarily a still deeper, more generally expressed contradiction, which lies at the base of commodity production. They could not know that the contradiction between social and private labour is only a historic form expressing this hidden contradiction, which then has still another, special appearance in a socialist economy, and therefore has also special socialist commodity-money or market relations as a result.

Only a dogmatic concept of Marxist-Leninist theory could lead one to deny the existence of certain new phenomena for the reason that they were not expressed and clarified at some time by the founders of Marxism. A scientific, creative conception of Marxism-Leninism, one which does justice to the real, scientific, methodological significance of this theory, requires its constant development and its constant enrichment by generalizing the findings in regard to new, actual phenomena. So it is not those who deny the existence of socialist commodity relationships because this contradicts the letter of doctrine drawn up by the classic writers of Marxism-Leninism, who are in harmony with the spirit of that philosophy, but those who, in accord with the realities, clarify the theory of these commodity relationships and thus help in their practical use and development.

It is understandable that, until socialist countries appeared, commodity production was, in the minds of Marxists throughout the world, linked with private property, and that the idea prevailed that it would disappear when socialist economies were built, being replaced by some sort of direct exchange or direct distribution of goods. The idea that building a socialist economy would mean replacing commodity relationships by a direct communist distribution of goods was widespread even after the October Revolution.[1]

But the necessity of developing commodity relationships between socialist industrial or trade organizations and the private farmers became plain. It was necessary to assure the development of production as fast as possible in a country that had been disrupted and laid waste in the long years of war, civil war, and the unparalleled plundering in the counter-revolutionary period. The masses of peasants, particularly, had to be interested in reviving agricultural production. Therefore it was necessary, first of all, to give the peasants the possibility of selling all their surplus products (on excess of the taxes in kind) on the market for cash, and at the same time to assure their purchases of the most necessary products of industry for the money obtained. Lenin recognized that only such a development of commodity exchange would make it possible to assure gradually the most

---

[1] "Born along on the crest of the wave of enthusiasm, rousing first the political enthusiasm and then the military enthusiasm of the people, we reckoned that by directly relying on this enthusiasm we would be able to accomplish economic tasks just as great as the political and military task we accomplished. We reckoned — or perhaps it would be truer to say that we presumed without reckoning adequately — on being able to organize the state production and the state distribution of products on Communist lines in a small-peasant country directly by an order of the proletarian state. Experience has proved that we were wrong." V. I. Lenin, "Fourth Anniversary of October Revolution," *Selected Works*, II, Part 2, Foreign Languages Publishing House, Moscow 1952, p. 601.

needed foodstuffs and raw materials for the towns, and on this basis in turn get back the industrial goods to the villages. This was necessary, in other words, to assure the necessary economic consolidation, revival, and, finally, advance, throughout the country.[1] The development of this commodity exchange between the socialist state enterprises and the private farmers was one of the essential characteristics of the new economic policy (NEP), which proved fully successful.

Lenin very early recognized, on the basis of the initial experiences of the Soviet State, that commodity-money relationships must be utilized. He pointed out the importance of cost accounting (Khozraschot) for the enterprises and considered that this was not just a simple accounting method for keeping records, but inseparably connected it with a utilization of the material interest of the enterprises. Unfortunately, he did not have time to elaborate this more deeply theoretically, giving the reasons for this method of management of the enterprises, and so he was unable to prevent the later oversimplifying and formalizing.

However, the utilization of the commodity-money relationships in the period of transition from capitalism did not mean that an end was put to the theoretical concept linking these relationships with private production, envisaging their elimination when private ownership was done away with. Even the re-introduction of market relationships in the NEP period was understood merely as a temporary retreat before the needs of the private farmers and handicraft producers, which, of course, compelled also the introduction of a commodity economy and cost accounting in socialist enterprises. It was quite logical, therefore, that, after collectivization had been achieved and private production had disappeared in the Soviet Union, the demands by theorists again emerged for the liquidation of commodities and currency and their replacement by a direct exchange of products.

---

[1] "…in essence the small peasant can be satisfied in two ways. In the first place, a certain freedom in circulation of goods is necessary, freedom for the small private entrepreneur, and in the second place goods and product must be supplied. What kind of freedom of circulation of goods would there be if we had nothing to circulate, and what kind of freedom of trade would there be if nothing to trade!" V. I. Lenin, "The Tenth Congress of the Communist Party (B) of Russia," *Writings*, vol. 32, p. 223 of edition in Czech.

Stalin did play a progressive role in opposing these speculative and sectarian ideas,[1] and defended the necessity of continuing to retain market relationships. But, in doing so, he committed another very important theoretical error which, to a certain degree, was a result of the state of the Soviet economy at the time (very limited extent of highly concentrated and mainly new industrial production arising in the midst of a clear predominance of agricultural production). This had a great effect for many years, not only in the subsequent trends in economic practice in the USSR, but also on the later economic development in all the other socialist countries. He outlined the theoretical concept that commodity-money relations are indeed an alien element in a socialist economy and are forced into being by the private ownership psychosis of the farmers who had not yet been transformed into socialist producers, even by collectivization. Market relationships must be tolerated only because they are necessarily brought by the existence of a "cooperative form of socialist ownership, a lower, insufficiently thorough-going socialist form."

In saying this, Stalin had as his point of departure the practical experiences that not only could production in highly concentrated new industry be directly managed, but that its products could be directly distributed again within industry. In contrast, all impediments on commodity exchange between town and country that would mean that farmers had not sufficient possibility of freely purchasing industrial goods would reduce their interest in increasing agricultural production and lead to stagnation in its development. Every development in commodity relations, purchasing of agricultural production by state organizations for money and the possibility of free purchase of industrial goods by the farmers, etc., led to a rapid development of agricultural production. The conclusion drawn from these practical experiences (confirmed later by the experiences of other socialist

[1] "Then we had to overcome prejudices of another kind. I have in mind the Leftist chatter that has gained currency among another section of our functionaries to the effect that Soviet trade is a superseded stage; that it is now necessary to organize the direct exchange of products, that money will soon be abolished, because it has become mere tokens; that it is unnecessary to develop trade, since the direct exchange of products is knocking at the door." J. Stalin, "Report to the Seventeenth Congress of the C.P.S.U. (B.)", *Problems of Leninism*, Foreign Languages Publishing House, Moscow 1947, p. 494.

states) was that at a socialist stage of development a market exchange between town and country must be fully and effectively developed. But the theoretical explanation of the necessity for commodity relations under socialism went no farther than this immediate experience. The thing that was most immediate and evident, the necessity for organizing commodity exchange between town and country, in order to assure a sufficiency of agricultural products, food for the town and raw materials from agriculture for industry, was taken generally as the explanation of the necessity for commodity relationships under socialism. In the period when differences of opinion were arising, in 1932–34, Stalin explained in essence the necessity to develop socialist trade and to use currency by the impossibility of organizing the direct exchange of products, for which a full development of Soviet trade must prepare the ground and for which conditions would arise only in the period of transition to communism.[1]

Stalin, therefore, was of the opinion that it was only the existence of kolkhozes that compelled the existence of market relationships, that socialist industry could get along without them, and that it is necessary to develop the trade outlets and organization of state trade to be later transformed into an instrument for direct exchange of goods in kind, and, finally, for direct distribution of products among enterprises and individuals.

Much later, Stalin expressed this opinion again in a more developed form, in connection with the famous discussion preparatory to issuing the *Textbook of Political Economy* in 1951. His comments on the *Textbook* were later published under the title, *Economic Problems of Socialism in the USSR*. Here again he gave the existence of two forms of ownership, the public or state ownership and the group or collective farm ownership, as the basic reason for commodity relations under socialism. He referred to certain statements by Engels and said

---

[1] "...They do not realize that money is the instrument of bourgeois economy which the Soviet government has taken over and adapted to the interests of Socialism for the purpose of expanding Soviet trade to the utmost, and of thus creating the conditions necessary for the direct exchange of products. They do not realize that the direct exchange of products can replace, and be the result of, only a perfectly organized system of Soviet trade, of which we have not a trace as yet, and are not likely to have for some time." *Ibid.*, pp. 494—5.

24

outright that — if it were not for these circumstances — it would be possible essentially to do away with commodity production.[1]

We see, then, that Stalin quite consistently derived the existence of socialist commodity relations from the existence of different, even though socialist, kinds of owners (the State and the collective farms). This seems to develop further Marx's doctrine on commodity relationships among private owners. Just as consistently, Stalin denied the commodity nature of exchange relationships within the state sector, between socialist state enterprises, because here there was no question of a relationship between different owners. In this case, he felt, there was only a *formal* likeness to commodity relationships (accounting, keeping records of values), which is derived from the existence of actual commodity relationships between the state and the collective farms or in external trade relationships with other states. At the same time, he believed that even the market relations between state and cooperative enterprises should be driven as soon as possible from the Soviet economy and liquidated as a remnant of the past, or should be changed in the first place into "direct exchange of products" (barter) and later into direct distribution of products' (communism).

This Stalinist theory, consistently put in practice during his lifetime, and to a considerable degree still today, has become a deeply rooted dogma which has greatly harmed socialist economic development. It has meant an immense exaggeration and magnifying of the particular quality of socialist production, a quality which, in its real, essential character, does indeed substantially distinguish socialist commodity production from private. But when this quality is magnified in a speculative way, this leads in practice to a crippling of the commodity character of socialist production and has as result an immense sharpening and very grave intensification of certain internal contradictions of this production.

---

[1] "It follows from this that Engels has in mind countries where capitalism and the concentration of production have advanced far enough both in industry and in agriculture to permit the expropriation of *all* the means of production in the country and their conversion into public property. Engels, consequently, considers that in *such* countries, parallel with the socialization of *all* the means of production, commodity production should be put an end to. And that, of course, is correct." *Economic Problems of Socialism in the U.S.S.R.*, Foreign Languages Publishing House, Moscow, p. 14. Emphasis in original.

Let us, for the time being, point out only the most obvious errors and the basic shortcomings of this theory.

According to Stalin, commodity relationships exist under socialism, because there is, on the one hand, state ownership and, on the other, collective farm ownership, because the state and the collective farmer stand opposed to each other. This argument limps at the very beginning, in opposing the two owners to each other. In reality, these relationships are much more complicated. For one thing, there is not just one collective owner, but a large number of individual cooperatives that, secondly, do not face one state owner, but a large number of state producers' enterprises and trade organizations, state administration, institutes, etc., with which the collective farms form individual and separate market relationships. The decisive factor is, however, the circumstance that the socialist state is the representative of all the working people, including the cooperative farmers, and cannot be set opposite them as some alien owner with whom they exchange the results of their work.

The basic error in Stalin's arguments is in the metaphysical concept of ownership itself. He did not conceive of it as a process of appropriating nature by means of a certain social mode of production, constantly appearing both in a certain conscious and legal relation of persons to things, and by means of these things to one another. He thought of it as a conscious relation of persons to things, not defined and accounted for in greater detail.

The process of appropriation of nature creates not only relations of persons to nature (things), but at the same time economic relations among persons, by means of which arise the legally separate owners of things. And it is these economic relations that form the basis for certain legal forms of ownership that must become the core of our investigations. The goal cannot be reached by a procedure that first sets up two owners (different people with different relations to things) and then, by this *a priori* relation, explain the relations between them.

This method of procedure usually characterizes ownership by the question: "Who decides the use of means of production, who decides on production, etc.?" But the decision maker, the governing body exists under various forms and types of ownership. The difference arises when different interests are made clear, the different aims that are followed by the deciding or governing body. As soon as we pose the question in this way, we see that we cannot remain merely on the surface of phenomena, in the legal or conscious sphere, but must plunge into the depths of economic relationships. If we pose the question: in whose favour does someone decide, what interests does he follow and what relation do his interests have as governing factors to the interests of the actual producers, we must analyse the economic relationships, the position of the pertinent subjects in these relationships and only then on the basis of this can we characterize in more detail the specific role of the given subject, his role in the process of appropriation. This means to answer the question of what the position of people is, whether they are in control or are producers in the appropriation (e.g., in a socialist economy, as distinct from capitalist). This question cannot be answered, of course, merely by the superficial statement that this person decides there and another decides here. It requires an over-all analysis and comparison of the two social modes of appropriation of nature by man, including an analysis of conscious (e.g., legal or political) relationships, but chiefly economic.

In order that someone might own, he must appropriate, in order to own permanently, he must appropriate permanently. For his method of appropriation to differ from others, it must differ not only in law, but primarily because of a difference in economic position. In brief, to appropriate does not only mean to get something by a single legal or illegal act, but to get something permanently by means of certain historically long-term economic relationships in which those who gain have a certain permanent economic position that is continually renewed. And even if the specific economic relationships are always effected by means of acts that have a specific legal expression, the specific nature of these economic relations themselves must be analysed to understand their legal aspect as well.

Explaining socialist relations of ownership means explaining first of all the socialist mode of production on the basis of a certain level in the development of production forces; explaining the necessary economic relationships, including the commodity relations arising from a given level of development of production forces.

In Stalin's thinking, however, commodity relationships were explained by conscious relationships, i.e. the will of people to decide about certain things and not to want to give them to others on a certain way. He said, for example:

"But the collective farms are unwilling to alienate their products except in the form of commodities, in exchange for which they desire to receive the commodities they need. At present the collective farms will not recognize any other economic relation with the town except the commodity relation — exchange through purchase and sale. Because of this commodity production and trade are as much a necessity with us today as they were..."[1]

This is, of course, an un-Marxist approach to the matter. His argumentation arises from the previously ascertained will of the collective farmers, the "acceptability or inacceptability" of commodity exchange for them. As if the existence of commodity exchange could depend on the will of people and were not a necessary, logical process growing out of the specific character of the production process. It is un-Marxist in general to separate some phenomena from the whole interconnections of the interwoven and interacting economic process, without taking account of the particular nature of commodity relationships in a given historical stage and their objectively necessary roles in solving certain economic contradictions. And this is true not only between the state sectors and the cooperatives, but also among the state enterprises.

If we are to disclose incorrect views in economic theory, we must study the laws of socialist production and proceed by the method of abstraction. Abstraction has been and must continue to be the method to help us recognize the essence of necessary economic interconnections that could be, even for a relatively lengthy period, concealed by erroneous economic practice. At the same time, it is impossible to use experimentation on a large enough scale, as it can be in most of the other sciences, especially in a way that demonstrates the existence of some broad and complicated economic interconnections, true of society as a whole. We cannot use experiments to refute the incorrect view that the reason for commodity production at the present stage of socialism is merely the existence of cooperative ownership. Nor would we be able to prove by the elimination of cooperative ownership in some region or district that the existence of this type of ownership had been or had not been the reason for commodity production in the state socialist sector. The adherents to

[1] Stalin, *ibid.*, p. 15.

this opinion will always see that it is the cooperatives in other regions that compel the form of commodity relations in the whole state sector. And to make the experiment of eliminating cooperative production throughout the country would, of course, be nonsense, because it has objective conditions for being and has an economic role to play.

Marx showed the force of abstraction in economic research when, in analysing capitalist commodity production, he had to abstract this from all elements of non-capitalist production (remnants of feudal production, small handicraft production, etc.), in order to demonstrate that certain relationships had their roots in the new capitalist mode of production.

Similarly, in studying socialist commodity production, we cannot make our conclusions depend primarily on cooperative ownership; on the contrary, we must leave out of consideration the particularities of cooperative production in a socialist society and then, only by this mental analysis can we arrive at a conclusion on whether certain relationships are or are not brought about by the cooperatives.

Even when we set aside, in our thinking, the particular qualities of cooperative production, and analysis of over-all socialist production brings us to the conclusion that, at the existing level of development, products cannot be distributed directly in kind among all the workers, but must be distributed indirectly by means of commodity relationships and currency. Of course, opponents will object that in this case currency would no longer be real, actual money, but a unit of calculation. Each unit would be determined by a time unit (according to how many hours had been worked by the worker concerned, or how much these hours would be worth if converted into simple time, and for this each person would receive time slips for which they would receive goods to the same value). Such argumentation attempts to show that currency is real only when cooperative ownership exists. The untenability of this argument is shown by the following reasons for the existence of socialist commodity relations.

According to Stalin, only consumer goods are commodities, because they are sold to members of the opposite "form of ownership" (industrial goods to the farmers and farm products to the workers). But no one is able to say what the difference is in selling, for instance, industrial goods to workers and to farmers. With these ideas of

Stalin's is connected the conclusion that means of production (which, according to Stalin, cannot be sold to farmers) are not commodities, and that when they are sold by one state enterprise to another only a form of commodity seems to appear. This form, in Stalin's view, arises from the need to calculate the labour expended to produce the means of production and to keep records of it in value terms; and when these means of production pass from one state enterprise to another, this does not represent a sale and purchase of a commodity.

At any rate, Stalin's whole argumentation to explain the existence of forms of value within the state sector by the need to keep account of the labour expended in value form, only for the existence of certain commodity relations brought into being by exterior influences, was constantly shown to be incorrect by economic practice itself. The total cost expressed in value form could not and cannot correspond to the actual amount of total labour expended. The real amount of labour contained in means of production never was expressed in the price. Nor did wages express the real amount or kinds of labour expended. There are several reasons for this, but the main one is that prices of means of production taken from the past were gradually changed in all socialist countries, not merely because, or even primarily because, there were changes in the total amount of labour contained in them, but by definite administrative measures (subject to ministerial or other non-economic influences). There has been a certain significance in the reciprocal relations and interchangeability of use values. In one way or another, the price relations and their movement was expressed more by everything else than by the relation and movement of the actual costs of the labour contained in them. Moreover, the very principles of a guided wage policy refute this theoretical conclusion. We cannot, by means of wage expenditures, calculate the actual amount of labour expended, because the workers in certain fields increase their productivity of labour more rapidly than in other fields, which also has an effect on a different development of wages. Regardless of this, wage policy must assure the necessary industrial wage differentials that correspond to other factors, as well as the differences in amount of labour expended in these branches.

But it is not merely or even primarily a matter of not having calculated or kept records of the actual amount of socially necessary labour expended on the products, but that, with this formal concept of value and prices in the enterprises, interest in the most economical production was completely lost, and so was the urge to find the most effective use of the means of production, ways of reducing costs of production and producing new and better products as the needs of the consumer developed. That is to say, the material interest of producers in furthering the socially necessary development of production was lost, an interest that had been emphasized in the NEP period and when cost accounting was introduced into socialist enterprises.

Both from the theoretical point of view and in the concrete method of management used in the past, cost accounting was restricted more and more to serve as an instrument for formally recording data without regard to the basic function, as outlined by Lenin, the use of the material interest of collectives of workers to promote more efficiency in the production processes. The material interest of the enterprise as a collective of producers was being less and less respected in the Stalin era, and the material incentives that would lead to reduction in costs of production and at the same time to the largest volume of created and realized value, corresponding to consumer demand, were very much weakened by the formalized application of cost accounting.

It is true that the enterprises did formally record the costs of production, the gross receipts and the return, but:

1. Their gross receipts did not depend on satisfying the real needs of the customers, their planning of production did not accord sufficiently with the needs of the customers, and often the latter were forced, not only for economic reasons, but also through administrative measures, to purchase what they did not need;

2. The gross receipts of the enterprise did not express the true value of the products, because prices did not correspond to their value. With the formation of prices which were to a considerable extent subjective, where prices were not related to production costs, some enterprises worked at a loss, through no fault of their own, and others had undeserved profits;

3. Enterprises obtained the necessary sums for wages and premiums, as well as for other production needs, according to whether they had fulfilled certain one-sided planning indicators, but independently of the actual value created. Sometimes, even when goods

remained unsalable in stockrooms, or when they had to be sold at great loss on the domestic market — or even more frequently abroad — the enterprises still got their planned amount of money for paying wages and other production needs.

In this way, commodity relations and commodity categories, including cost accounting, became a quite formal matter, entirely in the spirit of the Stalin theory. This meant the loss of the real essence of cost accounting, which was that every enterprise should be compelled to realize the true value in selling its goods, and to cover their main production costs, especially wages.

Stalin's concept, which rejected the idea that commodity relations really existed within the state sector, led necessarily to administrative relationships and administrative forms of management that intensified the contradictions among state enterprises. In the non-economic, administrative model of management, price no longer had its real economic function in the relations among enterprises, but became mainly a mere bookkeeping unit. This led to a situation where price did not resolve conflicts between enterprises, nor did it have the proper effect on demand and supply. The enterprises tend to be interested in higher prices for their products, in order to make possible a higher monetary volume of production, to show higher gross production. But this did not in any way assure an optimum development of production. On the contrary, it conduced to a socially undesirable rise in material costs, a disturbance in production proportions, a brake on technical development, etc. Under Stalin's concept, prices lost their meaning and became mere bookkeeping units, separating their movement from their economic basis.

It is the sum of the most essential laws of economic relationships among economic processes, characterizing a certain historically specific economic movement that we call *economic relationships*. The specific nature and the objective necessity of these laws result from a certain relatively long-range character of production forces. These are objectively necessary *methods* of cooperation and division of labour, distribution of means of production, exchange and distribution of objects of production, while the special methods of introducing the most fundamental economic processes into society always characterize certain historically specific economic relationships.[1] It is precisely by means of these economic relationships, or by means of certain specific laws of economic relationships and processes that production, distribution, exchange and consumption of all sources of production (means of production and manpower) and consumer goods are carried through. The special characteristics of these processes determine, in sum, the particularities of feudal, capitalist or socialist economic relationships.

One of the basic vulgarizations of the old administrative method of management consisted in the fact that there was an endeavour to administer the trends in production forces *directly* from the centre, without regard to the fact that production forces can develop only by means of economic relationships and that these relationships are not only a passive determination of the forces of production, but also have themselves an active and decisive influence on the development of production forces. But, while the development of production forces throughout society cannot be directly managed in a central social organization (it cannot determine the technique and the technology of every kind of production, every concrete type of product to be manufactured, etc.), the centre can have knowledge of the necessity for certain general economic relationships among economic processes (the necessary relationships among the most fundamental economic processes linking production with consumption) and can, by means of planned management of these economic processes, indirectly control the development of production forces (ascertained concretely in the enterprises).

The central body must, therefore, constantly make analyses in order to gain knowledge about the level of development of production forces and find out what changes in basic economic processes (respecting their complex mutual relationships) are needed to attain a further rapid and constant development of production forces and consumption. Instead of trying to directly manage the development of production forces by the purely quantitative method (by setting the rate of growth of production, the size of the production funds, number of workers, etc.) without paying attention to whether and

---

[1] For details on this, cf. O. Š i k, *Ekonomika, zájmy, politika* (Economics, Interests, Politics), Prague 1962.

how this development is conditioned by all internally related economic processes (by distribution of the national income, price policy, payments by the enterprises to the state, taxes, credit, interest, wages, investments, etc.), there should be instead a management of the development of basic economic processes and activities on the basis of a knowledge of these necessary economic relationships and their influence on the further development of production forces, and thus achieve a satisfactory and realistic development of production forces and consumption.

In explaining the development of the theory in regard to commodity problems under socialism, we must briefly mention another theory — the so-called distribution theory, which has also had quite a little popularity, even though it has not actually affected practice at all. But, it cannot be ignored, precisely because it is often presented as a counterbalance to the Stalinist theory, as it not only admits, but also justifies the necessity for the existence of commodity-money relations throughout the socialist economy, even within the state sector. It is not, however, a correct theory; it oversimplifies the very essence of market relations, does not explain their true reasons for existence or their function in a socialist economy. It is not a matter of chance that it makes no requirements or demands on practice and in essence tries only to give an apologia for what is done in reality. It is not based on a study of existing economic practices and does not see any contradictions in this practice. According to this theory, the commodity-money relationships, as they have worked so far, fulfil their function by distributing the products of labour.

It is because this theory is purely an apologia, seemingly anti-Stalinist, but superficial and incorrect, that it must be mentioned.

Attempts to explain the existence of commodity production by the special nature of distribution were sharply criticized by Stalin. The main argument in his criticism was that distribution cannot be brought about by a certain character of exchange, but only by a certain form of ownership. Even though we disagree with the distribution theory, still we must reject this incorrect argument raised against it. The incorrectness of Stalin's criticism of this theory lay in an undialectical concept of economic interrelationships, a purely one-sided causal derivation of some processes from others, and furthermore having an incorrectly conceived point of departure ("ownership"). Stalin postulated the primacy of production, without regard to the internal dialectical connections of the different phases of the production process. Marx always showed that e.g., a certain form of production not only determines the form of distribution, but is itself determined by it in turn, or is itself realized, by means of a certain form of distribution. In the same way, a certain form of distribution not only predestines a certain form of exchange, but is also realized by this means.

In criticizing the distribution theory, Stalin based his argument on his own erroneous opinions and methods, and therefore his criticism failed to show the real shortcomings of this theory.

We may consider J. A. Kronrod, one of the chief contemporary representatives of the distribution theory, and we will use his work to show the essence of this theory.

The first works by J. A. Kronrod known in our country were still to a certain degree influenced by Stalin's views.

In his later works he recognized that it is incorrect to explain the necessity for commodity production only or chiefly by the fact of collective farm ownership. Commodity production in the state socialist sector cannot be explained by saying that it is a form of production introduced from outside, nor by the fact that commodity production must be preserved under socialism as a technical means of bookkeeping. The conditions and causes of commodity production must be sought as a necessary, immanent form of socialist production.

In this respect, Kronrod directs his main arguments at the need for equivalence as the basis for commodity exchange, and asserts that "under socialism a product becomes a commodity if economic circulation is carried out on the basis of the equivalent compensation for labour materialized in it."[1]

He argues that "The non-antagonistic contradiction of the directly social labour at the socialist level of development, under conditions where an equivalent compensation for labour expended is needed, leads to the products being produced and exchanged as commodities.

[1] J. A. Kronrod, "Commodity Production under Socialism," *Voprosy ekonomiki*, No. 10, 1958, p. 110.

Production, distribution, and exchange of products as commodities, i.e., as values, are a form of solution to this contradiction; in this process the socially non-homogeneous, unequal labour, having various degrees of usefulness for society, is converted into socially homogeneous, average, social labour."[1]

So, it is a theory that, in explaining socialist commodity production, is based on the necessity to distribute according to labour and from that concludes that this distribution can be assured only on the basis of equivalent exchange — each person must receive for the amount of labour he has expended an equivalent amount of labour in another form (after certain deductions are made).

Explaining these basic necessities, of course, does not explain the need for and the essence of socialist commodity relationships. The fundamental shortcoming of this theory lies in the fact that, even if we accept the theoretical reasons for the necessity of equivalence, this can be fully abstracted from commodity relationships (the state could receive the records from the enterprises about the products, and then distribute the products among the workers according to work performed). That is, it does not explain why they cannot be equivalently distributed in a direct way, why money and prices must necessarily exist. Their exclusive function is not solely in the sphere of distribution. They also are necessary in solving certain contradictions in the entire production process under socialism, contradictions which, furthermore, cannot be solved merely by an equivalent exchange of the results of various kinds of labour in society, as we shall show later. This theory does not explain at all how commodity exchange differs from direct distribution according to work performed, or a mere equivalent exchange of the results of labour; nor does it say why this exchange must be a commodity exchange, using money and prices. In other words, this theory does not at all explain the special nature of socialist exchange relations.

According to Kronrod, the contradiction within socialist labour is a contradiction between general, homogeneous, average labour, expended on the entire social product, and individual or collective labour, expended on the production of the enterprise, which appears as special, socially non-homogeneous labour. Here the concept "non-

[1] *Ibid.*, p. 106.

36

homogeneous" is not clear. It can be interpreted to mean either that there is simple, less complicated, more complicated, and still more complicated labour, etc. In other words, that in the same period of time an unequal amount of work is performed. Or it can mean that different specific jobs of various usefulness are performed. These aspects of labour cannot, however, be combined in one abstract concept, without explaining their mutual contradictions.

We cannot seek the explanation for commodity relations merely in the non-homogeneous character of human labour, in its differing complexity or skill (as regards amounts of labour expended in the same time). It will not hold up with the assertion that in commodity exchange alone can various complicated jobs be converted to simple, socially average labour, and that therefore there must be commodity relations.

The relation of simple labour to complicated or skilled labour is not a relation that has only a technical and numerical aspect, but in it are projected very many developing social viewpoints, according to which one or another type of labour appears as simple labour and others as more complicated in varying degree. Therefore, it is too difficult to express directly the socially complicated labour as a multiple of simple labour, to express directly how much more work is represented by this complicated social labour expended in one hour than by one hour of simple labour.

To compare the differences in labour, it is not enough merely to judge the arduousness of the work. Various studies have been made from this standpoint, with comparative measurements of the job and the degree of arduousness. According to one study, for example, there are the following differences (Table 1).

But what is the significance of the finding that heavy work requires about double the amount of physical exertion that medium work requires, and about 2.2 fold more than light work? Converting complicated work to simple work can never be performed merely by measuring and converting one single (even though important) aspect of the work process, reducing it to a basic unit. Even less valid is a static calculation, without taking account of changing social conditions.

Not even if we succeeded in calculating or converting all types of socially complicated tasks to simple work, could we directly

TABLE I *Intensity of Work*

Type of work	Kilo calories consumed per hour	Example of job
Light work	Up to 75	Tailoring, stenography
Medium work	75-100	Bookbinding, machine mechanic, shoemaker, room painter
Heavy work	150-300	Carpenter, metal worker, miner
Very heavy work	Over 300	Quarry workers, lumbermen

Source: V. Halaxa, *Intensita práce in socialismu* (Intensity of Labour under Socialism), Prague, 1963, p. 15.

distribute by means of labour money (symbols) or by such distribution solve the contradictions that compel commodity production. The necessity of converting work of various degrees of complexity to simple or socially average work, and the necessity of renumerating workers according to their labour cannot be the essential reason for commodity production. Kronrod's theory cannot use this argument as answer to the question of the reasons for and the essence of commodity production under socialism.

Kronrod is imprecise in his argumentation and changes concepts when his arguments fail. First he asserts that "the contradiction in direct social labour under socialism is that as the sum of labour expended on the total social product it appears as a *general*, equivalent average labour; as individual and collective labour expended on the product of a given enterprise it appears as a *special* socially non-homogeneous labour." But then when he comes to the arguments for why socialist production is commodity production, why products are values, he says that the commodity form is "a form of solving the above-mentioned contradiction: in this process non-homogeneous, non-equivalent labour, having various degrees of necessity for society, becomes socially equivalent, average, social labour."[1]

What does it mean when there are various degrees of necessity? This could be understood only as an expression of the socially necessary or unnecessary work expended on the production of various

[1] Kronrod, *op. cit.*, p. 106.

types of use values that come about when more is produced of a certain amount of use values than society needs at the given value. There actually are no "differing degrees of necessity" to society. All the products that society at a given level can produce with the total amount of productive labour that is available, it can also consume, with the assumption that the different types of goods actually were produced in an amount needed by society, with a given socially useful amount of labour for each individual type of product. Under this assumption, every amount of labour expended is equally necessary. But as soon as more is produced of a certain type of product than corresponds to the demand at its given value, this means to expend more labour than is socially necessary. Labour can, therefore, be expended in the necessary quantity for various types of needed use values, and in this case all of it will be socially useful. It can, however, be expended for unneeded use values (either a range of goods that are not needed or in excessive amounts) and then this work would in fact be wasted and not socially necessary. This contradiction can be solved only as a contradiction between use value and value, between concrete labour expended on the production of certain use values and the testing of their usefulness in exchange, thereby testing the labour expended as abstract labour.

Kronrod does not do this. He attempts to convert the special, socially non-homogeneous labour into equal, average social labour. This is incorrect and cannot lead to the explanation of commodity production under socialism.

If Kronrod had explained the contradiction between abstract and concrete labour, the contradiction between labour and needs, as this has in turn an effect on the social usefulness of the labour expended, and therefore on the amount recognized and paid as social labour, then his view would be correct. But he presents these elements imprecisely, or rather tangled together. He says that this contradiction is solved only in commodity exchange. But this assertion remains unexplained. Furthermore, Kronrod is not consistent in his theory of commodity production under socialism. He did not venture to break completely with Stalin's concept of two forms of ownership as the reason for commodity production and inconsistently combined this with his own distribution theory. He seeks a solution, but has not yet found it.

There were very many important and interesting opinions, expressed in the economic discussions of the 1920's and 1930's, that dealt with one or another use of the money-commodity instruments, the law of value, etc. These are only gradually, and with some difficulty, becoming familiar to economists. In particular, the views of Soviet economists of that time that were for many years suppressed and silenced for the main part are very hard to obtain and are only partially known. Most of them dealt with the problem of commodity-money relations from the standpoint of the *transition* to a unified socialist economy, of the relation of private agricultural production to the construction of socialist industry, the securing of resources for a priority socialist industrialization, or the equilibrium and contradiction between industry and agriculture. The market is more or less repeatedly connected with the existence of a multi-sector economy of society. One discovers only very abstractly presented ideas that concern in general the necessity of a market in a socialist planned development.

Somewhat better known are the views of Western economists (Marxists and non-Marxists) about the problems of socialist planning, the system of management, centralism and decentralization, prices, market and so on of the 1930's and shortly after the war in the 1940's. The greatest credit for re-discovering these important theoretical ideas goes to the Polish economists, who in recent decades have been the first in the socialist countries to begin a more profound theoretical discussion on the models of a socialist economy and synthetic economic questions. Particularly important is the Polish economist W. Brus who, in his book (*Models of a Socialist Economy*)[1] contributed substantially to the development of contemporary theoretical thinking, by his attempt to reveal the chief contributions of these forgotten discussions and put them in the context of the present problems.

It is not the task of the present work to give a survey of all the views expressed on the question of commodity production and commodity categories under socialism. With the best will in the world I could not deal with all of them. For this I should need to write a special polemical work. But I have tried to generalize all the more

[1] W. Brus, *Modely socialistického hospodářství*, Prague 1964.

important ideas and arguments, either in criticism or defense, of the existing socialist practice, from the standpoint of the function of the plan and market, their mutual relationships and contradictions, to generalize and compare them with the present practical economic experiences and to give an opinion of them. I have usually tried to avoid making a concrete formulation of these views or to make any actual quotations, because this would have led away from the logical train of thought in the positive exposition of economic relations, to detailed polemics with individuals with considerably diverse theoretical views. But I have attempted to take a stand on the main essence of all important arguments that deal with the material, so that an economist who is familiar with these arguments can find them easily in their general features.

Since, however, my chief aim is to analyse socialist economic practice itself, to disclose the substance and the deeper reasons of certain serious contradictions, increasing in this economy, and to disclose the fundamental way to solve them, I have examined all previous theories, both from the point of view of their influence on present economic practice, and from the standpoint of their contribution toward revealing the fundamental methods of solving these contradictions. But from this standpoint it is possible to say that—for understandable reasons—no theoretical view had such strong influence on socialist economic practice—in a quite negative way—up to the present time as Stalin's ideas. Never yet has an integrated, over-all criticism of these views been made, especially of their profoundly incorrect methodological base that differed radically from really scientific methods of the founders of Marxist economics.

Of considerable interest is the feature, pointed out by Brus in his book, that Stalin, in making some of his later formulations of fundamental economic theories, actually repeats in somewhat altered form the views of Preobrazhensky of the 1920's[1] especially in regard to the formal nature of commodity relations within the socialist state sector and the concept of a socialist planned development that contradicts the working of the law of value that is supposedly connected solely with the cooperative, insufficiently consistent form of

[1] E. Preobrazhensky, *Novaya ekonomika*, Moscow 1926; quoted from English edition, *The New Economics*, Oxford 1965.

socialist ownership. The law of value was thus driven from "true socialist production" and conceded only as the result of a contradiction forced on socialism from outside. In this view, the law of value no longer determines the proportions of socialist state production, for they are determined solely by the planned activity of the state which follows the most rapid possible growth of production with the aim of the "maximum satisfaction of the needs of a socialist society."

It was this concept, denying the existence of internal, economic contradictions and conflicts of interest within state production and the necessity of solving them by means of market relations, which led socialist planning to take on an extremely subjective, mainly voluntarist exposition, in which the need for effective and qualitatively new development of a socialist economy was completely lost. Or else the question of effectiveness became merely a superficial matter of accounting, assured by the "khozrazchot" or cost accounting defined in a formal way. This is a form of theoretical apologetics for an extensive, purely quantitative growth of production, with formally balanced "proportional" harmonizing of sources and needs, which overlooks the inner contradictions in the development of social labour also within the state sector, completely one-sidedly over-simplifies the question of work and production incentives in enterprises, and therefore denies the role of market relations in solving these contradictions and assuring the optimal development of production.

One of the first Marxist economists, to try to combine socialist planning and the function of the market, and who brought out the significance of equilibrium prices to assure effective distribution of resources within the socialist production sphere, was the well-known Polish economist Oscar Lange. His greatest service was to stress the significance of the production structure, from the standpoint of the existence of substitutes in production and consumption and alternative solutions, as well as the role of prices in assuring the most effective solution. Unfortunately his approach to the question of the market did not reveal the social-economic substance of this phenomenon under socialism, is not based on the necessary internal contradictions in socialist labour and the economic interests, and therefore did not reveal prices as the necessary form for solving these contradictions.

Therefore he was prevented from disclosing the true economic substance of the market even under socialism, and the internal dialectical relationship between the plan and the market. This approach was derived from the general Marxist view of the time that the market mechanism could not act concomitantly with socialist planning. Therefore he seeks the solution in replacement of the function of the market by centrally formed equilibrium prices, where too many concessions are made to the priority administrative concept of socialist planning.

We grant that no theoretician can ever rise much higher than his times, escape *completely* the generally prevailing views, and express ideas that mature only on the basis of *accumulated* generalized and analy ed practical experiences. In the period when socialist production was growing at a rapid rate, when the internal, hidden contradictions of this growth did not appear so evidently on the surface, as they do today, a great service was done by Lange who pointed out the structural problems, the problems of efficiency, market and prices under socialism, even though he was at that time unable to attack some "axioms" of socialist theory, expose their errors and find a fundamental solution.

In the discussions of Polish economists in the 1950's, all these questions came to the fore much more clearly and concretely, and one may say in general that the recognition that the law of value applies to socialist state production was making way. A beginning was made in introducing a much more realistic view of the question of central and decentralized management of a socialist economy, using the law of value and commodity-money instruments. The most synthetic summary of these findings and an integrated elucidation of the advantages of the decentralized model of management in comparison with the centralized model, is given by Brus in his book cited above.

Despite the enormous theoretical contribution of these Polish discussions and studies, the *objective necessity* of the existence of commodity-money relations and the market under socialism was not explained. Furthermore the impossibility of solving the growing contradictions under conditions of restricting or suppressing these processes under the old administrative system of management by directive, was not made clear. Market relations are not elucidated on the basis of the internal contradictions of socialist labour at a given stage of development of production forces, and therefore the market does not appear as a necessary economic form of solving these contradictions within socialist planning. In this way, the decentralized model of management remains only one of the several possible models, while the relationship of the *central* to the *decentralized* management remains always a relation that is explained from the standpoint of the problem of *knowledge* in administration, not from the standpoint of the internal conflict of economic interests.

An immense number of articles and longer studies have been written about commodity production and commodity categories under socialism. One very interesting, although brief, article on socialist commodity production, giving reasons for it with which one must fully agree, is the article by the Hungarian economist Petr Erdös.[1] His conclusions about the function and utilization of these relationships under socialism, however, do not completely accord with hi own fundamental findings, and are obviously written still to a certain degree under the influence of the prejudices of the time and the political situation.

With the exception of some few theoretical studies (here we are referring only to those available in this country), the great majority give the reasons for, and the essence of, socialist commodity production in a way that approaches one or the other of the above-mentioned theories ("ownership" or "distribution") or move somewhere in between them. Some content themselves with a mere statement of the existence of commodity production under socialism, others have very abstract, unconvincing assertions (e.g., that commodity production comes about because of division of labour under socialism, or because of independently operating enterprises and administrations, etc.), without more detailed explanation or deeper evidence. All such assertions can be very easily refuted (e.g., by pointing out that division of labour for operational independence of enterprises will most probably exist under communism as well, from which it would result that commodity relations would continue permanently to exist, etc.). Therefore these cannot be accepted as sufficient ex-

---

[1] Petr Erdös, "Commodity Production and Value Categories in a Socialist Economy", *Voprosy ekonomiki*, No. 5, 1959.

planation of commodity problems. It is for these reasons that the Stalinist theory of commodity production has retained a sort of official character, with a few formal changes, such as the mere assertion that means of production that are manufactured in socialist state enterprises are also commodities. Along with these formal changes, it is still included in most of the textbooks of political economy of socialism, taught at schools in most of the socialist countries, and so on.

I shall, therefore, attempt in the subsequent positive exposition of my views on socialist commodity production to show more deeply the theoretical untenability and the practical harm done by the view that has hitherto prevailed concerning commodity problems under socialism.

2 Results of Applying Erroneous Commodity — Money Theories, and Management by Administrative Measures in the Economy of Czechoslovakia

A survey of the main theories of commodity production under socialism documents clearly the truth that the character of a given stage in social production cannot be explained without study of the actual facts, and an examination of the internal economic relationships. Insufficient knowledge of this has caused contradictions to grow in socialist economies. We cannot explain this by theories that accommodate themselves to existing economic practice and attempt to justify this practice as something that is fundamentally unchanging and inevitable. These theories will not clear up problems which we have not sufficiently considered in our conscious economic activity. If we were to give good theoretical reasons for what we *consciously* take account of in economic practice, there would be no such theoretical difficulty. But we should assume that our "conscious" management of the socialist economy still has many gaps if there are so many fundamental theoretical disputes among Marxist economists around questions of commodity production under socialism.

We shall now attempt, taking the Czechoslovak socialist economy as our example, to show that suppressing and formalizing commodity-money relationships by means of the centralized administrative system of planned management in the spirit of the Stalinist theories has really brought the economy to a situation where further development is no longer possible unless a clearcut stop is put to this erroneous system of management, and unless there is a basic change, respecting the necessary existence of socialist market relationships, and a fundamentally different concept of socialist planning. We do not intend to give a historical description of the post-war development of the Czechoslovak economy, but rather to gain insight by an economic analysis. We cannot always document individual statements with precise statistics and quantitative data, either because they were not studied and no records were kept, or because these data cannot, for various reasons, be published. Nevertheless, all important conclusions made here are either the result of statistical analyses or are based on quite obvious and generally known facts, so that the absence of statistical elaboration does not make them less reliable.

As we have already said, attempts to make integrated analyses of the Czechoslovak economy did not appear until contradictions and difficulties developed. This was taking place even before the 1960's, when the consequences of economic contradictions were already very serious and were obviously coming to the surface. From 1956 onwards there were already broad analyses and investigations of ways of overcoming certain economic deficiencies. Perhaps detailed historical analyses in the future will disclose that these symptoms of economic contradictions and errors in planning and management came much earlier. But we shall disregard this for the time being.

Difficulties in growth began to appear from 1960 onwards, climaxing in the period 1962–1963. The growth in over-all production began abruptly to slow down, as well as productivity of labour and national income, and in 1962–63 there was a general stagnation of economic activity. This is shown by the table on page 47.

Even though there was a serious decline in the rate of growth in 1953–54, it picked up again in 1955. It is true that the annual increments of production were gradually decreasing, but still there was rapid growth up to 1961, which was then suddenly interrupted.

TABLE 2   *Some Basic Indicators of the Economy of Czechoslovakia
In Comparable Prices*

Year	Global Social Product			National Income Originating from Production		
	In million crowns	Chain[3] index	Base index	In million crowns	Chain index	Base index
1948	130 568		100.0	70 160		100.0
1950	164 375	114.9	125.9	85 031	110.2	121.2
1953	206 864	105.8	158.4	109 691	106.4	156.3
1954	216 289	104.5	165.7	113 570	103.5	161.9
1955	238 390	110.2	182.6	125 249	110.3	178.5
1960	348 251[1]	106.2	266.7	176 027[1]	108.7	250.9
	338 958[2]			162 002[2]		
1961	362 583	106.1	285.3	172 974	106.8	207.9
1962	373 138	102.9	293.9	175 399	101.4	271.6
1963	373 145	100.0	293.9	171 595	97.8	265.6
1964	383 964	102.9	302.1	173 127	100.9	268.1

[1] In the period 1948–60 in comparable prices, using April 1, 1955 as base.
[2] In the period 1960–64 in comparable prices, using April 24, 1960 as base.
[3] Always expresses relation to preceding year, even if this is not included in the table.

Source: *Statistické přehledy* (Statistical Surveys), 2/1964 and 4/1964.

One of the most serious errors is to judge the success of economic development under socialism only by the rate of growth of over-all production, as we shall show later. Still, we must first answer two questions:
1. Why could socialist production increase rapidly for years and why did this rapid growth suddenly stop?
2. Was this development related to the system of planned management which did not change fundamentally throughout this period?

The decisive source for the growth of production is, on the one hand, the quantitative expansion of inputs, i.e. the volume of means of production and number of productive workers, and, on the other hand, the qualitative development of factors increasing the social productivity of labour, i.e. the technical improvement of means of production, increase in knowledge, abilities, and experience of the productive workers and leading personnel (by increasing their qualifications), the development of scientific knowledge and its application to technology, a progressive growth of social combination of labour (cooperation and division of labour).

It is quite possible to imagine a growth of production assured mainly by a quantitative expansion of sources of production, as distinct from the growth assured mainly by the qualitative development of production factors. Of course, in neither case will the development be purely quantitative or qualitative, because the two methods supplement each other and intermingle. But there actually are periods in the development of all industrial countries in the world when one or the other aspect has obviously *predominated*.

From the standpoint of society's development, there is great significance in whether the growth of production is assured to a relatively greater or lesser degree by extending material and labour inputs. The greater the production funds and manpower society requires to assure a certain growth of production, the greater the part of its global social product and potential manpower resources that must be devoted again and again to production. Therefore a relatively smaller part of the global product and manpower resources can be released for non-productive social needs. And *vice versa*, the more society can manage to decrease inputs in order to assure the same growth of production, the more effective the use of the part of production and labour that must be re-invested in production, the relatively greater is the part that remains for covering other needs. As we shall show later, however, there are special conditions under which it is more advantageous for a certain society to expand sources of production more rapidly, even at the price of a less efficient ratio between growth in volume of inputs and growth of production, than may be the case in another country.

From what has been said above, we can see that we are regarding the relation between the development of material and labour inputs and of production itself, from the standpoint of comparing the development of social production of different countries of the world. In certain countries, for certain reasons, a particular relation between the rate of growth of factor inputs and the rate of growth of production is established, and in other countries this ratio may be substantially higher or lower. At the same time, it is not a question of short-term, rapidly alternating, random differences in the ratio, but long-term, strikingly different trends — in which we see primarily the differences in ratio between the expansion of factor inputs and the growth of the social product, in which there are also substantial differences in the trends in social productivity of labour — must be distinguished by economic nomenclature. This is done by using the concepts "*extensive*" and "*intensive*" growth of production.

But, since it is a question of a category designating obvious differences between certain relatively long-term characteristics of growth, the concepts cannot be used except in comparative studies — comparing the long-term development of different countries in the world, or different stages of development of the same country. This international criterion that is used in characterizing extensive or intensive development is quite justified, because it expresses the completely realistic difference in the level of productive forces, especially in applying the newest scientific and technical findings in the development of various countries of the world. From this standpoint, there will be a certain number of countries which will attain the most rapid growth in production in relation to the rate of expansion of factor inputs, or that is to say, their growth in production will be assured by rapid rates of growth in social productivity of labour and the growth of production in the period studied is intensive. In comparison with these countries, then, other countries with slower rates of growth in production relative to the rates of extending factor inputs will have extensive development.

In brief, the dividing line between extensive and intensive development of production will fluctuate during the course of history, and to discover it for a certain historical period requires comparative studies. Under certain conditions of technical development, for instance, the major part of industrially advanced countries can assure the entire increment of its production (100 per cent) merely by a 20 to 30 per cent growth in input and this will mean that in countries where more than 30 per cent growth in volume of inputs is needed to assure the same growth in production, their development will be called extensive.

In this study we are not interested in comparing the mutual relations of the aspects of growth on a world scale, resulting in a precise and generally applicable characterization of the evidence of extensive development of production at the present period in history. We are only describing the development of the Czechoslovak economy in which there have obviously been certain periods of extensive development which resembled in many ways the development in other socialist countries.

Even though we need thorough international comparative studies in order to be able to say categorically whether development in Czechoslovakia immediately after the Second World War was extensive in nature, we must see that growth of production was assured from the beginning, to a large degree, by increasing input, with a relatively slow development in technique. Special circumstances compelled not only the extension of fixed capital units, but also insufficient scrapping of fully amortized machinery and equipment. While this development is only hypothetically called extensive (without making any international studies), we use the designation to indicate the special way production sources were rapidly extended, to assure the full use of manpower in the country.

Whether future comparative studies confirm the extensive nature of these post-war years or not, the fact is that, from about 1954–55, there began a development where growth of production was not only dependent on extending the factor input to an increasing degree, but also the capital output ratio worsened to such an extent that capital in this context refers not only to fixed capital but also to material and labour inputs. A serious economic contradiction began to arise, although at first only in a hidden and unnoticed way. The development not only became extensive from the standpoint of an international comparison, but also the extensive expansion of factors of production became completely uneconomical and negative.

Extensive development need not in itself be inefficient, nor need it lead to a growth of insoluble internal economic conflicts. From the standpoint of intensive development in advanced industrial countries, the extensive development of other countries will always, of course, appear less efficient. But it might be that, under certain production and economic conditions in that country, this will be the only possible and advantageous method of development. But, as soon as the extensive development has passed a certain limit, or goes further under specific economic conditions and brings insoluble internal economic contradictions, it is actually a special kind of ineffective, economically negative development, the consequence of an inadequate system of management which must be changed as soon as possible if there is not to be catastrophe.

We shall now try to show that the development of Czechoslovakia was favourable under the specific initial conditions, but that it changed at a certain point to an economically negative development which necessarily resulted in the above-mentioned events in 1962–63. At the same time, we shall try not only to show what is the essence of an economically negative extensive development, as distinct from normal extensive development, and also why extensive development will, if it is not supplanted in time by intensive development, necessarily change into a negative, extensive development with all the consequences. We shall at the same time show that the administrative system of planned management initiated a negative extensive growth of production and prevented a prompt change from extensive to intensive development.

GRAPH 1   *Trends in Basic Funds (Fixed Assets) in Czechoslovakia*

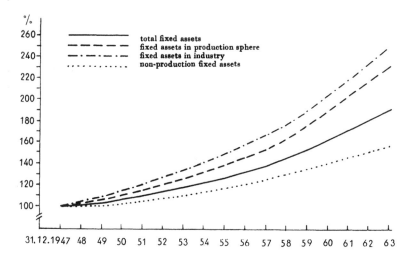

Source: *Statistická ročenka ČSSR* (Statistical Yearbook of the ČSSR) 1966, p. 174.

51

Since 1945, Czechoslovakia has been quantitatively expanding its sources of production very rapidly. The volume of basic funds[1] of production has more than doubled in the period 1948–63 (an increase of 133 per cent).

The same figure for industry alone increased two and a half times (see graph on page 51). The total number of employed workers increased in this period by 281 thousand, or by only 5.8 per cent. Agricultural employment declined and the increase in industry alone was more than three quarters of a million persons (771 thousand), which is a growth of 47 per cent.

Increase in total employment was accounted for primarily by the employment of housewives. The number of employed women rose from 2,097,000 in 1948 to 2,792,000 in 1963, reaching 44 per cent of the total number of employed persons. This is 74.3 per cent of the women in the ages between 15 and 55. As we have said, employment

TABLE 3   *Trends in Manpower in Agriculture, Agricultural Production and Productivity of Labour in Agriculture*

| Workers in agriculture | | Indices 1936 = 100 | | | | | |
| | | Gross agricultural production | | | Gross agricultural production per worker | | |
in 1000s	Index 1948 = 100	Total	Crop production	Live-stock production	Total	Crop production	Live-stock production
1948	2 239	100.0	76.48	4.2	67.1	111.3	122.7	97.8
1950	2 058	92.0	86.2	79.8	93.8	140.9	130.4	153.2
1953	1 858	83.0	84.9	91.2	77.4	167.0	179.5	152.3
1955	1 933	87.5	93.5	92.1	95.0	165.9	163.5	168.7
1958	1 764	78.8	98.5	92.6	105.6	191.3	179.8	205.0
1960	1 468	65.6	103.1	97.3	110.1	238.3	224.8	254.4
1962	1 380	61.6	103.1	94.5	113.3	252.4	231.4	257.7
1962	1 334	59.6	95.3	83.2	109.7	240.7	210.0	276.8
1963	1 316	59.6	102.3	95.7	110.1	261.6	244.7	281.5

Source: *Statistická ročenka* (Statistical Yearbook) 1961, 63, 64.

[1] fixed assets

in industry increased much more rapidly than employment in the whole sphere of production. The rapid decline in agricultural employment is shown in the table on page 52.

Productivity of labour grew rapidly in agriculture as a result of drawing off of latent reserves of surplus manpower that had accumulated there under capitalist conditions and, on the other hand, because of the development of collective large-scale agriculture which brought economies in manpower. With fundamentally the same volume of agricultural production as pre-war, this meant that productivity of labour increased considerably.

GRAPH 2   *Development of Industrial Production and of Productivity of Labour of Industry*

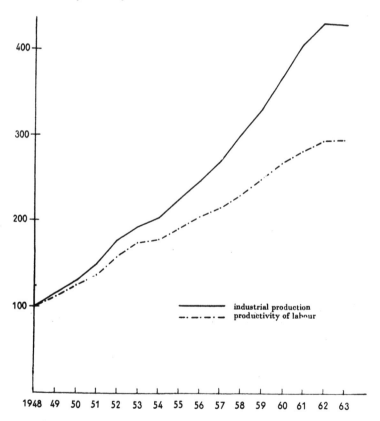

Source: Based on *Statistická ročenka* (Statistical Yearbook) 1965, pp. 26–27.

A rapid growth in manpower caused an abrupt rise in industrial production. When productive capacity was expanded through capital investment to use the increased manpower, production was also increased.

The extensive growth of industrial production required continuous enlargement of manpower until industrial production was suddenly reduced in 1962–63. (See graph 2.) At the same time, however, the sources of new manpower for industry became more and more exhausted. There was already a tremendously high level of employment of women, one of the highest in the world. The shift of workers from agriculture to industry is becoming more and more difficult under present conditions. The insufficient replacement of manpower by mechanization[1] of agriculture (particularly because mechanization was insufficiently integrated) created a situation in which the labour shortage and the high average age of agricultural workers became one of the main brakes to growth in total agricultural production.[2]

[1] We can see how insufficiently manual labour was replaced by mechanization in the following comparison:
Although there were considerably larger reserves of manpower in the German Federal Republic in the post-war period, for every 100 workers that left agriculture in the period 1949 to 1964 38 actual tractors took their place, whereas in Czechoslovakia only 9 (converted to units of 15 H.P. this is 15 tractors). One actual tractor falls to 3.5 workers in G.F.R., whereas in Czechoslovakia to 12 workers (one tractor unit of 15 H.P. to 7.9 workers).
J.Flek: "Počet pracovních sil v čs. zemědělství a faktory ovlivňující jejich potřebu" (Manpower in Czechoslovak Agriculture and Factors Influencing the Demand for It), Zemědělská ekonomika, 9, 1965.

[2] Economically Active Persons by Age Groups in the National Economy of Czechoslovakia, 1961 (in percentage)

Five-year group	Agriculture		Industry
up to 20 years	5.1		11.3
20—24	5.5		13.7
25—29	6.3		12.2
30—34	8.7		12.6
35—39	11.2		12.9
40—44	7.8	*(continued)*	7.6

When in a given country there is a large amount of unemployed or insufficiently used manpower which must be supported mainly or entirely by the results of labour of other members of the society (which means the consumption of the first group will necessarily be lower if the stimulus to work is not to be undermined), a rapid extension of the volume of means of production makes possible a rapid growth of employment and utilization of this manpower in an economically effective way. This is advantageous even when such an increase in factor inputs means a smaller growth in productivity of labour than if there were an intensive development, assuming, of course, that the overall social productivity of labour were to be increased (in other words, the growth of production in relation to the total amount of social labour, embodied and living, expended in production). The unutilized manpower need not appear only as an army of unemployed, but also can be hidden as insufficiently used manpower, in agriculture, for example.

Under the given conditions when there was a relative surplus of manpower (a latent reserve of insufficiently used manpower) in agriculture, which could be used in industry, this was temporarily justified. This extensive development necessitates a rapid expansion of the volume of fixed assets in industry, even at the price of slower scrapping using not only obsolescent, but also physically worn out machinery and equipment. Expansion of the volume of fixed assets is assured not only by new investment, but also partially by leaving fully depreciated machinery in production, while it becomes more and more outdated technically. In such a case, the growth in pro

(Footnote p. 54 continued)

Five-year group	Agriculture	Industry
45—49	12.1	9.9
50—54	14.0	9.7
55—59	12.7	6.3
over 60 years + not stated	16.6	4.8
	100.0	100.0

Source: Calculated on the basis of material from 1961 census, *Statistické informace* (Statistical Information), ÚKLKS 1962, No. 152.

ductivity of labour in industry will necessarily slow down because a growing portion of the workers are forced to work with outdated production means which make it more and more difficult to increase productivity of labour.

When such a development solves, on the one hand, the serious social problem of hidden unemployment in rural areas and when manpower in industry is increased by means of the expansion of production funds, and is capable of assuring a still more rapid growth in general social productivity of labour than there could be if there were more rapid scrapping and replacement of production equipment in industry, leaving substantially unused manpower in agriculture, such development is quite justified in economic terms. It is also feasible in a period of social change in rural areas, when there is a transition to socialist collective large-scale agriculture, when conditions for a rapid release of manpower from agriculture are being created and these could be utilized more productively in the expanding industrial base.

In this example, if in agriculture the conditions of production in a given period prevent the efficient use of manpower, it would be more efficient to shift workers to industry even if the employment in industry is expanded on an extensive basis.

Retardation and conditions of a slow growth of productivity of labour will necessarily set in if workers in industry are not provided in time with modern machinery and equipment. Of course, under condition of rapid technical development, and with efficient machinery and equipment it may not be necessary to increase the proportion of accumulation (or there can even be a relative decline), and still the equipment of all workers with modern machinery can be assured. Extensive expansion of the basic fund of production and of production itself has no sense under conditions where there is a general shortage of manpower and the over-all costs of social labour (embodied and living) begin to grow faster than the growth of social production. Under these conditions and in this way normal extensive development turns into negative development that creates insurmountable obstacles to the economic covering of the rapidly growing input requirements and, in the end, will undermine the process of growth completely.

If, therefore, conditions for extensive development that in a certain initial period were justified are now gradually disappearing, and their changed conditions are not recognized in time, then the continuing orientation of economic policy, and planning and management procedures, in the direction of extensive growth must at a certain moment fail. Together with the exhaustion of extensive sources of growth, independent of the planning directives (setting rapid rates of growth on the basis of experience in the period of a thoroughly extensive growth) the rate of growth will slow down and, at the same time, contradictions will grow to the extreme between the constantly lagging social productivity of labour and the much more rapidly growing material inputs connected with extensive development.

This is the experience that the economy of Czechoslovakia has gone through. Let us see how the orientation on extensive growth of production appeared under conditions when the sources for such a development began to disappear and in which, at the same time, there was a system of management which prevented the prompt re-orientation and transition to a highly intensive and qualitative development.

In the first post-war years there was a possibility to rapidly draw off manpower from agriculture to industry, since it had been accumulating there before the war,[1] during the war, and shortly afterwards. Also the rapid collectivization in agriculture released a large number of workers for industry. In order that this manpower might be utilized productively, a certain amount of plant and equipment was not scrapped even after full amortization, but was left in operation. The bulk of new investments were not used to replace machinery, for modernization and technical reconstruction of production equipment, but for expanding production capacities requiring new manpower. As a result, plant and equipment grew very rapidly in industry, but at the same time the machinery pool became outmoded, as shown by Table 4.

[1] On the territory of the former Protectorate Bohemia and Moravia alone, the population in villages with less than 10,000 inhabitants increased in the decade 1930–40 by about 400,000 persons, which was 290,000 persons more than the increment in the decade 1920–30.
Source: *Statistická ročenka Protektorátu Čechy a Morava* (Statistical Yearbook of the Protectorate Bohemia and Moravia), Prague 1942, p. 9.

TABLE 4   *Machinery and Equipment in Industry by Age (as of end of year)*
(Percentages in terms of 1955 prices)

| | Proportion of machines and equipment, aged: | | |
	up to 2 years	up to 10 years	over 10 years
1955	20.6	45.8	33.6
1958	20.8	54.9	25.1
1960	22.9	51.8	25.6
1963	18.3	54.6	27.1

Source: *Statistické ročenky ČSSR* (Statistical Yearbooks of the ČSSR), 1955–1963.

The proportion of the older age groups is considerably higher when expressed in number of machines and equipment than when expressed in value.

According to an extensive inventory of machines and equipment carried out by the Statistical Office at the beginning of 1960, covering over 2,000,000 machines and almost half the total amount of the purchase price of machines and equipment, 52.0 per cent were older than twenty, 13.4 per cent older than 30, and 6.1 per cent older than 40 years.

Of course, in some groups of machines these proportions were even higher. This can be seen in Table 5, p. 59.

For a certain time, the increase in production in newly built factories was very large and contributed to a more rapid growth of social productivity of labour than could have been achieved with a slower expansion of the volume of plant and equipment or an insufficient transfer of manpower from agriculture to industry.

Furthermore, productivity of labour increased rapidly in the old factories as well, on the basis of a partial improvement in technique and organization of their production, a partial increase in intensity of labour, a relative reduction in costs of administration and so on. The relatively rapid initial growth of social productivity of labour succeeded in fully covering the material requirements of growing productive and non-productive needs. In the course of time, however, together with a continuing extensive development of production,

TABLE 5   *Age of Czechoslovak Machinery, Selected Types*
            (Percentage of total amount of given type)

	Proportion of machines aged more than			
	10,	20,	30,	40 years
Steam boilers	74.7	57.3	46.1	31.6
Machinery and equipment:				
in textile and clothing industry	78.4	57.3	37.3	22.8
in food industry	69.2	47.3	29.7	12.7
in production of cellulose and paper	73.6	55.7	28.8	12.8
in polygraphic industry	69.9	52.0		7.3
machine tools	59.5	23.9	7.7	2.4

Source: *Statistický obzor* (Statistical Review), 1961/6, p. 247—8.

a certain contradiction began to grow up, which we may give the over-all designation of "contradiction between the development of material needs and of material resources". This should, however, be analysed in more detail.

In the first place, the extensive growth of production led gradually to a slowing down in the increase of output per worker in industry. There was an obvious trend toward an absolute slowing down in growth of industrial output per worker as shown on the graph on page 63. In addition to the annual increments in productivity of labour and in number of workers engaged in industry, the graph also shows the moving averages of productivity of labour, thus smoothing out annual discrepancies and showing more clearly the trends of development. This development shows that the technical level of industry started gradually to fall behind and that, on the whole, the qualitative factors of growth were inadequately developed. In the old factories it was more and more difficult to increase the productivity of labour by small technical and organizational changes, by intensification of labour and so forth, and substantial qualitative changes in the technical base became quite exceptional. The result of this is that a growing number of old, experienced and skilled workers were equipped with obsolete production equipment, whereas the new factories, where there was the relatively greatest amount of modern equipment (even though not always at the highest world technical level), had mainly new, less experienced and less skilled manpower. As a result of this, many new factories did not exceed or did not even attain the productivity of labour of the old factories. Furthermore, the worsening of natural conditions (for instance in the mining of coal, etc.) had an effect on this slower development of output per worker.

Although a slowing down of the rate of growth of labour productivity is not a positive development, it need not cause economic contradiction. But if it results from a decline in efficiency of machinery and equipment, and if the plant and equipment per worker are increasing, there must necessarily occur at a certain moment a deformation of the reproduction process.

If efficiency of machinery in industry is expressed by the production ratio per machine unit (e.g., the volume of production per 1,000 crowns' worth of industrial machinery and equipment), we find that this efficiency is declining sharply, as we see in the graph on page 61. This graph shows the rapid decline of total volume of production in relation to the total number of machine units used for this production. A certain deviation from this relationship could be explained by structural changes in production, allowing for substantial differences in price level of capital and consumer goods. Furthermore, one must take into account the changes in old products and introduction of new ones. But neither of these factors explains the rapid decline in efficiency of machinery and equipment.

Even if the prices of means of production were substantially higher (corresponding, e.g., to their actual value), the trend of development would not change significantly, because the relatively more rapid growth of total production would correspond over a long period of time to a more rapid growth in the volume of machinery necessary for production as a whole (expressed by correspondingly higher prices).[1]

---

[1] Although an estimate of a certain volume of machine units expressed in comparable prices can be distorted, e.g., by new machinery sold at new prices, while the sum of these new prices would express many more (or fewer) machine units than the same sum of comparable prices representing the old machinery, this does not deny the general tendency described above, because here again the prices of newly manufactured means of production can express in reality fewer (or more) units of production than the comparable prices for the old production.

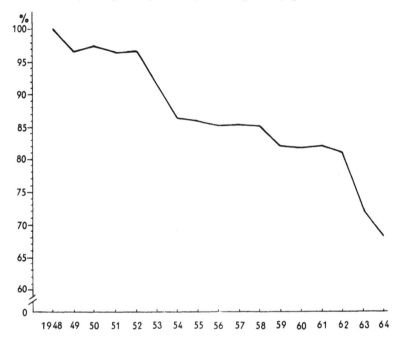

Source: Based on *Statistická ročenka* (Statistical Yearbook) 1966, pp. 124, 179.

The ratio of the actual value of machinery (the socially necessary amount of labour embodied in the machines) to the volume of its production is not expressed precisely, although this would approximate the concept of development of total social productivity of labour. But this would require, on the one hand, registering only the depreciated value of machinery in relation to volume of production, distorted not only by price influences but also by changes in depreciation practices. On the other hand, it would require the use of actual value prices. The above-mentioned relationship can, therefore, give us only the increasing amount of labour embodied in the growing volume of materials, plant and equipment, necessary to produce a certain quantity of use values.

We are not trying here to show that social productivity of labour is declining constantly, but to clarify the reasons for our difficulties. Nor are we trying to express the relation of actual value of machinery to production, but to show that the rate of expansion (accumulation) of machinery funds is more rapid than would correspond to the growth of total industrial production, and that this accumulation of machinery is inversely related to the development of productivity of labour. The same tendency can be seen in the following table which shows the relationship of productive investment to increments of global social product and national income (in "Western" terminology incremental capital-output ratio).

TABLE 6   *Trends in Investment Costs per Increment of Social Product and of National Income*

| Year | Investment in production per crown of annual increment of: | |
	Social product[1]	National income[1]
1950	0.49	1.33
1953	1.27	2.18
1955	0.67	1.27
1958	1.05	2.01
1960	1.09	2.41
1961	1.46	3.14
1962	3.09	13.90
1963	2.58	18.22

[1] 1950–60 in prices of the base year 1955, 1961–63 in prices of 1960. The whole series of investments are considered in prices of 1963.
Source: *Statistické přehledy* (Statistical Surveys), 2/1964, *Statistická ročenka* (Statistical Yearbook), 1964.

But, as we have already said, much more important than the general decline in efficiency of machinery and equipment was their decline in efficiency in relation to the development in productivity of living labour. The volume of machinery funds per worker (or "Equipment of workers with machinery"), necessary to assure a certain growth in productivity of living labour, increased, while the rate of growth in productivity of labour declined. The following survey of development in the period 1951–1964, and in different shorter intervals of time, shows a general decline in expressed efficiency of machinery, although there was a moderate increase in 1956–60. In this table, the trends in productivity of labour are calculated only in wholesale prices; while in the preceding graph consumer goods, as part of total production, are calculated in retail prices.

GRAPH 4   *Annual Increments in Productivity of Labour and in Number of Workers in Industry*

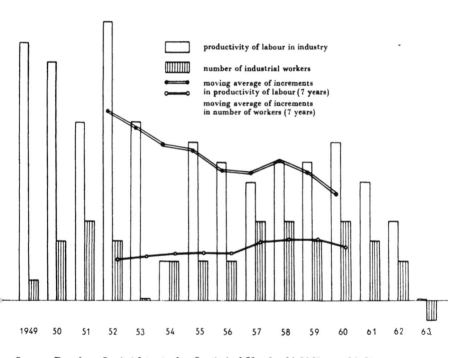

Source: Based on *Statistická ročenka* (Statistical Yearbook) 1965, pp. 26–27.

Such trends of development necessarily lead to growing economic conflicts which at a certain moment culminate in intolerable difficulties. The disproportionately rapid rate of growth in machinery stocks and fixed assets is generally related not only to a large absolute growth of demands in the engineering industry and its material, fuel and power base, but also to the *relative* share of the

63

TABLE 7   *Mutual Relationship of Growth of Productivity of Labour and Equipment of Industrial Workers with Machinery and Equipment*
(in percentages at constant prices)

Average rate of growth	1951–55	1956–60	1961–64	1951–64
1) Output per production worker	108.5	107.0	103.4	106.5
2) Machinery and equipment per worker	108.8	106.4	107.5	107.5
3) Efficiency of machinery	99.7	100.6	96.2	99.1

Sources: *Statistické ročenky* (Statistical Yearbooks), 1961 and 1965, Statistické publikace ÚKLKS – Základní fondy v letech 1948–1963 (Statistical Publications of ÚKLKS – Basic Funds in the Years 1948–1963).

social product necessary to cover the material inputs for this production.[1]

To understand this contradiction, it is not enough to study only the trends in value of units of production, or the production costs of individual products (even if we assume it would be possible to calculate precisely and keep exact records), because production costs do not include the entire value of the increases in basic production funds — only the part of the value going to amortization. But from the standpoint of social reproduction process and growth of production, it is of prime importance to follow trends in total costs of social labour that must be spent annually by society in order to obtain a given magnitude of annual social product. In other words, society must know how much total social labour (embodied and living) is needed to create the social product and, particularly, how much this

[1] Of course, the part of social product necessary for the reproduction of the basic production funds consumed during the production process serves also partly for the extension of these production funds, because the scrapping of depreciated assets is not proportionate to the increase of new assets financed by amortization. The part of the social product needed for reproduction could not cover the more rapidly growing needs of the basic production funds under conditions of extensive development, and their expansion swallows up a constantly growing share of the surplus product.

social labour must be extended for a specific growth of social product.

Here, again, the problems of extensive and intensive development enter the picture, as well as the positive or the negative features of extensive development. The more rapid the development of the quality factor in production, and especially the greater the effectiveness of basic production funds, the relatively less need to extend the volume of production input, to extend fixed assets as well as labour and material, to assure a certain growth in production. Even an extensive development could be economically feasible, as long as the extension of production input guarantees an even more rapid growth of social production, enabling society to cover the growing production needs without limiting consumption relatively or absolutely. An intensive development, on the other hand, would guarantee a more rapid increase in final consumption. Such a development could, under certain conditions, be less favourable than a more rapid growth of employment.

But when the total production input increases more rapidly than social product and society must spend an increasing share of the relatively smaller increment of product to extend fixed assets and material inputs, without making any saving in living labour, this would necessarily mean a relative (sometimes even absolute) diminishing of general consumption. This begins with restrictions of social consumption, but as it proceeds further it compels a retardation in growth of real wages, a levelling out of wages and this, sooner or later, retards the growth of production. From the moment when factors of production increase at a more rapid rate than output, extensive development is a negative feature. This may be unnoticed at first.

In capitalist countries growth theories, the marginal capital coefficient concept is usually used $\left(\dfrac{K'}{P} \right)$. But this is not sufficient. Total social costs of production should include:

1. The value part of the production funds consumed in production during the year (usually called in Marxist literature the consumed part of constant capital $= c$) plus the value part by which fixed assets had to expand in the given year, but did not enter into production entirely (extension of fixed assets, including the amortization already computed in total c, and the increase in inventories — the sum of embodied labour) which society had to transfer from its social

product to the production sphere to assure further growth in production;

2. The value of living labour necessary to assure social production. The more embodied labour must be expended to assure the growth of social product, the more must be saved from living labour and *vice versa*.

Only the total amount of material inputs and labour taken together, which society must invest annually in the production sphere in order to achieve the necessary growth in social production, can characterize this production process.

For example, one can imagine quite easily that a growth in the capital coefficient will be more than compensated under certain conditions by savings in material and manpower (going over from simple machines of a certain value to technologically advanced semiautomated or automated mechanisms which are so expensive that, in relation to their production, the capital coefficient rises, but which, on the other hand, may save so much manpower or materials that total costs of production declines and efficiency increases). On the other hand, a technological lag or a disadvantageous structure of investments may lead to an increase of the capital coefficient, but the productivity of labour may simultaneously stagnate or even decline, with increasing consumption of materials, etc. In such cases there is a disproportionate rise in yearly costs required to assure growth of production and insoluble contradictions will arise.

In order to recognize the reasons for such contradictions and to characterize them more precisely, we must first analyse the total *reproduction costs*.

These include, first of all, the costs that are usually called production consumption, i.e., the circulating funds used, plus amortization (symbol "c"). This is materialized labour that must be expended and is consumed in production during a given year. But society must expend each year a much greater volume of means of production than is used up in the production process. These are the means of production that expand the production base (increment or accumulation of fixed assets = symbol "a"). In the case of circulating funds it is actually the increase in stocks during the year. In the case of basic funds it is the net increase in fixed assets. It is, however, difficult to make such deduction under present statistical practice and therefore some items are counted twice. But this is only a small part of the value (the annual amortization of newly acquired basic funds) and cannot distort the over-all developmental trends. It can, therefore, be disregarded.

It is somewhat more complicated to calculate labour costs. Since we are not interested in an unrealistic calculation of social productivity of labour (price difficulties, etc.), but in clarifying the ineffectiveness of a specific extensive development and its unfavourable consequences in reproduction, we cannot be primarily interested in the development of the *value* of living labour in relation to the product, but in the costs that society as a whole must pay annually for labour in the production sphere. These costs are represented by the sum of the wages paid out in production (symbol "v") which partly reflects the trends in quantity and quality of labour expended, but which is also affected by other factors. One of these factors, in particular, is the necessity to raise wages in relation to growth of productivity of labour, as an incentive to this growth. Another factor is the tendency to project into the wages the general conditions of the development of living standards (the existing possibilities of a rise in individual consumption).

Even if we assume that average nominal wages per worker in production rise relatively fast and their increment per capita is constant (e.g., four per cent a year), or even that the rate increased as an expression of the general rise in living standards, still, the sum of production consumption, production accumulation and production wages (the social costs of reproduction or $c + a + v$) should not rise in the long-run more rapidly than the social product. In other words, in the long-run there should not be an increase of the reproduction coefficient $R = \dfrac{c + a + v}{P}$. Such an increase would relatively diminish the part of social production that covers the non-production needs (such as free services, social grants for housing and personal transportation, roads and other public facilities, schools, health services, social services, science and research, cultural activity, defense expenditures, etc.). In modern society, not only must all this social consumption and the non-production accumulation keep pace with production, but it must increase relatively, if there are not to be serious disproportions and shortcomings in the trends in living standards. But wherever reproduction costs grow more rapidly than the social product, meaning a growth of the reproduction coefficient, with a constant slowing down in growth of average wages per worker in production, and where, as a result of this, the negligible growth in wages does not stimulate sufficiently the increase in productivity

GRAPH 5.   *Development of Social and of Reproduction Costs*
(in constant prices, 1955 and 1960)

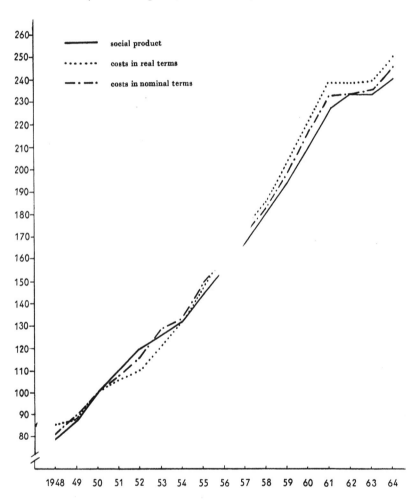

Source: Based on *Sattistická ročenka* (Statistical Yearbook) 1965, pp. 136–137.

of labour, the unhealthy development in reproduction costs becomes at a certain moment a *direct* brake on further growth.

But, since the nominal wages themselves do not tell us much about the actual reproduction costs of labour, which are dependent also on the trends in living costs, it is important to study also the real wages. We shall therefore proceed to a graphic survey of the development of the social product and of reproduction costs (including both nominal and real wages) in Czechoslovakia in the period 1948–64.

As shown in Graph 5, the rate of growth of reproduction costs (in real terms) passed up the rate of growth of social product in about 1954, was considerably higher in 1956–7, approached it in 1958, and then again grew considerably more rapidly up to 1961. The extreme sharpening of this contradiction in 1961 required extraordinary measures that brought the two trends closer together in 1962–3, but in 1964 the contradiction began to grow again. The reproduction coefficient increased from 0.80 in 1950 to 0.84 in 1961. At the same time — as we shall show later — there was a retardation of the annual increment in average nominal wages which actually declined in the 1960–64 period to a level that no longer provided sufficient wage-incentive for an increase in productivity of labour, making 1.95 per cent increment in branches of production, not including co-operative farms and

TABLE 8   *Comparison of the Average Yearly Increments of Social Product and of National Income* (in percentage at comparable prices)[1]

Average yearly increments:	1949–55	1954–58	1959–64
of social product	9.6	7.5	4.9
of national income	9.3	7.2	3.5
Index of average yearly increments (First 5-Year Plan average = 100)			
of social product	100.0	78.1	51.0
of national income	100.0	77.4	37.6

[1] 1948–60 in prices comparable with 1955, in 1960–64 in prices comparable with 1960.

Source: *Statistická ročenka* (Statistical Yearbook) 1965, pp. 136 and 139.

apprentices. On the other hand, the growth of production accumulation (a) was more rapid than the growth of any other element in the reproduction costs. If (a) in 1950 = 100, it grew to 691 in 1961.

The disproportionate growth of reproduction costs, of course, was felt first in a disproportionate rise in cost of machinery and raw material used in production consumption. As a result, social product grows more rapidly than national income, and the national income share in the social product declines, as shown by the table and graph on pp. 69 and 70.

A too rapid growth in the increments of production funds requires

GRAPH 6.   *Share of National Income in the Social Product* $\dfrac{N\ I}{S\ P}$

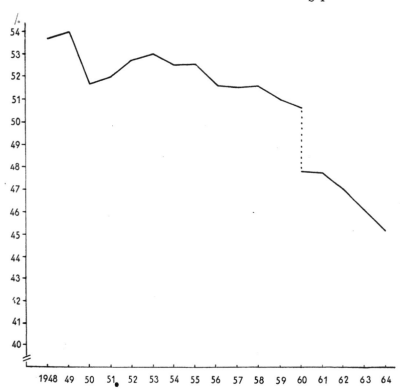

Source: Based on *Statistická ročenka* (Statistical Yearbook) 1965, pp. 136–139

a growth in the share of national income going to production accumulation. This share increased as follows:

TABLE 9   *Share of National Income Going to Production Accumulation*

1950	1951	1952	1953	1954	1955	1956	1957	1958	1959	1960	1961
5.6	6.5	7.4	9.7	5.5	8.3	9.0	10.9	12.0	15.3	14.4	
										13.5	16.1

Note: Development up to 1960 in 1955 prices, data for 1960–61 in 1960 prices.
Source: *Plánované hospodářství* (Planned Economy) No. 12/64, p. 12.

The above analysis shows how a negative extensive growth must necessarily undermine the basis for further extensive growth or economic growth of any kind. On the one hand, it produces an excessive increase in expenditure of labour and on the other hand, the rise in productivity of labour and in production slows down, and therefore these needs are unadequately covered. For a certain time this contradiction can be surmounted at the price of an absolute and relative retardation in the rate of growth in personal and social consumption. This development becomes itself a brake on further increases in productivity of labour, and therefore at a certain moment the development must lead to stagnation of production, of productivity of labour and of national income.

Let us summarize what is the direct cause of the increasing contradictions between the retarding growth of production, and productivity of labour, on the one hand, and accelerating reproduction costs and material inputs on the other. Then we shall show why inadequate development of personal and social consumption sharpens this contradiction.

The first point we must give consideration to is the incorrect structure of production (macro- and microstructure), resulting from extensive development and having a decisive influence on the decline in efficiency of machinery funds, as well as to the disproportionate growth of production consumption. A too high and a constantly growing share going to mining and heavy industry results in a growth of the kind of industrial production which requires relatively high investments with long-term realization without ensuring a proportionate

71

increase in production. The volume of production per unit of investment declines most rapidly in this case, because of the disproportionate growth in costs of new production equipment in comparison with improvements in technology, but also because of the rapidly worsening situation in regard to natural resources. The higher the proportion of investments made in these branches of production, the lower the total effectiveness of investments and of basic production funds.

Our survey compares the development of extractive and heavy industry (chemistry is added as a matter of interest) with the global trend in industrial investments.

Taking the volume of investments in 1950 as 100, the average annual volume of investment in the various periods in different branches of production was as follows:

TABLE 10   *Indexes of Annual Investment by Industries* (1950 = 100)

	1951–1955	1956–60	1961–63	1951–63
Industry total	134	198	262	192
power production	164	278	300	239
fuel extraction	196	404	451	335
fuel processing	179	848	766	572
mining and treating ferrous metals	146	174	514	242
mining and treating non-ferrous metals	486	594	3 740	1 278
metallurgy of ferrous metals	148	182	278	191
metallurgy of non-ferrous metals	465	584	657	555
engineering	104	256	246	195
chemical industry	137	151	333	188

Source: *Statistické ročenky* (Statistical Yearbooks), 1960 and 1964.

Naturally we cannot avoid investing in less effective branches of production with a slower turnover. But their share in the total can develop only as much as the economy can bear, in a way that does not hamper its future development. When the structure of production is determined, however, by simplified, one-sided planning methods, and production incentives prevail which do not reflect aspects and calculations of highest return on investment, then the structure of production inevitably develops counter to the requirements of an optimum economic development.

In addition to the low efficiency in the development of the material inputs, the process of scrapping worn-out machinery was slow and the average age of machines rose. Furthermore, there was little progressive technical change in many newly introduced machines and equipment. Even the scrapped machines and equipment were usually not replaced by really advanced ones. Year by year the technical development of our production lagged farther behind the world technical development and did not use sufficiently the newest findings of science and research that had already been applied throughout the industrially advanced world.

Moreover, there was the fact that the average length of time for realizing capital investments was growing and there was a greater volume of construction that had been started and not finished.[1] This, of course, greatly increased investment costs and the general costs of production and material inputs.

Finally, we must tell of the ineffective use of fixed assets by the enterprises and the way unused capacity increased. The enterprises exaggerated their demands for investment capital, to create the most favourable conditions for carrying out the growing quantitative targets of the production plans. Together with the continually higher annual production targets which ignored the fact that great reconstruction and modernization in the enterprises leads to a temporary slowing down in the growth of production, there was a rapid increase in claims made by enterprises for investment capital for *development* which added to the existing production base. To a certain extent at the same time under-used capacity became a reserve to meet unforeseen imposed changes in production targets and this also contributed to gross production costs.

[1] In the period 1960–63 the volume of uncompleted construction grew by 13,300 million crowns, and the total was estimated at the end of 1963 at 40,800 million crowns.

Source: *Dvacet let rozvoje ČSSR* (Twenty Years of Czechoslovak Development), Prague 1965.

73

The excessive and ineffective expansion of plant and machinery was accompanied, of course, by a large, superfluous consumption of material. On the one hand, the disproportionate increase in investment itself caused rapidly growing demands for raw and other material (for engineering and construction), on the other hand, the outdated machines consumed too large quantities of raw materials that were not efficiently processed. Furthermore, the enterprises were interested in producing goods at as high as possible material costs and in general using a superfluous amount of material. We shall return to this later.

The disproportionately growing needs for raw and other materials, especially for engineering and other capital production branches, in turn caused a disproportionate growth of investments in these raw material branches (extractive, power, metallurgical, etc.). The rapid extension of the basic fixed assets in these branches caused in turn immense demands on manpower, buildings, machinery, and equipment, that is, of demands on engineering and construction branches. Thus there arose to a certain degree a type of production useless for final consumption.

One may say, in general, that the extensive development of the economy in Czechoslovakia in the past years was characterized by relatively high material inputs, ineffective use of the plant and machinery, a disproportionate growth in investment costs, a slowing down in productivity of labour, a more marked decline in growth of national income than in the global product, and a growing share of net investment in the national income. The most synthetic expression of this development was the more rapid rise in total production costs[1] than in social production, and of the overall input-output ratio.

Anyone who wants to deny that there was an extensive development and that it had negative results in our country, by pointing to the considerable rise in productivity of labour in industry, and the assurance of growth in industrial production by a greater rise in productivity of labour than growth in employment, is obscuring the facts with his apologetics. In the first place, he is speaking only of the rise in productivity of labour and not of general social productivity,

---

[1] Including costs of investments under construction.

ignoring the fact that a growing part of the savings in labour in production was eaten up by the huge costs of reproduction, including material inputs, so that there remained less and less for final consumption. In the second place, he does not speak of the fact that even the rise in productivity of labour was slowing down more and more and that it could have risen much more sharply if scrapping of outdated plant and equipment, and their replacement by more modern and technically more progressive machinery had been more rapid. Only in a period of surplus manpower in agriculture could a slower rise in productivity of labour in industry (as a result of extensive expansion of industrial production funds) assure a more rapid rise of total production per producer than with an intensive development of industrial funds. But when manpower continued to leave agriculture for industry, there resulted an actual retardation of the rise in productivity f industrial labour, whereas in agriculture the relative shortage of manpower (in relation to the technical level of agriculture) became the main bstacle to a more rapid growth of agricultural production, and the *extensive* expansion of industrial plant ceased to have any economic sense.

Even more serious, of course, is the fact that industry absorbs almost all increases in manpower coming from agriculture, while the non-production sphere, especially the paid and free services, did not develop, because there was an absolute shortage of manpower. Furthermore, the lack of material interest retarded their development. This also is a typical expression of the extensive development of production whose detrimental consequence was not recognized in time.[1]

The gradual realization by planning agencies that sources of exten-

---

[1] A comparison with countries with highly intensive development of production shows quite clearly the excessively high proportion of workers in Czechoslovak industry, and the too low proportion of workers in the non-production sphere. In the United States the percentage of workers in industry was 26.7 per cent in 1950 and 25.6 per cent in 1963, while the proportion of workers in services and public administration rose from 23.6 per cent to 25.2 per cent. In the German Federal Republic about 20 per cent of the workers were in the non-production sphere and by 1963 22 per cent.

Even though we cannot always compare precisely certain aggregated items, still the development in Czechoslovakia is an example of a typical extensive development. (Continued on next page.)

sive development were being exhausted and attempts to restrict the shift of manpower to industry not only came too late, but also could not have any hope of realization because the objective conditions were not prepared for them. There were no technical facilities for a rapid and substantial increase in productivity of labour, and therefore all industrial departments and enterprises forced through further additions of manpower, so that they could assure the required growth in production. The old system of management definitely obstructed a transition to intensive development.

It is quite clear that a substantial rise in productivity of labour requires a lengthy preparatory period of technical adjustments. Minor technical and organizational changes in the enterprises are inadequate. Instead there must be truly fundamental technical and technological changes, often linked with basic replacement, reconstruction, and modernization of the entire production equipment. But such an intensive technical development of production requires, first of all, that the enterprises have a real economic interest in such development and the indispensable conditions to carry it out, the most important employees (technicians, designers, planners, researchers, etc.) must have sufficient financial motivation and the necessary requirements for their work. Finally, the personnel in the non-production sphere that provides the necessary prerequisites for such a development of production (schools, science, research, etc.) must have the necessary scope, prior training, and all the material conditions for their work.

But it is precisely these prerequisites for a qualitative and intensive development of production that could not be created under condi-

(cont.)

Percentage of workers in industry and in the non-production sphere of the total number of workers in the national economy.

Workers	1950	1955	1960	1964
in industry	30.0	32.6	37.3	38.1
in the non-production sphere	13.4	14.9	16.7	18.8

Source: *Statistické ročenky ČSSR* (Statistical Yearbooks of the ČSSR), 1950–1964.

tions of extensive development and the old administrative system of management. In the first place, the enterprises did not have the possibility for, or the necessary interest in, such development, as we shall discuss later in more detail. To the inadequate creation of material conditions throughout our society, there was added the insufficient interest in creating sources of qualitative development in the production units themselves.

The continually slowing rate of growth of national income, with a relative decline in consumption funds, meant that the means to cover personal and social consumption did not grow fast enough. The rise in average wages had to be restricted and gradually slowed down, as shown by the following table.

TABLE 11   *Average Annual Increment in Average Wages:*

Average annual increments	1949–53	1954–58	1959–64
Average monthly wages of workers in the socialist sector of the national economy (excluding co-operative farms)	5.9	3.4	1.8
Average monthly wages of workers in the socialist sector of industry only	—	2.9	1.9

Source: *Statistická ročenka* (Statistical Yearbook), 1965, p. 22.

In 1963 there was an absolute decline in average nominal and real wages of workers and employees. Whereas the index of nominal wages in 1962 was 128.2 (1953 = 100), it declined in 1963 to 128.1, and in real wages the decline was from 148.4 in 1962 to 147.5 in 1963. To a much greater extent than in wages of workers (where a rise is an essential stimulus to raising productivity of labour) there was a restriction of financial sources for assuring the necessary rise in salaries of technicians, educators, scientists, medical personnel, etc. Thus for years, especially since 1959 there has been more and more of a harmful tendency to level out incomes, which had the effect, in turn, of hampering scientific and technical development. This can be seen in Table 12.

TABLE 12   *Relations between Different Categories of Average Monthly Wages* (average wage of workers = 100)

Average wage for:

Year	Workers in industry	Engineers & technical personnel	Office employees in industry	Employees in non-production sphere
1955	100	126.2	85.1	87.0
1956	100	127.2	84.7	86.9
1957	100	127.7	85.4	91.0
1958	100	131.5	88.2	90.7
1959	100	133.6	88.6	90.0
1960	100	132.7	87.2	89.0
1961	100	130.7	85.7	87.8
1962	100	127.3	83.9	86.9
1963	100	126.6	83.7	87.5

Source: *Statistická ročenka ČSSR* (Statistical Yearbook of the ČSSR), 1964, pp. 122 and 171.

Nevertheless, attempts to prevent a growth of the demand-supply disparity could not be successful and this resulted in a number of supply difficulties. On the one hand, the unrealistic plans for agricultural production had not been carried out for years[1], so that year after year there was a deficiency in the planned market stocks, and, on the other hand, the structural discrepancy between the market

[1] *Percentage Fulfilment of the Plan of Gross Agricultural Production*

Year	Crop production	Livestock production	Total
1960	93	96	95
1961	89	97	93
1962	81	92	86
1963	94	99	96

Source: *Statistical Report of the Central Commision of People's Control and Statistics.*

78

supplies and demand continued to grow. This brought about a situation of unconvertible purchasing power with people losing time unnecessarily in looking for various types of goods.

True, there was a planned restriction of growth of nominal wages, but since the payment of wages depended on fulfilling the plan of production and not on actual sale of goods, wages were paid even when part of the goods were not sold at all, or were sold — particularly with regard to exports — at a considerable loss. This resulted in a failure to comply with market demands and in amassing stocks of undesirable goods.

The inner development in Czechoslovakia reflected itself, naturally, in foreign trade as well.

Here, too, there were structural problems. Trends in structure of goods produced and exported did not correspond sufficiently to the development of goods demanded on the world markets. In particular, the structure of our production was not fully directed toward the most effective exploitation of home raw-materials and toward the importation of raw materials that could be most advantageously processed (crude oil, natural gas, etc.). Instead raw materials were imported and processed that could be least efficiently used. Therefore, the share of labour added to the value of imported raw materials (processed and re-exported) was small and even began to show a relative decline.

In many branches of production the development of social productivity of labour fell behind world trends. Consequently our costs of production were higher than the world level. Since world prices at which we had to sell these products were determined by world production costs, we had mounting losses. Further losses were caused by the technological backwardness in many branches of production, by inadequate systems of services and spare parts.

This means, in general, that for a certain quantity of labour contained in the imported products we had to export year by year more of our own labour. All this meant mounting losses in foreign trade. Relatively, an increasing quantity of machines, of industrial consumer goods, and other products had to be exported to cover imports. This meant that national income, itself increasing only slowly, declined further in relation to the gross product. The same applies to final consumption and accumulation, because with ineffective use of imported raw materials a point was reached at which the resulting exports did not cover their costs. An example was the ineffective use of imported raw materials by building overheavy machines for export.

Machinery export is an important item by which Czechoslovakia covers its growing imports of agricultural products and raw materials, both for metallurgical and engineering production and for light industry (especially the textile and leather goods industry). We must also realize that the growing exports of machines, necessary also to cover the importation of agricultural products, were made partly at the price of a slower mechanization of agriculture and were decidedly less effective than would have been a rapid rise in intensity of agriculture in this country.

Under these conditions, further extension of the proportion of engineering production, especially heavy engineering and metallurgy in industry in this country, as some economists suggested, would have been ruinous, for the passive balance of imports of raw material for all our industry (including engineering) would have grown more rapidly than the active balance of exports of our processing industry.[1] Experience of recent years demonstrated the need for changing the structure of our foreign trade, for increasing exports of consumer goods and the imports of machinery (imports of special machinery in return for our special machines). This assumes an increase in specialization in the production of machines, that the proportion of

[1] *Balance-Sheet of Imports and Exports of Some Groups of Goods*

	1953	1955	1956	1961	1962
1. Net imports: Fuels, mineral raw materials and metals	—796	—739	—1011	—3836	—3132
2. Net exports: Machinery, equipment and tools	+2142	+2675	+2557	+3141	+3614
Sum of rows 1 + 2	+1346	+1936	+1546	—695	+482

Source: *Statistická ročenka* (Statistical Yearbook), 1963, pp. 358 – 370.

machinery in industrial production may not continue to rise, and that specialization may now be the rule.

It is often given as an argument to explain our growing difficulties that the external conditions for foreign trade have grown worse. They say that, whereas shortly after the war conditions were favourable for marketing our engineering products (reconstruction in capitalist countries, industrialization in socialist countries), these conditions have disappeared in recent years. Competition has sharpened on capitalist markets and socialist countries are demanding more and more that we import their engineering products as a condition for their taking our machines (machine for machine, raw material for raw material).

Even though this change in external conditions is a fact, we cannot use this to excuse the structural inflexibility and lack of adaptation in our production. No foreign trade partner will import our products unless he gains also by the trade. The world markets are ruled by market laws and the inability of our production to adjust itself sufficiently fast to market trends is necessarily a domestic matter of our system of management, as we shall show later. We can assure the necessary exports without increasing losses only if the development of our macro- and microstructure corresponds to the demand on world markets (or even anticipates it), only if it assures a growing specialization of production (particularly in engineering), so that our exports may adapt better to the import possibilities of other countries and assure the development of production costs in accord with world costs.

With the growing competition and anarchy in capitalist markets, we can meet the problem only if we produce on a mass basis, keeping pace with the trends in world production costs, so that there will be no losses when we sell at world prices. In a small country like ours this is possible in a very limited number of production branches. Or we can also orient our production on small-scale or piece production, that is so advanced and changes so flexibly that the products will always be at the highest world level in technique and quality, and thus can be sold at relatively high prices. In one way or another, each export branch must have its own clear conception and method of meeting world competition. At the same time, it is necessary to see that the growth of foreign trade with socialist partners will also require us to offer more attractive goods that are of greater benefit to these countries, which, again, is possible only in one of the ways outlined above.

To surmount the problems in foreign trade — and, if it does not expand, the Czechoslovak economy cannot grow — it is essential to change the structure of the national economy and make its development more flexible, especially to change the proportions between the share of domestic and imported input in the value of exports and to increase the effectiveness of foreign trade. Of course, this requires a better relation between domestic production costs and prices on world markets. And this, in turn, requires that gains or losses from a specific development of foreign trade have direct effect on income, both of the production enterprises and the foreign-trade enterprises — instead of going directly to the state budget.

If we think over the general contradictions, it is quite clear why there had to be a cessation of growth in the years 1962–63 and had to be great economic difficulties. These contradictions caused extreme tension between resources and needs.

Another look at the course of development of our basic contradiction will show us why the rapid growth of necessary production costs in relation to the growth of social product (especially of investment costs, which reflected the low efficiency of fixed assets) had, finally, to come to a stop. A progressing development in this direction would have brought about — at a definite moment — a decline of non-production social and individual consumption, both in relative and in absolute terms. This interruption may take place "sooner or later" often depending on casual circumstances. But, as we know, every casual event is one of many expressions of the inevitable. The immediate causes of the sharp retardation in growth of production were great, inadequately coordinated changes in foreign trade and a non-fulfilment of the tasks of the first year of the third Five-Year Plan, especially in capital investments. This was merely a concrete expression of the unrealistic conception of the plan, set up on premises of extensive growth under conditions when this type of development was no longer possible at all.

The high investments, intended in the third Five-Year Plan, according to the old methods of planning, as assurance of a rapid rate of growth, remained, as early as 1961, to a large degree unrealized. They were set up on unrealistic plans of growth of production, of labour productivity and on plans of declining production costs in all the supply branches and in construction itself. Capital investments were largely dispersed, and not putting many planned investment projects into operation meant serious disproportions of all inter-branch and purchaser-supplier relationships.

The long-term growth of heavy industry, together with sudden and considerably higher investments in 1961–62 forced us to import a huge quantity of material that could not be fully covered by labour embodied in goods we exported.

At the same time, this development was inevitably accompanied by a further rapid growth of purchasing power (increase in wage payments, due especially to a rise in manpower) which was insufficiently covered by market supplies. The non-fulfilment of exaggerated plans of agriculture production, the structurally unfavourable and unvariegated development of production of industrial consumer goods together with a considerable rise in total wages not covered by corresponding production (wages having been paid out for production of outdated, unwanted goods, for products sold with lo s, for uncompleted projects) — all this resulted in a situation where the tension on the market and the dissatisfaction of consumers increased.

Deficiencies of agricultural production, compared with the plan, caused considerable supply difficulties and required unforeseen increases in imports of agricultural products. In order not to deteriorate the already passive foreign trade balance we had to reduce the importation of necessary raw materials, which immediately increased difficulties in production, causing a sharp decline of growth of production. This reflected itself in turn in foreign trade and brought about a further chain reaction. Thus foreign trade became at a certain moment the direct cause for interruption of growth of production, although the foreign trade situation itself was a reflection of the former erroneous extensive development of production.

It is absolutely impossible to understand the long-term negative effect of the extensive development in our production, if we do not think of it as an inevitable result of the old directive system of management and of suppressing socialist market relationships. This could only lead to an extensive economic development. Some economists, both theoretical and practical workers, while realizing the detrimental character of the past economic development, do not see its causal relation with the directive system of management. They believe that it would suffice merely to draw up other economic-political directives, than those in the past, a new production structure, to appoint more capable management personnel in the enterprises and to use more computer technique in management.

We must see that each of the proposed measures is relatively justified and important, but also that they are interrelated with other economic and management processes. Setting up of such requirements by themselves, without changing the whole system of planned management, is to propose measures that simply will not be carried out, to distract attention from a complex, qualitative change that alone can bring about a fundamental change in our economic development. Only someone who is incapable of reflecting on the economic and social relationships will suggest isolated and therefore ineffective measures, instead of trying to solve the problem in a complete way.

Economic-political directives and plans determining the production structure are an indispensable part of the entire management system. In a given system they follow the aims that correspond to that system, using appropriate means for drawing up these goals, relying on quite specific data and methods of work. They are forced to base their work on the information and interests of the lower management bodies and production units, which are, in turn, a product of the general system; they must use appropriate methods of carrying out the aims, etc. Therefore, to demand a change in content of the economic-political directives and plans, leaving the general system of management unchanged, is to demand the impossible.

Using theoretically and practically well trained management personnel in all the economic management positions (not just in the enterprises) is of great importance. At a certain moment in the development, especially when the transition to a new system of management had been decided on, good personnel can be the chief means for carrying out the new system of management. But when conceived of separately from the total system of management, e.g., when the old directive system of management is still in effect, the demand for better trained leading personnel is quite illusory and ineffective, because the most capable manager will have to conform to the existing directive system of management and will gradually lose, not only his qualifications, but also his initiative and zeal for changing what appears to be an unsurmountable, objective, external force.

The same applies to the new mathematical methods that are used in economics and to advanced computer techniques. Unquestionably, transition to a more scientific method of planning and management cannot be imagined without applying new methods and techniques. But, unless there is a well-integrated transition, completely new methods of setting up the goals of economic development, of setting up plans, and methods of carrying them out, unless there is a change in the interests and capabilities of the management bodies, the level of the production units and of all employees, and a consistent utilization of socialist market relationships, the new computer technology would not only fail to assure an optimum economic development, but could even serve to justify a completely one-sided development aimed at simplified goals that do not accord with social interests.

Therefore the system of management must be conceived as an integrated system with mutual relations, obligations and jurisdiction, as ways and methods of setting up goals and tasks, as the instruments and means for carrying them out and checking on them; as a system of utilizing the interests between leading and lower bodies, forming the relationships between the interests and rational cognition by both management and rank and file. Only with such a complex concept can one grasp the fundamental difference between an administrative and the genuinely economic system of managing a socialist economy. And only thus can we understand the causal relation between the previous extensive development and the directive system of management.

Characteristic of this system are the over-simplified criteria and goals observed by all economic, political, planning and management directives, on which all material and moral stimuli were oriented; furthermore the general over-estimation of the interests and initiative of the production workers and collectives in the enterprises, together with the suppression of market relationships between purchasers and suppliers, all played their part.

Two factors were decisive when evaluating any economic development: the rate of growth of total volume of production, and within this aggregate, the growth of certain, selected highly important products. All plans, directives, controls, rewards, moral-political appeals, etc., were to assure that priority was given to these selected products. From this standpoint the directive system of management can also be characterized as a preferential system of management. To safeguard this preference, priority growth of production with a structure decided by the central will, disregarding all other criteria and aspects, is the most characteristic trait of this system.

Plans, setting by directives the tasks for increasing production, were not based on analyses of future possibilities for development of production factors in the different branches of the economy, nor on selection of the most efficient variant of development that would assure the most economical development, and that would correspond to trends in demand and stimulate new demands. Instead they were based on more or less empirical findings on the maximum possible rates of growth of production. These empirical findings originated mainly from experiences during the period of extensive growth. On the basis of these empirically envisaged possibilities for the growth of production in the main branches (engineering, metallurgy, coal mining, energy, etc., and experiences in the mutual relationship of volume of investment and increments of production), as well as by a method of subjectively summarizing the requirements for investments coming from the enterprises, the directive plans were designed, setting the rate of growth of production. Enterprises and departments, relying on the experiences of the previous extensive development, demanded the greatest possible volume of investments, the most manpower and the lowest production targets they could, so that they could fulfil the plans easily. The central planning body, having had experience with exaggerated demands, tried to reduce and limit the demands for investments, for manpower, and to push the targets higher. A compromise directive came out of this conflicting negotiation on the plan and, while it had a good deal of subjective considerations, corresponded on the whole to the possibilities of extensive development and stimulated it.

Furthermore, setting the structure of production by plan had much empiricism and conservatism, based on a very simplified idea of reproduction theories. By balancing sources and needs between the individual branches of production, by more or less unchanging ideas of the norms of material consumption, stressing the chief growth factors (steel, coal, energy, etc.) concepts arose about the basic proportions of growth of individual branches producing means of production. It was thus quite possible to meet the increased production plans, without significant structural changes in engineering, metallurgical, power, extractive, and other industries, and using a very conservative form of distribution of investment sources. The limiting factor was the growing demand for raw materials and fuels, with increasing demand for investments. In sum, this was not a concept of the most effective production structure, based on a constant search for new technical orientation and development of production in all branches, that caused changes both in material inputs and in the mutual inter-branch relations and therefore gradual changes in the basic production structure. Instead it was merely a balancing of the inter-branch global quantities, based on preconceived growth requirements.

At the same time the high and growing proportion of investments made in heavy industry — especially in the heavy extractive industries — was theoretically justified by the very over-simplified concept of the necessity of giving priority to a growth in production of means of production, rather than the production of consumer goods. This, of course, cannot be shown actually by any concrete production structure (e.g., chemical or agricultural production is mainly the production of raw material for production). Moreover the endeavour to balance out the plan in order to prove its correctness is quite erroneous, since for quite different variants of technical and economic development one can achieve internal balance.

The centrally drawn up five-year plans, with the administrative settling of conflicts in negotiations between the central, department and enterprise bodies, were then — after adoption by the government and the National Assembly — quite mechanically disaggregated to the enterprises. Here they often came in conflict with the actual production conditions. The large number of detailed directive indicators (planned rise in gross production, selection of specific products, productivity of labour, investments, manpower, wage funds, etc.) were usually not really coordinated within the enterprises, since no one was able to make an analysis for years ahead of the development of all these individual, inter-related economic factors. Therefore, the targets for growth in production were too high for some enterprises in relation to the planned investments, and for others in relation to the number of workers, and still others might have too high targets in productivity of labour in relation to the range of goods required of it, etc. The enterprises that benefited most were those which managed to fight and win targets in a plan that guaranteed the largest volume of investment, the highest number of workers, and the lowest production tasks.

With this method of detailed, directive planning, the five-year plans were too rigid, and therefore had to be changed. The actual economic development deviated considerably from the long-range plan and, for this reason, the annual plans became of prime importance. Year after year, on the basis of concrete experience, in the central planning body detailed directive plans were drawn up, while the five-year plan changed into a sum of abstract and dead figures. Because of this, the enterprises in fact lost their perspective and the main pressure on them was the control by the higher departmental agencies of fulfilment of annual plans. Moreover, the decisive material interest was linked with the fulfilment of annual planned production targets.

The control and the material interest of the enterprises were aimed primarily at the fulfilment of a planned increase in volume of production and of productivity of labour. Volume of production was expressed by means of an indicator of "gross production" which contained the total costs, not only of actual final production, but also of semi-finished production. Productivity of labour was usually measured by gross production relation to the number of workers. Whether the development of the wage fund was planned at a certain ratio to the development of gross production directly or of productivity of labour, it was found necessary to stimulate a decisive material interest on the part of the enterprises in achieving as large as possible a volume of gross production, in fulfilling and over-fulfilling the plan of gross production.

The instability of the five-year plans and the loss of perspective in the enterprises resulted in indecision, ignorance and neglect of necessary technical developments. Carrying out annual plans of production made the enterprises lose interest in technical changes because on a short-term temporary basis they would slow up growth in production and the fulfilment of the year's plan. In important departments the enterprises were therefore willing, at the most, to introduce only minor technological changes in the important workshops, while the greater part of investments were aimed at expanding plant capacity. Thus the appeals of the superior agencies regarding technological progress — except for a few, selected technical targets set by directive — were only general and rather ineffective proclamations.

The less the attention paid to technical measures conditioning the rise in productivity of labour, the greater the contradiction between the socially necessary development of production and the material interest, as well as the activity of the enterprises. The interest of the enterprises in fulfilling the plan of productivity of labour under worsening technical conditions and a gradual exhaustion of the partial and organizational improvements that could be made, led not only to a frantic avoidance of everything that could, during the year, threaten the plan's fulfilment (this meant any large technological change), but also to production methods that came more and more into conflict with the trends in production needed by society.

The enterprises had an interest in narrowing down the range of goods produced. This did not always lead to a rise in productivity of labour, or to better satisfaction of the purchasers' needs, but it did make it easier to carry out the plan. For the same reason they avoided the introduction of new products, preferred to persist in producing the old, standardized products, preferred to produce goods that used large quantities of material that could be counted in the price of the product and thus higher volumes of gross production[1] could be attained.

[1] We could list innumerable examples from almost every production branch and enterprise. An enterprise manufacturing tractors avoided introducing a new type of tractor that would save in metal, merely because it could not fulfil the plan of gross production if it did; a metallurgical enterprise produced heavy rolled products that were costly in material and refused to introduce thinner sheets; a chemical enterprise was interested in getting expensive chemical raw materials and semi-finished products, using them to produce goods with low labour input — floor coverings — avoiding the products with higher labour input; a textile enterprise disproportionately increased the production of material made from expensive, imported wool and restricted the production from cheaper material; for a long while heavy shoes requiring expensive material were produced, although world fashions had long given preference to light, airy footwear; construction enterprises gave priority to mechanized basic construction work that required lower labour input, that was more costly in material (excavation, heavy walls, etc.), and did not finish construction because the work connected with this had a higher proportion of labour and was therefore not advantageous; enterprises doing repairs avoided performing minor repairs in the homes with lower consumption of material or they tried to make unnecessary replacements of sound parts, and so on.

Furthermore, the disproportionate and unnecessary inter-change between enterprises of products during production made possible double counting of gross production. Any sort of price rise which the enterprises succeeded in attaining (e.g., by slight changes in the products manufactured, etc.) enabled them to increase gross production; and, finally, enterprises were interested in expanding the volume of half-finished, uncompleted production (in the case of construction enterprises, this practice led to extremely detrimental consequences — there was a continual increase of the number of half-finished uncompleted construction projects).

This incorrect orientation of interest and work of the enterprise on mere quantitative growth and, often, only on a fictitious expression of this in accounts, retarded any qualitative development in production, increased the disproportions in production, led to uneconomical operation, great losses and limitations on technical development. Not only were the enterprises not interested in efficiency of investments, but their exaggerated and usually extensively directed investment demands backed by distorted information and reports to central bodies, hampered every effort to make planning more scientific by means of modern mathematical methods, etc.

This system acted as an economic force which compelled the purchasers (either enterprises or the population) to purchase products that did not completely correspond to their needs.[1] (The enterprises were often compelled to do so by administrative measures.)

---

[1] The system of economic contracts, introduced here in 1950 and fully in effect until 1958, was designed so that in the centralized model of management only a few minor data were to be filled in to conclude the concrete planning act. This incorrect conception of a system of economic contracts was fully in accord with the strict centralization of planning and management and the concept of the plan was not regarded as a plan of overall development but for the sector of economic obligations almost exclusively as an allocating balance sheet without regard to whether the scheduling was or was not in harmony with other parts of the plan. If it charged the suppliers with the task of delivering 1000 units, the purchasers were obliged to take these 1000 units, too. This means that both purchaser and supplier were legally obliged to sign the contract, without regard to whether the supplier had the conditions for producing the 1000 units or whether the purchaser could use the 1000 units. Naturally, this means that production enterprises and trade organizations had to purchase a whole series of products that they did not need at all and that remained unused for years in warehouses until they were written off and destroyed.

Sometimes the purchasing enterprises had to re-work the products purchased and adapt them to the actual needs (e.g., to roll thinner the supplied sheet metal which the suppliers preferred to produce because the thicker sheets made it easier to fulfil the plan). Many times consumers had to buy types of goods that did not suit their needs or taste because for a long time they were not able to obtain the goods they wished.

Prices, their movements and relationships, did not *influence* the enterprises in selecting the line of production. Furthermore they did not *interest* the enterprises in cutting production costs and in meeting market demand. And the economically unjustified relations of prices resulted in enterprises producing types of goods that were unrelated to market demands — products that had the most advantageous prices in relation to wage costs. In the first place, this advantage was not harmonized with the trends in demands of customers (often quite the opposite). In the second place, this advantage was not just because of relatively higher net return in relation to wage costs, but also because of relatively higher material costs (the greater the consumption of material in the product the more favourable for the enterprise was the price).

Finally, the price did not exert any prior pressure on cutting production costs in the enterprises on the basis of competitive production, but more or less sanctioned *ex post facto* the production costs calculated by the enterprises.

Of particular importance is the fact that the production enterprises were completely isolated from trends in world prices. They sold goods to Czechoslovak foreign trade enterprises at domestic wholesale prices, not even knowing the prices at which these goods were sold on world markets. They did not know the relation between production costs in this country and world prices, or the amount of loss or profit for the different types of goods. This made them even less interested in increasing the return from foreign trade. Furthermore, not even the foreign trade enterprises had an interest in the real effectiveness of foreign trade, because the profit and loss figures disappeared anonymously into the state budget.

In this way, foreign trade did not exert sufficient pressure to adapt Czechoslovak production costs to world costs, to conform the parameters of technical advance, quality and usefulness to world parameters, and this country's production and export structures to the world trends in demand. Quite the contrary, foreign trade acted as a barrier, preserving the lag in many home products and the rigidity of the commodity production structure in our country.

With this given system of management, plans were inevitably set up subjectively. The actual production units, the enterprises, had no interest in seeking and adopting the ways of developing production that would give the highest return, covering and stimulating real consumer demand; instead, there was an endeavour and a possibility to hide all the more effective production changes that would be desirable for the market, as well as all reserves for using productive sources. And on the other hand, the political organizations were following simplified and one-sided criteria of economic development (the quantitative growth of production), regarding plans only as the decisive instruments for enforcing the centre's wishes. Under such conditions the plans had to be set up in the way we have described. As long as there were extensive sources of growth, the plans could continue to be carried out in this way and there was no pressure to change the ways of planning, nor to change the incentives for the enterprises.

Although the economic waste, the disproportions and the hampering of qualitative development continued to grow, the economic development was considered good on the whole, as long as the planned rise in production was carried out. But in the years 1956–57 the first very serious signs appeared. The sources for extensive development were being exhausted, and therefore there began a political orientation, with the accompanying resolutions and appeals to speed up the technical development and increase the effectiveness of production. This was the aim of the reorganization in planning, management and financing in 1958.

But neither the resolutions nor the reorganization could assure the necessary technical development and a shift over to intensive production, because they did not essentially eliminate the old way of planning or stimulate the material interest of the enterprises. The main line of the reorganization did have the correct goal of lessening the purely quantitative orientation of the plans, of doing away with indicators of gross production, of extending the independence of the enterprises and increasing their interest in a higher return. But the halfway measures and the lack of thoroughness in carrying out the changes, and especially the reluctance to abandon the detailed directives in the central plan, all condemned in advance these partial progressive changes to failure.

The endeavour to increase the enterprises' material interest in an increase in return by tying this to a certain bonus and premium fund, depending on the size of increment in returns, was nullified by the fact that the decisive material interest of the enterprise collectives, together with the development of wage funds, continued to be aimed at growth in productivity of labour (tying the wage funds in a certain quantitive relationship to the indicator of productivity of labour). Since productivity of labour was not only planned by directives in the old way from above, but was also mostly measured by gross production in relation to manpower, the material interest of the enterprise continued to be primarily aimed at one-sided quantitative and extensive development.

The main drawback, however, was that nothing had substantially changed in the old system of planning. Putting in operation some of the new production capacities in the period 1958–59, a certain lessening of the tightness of material supplies, together with higher initiative on the part of the enterprises, which resulted in the fulfilment and over-fulfilment of the planned targets for growth, ended by shifting over to the third five-year plan (1961 to 1965 inclusive). This plan did not ensure a balanced and efficient development. Rates of growth of production, volume of investment, the distribution of investment means and the basic structure of production were set by means of the above-described over-simplified planning method. The growth targets for production were based essentially on experience with extensive growth. The fact that sources for manpower were exhausted, and that there was a necessary limitation on increases of manpower in the plan, meant that higher goals were set for a rise in productivity of labour. The insufficient technical preparedness in production could not be surmounted by higher machinery deliveries, because it was necessary to increase exports of engineering products as the chief means of obtaining foreign currency payments.

The growing demands for new investments in machinery (in manufacturing and in agriculture) brought about — under the simplified method of balancing out and the conservative concept of technol-

93

ogical and structural development — the need for still greater investments in the metallurgical and extractive industries, with a huge backlog of investment tasks for the first years of the five-year plan. With the great problems that existed merely in the balancing out of these excessive tasks in production and investment which could be surmounted on paper only by unrealistic targets in productivity of labour and growth of agricultural production, there had to be a failure of the third Five-Year Plan. The necessary proportional development of production was not assured as required for carrying out the great investment tasks. This was especially because the necessary preceding qualitative technical development had not been assured, and, for this reason, there were no realistic possibilities for the necessary growth in productivity of labour. But there was not even enough manpower available to assure a more rapid extensive growth in the old way.

For these reasons, the third Five-Year Plan did not succeed and the growing contradictions culminated in 1962–63, as we have described. Despite the numerous reorganizations of management, despite the changes introduced in 1958, there was no essential change in the old model of administrative management. Any basic change was prevented — although there had been warning signals from the economy — by the dogmatically conceived idea of a socialist economy and of a socialist society in general that had arisen in the period in which Stalinist economic theories absolutized certain historically specific socialist forms of development. The incorrect ideological conceptions prevented the consistent and thorough-going change in the system of management which — whether or not it fully corresponded to a certain specific stage of development — became the most serious hindrance to the development of a socialist economy in Czechoslovakia.

But the old methods of management are so entrenched that it will not be easy to overcome them definitively and to wipe them out from our society. Again and again, their proponents try to show that these methods are justified and critics of them wrong. They seize every opportunity for this. They attempted to use the fact that in 1964–65 there was again a rise in industrial production as an argument to show the vitality of the old method of management and that it was unnecessary to shift to a new system of economic management.

A critical evaluation of the previous development in 1962–63 was called "pessimism and a blackening of our past." Although it is obvious that one cannot use abstract moral categories, strongly tinged by desires and narrow interests, to refute facts and results of objective analyses, they were again evaluating the rise in industrial production in just as one-sided and simplified a way as in the past.

In the years 1964–65, extensive growth continued with negative effect in the production sphere, where certain temporary conditions had once more been created for it.

First, there was success in putting in operation some new production capacities that had been started in previous years. In the years 1961–64, new production capacities amounting to 125,400 million crowns were put in operation. This is roughly 10 per cent higher than in 1956–60. Thus the work of past years served again to expand the production base that helps to assure a certain increase in production. The new capacities, of course, meant a further drawing off of manpower and the situation in manpower was rapidly growing worse. In general, the new capacities were not given the full, planned number of workers, and this was one of the reasons that factory output did not come up to planned capacity.

Therefore, the sharp decline in effectiveness of the basic means of production continued; in 1964 there was 5 per cent less production per unit of industrial means of production than in 1963. The most serious, however, was the fact that the increase in production was accompanied by an immense rise in material inputs; there was only a slight rise in national income which remained at substantially the same level as in 1961. The total increase in social product in 1964 to the amount of 10,800 million crowns was swallowed up by the increment in inputs and depreciation, totalling 9,300 crowns, and for the increment in national income only 1,500 million crowns remained.

With this purely extensive development, the enterprises were driven to fulfil and over-fulfil the plan of volume of production, without regard to the efficiency of the development. For this reason, the contradiction between the trends in production costs and in growth of production had not been surmounted, and there was a growing contradiction between the rapid increase in consumer purchasing power and the structure of market supplies. There still was a slight improvement and the supplies to consumers were maintained, but only because in the last few years the share of the national income going to accumulation declined markedly — by one third from 1961 to 1964. This reduction of accumulation is not an expression of higher effectiveness of the basic means of production, but simply a result of limitation on volume of capital investment. This marked decline in accumulation explains a certain temporary alleviation of the situation in foreign trade.

Even though the substantial cut in accumulation was a necessary measure for a transitional solution of the problems of foreign trade and dispersal of investment projects, it is important to realize it is only a temporary measure. After several years' decline in accumulation it would scarcely be possible to continue to maintain consumption at the expense of the fund of accumulation, because this would retard the growth of production in future years. We could tolerate a longer term of relative decline in accumulation only as a result of real technical progress, structural changes and a general rise in the effectiveness of production, especially of basic means of production.

But the point is that we could not think of going over to such an active and intensive economic development under conditions where the administrative forms of management persisted. Only if they are actually replaced by economic management, with a consistent use of socialist market relations, can the gradual changes in the economic development in this country be attained. The succeeding part of this book is to be devoted to a theoretical interpretation of these new methods of planned management and use of market relationships.

Summary

Until the first socialist state arose, Marxist economic theory assumed that commodity-money relationships would disappear with the end of the capitalist economy. Shortly after the Soviet Union came into being, towards the end of the period called War Communism, Lenin recognized the necessity of utilizing market relations to assure the development of the Soviet economy. But he thought the reason they continued to exist was that extensive and dispersed small-scale production, especially in agriculture, persisted.

After agriculture had been generally collectivized, it was found necessary to continue retaining and utilizing market relationships, but these, Stalin felt, derived their existence from cooperative production, particularly in agriculture which, as "a less consistent form of socialist production and socialist ownership compelled market relationships with the state socialist production." This theory resulted in an attitude of tolerating market relationships as a hangover from the past, which must be driven as soon as possible from a socialist economy. It meant also the denial of intrinsic reasons for the existence of commodity-money relationships within socialist state production and the suppression and formalizing of these relationships by administrative forms of management.

After the death of Stalin, it was recognized that commodity-money relationships were necessary, even between state enterprises, but there was actually no success in refuting the Stalinist theory of the causes for the existence of socialist commodity-money relationships. Nor did the "distribution theory" serve this purpose, for it did not manage to explain the real reasons and essence of socialist market relationships, and therefore was unable to do away completely with the entrenched Stalinist ideas. Furthermore, it did not demand alteration in exchange methods and forms prevailing in economic practice; therefore, it did not demand change in the administrative form of management that continued to suppress and formalize market relationships.

The e administrative forms of planning and management, restricting market relationships, also began to be applied after the Second World War in the socialist economy of Czechoslovakia. They assured in this country a rapid extensive growth in industrial production and, for a number of years, a rapid rise in consumption and living standards as well. But this extensive development continued, even under conditions where the sources for it had long been exhausted and therefore its preservation led to great economic losses.

The development of the Czechoslovak socialist economy in recent years has shown the necessity to overcome the negative extensive growth and to go over to a highly intensive development. Of course, the fact that the recognition of this necessity came rather late and that the sources for extensive growth had been not only exhausted but even, one might say, overdrawn (at the expense of agriculture, services, the infra-structure, even at the price of investment and foreign trade losses and a retarded rise in living standards, etc.), makes it more difficult to effectuate these changes.

The basis for a transition to intensive growth in the present situation is to carry out basic structural changes in production, to assure a genuine, qualitative development of production factors.

A basic prerequisite for this is doing away with the system of administrative planned management which had caused a loss of perspective because of the instability in the long-range plans, and also determined production by one-sided, mainly quantitative and uneconomic orientation of activity and incentives. It led to quite unnecessary investments and needlessly expensive growth of production; needless consumption of material; an avoidance of technical and qualitative development; growing disproportions, or a continual state of emergency and shortages; a lag in services, science, research, in the educational system; retarded the rise in consumption, and levels wage and salary scales, which again slows down qualitative development.

But, especially, the administrative system of management restricts the enterprises' independence and undermines the optimum development of their initiative. Management bodies in the enterprises could seldom decide independently and flexibly on any economic process according to the rapidly changing economic conditions, but were primarily compelled to keep formal records of carrying out the administratively prescribed quantitative indicators. The increase in contracts required still further formal record-keeping, because, again, it was directed toward the fulfilment of the indicators set by the higher bodies and they could not evaluate the directives themselves (judge how far they corresponded or not to the concrete economic conditions and possibilities) and could not at all discover the actual economic possibilities for the individual enterprises (for example, the possibilities of improving products, introducing new ones, perfecting technology, etc.).

Changing over to genuinely planned management and a consistent use of socialist market relationships is a condition for a lasting improvement in a socialist economy. But this requires the surmounting of entrenched ideas and methods of socialist planning that have hitherto prevailed, and the understanding of the necessity, essence and particular features of socialist commodity-money relationships, utilizing them in macroeconomic planning.

II A PLANNED ECONOMY AND MARKET RELATIONSHIPS

1 The General and Direct Social Orientation of Labour under Socialism

In Marxist economics, socialist planning is usually treated as an expression of the direct social character of labour under socialism. This is the negation of the indirect social character of labour under private commodity production. With private ownership the work of individual members of society could not be directly expended in a *planned* way as social labour, although it was always necessarily designed to satisfy the needs of the other members of society. Under socialism, labour is expended *directly* as social labour.

Hitherto the substantial change actually occurring under socialism when labour has become socialized has always been explained too abstractly and with too great over-simplification. The so-called direct social character of labour was considered an *absolute* antithesis of indirect social labour, as an expression of the idea that national planning of the economy would in itself assure that labour expended in any socialist enterprise or factory would always be socially necessary labour. The fact that this has not been true in every case was considered to be merely one of the temporary, transitional shortcomings of our economic understanding and planning, which would be overcome in time, when planning bodies would have greater proficiency and experience.

It was, however, never conceded that it was more than just insufficient knowledge (and this problem was also immensely simplified), or that definite, objectively necessary conflicts of interest could prevent labour from being fully expended as socially necessary labour. On the contrary, the existence of such contradictions was strictly denied and the unity of interests of members of socialist society was again declared to be absolute. The logical result of such thinking was then, naturally, the rejection of real commodity-money relations and, of a market mechanism within a "thoroughly socialist (state) production". Commodity-money relations were reduced to a formality in deriving certain commodity forms only from the external relations of state enterprises (with cooperatives or with foreign states).

First, it is a matter of analysing in more detail the Marxist category "direct social labour", to show what is really changed when labour is expended as a consequence of socialist nationalization of the means of production, and why planned development under socialism must be conceived of in a different way than hitherto. This will show, at the same time, that the identification of the category "socially necessary labour" with the category "direct or planned expenditure of labour" is incorrect. We consider it, moreover, more correct to use, right from the start, the expression "general and direct social orientation of labour" rather than "direct social character of labour". I shall attempt to explain why.

In the second part of this study we will explain the necessary contradiction arising within socialist labour, which cannot be eliminated by socialist planning and must be solved by specific commodity-money relations.

a Planned Management of Economic Activity under Socialism

The socialist nationalization of labour means, first of all, to do away with the class distribution of the means of production that had in the past divided society into antagonistic classes, non-owners and owners, workers and those who exploit workers. The socialist mode of distributing means of production prevents them from becoming private property, makes it impossible for people to decide their use according to private interests and will, against the interests and will of other people, using the means of production to exploit the labour of others. Means of production are appropriated in a socialist way, i.e., they are produced, distributed, exchanged and used throughout society in accordance with the needs and interests of society as a whole and according to society's plans.

When private appropriation of means of production is done away with, all members of society are put on a mutually equal basis as regards the fundamental mode of appropriation of necessities of life. All members of society, except those who are disabled, are required to earn their living by labour. With the immensely developed and widely ramified division of labour, where no one can obtain all the necessary means of subsistence by his own work, there arises the necessity of cooperation among all members of society following a common goal, i.e., a goal that corresponds to the general interest of all members of society.

It is in this sense that direct cooperation among all members of the whole of society arises. Within the limits of society as a whole people must proceed in their work in a mutually purposeful way, in order that their different types of work might supplement and complement each other.

A purposeful determination of the development of social production under socialism is assured primarily by the planned economic activity of production, exchange and distribution.

Of course, there is a certain planning of economic activity under capitalism, too. Here, also, the individual capitalists or corporations set up a goal and procedure for future economic activity. Some capitalist states also attempt, mainly by fiscal and monetary policies and other measures, to direct the economy's development in a planned way within a given state or in economic regions. If we want, then, to express the special feature of planning under socialism, we must resort to more concrete definition. How does the purposeful direction of economic activity under socialism differ from that under capitalism?

In the first place, under socialism there is planning of *all* economic activity for *the entire* national economy. Under capitalist private-property relations, only the activity of separate units is planned within the framework of one or another private capitalist enterprise or capital corporation. But even when the capitalist state attempts to direct the development of the entire national economy, private decisions remain decisive in the orientation of economic activity, which leads to insurmountable contradictions between the state plans and the over-all development of the national economy. Under capitalism, therefore, the entire activity of the national economy cannot be planned as it can under socialism, because there necessarily are not only contradictory class interests, but also the contradictions among the different private owners of capital (or the large corporations). It is true that they can and do at various times come to an agreement on some specific joint planned operation, but their private or group interests, their will and decisions are always in the final analysis *decisive* for their actual economic activity. This is one of the main phenomena of private ownership.

The contrary is true under socialism, where there is socialist distribution of the means of production and socialist division of labour, and where, therefore, there is no contradiction between labour and ownership, and where consumer goods are distributed on a socialist basis, according to work performed and partly also according to the needs of the members of society. Here exists a unified basic interest of all workers, an interest in the socially necessary optimum development of labour cooperation throughout all of society, and in a socialist distribution of the results of this labour.

The repeated perception of economic phenomena, the experiences of different members of society, and then, of course, the expanding theoretical understanding of economic relationships lead people to recognize that all production is directly and mutually linked and that the results of social production are distributed substantially according to labour. Therefore, there is a fundamental common interest of all members of society to subordinate their work to the goal which is set by society and which determines the trends in general social production. That means at the same time that the goals and the procedure, that is, the plans of smaller social groups, regional or on the level of enterprise, factory or shop, or of individuals, are subordinated to the more general plans, the plans for society as a whole, and also that, within the limits of the society, there is a uniform approach.

The system of planning for society as a whole is, therefore, an expression of the fundamental unity of interests of society, and that, again, is an expression of socialist production relations. As we shall show later, the unity of interests is not absolute. Even under socialism there are conflicts of people's interests, and hence in their activities as well. Of course, if we compare this with capitalism, we see a substantial difference. The antagonistic conflicts of interest between classes have disappeared and the antagonisms between private owners, too. Conflicts among workers under socialism are insignificant compared with those under capitalism, and the interests of the people appear as coordinated, united interests. Naturally, when we compare socialism with communism at some future date, the internal conflicts under socialism will seem substantial as compared with those under communism.[1] It is in this relative sense that we must understand the unity of interests under socialism.

The first particular characteristic of socialist economics, therefore, lies in the fact that there is planned management of the main economic activities within society as a whole, as the expression of the unity of fundamental interests of all members of society.

The second special feature is that under socialism there is a possibility to foresee the essential inter-relationships between the main economic activities, and, precisely because of this, there exist conditions for basic agreement between the plans and the subsequent actual economic activity.

The development of the main economic activities can be so planned that they will evolve basically in intrinsic harmony with these economic activities, with which they are connected. Precisely this is what it means to respect economic laws. The formula, "utilize or apply socialist economic laws," is very often used in our everyday life, but, for the most part, very abstractly and with little idea of its content. As we know, laws are the essential, necessary relationships between phenomena or things and when we speak of economic laws, these are the essential, necessary relationships of various economic activities. If we want to apply purposefully these logical relationships, we must respect these laws. This does not mean that we must create

---

[1] "In its first phase, or first stage, Communism *cannot* as yet be fully ripe economically and entirely free from traditions or traces of capitalism... But it is important to realize how infinitely mendacious is the ordinary bourgeois conception of Socialism as something lifeless, petrified, fixed once for all, whereas in reality *only* under Socialism will a rapid, genuine, really mass forward movement, embracing first the majority and then the whole of the population, commence in all spheres of public and personal life." V. I. Lenin, "The State and Revolution," *Selected Works*, Vol. II, Part 1, Foreign Languages Publishing House, Moscow 1951.

them, they exist objectively, independent of our will. This means directing economic activity in such a way that essentially interrelated economic activity will develop, as much as possible, in mutual harmony.

Under capitalism this is rarely possible. For example, it is not feasible to determine wages in all enterprises in a way that will harmonize with the development of production programs of all enterprises. And yet there is an essential relationship between wage policy and the production programs of the individual enterprises. Wage trends are the basic determining factor in the development of market demand. And market demand, in turn, must be met by a certain supply of consumer goods. And this supply of goods on the market is, again, dependent on the previous development of production programs in all the enterprises. In the final analysis, the attaining of harmony between demand and supply in the future period means to plan general wage trends to conform with production programs for all enterprises.

There are too many "unknowns" under capitalism and, unlike socialism, it is not possible, either, to coordinate sufficiently in advance the trends in production capacities among the various private entrepreneurs or to harmonize the distribution of the national income between capitalists and workers. No one can prevent the struggle of the working class for higher wages and better working and living conditions. The distribution of income into savings, investments and personal consumption, according to the will of the capitalists, cannot be sufficiently foreseen, and the indirect measures that influence the development of these processes are only partly effective, although it does have decisive influence on the future relationship between over-all supply and demand.

Of course, this is not to say that central planning under capitalism could not affect the development of these processes, with the aim of assuring a dynamic equilibrium of the economy. It is certainly true that the present level of capitalist development and the state-monopolist measures create conditions which had no counterpart under the older type of capitalism. Moreover, it is necessary to support all progressive political forces that attempt, and are able, to act on capitalist states and influence the economic-political measures taken for the welfare of the people and to raise their standard of living.

We cannot, on the basis of present-day experiences, estimate how far such states, under the pressure of these progressive forces, can really succeed in subordinating private interests and decisions to the broader interests of the workers in society and assure certain generally beneficial aims by planning. But it would not be right to give up these immediate goals in the political endeavours of progressive forces.

Socialism makes it possible to purposefully coordinate the development of the economy, determine by plan the main economic activities in such a way that the development of some need not hinder the development of others. And it is precisely because we take account, in advance of the essential relations of the main economic activities that these can develop fundamentally according to plan.

But it would be a mistake to mechanically identify with reality the above-described possibilities for a planned development under socialism. Although there are indubitably more favourable social conditions for a social, planned orientation of all main economic processes than there are under capitalism, this does not mean that the economic development in socialist countries is always in harmony with the plans. Here also there are necessary contradictions between the plans and reality. If we leave aside some conflicts of interest which we shall discuss later, in particular those caused by the fact that we still are far from being able to foresee all essential relationships, and even less so the minor relations, and therefore many economic processes still develop otherwise than we planned or anticipated. For example, general purchasing power has often developed in a way quite different from our expectations; we are not yet able to predict the structure of demand and thereby the retail turnover, etc. If we are not able to predict correctly future economic needs in our planning, it can happen that certain processes will arise spontaneously, deviating from our ideas expressed in the plan.

Even now, although we can speak historically only of the initial experience of our economic planning, we may say that the existence of socialist production relations makes it possible to plan the whole social production process and do away, as Marx and Engels said, with the contradiction between planning in an individual enterprise and anarchy throughout society. This means to plan not only on the enterprise level, but also to subordinate these individual plans to the plans for society as a whole.

At the same time, we must overcome the over-simplified views on socialist planning that have been widespread in our theory and, to some extent, in our practice as well.

What are these over-simplified ideas?

Planning all economic activity in a purposeful way means determining its development, taking into account the main internal economic relationships. As much as possible we must respect all fundamental economic relationships to be able to direct as precisely as possible the necessary development of the different economic programs. The over-simplification occurred when we considered planning to be something to be assured merely by proportional development. At the same time we had an over-simplified understanding of proportional development itself. This was considerably furthered by the Stalinist formulation of the "law of planned, proportional development of the national economy".

Why did this formulation bring with it an over-simplified conception?

Planned development of the national economy under socialism is indeed an objective necessity, a law. Socialism cannot develop without planning on a society-wide scale. A definite concrete form of planning in a specific period in a definite country is, it is true, always subjective activity and is influenced by the subjective characteristics of the people who are doing the planning, but without these plans in one form or another, a socialist economy cannot develop at all.

Of course this can be genuine planning only when there is an essential agreement between what is planned and the real needs and possibilities or the real economic development. If there were no fundamental agreement between the plans and the actual development, it would be impossible to speak of a system of planning. Instead, it would be a question of goals that actually cannot be realized or, in other words, pious wishes. Moreover, it is not enough to narrow down one's attention to proportional development if there is to be agreement between the desired and the real development. We must take account of all fundamental economic relationships by which the proportions are achieved, as well as all other concrete economic relationships.

We must purposefully assure, in planning, that, especially, general economic laws are respected, laws that operate more or less on all levels of development of social economy, under all social and economic conditions. These are *the most general laws*, that appear under various economic conditions in various forms, operating through a large number of different specific economic processes, with varying force and consistency. Often these cannot even be traced in a short period, but over a longer historical period they must, in the final analysis, prevail, even though, perhaps, merely as long-term trends.

The most general economic laws cannot be disregarded by any economic system, if it is to persist historically, although they may be ignored or suppressed for a short period. They must be respected all the more in planned management of socialist economic activity. We shall attempt to formulate some of these more general economic laws, without making any claim in this study to a detailed analysis or historical demonstration. We are, however, convinced that a socialist economy must also primarily assure the operation of these laws.

These fundamental, general economic laws of development of production and all other economic activity are:

1. Social production must assure constant expansion and development of use values (material products of certain specific usefulness) in such a way that the existing needs of society are qualitatively satisfied, but also so that new needs are stimulated by new products and a continually rising level of consumption is assured (the law of development of use values).

2. Social production must develop in a way that will assure that the different types of use values are always produced in economic proportions. This means in amounts corresponding, in the final analysis, to the amounts of the social, economically realistic (given by the distribution processes) need for these use values (law of proportionality).

3. Social production must develop so that use values are produced with constantly increasing productivity of labour and with full utilization and reproduction of all the means of production of society (the law of economy of time).

4. Finally, social production must serve final consumption and its growth, and not "production for production's sake". This predetermines the basic relationship between producing means of production and consumer goods (law of reproduction).

These are laws that essentially determine, over a longer period of time, the basic tendencies of development of production activities (productive labour), the distribution, exchange and consumption in their mutual connections and relations. Or, in other words, these are basic economic relations that must prevail by means of these activities over a longer period of time.

These are also laws that determine generally the development of productive labour. Therefore, when we speak of the socially necessary development of labour (or, what is the same thing, the objectively necessary development of social labour), we have in mind the development that is determined by the objectively existing economic laws and which operates, *in the final analysis*, over a long period, whether people are aware of the existence of these laws or not. The existing economic system with its own mechanism always compels the objectively necessary development of production (and therefore of productive labour), because otherwise social production would break down and human society would perish. An economic system of society where over a longer historical period the law of economy of time was not observed, if, for instance, goods were produced by lower and lower productivity of labour, with worse and worse utilization of the potential productive forces, a growing waste of productive forces, etc., would necessarily disappear and be replaced by another, more progressive economic system.

But we should bear in mind that we formulate as the most general laws what objectively appears only as a certain fundamental tendency of development, what at any moment of development prevails *more or less* by means of concrete human activity. This means, in other words, that concrete human labour develops so that it is never *absolutely* identical with the objectively necessary development of social labour. The objectively necessary development of social labour is really only a concept which expresses a definite general tendency which is abstracted from reality, and which can be demonstrated by an analysis of the long-range development of the economy of any country.

But it is necessary to recognize the existence and the essence of certain economic laws, in order to study and determine the specific forms of their expression, or to determine the sum of economic processes through which the laws can prevail, if we are to speak at all of purposeful, planned management of the economy. This means to study under actual conditions the necessary development of all economic activities in such a way that, through them, it would be possible to attain the necessary development of social production.

This means, however, respecting far more specific objective economic relationships than we have described, for we were attempting to formulate only the most general, most fundamental economic requirements. In any historical period of development of the society's economy there are an enormous number of more specific economic relationships which conscious economic management should respect and which economic science tries to disclose and to clarify. The immense over-simplification is all the more striking when we realize that socialist planning, under the influence of Stalin, was concerned only with proportional development which — as we have tried to demonstrate — is only one of many of *the most general* economic laws.

When we want to express the specific essence of socialist planning of the national economy, we should put it about as follows: *Socialist planning of the national economy means a unified, social, purposeful determination of the development of economic activity within the framework of the whole national economy, taking account of all its fundamental intrinsic economic relationships, in such a way as to achieve the most consistent harmony of all planned economic activity and its actual future development.*

A more precise concept of socialist planning is not only of theoretical importance, but is also of immense significance in practical work. How was the over-simplified theoretical view of these problems reflected in practice? Assuring proportions in a planned way was understood in practice to be purely a matter of departmental concern. A certain department or a certain sector was responsible for planning and assuring proportionality, while all the other governing bodies or departments were concerned about some "other" management, took charge of "the rest". Some saw to technology, others to "market and supplies," still others to "wages and labour matters," etc. And someone had charge of "planning". That is the way it looked, also, between ministries: among them the State Planning Office was competent to plan, whereas the main concern of the other ministries was to "direct production". And all this was a reflection of the fact

109

that the planned assurance of proportion was understood to be only one of several other economic processes.

But it is impossible to get along without planned management of all economic activity in mutual harmony. By means of all the economic activities more or less consistent proportional development will come about. The development of any economic activity has an influence on the development of economic proportions. And therefore it is impossible for someone to be responsible only for the development of proportions, someone only for the development of "other" economic activities.

The result of all this is that planning cannot be conceived as standing separate from economic management. There can be no planning without management, just as there can be no management under socialism that does not have planned direction, taking into account all existing economic relationships. Economic planning always has two inseparable aspects.

One aspect is cognition, learning to know the existing conditions, the state of the economy, the economic level that has been attained, etc., and to perceive the necessary development of economic activity in the future, with regard to the envisaged internal relationships. It is necessary to study, not only what has been achieved, the stage of development we are now in, but also where economic activity is to develop in the future, in view of its presumed intrinsic relations. This is one aspect of planning. Of course it is clear to everyone that we cannot stop at this point, or it would not be planning. The direction of the development of economic activity, according to recognized necessity, is the other aspect of planning-management, direction of the development of economic activity, inseparably connected with planning. And an essential part of this is the checks and controls, finding again what are the results achieved, observing the actual development. This means new understanding, again new ways of management and on and on.

But we must distinguish in the extent of economic activities that are directed in a planned way. Sometimes a great number of economic activities can be directed in a planned way at a certain moment, simultaneously, and sometimes only isolated economic activities. Nevertheless, planning and management cannot be opposed to each other or set separately side by side. All our management, whether it is on a broader or a narrower scale of economic activity, must be understood as planned management.

If I stress this conception of planned management, this is merely to underline the fundamental, intrinsic unity of management in the national economy. I am aiming the argument against what has been the greatest evil, one that has not yet been overcome — against departmentalizing, against a division of labour in management, that limits recognition, that sees no essential connection between the different sectors of work, and develops without understanding the relations between them. But to govern in a socialist way means to see correctly the interrelationships, because the direction of labour results in economic activity and all kinds of economic activity are mutually dependent. That is why it is necessary to emphasize so strongly the internal unity of all economic management and the planned nature of all management.

Planned management is carried on by means of various instruments, one of the most important being the plan, and therefore the concept of "plan" in the narrow sense cannot be repudiated. Plans as definite, over-all, governing directives, determine periodically (occurring regularly at certain periods) the development of a large number of varied, mutually dependent economic activities in the framework of socialist units for a certain period in advance. This unit could be either the entire national economy, or individual narrower units, such as groups of enterprises, one enterprise or factory, etc. But it always determines the over-all development of many aspects, of many types of economic activity in their mutual relation, whether it is a plan on a national scale, a branch of industry or any level of cooperation.

There are also other forms or instruments of planned management besides the plan. There are governing directives, orders, financial or other economic stimuli that currently determine or act on the development of the individual types of economic activities. These single governing directives cannot be called a plan. Looking at the surface phenomena, we must, therefore, distinguish various forms and instruments of planned management.

Every governing order, if it is genuinely part of planned management, must be based on a knowledge of the internal relations of economic activities. It cannot ignore them. We cannot suppose that by planning in the narrow sense of the word we are assuring the proper proportions, and that the other economic and government directives have nothing to do with it. Any sort of economic activity that has not been set by the plan, or was set by the plan and then afterwards changed in any way by another governing order, has an effect, in turn, on other economic activities that are related to it and affects their development. If all such relationships are not considered in advance and the development of economic activities is not directed with a view to these relationships, we will inevitably have a growing number of contradictions.

Any growth in contradictions hampers the development of any economic activity, any economic processes. And they must, on the whole, have a retarding effect on the mutually related development of production and consumption by society. If, for instance, we change in some way the trends in wages, thinking that this will not affect the development of proportions in production, this is a gross error, because the wage trends will be reflected in the development of the purchasing power on the market, which in the end is fundamentally connected with the development of proportions in production. Wages can develop more or less in harmony with the development of division of labour, or more or less in conflict with it. We cannot, therefore, plan the development of proportions in production independent of wage trends or independent of price trends, etc. This was the way, however, economic practice has developed and often still does, in spite of the fact that socialist management is alien to and incompatible with departmentalized ways of working.

No form of management can be separated from the plan as one of the basic forms of management; consideration must be given to what relationships the plan respects and how a certain order is linked with the plan. When the individual orders merely concretize the general provisions of the plan, then there need be no contradictions. But if they change the trends of certain economic activity contrary to the plan and do so without coordination with the related activity, there must occur a growth in contradictions. For instance, if an order is issued on the basis of the internal conditions of the enterprise and changes the term for finishing certain kinds of products, this must necessarily interfere with the production in the customer enterprise. And these conflicts can grow to a scale that will adversely affect the whole national economy. If directives only change somewhat the concrete aspect of qualities of certain products, as compared with the plan that preceded production, contradictions must arise in the trends of demand for these products. Or if directives speed up somewhat a certain production as compared with the plan, and this is not coordinated with other related economic activity, they must cause growing contradictions, because there will either be delays in deliveries of raw materials for this faster production, or else difficulties with transportation, marketing, etc. From this we can see clearly that no governing directive can change any economic activity without taking account of the internal relationships.

But it is not just a question of the immediate surface relationships. Merely to bring the point home I have given some of the most immediate, surface relationships of one enterprise with another. It is evident that if products are not finished by the time set and are not delivered to the customer in time, conflicts must arise. But there will be certain individual contradictions that concern, e.g., a limited group of enterprises, and these had generally been taken into account. But we are interested in deeper, hidden relations that are always crucial. Let us consider the example given above of the relation between wage trends and the development of production, as reflected in a certain development of supply and demand on the market. Paying higher wages in the individual enterprise than had been set by the plan in relation to the development of production, assuming that the plan had properly delimited the relation between wage trends and a certain development of production or of stocks of goods, means that—for one reason or another—this basic relationship is not respected. A wage rise means necessarily an increase in purchasing power and a change in its internal structure. And vice versa, the development of stocks of goods is dependent on trends in production. If these two processes are not coordinated, the growth in contradictions between them results either in a more rapid growth of some stocks of goods as compared with the purchasing power or on the contrary in inflationary tendencies, a more rapid growth of purchasing power and a relative shortage of goods.

These internal deeper relationships are usually not studied by the different governing bodies. They see only their direct departmental, branch, or enterprise problems and for the most part do not consider the individual changes as important enough. Of course, if wages increase too rapidly only in one enterprise, this causes only minor disturbances in the broader relationships, and is not reflected at all in the general relation of purchasing power to stocks of goods. But as soon as more enterprises are concerned, there is a substantial growth in contradictions. In other words the essential relationships in the national economy have been ignored.

When certain changes cause only isolated and minor contradictions they can be solved by means of reserves and no great difficulties arise. A somewhat more rapid rise of wages in two or three enterprises can be balanced by a decrease in some stocks. But substantial changes usually come to the surface through a large mass of insignificant changes. Every substantial change occurs by means of the changes made in individual enterprises, changes in individual activities, etc. But as soon as these individual changes go beyond a certain degree, a growing contradiction arises. This is why it is so harmful when the planned development of the socialist national economy is linked only with setting up and carrying out of the plans as a mere totalling of data and tasks, and when one does not see that planned development is put into effect by means of all economic activity, and therefore also by means of all governing orders that determine the development of this economic activity.

But, in practice, planning was linked only in a simplified way with the assurance of proportions in production, and the very concept of proportionality was over-simplified. It was understood only as a quantitative relationship, in which the different types of goods are produced and it was not clear enough that the proportions of production are tested only in their relation to needs. That is to say, they are tested by the degree to which they satisfy economically justified social needs. Only labour which satisfies human needs is socially useful labour. And only the amount of labour expended on the different types of products which develop in harmony with the economically justified needs for those products can be called — without making absolute generalizations — proportionally expended amounts of labour.

Since needs are not merely a passive reflection of production, but have a relatively independent development, the proportions of production cannot be properly determined without studying the probable development of demand. Anyone who wants to determine the proportions of production without forecasts of the development of proportions in demand overlooks what it means to assure purposefully proportional development. The relative independence in trends of demand has not been fully appreciated in practice for a long period of time. The main effort was to cover needs of production and to see to it that the production of individual branches was mutually balanced. But the rates of development of the branches producing consumer goods were set as a more or less derivative result of certain over-simplified and one-sided balancing methods and by very empirical estimates, without any scientific investigation as to how the internal structure of purchasing power will develop.

It was expected that personal consumption could adapt itself to the possibilities of production. It was assumed that we will be able to produce all the necessary consumer goods if we have a certain production base. It was not realized that with the growth in real income of all members of the society, there would be large changes in the structure of demand. For example: with a given growth of average real income there is a relatively more rapid increase of demand for automobiles, dwellings, furniture, services, etc., than for other products.

We see that it is impossible to direct purposefully the development of production proportions without at the same time making a study of the probable development of demand, resulting from a given rate of development of production. Therefore, also, planning practice must give regard to the fact that, while production does determine trends in demand, demand is not just a passive reflection of the development of production, and its relative independence must be considered in planning the proportions of production. We must keep in view all the relationships which determine the development of demand, not only for purpose of production but also for distribution, exchange and the most important non-economic processes that have an influence on the development of demand. And again, the development of production must be in harmony with a forecast of all these factors.

It is necessary to realize that proportionality must be understood as the relation between production and needs, that the proportionality of production must not be separated from the proportionality of demand, and that this relation of production with demand and with consumption is carried out through every type of economic activity. We cannot therefore assure this relationship only by narrow production directives, but only by directives that determine the trends in wages, prices, trade development, financial processes, etc. The management of all this economic activity must respect the laws of economic relationships and therefore the laws of proportionality.

It must always be emphasized that economic thinking is a reflection of economic *relationships*. All economic laws are — as we have said — abstractions of certain real *relationships* between economic processes and anyone who has not learned to think in terms of economic relationships cannot foresee the development of any economic process. Even the individual economic laws which express the *selected* or abstracted fundamental relationships are again mutually connected and mutually related. All the above-mentioned universal economic laws operate only in a certain mutual relationship and if for a long period one of them does not appear the others cannot, after a certain period, appear either.

The sum of the most essential laws of economic relationships among economic processes, characterizing a certain historically specific economic movement, we call *economic relationships*. The specific nature and the objective necessity of these laws result from a certain relatively long-range character of production forces. These are the objectively necessary *methods* of cooperation and division of labour, distribution of means of production, exchange and distribution of objects of production, while the special methods of introducing the most fundamental economic processes into society always characterize certain historically specific economic relationships.[1] It is precisely by means of these economic relationships, or by means of certain specific laws of economic relationships and processes that production, distribution, exchange and consumption of all sources of production (means of production and manpower) and consumer goods are carried through. The special characteristics of these processes determine generally the particular nature of feudal, capitalist or socialist economic relationships.

One of the chief vulgarizations of the old administrative method of management was seen in the fact that an attempt was made to administer the trends in production forces *directly* from the centre, without regard to the fact that production forces can develop only

[1] For details on this, cf. O. Šik, *Ekonomika, zájmy, politika* (Economics, Interests, Politics), Prague 1962.

by means of economic relationships and that these relationships are not only a passive determination of the forces of production, but also have themselves an active and decisive influence on the development of production forces. But, while the development of production forces throughout society cannot be directly managed by a central governmental organization (it cannot determine the technology of every kind of production, every specific type of product to be manufactured, etc.), the centre can have knowledge of the necessity for certain general economic relationships among economic processes (the necessary relationships among the most fundamental economic processes linking production with consumption) and can, by means of planned management of these economic processes, indirectly guide the development of production forces (ascertained concretely in the enterprises).

The central body must, therefore, constantly make analyses in order to gain knowledge about the level of development of production forces and find out what changes in basic economic processes (respecting their complex mutual relationships) are needed to attain a further rapid and constant development of production forces and consumption. Instead of trying to manage the development of production forces directly by the purely quantitative method (setting the rate of growth of production, the size of the production funds, number of workers, etc.), without paying attention to whether, and how, this development is conditioned by all internally related economic processes (by distribution of the national income, price policy, payments by the enterprises to the state, taxes, credit, interest, wages, investments, etc.), there should be instead a management of basic economic processes and activities on the basis of a knowledge of these necessary economic relationships and their influence on the further development of production forces, and thus achieve a satisfactory and realistic development of production forces and consumption.

b   Relation of the General and the Individual in Planned Development

Economic activity is the activity of millions of people in the whole national economy, a tremendously extensive, varied, constantly changing activity. And among all these activities there are a vast number of mutual relationships. In order to bring the point home, it suffices to imagine the mass of economic activities in enterprises, factories and shops, the great number of trade outlets, transportation enterprises, agricultural enterprises, banks, financial institutions, and so forth. The management of this activity of millions of people in all its details cannot be done by one governing body. At the same time, it must all have uniform direction, in order to develop harmoniously, intrinsically coordinated with the existing internal relationships. If every minor cooperation, let us say, every enterprise or every group of people had its own independent isolated direction this would lead in fact to anarchy throughout the whole economy, and a growth in major economic contradictions would be unavoidable. Development would be possible only by means of elemental solution of the growing contradictions, that is, by means of crises.

If spontaneous growth and spontaneous solution of the contradictions is to be avoided, if there is not to be anarchy, there must be a unified direction of economic activity in the framework of the whole national economy. This requires that there be governing bodies standing above the individual groups of production units. In other words, the necessity arises for management bodies that are separate from the actual economic activity.

In my whole exposition, so far, I have been abstracting from the particular qualities of socialist cooperative production which I shall mention in a special section. I conceive here of unified management of economic activities in a simplified way as the unified management of activity developing within nation-wide cooperation without regard to the specifics of this management in relation to cooperative enterprises and cooperative workers.

Uniform management of the economic activity of society requires in the first place that there be a central governing body coordinating its conscious directive activity with the basic interests of all workers and assuring a uniform fundamental management of all subordinate bodies and, finally, of all economic activity. Neither this central management nor the management activities of all subordinate bodies can be performed (at least not to a decisive degree) by people who are directly active in the economy (workers in product distribution or exchange of products, etc.), but must be by people who are performing this managerial work as a special activity within the social division of labour. At the socialist level of development, the economic management body must still necessarily be a state governing body which is the expression of inter-relationships that will not be analysed further within the limits of this study.

The fact, however, that we must distinguish between the economically active people and the specific management bodies which operate on their behalf and in accord with their fundamental interests, is primarily because of the given level of development of productive forces.

It is both possible and probable that, one day in the communist future, the distinction between the economic supervisory and economic operational activity will disappear, in the sense that the actual work will more or less be transformed into the tending of automatic machinery and other complicated mechanisms. This does not mean, however, that it would no longer be necessary for one group of people to give orders to another group. There will always be a relation of superior and subordinate. But this relationship of management will have quite a different character than it still necessarily has today. Not only will it no longer have its present political character but also it will not be connected with now still indispensable differences between the supervisory and operational activity which reflect also the substantial differences between mental and physical work and in general the difference between work of greatly varied complexity and attractiveness. Furthermore, a substantial increase in the level of education of all people, the possibility of going more frequently from one specific activity to another, the overcoming of the present rigid division of labour in society and the beginnings of communist consumption relationships will completely change the situation of superiority and subordination, ridding it of all hangovers of dependence of the subordinate on a superior. The demands for knowledge and capabilities of everyone whom society selects for a directive position will increase substantially and society will to a much greater degree and more thoroughly judge and check on them.

However, the present division of labour between the economically directive activity and economic operational activity is necessary for the time being, because the character of labour itself, linked with the present stage of development of productive forces, has not yet been overcome. Also the great differences between these two groups of activities cannot be done away with; to a considerable degree people are bound for their whole lives to a certain profession. The producers themselves cannot take part in management work with the necessary level of knowledge and their participation in management is restricted by the relatively long working hours and their rather narrow field of knowledge. If the management bodies were, under these circumstances, to be producers, too, they would, of course, get no work done. Therefore, for the time being, it is necessary to have special bodies for management alone; this, of course, has its disadvantage, as we shall show later.

For the time being, there must be a division of labour between people who are economically active and people who are supervisors, although it will be possible and necessary to have a sort of sporadic participation of producers (during the work-day) in the activity of management bodies. This transitory participation will not do away with the necessity for having people who deal only with management, for the existence of a certain special governing apparatus.

As we have already said, there cannot be only one management body for it would be unable to cope with the management of millions of economic operations. But, in order to assure uniformity and harmony of economic activities, the management bodies must be coordinated. The consequence of this is the necessity for a uniform system of internally connected and coordinated management bodies representing the producers and taking them into participation in management as much as possible. For the various links in the social division of labour, for the different levels of cooperation, or, at the same time, for the varied specific economic activities, there must exist separate management bodies. Even a unit such as the shop must have its own specific management, must have its own foreman, if it is to have intrinsically coordinated procedure. This is even more true for a factory, enterprise, group of enterprises, and so on.

Every such governing body must always be as closely connected as possible with the sphere of economic activity it must direct. It must have as complete knowledge as possible of the particular features of the economic activity or sphere of economic activities it must direct—in this sense it must be specific management.

The direction of various bodies of management will always have something in common and at the same time there will always be something specific, something in its economic activity that will distinguish it from others. In some ways it will differ and will express the general basis for various production activities. To consciously attain this unity and common approach cannot be done by all specific management bodies meeting and coordinating their management. This is unthinkable, because there are so many cooperations and relationships that coordination on mass meetings would be impossible to carry out. Therefore, specific management bodies must have a higher coordinating management body for several such lower units. And these, in turn, should be combined in a still higher body. Thus we arrive hierarchically at the need for a single central management body.

Every lower supervisory body must be guided by as concrete knowledge of matters as possible. This is why we call it a specific body. It cannot operate by the same generalized directives as the higher body of management. It must consider the specific conditions for managing its sphere and must try to direct the development of a given economic activity with as concrete knowledge of the matter as possible. The more general, higher management bodies exist only to facilitate *a priori* coordination of activity and to assure a development in accordance with the needs of society as a whole.

But if centralized management is not properly understood, there are great dangers concealed in it. If centralism were understood to mean that the higher, more general, body is to supplant the lower specific management body and to make decisions for it, then there will be bureaucratic management and the lower bodies will become ineffective. Substitution or duplication of management activity occurs when the higher body makes decisions in as great detail and as concretely as the lower. This incorrect comprehension of centralism reveals itself in a system of massing detailed matter to be decided from the lower tiers to the centre and a mechanical passing on of unchangeable orders from the centre to the bottom. This necessarily leads to an erroneous and bureaucratic form of management.

In a system of unified management we must respect the relative independence of the lower specific bodies of management from the higher and more general bodies. The lower must have the possibility of deciding to an extent that will enable them to apply to the maximum their knowledge of specific conditions in the sphere which they are managing. Of course, without disturbing the interrelationship between them and the general necessary development. At the same time, it is necessary to make use as much as possible of the experience and the knowledge of the producers themselves, the workers, technicians and other employees, and to assure their direct, though necessarily only occasional, participation in the active work of management.

This relative independence in making decisions, together with the active participation of workers is, then, the generally defined trend of development which we consider to be the other aspect of a socialist system of management, which we call democratism. The unified socialist system of management is, therefore, a unity of two aspects, a democratic centralized form of management. Democratic centralism in socialist management means the subordination of specific management bodies to more and more generalized supervisory bodies, creating a hierarchy up to one central body of management to assure the socially necessary trend of development of all economic activity, and its internal harmony. At the same time there must be a maximum possible relative independence of these lower specific bodies of management and a co-opting of economically active people to help in the management, to make possible a flexible management of the different economic operations, taking account of their particular features and respecting to the maximum the different specific conditions.[1]

This relationship between the central and the peripheral decision-making and management, the proper delimitation and co-ordination, is one of the most important and unique problems of socialist economy and of socialist society in general. It is around this question that the greatest disputes between Marxist economists occur, disputes between

---

[1] "But Engels did not at all understand democratic centralism in the bureaucratic sense in which this term is used by bourgeois and petty bourgeois ideologists, the anarchists among the latter. His idea of centralism did not in the least preclude such broad local self-government as would combine the voluntary defence of the unity of the state by the 'communes' and districts, with the complete abolition of all bureaucracy and all 'ordering' from above." V. I. Lenin, "The State and Revolution", *Selected Works*, Vol. II, Part 1, pp. 274–5, Foreign Languages Publishing House, Moscow 1951.

the economists who adopted, in the Stalinist era, the over-simplified and metaphysical mode of thinking which rigidly absolutized lifeless schemes of unity and contradiction, with those who are trying to overcome this simplified way of thinking and its theoretical results, and to view a new reality in all its complex, conflicting and dialectical unity, which corresponds to the essential principle of scientific Marxism.

A metaphysical concept of the relation of central to non-central (peripheral) decision-making and management absolutizes the unity of both these aspects, which leads to identification of content with method in the decision-making by central and peripheral bodies of management. The representatives of these views believe that the central body must gather as much detailed information as possible on the economic activity and economic events from all the smaller units (enterprises, etc.) and coordinate their activity in as concrete a form as possible and then direct the development of this activity again in detailed and specific fashion. They consider that the expansion of such a system of central decision-making is a necessary development, caused not only by the process of socializing labour but also by progress in the techniques of management (new computing techniques, automation of communication processes, etc.). The very origin of detailed central economic decision-making they consider as the most characteristic aspect of a socialist economy and the concomitant technical progress as a factor of a constantly expanding process of central decision-making. One of the most striking conclusions of these ideas is the assertion that central, planned decision-making can fully replace the market mechanism among enterprises because it enables the planning commission to coordinate in advance the relations between suppliers and purchasers and the full coordination of production and demand by means of preliminary direct negotiation.

It is obvious at first glance that these ideas are abstract and remote from life. A huge number of individual relationships exist between the sources and the needs in social production, which is the output of several million different types of products. Furthermore these products as well as the methods of their production, the material composition, cost of production, complexity of labour process, and so forth, are constantly changing. These relationships cannot all be recognized by one planning centre, in every detail and in full concreteness, not to speak of coordinating them in advance (and considering them in the process of management). This is not a simple relationship between changes in *demand* for a certain means of production and manpower, and the necessary changes in the sources to cover them, but is at the same time a relation of the changes in the useful properties and the utility of certain products and the changes in needs and consumption by these.

No individual central body can constantly study in all detail the changing needs, technical, production and labour conditions, decide on all these changes and coordinate them in all economic relationships. If we realize that every decision on changes in technique and technology of production, in character and qualities of products causes changes in economic relationships and thus must always be considered and studied economically in detail, we can see that there must be specific bodies of management connected with the different productive units which differ in technique, and which must not only decide the development of the technical side of production, but also study the direct, concrete economic relationships and causality. In this detailed direct decision-making no central body can replace the specific peripheral bodies of management.

Even the most pro-centralist of the economists can see how abstract and impractical it would be to carry to its logical conclusion the idea of central management, when the central body would decide on all the individual concrete economic relationships. No less simplified are the theories viewing the problem as solved by the division of labour between central and peripheral bodies according to the possibility of being sufficiently informed. In their opinion it is necessary only to limit the extent of specific decision-making by the central bodies with regard to production, since they cannot obtain information rapidly and reliably enough about all the changing conditions in production and consumption.

This theoretical standpoint usually results in an endeavour merely to limit the number of directive tasks and indicators set by the central planning and managing body to what is called a reasonable degree. For instance reducing the number of indicators that directly determine the volume of production of certain types of products. Or, in some cases, there would be a replacement of some indicators that are the result of a too simplified, one-sided and abstract concept of trends in production in the central body and which cause a line of products to be produced that does not suit the needs of society, using in their stead "improved" indicators. An example would be replacing the directive indicators of "gross production" with a directive indicator for "net production" or with a directive indicator for "commodity production", subdivided according to sales in the foreign market, domestic market, and earmarked investments.

All such efforts to limit exaggerated centralized making of decisions and to improve the system of centrally planned tasks and indicators, which we now see being made in all socialist countries, are not based on sufficiently profound analyses of the relation between the central and the peripheral management and, therefore, usually have led or lead to rather ineffective reforms and reorganizations. The theory that views the problem as a question of the division of labour between the central and the peripheral management, merely from the standpoint of the possibility of gathering and processing information, simplifies the whole matter to an intolerable degree and cannot lead to correct conclusions.

In the first place, this theory does not analy e the question of information and decision-making from the standpoint of the relation of the "general and the individual" and the relation of the "long-term and short-term," but merely assumes the reception of all information and all decisions that the central and the peripheral bodies can obtain and act on, on an equal and undifferentiated basis as *concrete* information and as decisions on the *concrete, individual* economic acts and activities. Even though some adherents to these theories do tacitly assume the existence of a certain difference between the nature of a central and peripheral making of decisions, this difference is not explicitly analysed and explained and in practice leads, not to a dialectical and logical solution of the division of labour in decision-making, but to incorrect, purely superficial division of labour giving rise to so-called preferential management.

Before we discuss in more detail this erroneous concept of division of labour between the central and peripheral bodies of management, let us mention another fundamental error in this theory. This is the complete neglect of the problem of *economic interests* in solving this division of labour. This leads necessarily to erroneous conclusions in regard to management. Anyone who thinks that division of labour

125

in economic management can be decided merely from the standpoint of studying the problem of gathering and processing information, and assumes tacitly that those who furnish the information and those who receive it (and, on the other hand, those who issue directives and those who receive them) have completely unified interest, so that we can pass over the question of interests, is profoundly mistaken. If the question of division of labour among different bodies of economic management is to be properly solved, it is not possible to abstract from the interests of those who manage and those who are governed. On the contrary, a serious study of these interests, the conditions that give rise to them and their development, their orientation and in-fluence on economic decisions are the main prerequisite for a correct solution of the problem of central and peripheral management.

The problem of economic interests, their basic connection with economic management, and the need to respect them in solving the division of labour between the central and peripheral bodies will be dealt with in a later chapter. Now we should return to the super-ficial concept of management which results in preferential central management.

Characteristic of this concept of management is the fact that it is able to consider only the concrete management of economic details; and thinks that a general program of economic development on the basis of aggregate information and by means of aggregate indicators or other economic instruments is something unsocialist. The naive striving for "concreteness" at any price and at every level of manage-ment leads to the duplication of the same detailed decision-making from the lowest bodies, the enterprises, through the various depart-ments on up to the central body. What endeavour there is to "im-prove" this situation and find some sort of division of labour between the central and the peripheral bodies of management, is done only in the purely specific sphere, in the sense that determination must be made on what the central body is to decide (the production of certain commodities, the distribution of certain products, the capital invest-ment for certain purposes, a specified technical development, and so on) and what — again in specific fashion — is to be decided by the peripheral bodies.

This is a purely superficial consideration, with no idea that the central and peripheral bodies should actually decide about the

126

development of the same economic activity, but at different levels of more specific or more general consideration for different time periods and various degrees of obligation. Instead of this correct view of the relation between the specific and the general in understanding and managing economic realities that must be respected in delimiting the mutual relationship of higher and lower management bodies, the usual practice has been for the central body to decide as concretely as possible about production, or at least in such a way as to assure the priority in fulfilling the plan of certain most important specific productive tasks.

This type of central management in which the highest planning and administrative bodies determined the targets of specific development, production in concrete and binding directives for a relatively short period of time or decided certain aspects of production, and used pressure to ensure their priority fulfilment by the enterprises, at the price of the neglect of other products or aspects of production, which had not been set in a concrete fashion by the central bodies, can be fittingly entitled *the preferential system of management.* In this system the most rapid, purely quantitative growth of production, particularly of industrial production as a whole, is the aim. And within this purely quantitative growth there are certain selected spheres of production and types of products that are preferred, even at the cost of neglecting other products or a lag in the qualitative and rational development of production as a whole.

Under certain extraordinary political or economic conditions this preferential management can be for a short period desirable and even advantageous. For example, in wartime or under threat of war, when preference is given to production that is important for the war effort. Or it can be a means for speeding up the economic consolidation of a new, still politically weak regime, to assure the rapid overcoming of unemployment or of insufficient employment, of poverty, and to assure economic independence from hostile states, etc. Under such conditions, preferential management can achieve a rapid priority growth of the necessary production at any price, even at the price of a temporary growth in disproportions and other economic losses. But as soon as this extraordinary system of management, possible only for a short term, is raised to a generally applicable system that is essential for socialism, it must sooner or later act as a brake on

127

growth or cause an absolute decline, as was shown by the example of the ČSSR in 1963.

With preferential management, the most effective alternative paths of economic development are not calculated and the national plan does not arise on the basis of an analysis of the optimum development of the different spheres of production and the entire national economy. The structure of production is established on the basis of the decisive influence of indicators expressing the maximum growth of production. The absence of prices that are based on economic realities makes it impossible to make any calculation of efficiency. The main responsibility and material interest of the enterprises drive them to achieve a quantitative growth of production even at the price of uneconomical activity, of neglecting technical development and the improvement of products, or with no regard to market demands, etc.

One of the gnoseological roots of this incorrect absolutizing of temporary preferential management in the socialist system in general is — among other things — a misunderstanding of the relation between the general and the specific aspects in the course of gaining insight into and of controlling economic realities, and a disregard of this relation in determining the division of labour and cooperation between the central and peripheral bodies of management.

The central authority cannot decide all the details which should be decided by the lower body. There must be some process of generalization. Generalization and specifying cease to be only a philosophical problem and become a matter of social practice. What generalization is there in the management of the economy? Mainly in generalizing various perceptions based on detailed information about the existing economic situation, and its trends of development.

Socialist management requires the bodies or agencies of management that are closest to the actual economic activity to decide on the basis of their most *concrete* knowledge. It is, of course, a matter of the Leninist concept of "concreteness", the fullest knowledge of a given phenomenon, a given activity, a knowledge of all the relationships, even the most general, that determine the long-term trend of development of individual activities. The management agencies that are closest to the economic activity cannot know by direct experience the more general relationships nor, therefore, about the basic trend of development of the economic activity. The enterprises, for example,

128

cannot know the *long-range needs for their products and the necessary growth of their production*, the investment funds that they will have at their disposal in the future, the available manpower, wage trends, etc. Therefore the trend of this development must be set by the more general management bodies in rough outline. But in order to do so the higher bodies must be informed about certain general production conditions, the general needs, the general possibilities for growth of production and of labour productivity, etc., and in turn must determine the general trend of development for production, distribution, exchange, using these outlines to coordinate in the best possible way the trends of production and demand, getting more concrete as the directives are sent on down.

Of course it is very difficult to apply this relation between the general, the special and the individual in practice. The general is not something separate from the individual, but expresses the common fundamentals of many individual economic phenomena; the general tendency prevails by means of a mass of individual phenomena.

Let us take the case of the production of specific products, proceeding from the fact that there are hundreds of thousands, millions of these products and just as many concrete, individual proportions. Each individual product, type, range of goods, must be produced in certain amounts. Consumers do not have a general demand for shoes, but always a certain specific need for specific shoes of a certain colour, a certain style, size, etc. But when production of these goods does not correspond generally to the demand for the product, the consumers feel this as a shortage, although there is a sufficiency of other kinds of shoes. Or, for instance, it is not enough to balance production and consumption of textiles in general without ascertaining precisely the necessary amount of each kind and range of textile materials. If, on the one hand, there is a surplus of cotton material in relation to demand, and, on the other hand, there will be a lack of a certain woollen or silk material that is in greater demand, then it is useless to explain that we are producing the planned amount of textiles. As soon as disproportions arise in the production of textiles the figures for total production will not mean anything.

The central management body cannot decide on the huge number of different concrete proportions. Not only because this would require an enormous number of operations, but also because time plays an important role. The concrete needs, expressed in detail, change very rapidly and at the same time the actual production conditions change very rapidly, as well. No general body, especially not a central one, could change detailed governing directives promptly enough or as rapidly as the actual technical production conditions or as demand changes. Therefore bureaucracy also means a delay, inflexibility, insufficient change in orders, in view of the more rapid changes occurring in economic conditions. From the standpoint of time, as we shall show later in more detail, it is impossible for the more general governing agencies to decide so many concrete matters and, in the final analysis, the unit of government that is closest to this economic activity must make the decision.

Nor is it necessary for the central bodies to decide these details. This is not the sense and meaning of socialism. Their task is to decide on the general, over-all trend of development in production, keeping in mind the forecasts of social needs for a very broad, general group of products. It is therefore necessary for a certain amount of homogeneous types of production to be classified into broader groups of products so that the higher governing bodies can direct the extent of production of this broader group. This figure can be set for a longer period, so that decisions on production need not be changed so rapidly. But the concrete extent, within this broader group, of each individual type of product and the range of goods in it, must be determined by a specific management body which is closest to production.

Social production can grow at a rate which is in general dependent on the extent and quality of the sources of production (especially on the amount and technical quality of the means of production) which can be introduced into production and extend the capacity of existing means of production, or, in other words, on the accumulation in production funds in the enterprise itself, the amount and skills of the workers, the extent of the scientific knowledge which can be applied to the technology of production, the process of concentration and specialization of production and its contribution to production. Over-all production must develop within the structure and proportionally to the basic direction of trends in demand, both on the domestic and on foreign markets, to the demand for consumer goods and for means of production. No individual enterprise can know all these basic prerequisites for growth in production, nor can it make a survey of the possibilities of development of other branches of production, the general social possibilities for accumulation, the over-all growth in income of the population, changes in the structure of demand, etc. If the lower bodies were to decide entirely by themselves on the trend of production there would be anarchy, because each one would produce without any previous knowledge of the over-all long-term trends in demand and the necessary development of production. Connected with this, there are tremendously great superfluous reserves in capitalist countries, where there is no central planned direction and furthermore, there are spontaneous failures of all those enterprises who have made mistakes in their independent private decisions.

Opponents of economic planning of any kind who defend pure market economies (even among non-Marxist economists there are today very few of this view) object usually to the principle of planning giving this argument:

"The market mechanism by itself creates in the respective industries all the necessary means (commodities) in harmony with trends in market demand. If too little is produced in one branch in relation to an increased demand, prices are relatively increased, profits rise, and thus there is greater inflow of capital into the industry, which again permits an expansion of investments in this field, a shift to it of manpower, and thereby the needed expansion of production in accordance with trends in demand. This means that there is a mechanism for the distribution of means (resources of production) between branches, the possibility for a proportional development of investments, and so there is no need for any economic planning."

Against these very over-simplified views we may point out the following facts that at the same time clarify in sum the necessity and progressivity of planning for the whole economy:

(a) Distribution of means (production resources) simply by the market mechanism is distributing only according to past or present demand in the market and not in accordance with future demand that has its own relatively independent development and goes through inevitable changes;

(b) Growth in demand for certain groups of commodities, e.g., A, B, C, D, that can be ascertained at that moment of development cannot at the same time be extended to an increased demand for all products which are prerequisite for the increased production of A, B, C, D. This demand cannot be forecast by the market mechanism at all, so the continuous re-distribution of sources must also change the originally existing situation in the market (the growing volume of investment changes also the demand for consumption goods that originally caused the greater investment);

(c) Not every spontaneous change in the production structure that follows the trend in demand is necessarily the most efficient change in the structure. In every economy there is a huge number of possibilities for substituting goods that will satisfy the final demand and that are appropriate from the technological point of view. If there is no possibility of considering in advance the various alternatives and of seeking the most effective variant, random circumstances will often decide the changes in the production structure that will be far from the most effective one;

(d) There will always be spheres of demand that are socially important but depend on nation-wide, political decisions and interventions in the distribution of national income (in the sphere of social consumption, defence of the country, state investments, etc.). These needs cannot appear spontaneously on the market and if they cannot be foreseen it may be difficult for production to satisfy them immediately.

Planning on a nation-wide scale makes it possible:

1. By means of scientific analyses to study the trends of future market demand, meaning the changes in the *macrostructure* of demand brought about by the future growth and qualitative changes in production by fundamental processes of distribution of the national income and the relatively independent trends in consumption;

2. Promptly to set the changes in the macrostructure of production to make possible not only the future satisfaction of market demand, but also timely investments for all the branches of production that have been affected, which are needed for the rise in production that would satisfy final demand;

3. In deciding the future structure of production, to consider in advance alternative developments that will make it possible in one way or another to satisfy the future market demand and to decide

which is the most effective alternative. The number of possible alternatives of developments is substantially increased if we take into consideration all the possibilities of development of foreign trade (replacing domestic production by more efficient imports).

4. To forecast the emergence of all needs outside the market that arise from some social consumption and in time to assure the development of production and distribution, making possible the satisfaction of these priority needs. (This is not, of course, to deny the decisive role of future *market demand*, even under socialism, for the development of production   to which problem we shall return.)

It is, therefore, a question of using certain scientific methods in the centre to ascertain the trend of development of any general group of products or any branch of production. Within the general long-term trend of development in the branch that has been outlined, the individual enterprises can, on the basis of negotiations with their customers (everyone of whom will know his own general orientation), decide concretely the over-all production and the production of individual types of products, range of products, and so on. Concretizing production on the basis of negotiations between the different suppliers and customers is possible only because the general trend of development had been set in advance. After all, it is the essence of socialist planning that the general essential relationships need not spontaneously prevail with great losses, but can, and should, be foreseen and taken account of by means of scientific methods. For this to occur, there must be — among other things — method of generalizing or aggregating the products and the different aspects of production from the lower levels up to the central body of management.

The question arises, from what standpoint must the groupings be made, according to what aspects should products be classified in broader groups, whether this is to be according to their properties as use values, that is from the standpoint of consumption, or, on the other hand, according to technique and specialization of production. Usually the two points of view coincide. Products that can be combined in one common group from the standpoint of related technique of production, which generally need the same machinery or the same raw materials, technical procedures and so on, for their production, have usually a similar value that satisfies related needs. If we, for example, include certain products in broader groups and call them

133

textile products, we make this classification from the standpoint of technique of production. And all the products that belong to the textile group have roughly the same properties even from the standpoint of consumption. They serve for clothing, to protect against the cold, etc. But they are not always fully identical. And, therefore, we must also distinguish these two standpoints of generalization, as well as combine them with a purpose.

If we group the products from the standpoint of studying the trends in demand we cannot always form the same groups as we would if we were grouping them according to technique of production. But we must coordinate the groups of production quantitatively with demand. Even though the contradictions are not great, it is necessary in practice to make as precise as possible a study of demand and harmonize this as much as possible with the amounts in the different groups of products from the standpoint of production. Therefore, we must form groups from both standpoints, consumption and technique of production, and join these groups. For example: the need for summer shirts and jersey pullovers must be classified as a certain quantity of shirts for the clothing industry and a certain quantity of jersey pullovers for the knitted goods industry. This means to transfer the production groups to the consumption groups and then in turn transfer the consumption groups to the production groups. The determining factor will be, however, the groups which are formed from the standpoint of production.

Without this generalization, it is not possible to direct and manage socialist production, for all substantial relationships must be considered in advance, especially the most general relationships — between production and consumption.

c Organization of Management and Proportions of Production

The relation between the different concrete products and the generalized groups of products must be understood in connection with the relation between individual, general, and even more general proportions. If we distinguish between the individual, the general, the still more general and the most general proportions, this does not mean that we consider them to exist side by side but in their internal unity. The different proportions are actually the ratios in which the different specific types of products are produced. Just as there exists a huge number of individual types of products, so also does there exist vast numbers of different individual proportions. If we proceed from these individual products by generalization to broader generalized groups of products we thereby gain also insight of more general proportions.

The most generalized proportions of production are the quantitative ratios of producing the most generalized groups of products in relation to demand.

Such most generalized proportions are, for example, the ratios for producing means of production, on the one hand, and consumer goods, on the other. Since products cannot be gathered into broader, more general groups than groups of "means of production" and "consumer goods" (further aggregation would create only a group of "Products").

From a somewhat different standpoint, we arrive at rather more concrete groups, the groups of industrial and agricultural products. Of course, the proportion of production of these two groups is still one of the most generalized. Another very generalized proportion would be the proportion of extractive and processing industry or the proportion of industrial production of means of production of consumer goods, the proportion of crop production in agriculture, or of livestock production. All these more generalized proportions come about by means of a huge mass of special individual proportions. Just as we can go from the individual, concrete types of production to the above-mentioned generalized groups of products, so we can also proceed by generalization from the individual concrete proportion to constantly more general proportions until we arrive at the above-described most general proportion of production.

A group of individual proportions is always a form of expression of certain more general proportions. This also means that our proper aggregation of products into constantly more generalized groups and the planned orientation of their production is a prerequisite for increasingly more purposeful planned management of production of each individual type of product. Producing in the proper proportions each individual type of product presupposes the establishment of proper proportions in a broader group of products to which this specific type belongs. If we want, for instance, to produce in proper proportions

135

all types of clothing, including men's shirts, we must establish in advance the proper proportions of production for the clothing industry which, in turn, presupposes a setting of the proper proportions for textile production, etc.

Generalizing in the direction of the centre does not, of course, apply only to products and proportion of production but also to all aspects of social production. This includes all aspects of economic activity, everything that is a prerequisite for purposeful coordination of these economic activities in society, e.g. aggregating the costs of production of the necessary amount of materialized and living labour for an ever broader group of products. Time is not economized under socialism in a spontaneous way. Economy of time has to be constantly safeguarded in production and planning. In the centre, however, the individual amounts of materialized and living labour cannot be determined for each individual product. Orienting trends of costs also requires generalization. Knowledge of the costs necessary for the more general groups of products must be generalized, and their development on the basis of an analysis of the generalized factors of growth of social productivity must be taken into consideration when determining the proportions between branches. And the same is true in central forecasts and planning of all decisive aspects of production and distribution.

This does not mean to say, however, that cognition of all aspects of production must be carried on up to the central planning body in a generalized form and from there, after coordination, must in turn, by means of certain concretized disaggregated indicators, be directly distributed among the individual enterprises by means of directives. Here lay, and in many cases still lies, the over-simplified concept of socialist planning, based on the idea that if every individual aspect of production or of other economic processes has not been scheduled by directive from top to bottom, the proportional development of socialist production cannot be assured.

But actually we see that this over-simplified idea and its practical application hindered the socially necessary development, and a large number of disproportions were mounting over a long period. This was furthered by the over-simplified idea of the process of aggregation and disaggregation.

The entire concept of planning will be discredited if it is not understood that the transition to a more general aggregation in planning by way of quantification of a given process (for example, in the quantitative determination of the necessary amount of clothing or the over-all pay-roll level necessary for the clothing industry, etc.), implies also a transition to increasingly less precise figures. An approximate magnitude that is forecast and planned for a certain future period always contains within itself a possibility of a plus or minus deviation which must be the greater, the less precise the information for determining this magnitude, and the less precise are the calculations of all economic relationships that influence the development of the given magnitude.

To ignore these inevitable imprecisions in the individual aggregated planning magnitudes and their mechanical assignment by directive from the centre to the enterprises must, instead of mutually coordinated development, result in contradictions in interrelated economic processes.

Instead of a specific determination of the individual economic activities, in harmony with rapidly changing conditions of production and demand within general approximate quantitative limits, these concrete specifications originated as the final result of central figures, considered to be precise, final and absolute. In addition, these figures were assigned in a rather mechanical way. If, moreover, the central figures arose more under the influence of subjective desires (maximum rate of growth, etc.) than from a sober technical-economic analysis and realistic evaluation or search for the most effective development of production, then mechanical assignment of these figures necessarily creates unrealistic goals and tasks for many enterprises. This is one of the characteristics of administrative, bureaucratic planning which runs counter to socialist planning.

There is, therefore, a need for a certain progressive generalization and aggregation of qualitative and quantitative findings on all basic aspects of development of production from the individual workplaces up to the planning centre, in order to determine the general long-term trends of development in production and the basic distribution processes. But this does not mean that the determination of individual concrete tasks and magnitudes corresponding to the centrally planned trend of development can be achieved only by centrally scheduling and assuring of a large number of obligatory indicators.

We shall speak in more detail about the possibility of using other methods for assuring harmony between the concrete production programs of the enterprises and the central plans.

In connection with an analysis of the relation of the general and the individual in socialist planned management, we must question the very existence of certain management bodies, because the organization of management bodies has substantial influence on the method of management, on the possibility of more or less consistent observance of objective economic relations.

The question arises as to how many management units there should be and where they should be, and what determines, actually, the system of management units.

The existence of specific management units should not be decided by chance. Their number, location, jurisdiction, the division of labour among them and their mutual relationship — all this is objectively determined in rough outline. It is determined by economic relationships and the need to consciously respect these relationships in the process of management. That is to say, in setting up the economic bodies of management and delimiting their main activities, it is necessary to proceed from a knowledge of the essential economic relations and to consider which system of management will help most to apply effectively these economic relations.

Of course, not all the fundamental economic relations can be analysed in this work — that would be the whole political economy of socialism. But it is a question of making this problem more comprehensible and of taking account of some of the more general economic relations in a way that will again bring out the objective determination of a specific organization of management bodies.

Factory management bodies are essential because of local production problems. The size and location of these units must be carefully determined. At the same time, however, the objective determination of the character of the factories cannot be understood to be absolute. Especially in its beginnings, socialism takes over factories, enterprises, etc., just as capitalism left them, and as a result also takes over a certain random and irrational quality which was connected with their origin under capitalism. We are here considering new units of production.

The main criterion in founding factories must be to assure the most productive output of certain commodities. But there are usually certain contradictory circumstances which must be recognized and investigated, arriving at solutions that will assure the most productive production. Generally speaking, larger units increase productivity of labour. From this standpoint, it is necessary to create the greatest possible concentration of production in special factories. But there are certain limits to it if one wants to avoid contradictions. Too large concentrations, too large factories, reduce productivity because of a number of specific factors. Too large plants, for example, usually require a complicated organization of labour, expensive transportation of workers from remote places, tremendously extensive housing construction, too great distances in the transportation of raw materials, etc. If we analyse this and disclose all the specific, contradictory relations, we shall arrive at the most advantageous size for the factories. Most advantageous in the sense that we shall find out the conditions for the most efficient production, with the least cost. The existing economic relationships decide the size of one or another basic production unit that must, of course, have its own management. In other words, the existence of plant management bodies is determined by the same objective relations which compel the formation of separate production units.

Over the factory's management there must be another management agency which will assure the most economical distribution of production programs, of means of production and manpower among factories of the same type. A larger demand for certain products than can be met by one factory requires that there be more factories. If analysis should lead us to the most advantageous size for one factory, that would have the capacity to satisfy demand for products of a specific type, then there would be no need for other factories of the same type. On the other hand, if the existence of several factories producing the same or similar goods was found to be indispensable, then this shows the necessity for a management unit to coordinate their activity. This necessity arises because there must be purposeful distribution of the production programs, means of production, manpower, etc., among plants of a like type, if there is not to be unbridled competition. The higher management bodies must simultaneously assure a certain connection between all the subordinate units and their customers or suppliers, an inter-branch exchange, the most rational joint research development and design. And all this is in essence the task of the enterprise management. Therefore the objective economic relations between factories of like type, between them as a whole and their customers or suppliers, necessitates the existence of enterprises and their management bodies.

The same circumstances, however, could force into existence still higher management bodies, directorships over enterprises of the same type — call them chief directorships, branch or general director-ships, or otherwise. Wherever there are too many dispersed factories, it would be uneconomical to set up a single enterprise. A great number of dispersed factories, even of a similar type, cannot be grouped into one enterprise, for this would be very uneconomical and the manage-ment would be too general, too far removed from the specific, in-dividual units. For this reason, several enterprises must be set up, each including a smaller number of factories. In this way, enterprises of the same type will grow up side by side, or enterprises with a similar production plan, subordinated to the branch directionship.

This branch management body, placed above the enterprises, is especially necessary to assure the most effective technical develop-ment of the given branch, coordinated use of the technical research, concentrated and most effective use of funds for investment, research in trends in the domestic and foreign markets, training of specialized personnel, and analysis of the most advantageous allocation of pro-duction capacities, etc.

In particular, the branch management should study and guide these basic developmental economic processes. On the other hand, the concrete decisions of the production program, making of contracts with customers, hiring and discharge of workers, etc., should be largely left to the management of the enterprises, without the directive interference from the branch management. But as soon as the branch directorships begin to determine concretely the production pro-gram and the extent of production of the different enterprises, this would not only restrict the independence of enterprises but, also prevent competition between them, and thereby, also, the necessary market relationship between trade and production of which we shall speak later.

Of course, it is not essential for the branch management to include only completely homogeneous enterprises. There can also be a certain

140

division of labour among the enterprises in the same directorship, so that it actually is a question of combining similar enterprises producing together a certain general group of products. (For instance, one such directorship could serve for all the enterprises in the cotton processing industry, producing cotton yarn, cotton thread, cotton material, cotton wool, and goods for the medical services, piece goods made of cotton, such as handkerchiefs, towels, diapers, etc.)

These directorships would be the management bodies over several similar branches of production, where production is greatly dispersed.

Over these branch directorships there must necessarily be a central body for the state as a whole, so that production will be harmonized with the developing needs of society. Under certain conditions, there could be therefore two or three tiers of management bodies, each covering a broader and more generalized sector of production. Under certain conditions, as at the present time in Czechoslovakia, there are ministries above the enterprises or the groups of enterprises which represent an industry branch or several branches.

The task of these broader management bodies is to direct the general, long-term trend of development of certain like enterprises. Here, again, the generalization and the disclosure of still more fundamental social aspects in the technique of production, in the use of raw materials, in the use value of the products, etc., leads to a delimitation of broad branches of departments, which link still more heterogeneous enterprises and groups of enterprises, which have something in common in their very general characteristics. It would be a mistake to consider the departmental managing bodies or any specific management bodies as the only logical and necessary arrangement. They are changing and transitory forms of management, determined by history, always having a longer or shorter period of existence, and it would be dogmatic to consider any management body or any system of management as something permanent.

Although there have been certain feelings against reorganization in the system of management, arising mainly from some subjective shortcomings in former reorganizations made in response to changing economic conditions, it will be necessary from time to time to reorganize the system of management in Czechoslovakia. There are changes in the technique of production, in consumption, in division of labour, and, if contradictions are not to occur between these economic conditions and the form of management, there must necessarily be, from time to time, a change in forms of management.

Of course, this reorganization must be carried out on the basis of a deep analysis, with thorough preparation, etc., in order that there will be as little as possible subjectivism and empiricism. But we cannot retreat in the face of feelings against reorganization in general, because this is really evidence of dogmatic conservatism, a failure to understand the necessity for continuous economic change and a consequent necessity to change the forms of management. If, for example, ministerial management bodies were necessary for a certain period, this does not mean that they are eternally necessary. Instead of independent ministries, there could also be branch departments or administrations within one central economic management body, etc. Determining the system of management bodies requires a constant study of the relationships between economic development and forms of management. As soon as we see that there is a growth in contradictions, that certain forms of management are hindering the most effective and thorough consideration of economic relationships, the consequence is that new forms of management must be sought.

The necessity of having these branch management bodies arises from the social division of labour, that is to say, the existence of like or similar types of production which must be coordinated in advance. The decisive factor is not whether these are relatively independent management bodies for a certain area, or only departments, units of administration, etc., within a single management body for the area. The particular form must always correspond as much as possible with the particular conditions.

It is not possible to give a general answer to the question of how broad the production groups to be included under one branch management body must be. But we can never follow a single, simplified criterion. Instead it must be all the main production technological and economic relationships that must be consciously respected under unified management. For example, we once (1951) dissolved the former general directorships with the simplified concept of bringing management as close as possible to production, and then we formed a large number of similar enterprises, which, however, were not able themselves to solve the huge number of economic problems. Not only were these small enterprises unable to determine the proportions of production, because they could not find out the proportions of consumption, but they could not arrange for the research, development, etc., except at a huge waste in expenditure. They could not separately decide on investments, because this would have led to a great dispersal of investment funds and a hindrance to concentration of production. They could not even independently provide for the sale and purchase of goods, etc. As a result, it was necessary to transfer a vast number of concrete decisions to the ministries. These in turn could not decide such a large mass of questions for their entire extensive sphere of competence, and therefore the chief administrations were set up to direct certain branches within the ministries. The branches governed by the chief administrations were, however, broader than the former branches administered by the general directorships, and became even more bureaucratic and cumbersome in their work. This, in fact, brought greater separation of management from production than there had been before. Furthermore, the material responsibility and interest in result disappeared from these administrations. The significance of this fact we shall speak of later.

As long as there must be several enterprises within one branch of production (as a result of scattered production in this branch), there can be several enterprises included under one coordinating management body that would be materially interested in, and responsible for, results (branch or general directorships, etc.). The larger and more concentrated, but at the same time the more specialized or combined the enterprises, the more economical will be the decisions in regard to future development (research, trends, designs, investment, marketing, supplies, etc.), and the less necessary will be the special directorships over the enterprises. At the same time, however, the greater the specialization of production in the enterprise, the greater the number of proportions that must be decided on and the broader the price problem, on the one hand, the greater will be the number of distribution processes to be decided (assignment of income in the enterprises to the different enterprise funds) and the greater the need for control, on the other hand. Therefore, there must be a decided effort to extend jurisdiction and responsibility of the lower management links, with a genuinely scientific preparation and application of the system of aggregation and disaggregation of qualitative and quantitative economic findings, an effort to prevent any duplication of management activity in the various management bodies and an assurance that the decisions made in the higher bodies will be only on the more general macroeconomic processes, of interest to all society, decisions which the lower bodies cannot make with any knowledge of the matter.

In brief, the allocation of decisions must be made on the basis of an analysis of the relations between the peripheral (enterprise) bodies and the central management body under socialism, a relationship which necessarily results, because of the relations between a large number of specific production management bodies and the central management body, in a system whereby the central management body would, on the basis of its plans and other instruments of administration and stimuli, orient only the development of the most fundamental and general economic processes and would decidedly avoid administering the individual concrete economic activities (but for those exceptions caused by special political circumstances). In this sense, the central economic plans should be expressly *macroeconomic* plans giving direction only to the basic structure and most general proportions of branches of production, the fundamental regional allocation of production forces, the basic processes of distributing the national income, the basic proportion between domestic production and foreign trade, etc. At the same time, the central body must provide over-all policies, in accordance with the plan and with the aim of carrying it into effect, in regard to finances, prices, wages, foreign trade, but leaving to local management the details in regard to all these factors. But we shall speak of these problems in a separate section.

It is important to see, however, that only a transition to planned orientation of *macroeconomic* processes by the central body can lead to real materialization of this guiding activity and can surmount bureaucracy. In practice this does not mean just a small change, but a fundamental change of the whole system of socialist management. The logic of the objective economic relationships requires this.

There necessarily exists a reverse influence of the principal, and basic forms of management on carrying through definite, necessary, economic relationships. Certain basic forms of management can, to a certain degree and, for a limited time, prevent the conscious co-

144

ordination of objectively related activities, which will appear in the form of growing contradictions. Under socialism, where objective relationships must be carried through by means of economic activities which are all guided by a united system of management, the shortcomings in the basic forms of management, that is to say, insufficient regard given to the various fundamental objective relationships, must result in insufficient coordination of the related activities or in growing contradictions among them. The necessity for coordinating these by changing the principal and basic forms of management becomes apparent only over a relatively long period, not immediately, and is felt only when contradictions are growing. This means that not every growth in contradictions can lead immediately to a change in policy and that we cannot wholly avoid a long-term growth of some contradictions. There must be a certain generalizing of the specific contradictions and only by this generalizing can we arrive at a knowledge of their causes.

The causes of certain repeating phenomena do not usually appear on the surface. They cannot be recognized immediately and therefore we need more profound analyses to disclose them. An inadequate analysis leads only to ineffective "orders," "command·," "appeals," etc., which do not prevent other contradictions from piling up. Only when the individual negative phenomena are generalized and their deeper general causes are discovered can there be any fundamental change and can they really be done away with. Of course, they can persist in individual factories for a relatively long time and hamper activity. Nor can the changes recognized as necessary always be made easily and promptly, and even under socialism we must realize that various narrow interests have temporary influence in delaying these changes. They must, however, eventually give way to the basic interests of all the people.

Changes in management or in the entire system of management, therefore, can be brought about for two reasons: 1) when there occur substantial changes in economic activities, i.e., changes in production, technique, division of labour, and exchange among individual enterprises, etc., which compel, at a given moment in their development, also change in the management or system of management; 2) a deeper knowledge of certain economic relations that have formerly been insufficiently respected. The growth of economic contradictions makes these economic relations more evident and compels changes in management.

At the same time, the possibility cannot be excluded that under certain conditions there could be new findings about an unsuitable or outworn system of management, but the necessary reform cannot immediately be carried out in practice because of the temporary opposition of some leading economic or other social bodies. Under socialism, however, every progressive social finding will prevail sooner or later, as a prerequisite for overcoming the growing economic or social contradictions.

d Relation of the Short-term and the Long-term Aspect in Planned Development

As we have already said, planning means the purposeful management and coordination of mutually related economic activities. These activities, however, are related at a specific time and we must reckon with this time relationship in planning.

Among the various economic activities there exists an immediate, uninterrupted time relationship. There is an apparent surface interrelationship between one phenomenon and another. For example, for a certain amount of work a certain payment is made. The immediate time relationship between the work and the payment is apparently visible on the surface. Usually all external, surface relationships are also direct time relationships, which means that certain economic phenomena follow on one another in a short period of time.

But economics is not a question only of these direct, external relations that exist between economic activities that are directly related, but of deeper, intermediate relations that do not follow one another, that are seemingly unrelated economic activities. And these are the fundamental, deep relationships that determine the basis for whole groups of individual economic activities. The outward aspect expresses the direct relationship, e.g., "for certain work a certain sum of money is paid." But should anything be given in return for work? Why should it be money? Why this amount and not another sum of money? We will not understand all this from the external relationship. The essence of money payment is determined by much deeper and broader relationships. All have something fundamental in common, something that is given by certain basic relations, not to be learned from ordinary observation. Moreover, socialism is characterized by the very fact that economic activities are directed, not only according to the immediate external relationships, but also by taking account of the hidden, basic relations. Capitalists must also reckon with the immediate external relationships when directing economic activities. But they cannot take account of the hidden, basic economic relationships on a society-wide basis, for these occur spontaneously, beyond the capitalists' sphere of activity and often against their will. Under socialism, however, these relationships must be recognized and consciously respected as much as possible in determining economic activities, because there is no such mechanism for assuring that they operate spontaneously, as they do under capitalism.

When, for instance, specific individual wages are set, then this cannot be as a consequence of spontaneous development or the competitive struggle of labour on the market, a struggle between labour and capital, nor can it be the consequence of a mere subjective comparison of work performed in an individual factory. An enterprise cannot set wages only by comparing the work processes that are directly related. Each individual wage is, and must be, the result of the action of much deeper relationships.

We cannot examine all these relationships again in detail. But, merely to make it clear, we shall list some of the chief of these. Every wage must be the result of the basic relations between the general wage fund of society as a whole and the over-all market supplies, on the one hand, and the relations between the various kinds of work that exist in all of society and the wage relationships for this work, on the other hand. If we are to set wages properly, we must base this primarily on the essential relationship trends of the general market supplies and wage funds. In this way we arrive at a certain level of the general wage fund. If we take account of much more concrete relations, if we compare all the different groups of labour throughout all society and consider the various types of work more concretely, we arrive at the most concrete types that exist, side by side, in every factory. Thus we also arrive at a recognition of the necessary wage relationships and the specific individual wages. Each individual wage is, therefore, the result of recognizing both the most fundamental and the most concrete relationships. Only by taking account of everything, that is, even these general, basic relations, can we achieve a fundamentally coordinated development of related economic activities. Only thus, furthermore, will the actual development correspond to the desired development.

But respecting the general, fundamental relations means understanding that they come about through a mass of individual economic activities that are not directly connected, possibly not even in time. These can be specific economic activities that even occur in quite different spheres and at quite different times. I shall make this clearer by giving an example:

In a certain period of years an enterprise for the production of synthetic fibres is built; not until later will it begin to produce large quantities of synthetic fibres. This is a specific activity that occurs at a certain time. And now, seemingly independent of this, in completely different enterprises and at a quite different period of time, the workers' wages are increased. In a certain year, however, there is a higher demand for a larger amount and higher quality of textile products made of synthetic fibres. And now it is seen how well coordinated is the building of the factory for synthetic fibres (and the textile production based on it) with the rise in wages and the living standards at a certain time throughout the whole national economy. The possible growth of contradictions between the supply of textile products and the demand for them would, on the contrary, show that the fundamental mutual economic relationships had not been sufficiently respected. Naturally, this example is considerably simplified but it serves as illustration.

The more fundamental the economic relations, the relatively more stable is their validity and the more slowly they change. Of course their concrete forms of expression constantly change. For example, the relation between the wage funds and the market supplies determines the basis of socialist wages which are the workers' share in a certain part of the social product destined for personal consumption, and applies   under socialism   as long as wages continue to be paid. These most basic relationships that are in effect throughout the whole period of existence of socialism and which are the special quality of socialist economic relations, are what we call socialist economic laws. However, it is not enough, in planned management, to know this or that logical connection in a general way. It is necessary to foresee in what concrete form it will appear in the course of the next few years. That means, for instance, to ascertain what will be the trend of growth of market supplies in the next five years and how, in view of this, wage funds must grow in the same period of time, taking account of other relationships. These long-term relationships must be respected in planning the huge numbers of general wages paid out at certain periodic time intervals, at the various places throughout the national economy.

In order to harmonize the various economic activities that are essentially related, it is usually not enough to take a short period of time, even if we do know these essential economic relationships. If we should, for instance, want to assure in the course of a month the harmony between the purchasing power and the stocks of goods, when we had not thought of this before and had not built in time a factory to produce artificial fibres, a spinning mill, weaving mill and other necessary enterprises we should not succeed. A long-term perspective is necessary. To illustrate, we must decide today on various economic activities, in order that many years hence we will have harmony between quite different economic activities that do not have their beginning at the present time. So, in order that different kinds of economic activities be started that may at a given time seem even superfluous, we must necessarily look some years ahead and forecast how other economic activities that depend on the former are going to develop in direct mutual relationship.

Where lies the difficulty in this problem? It is impossible to foresee for a long period in advance all the concrete economic activities in detail. Only very general processes can be forecast, which constitute the essence of a certain mass of individual concrete economic activities. The longer the range of perspective, the more general the indicators of development that make it possible to express the essence of the future development. The longer the period of time, the less detailed the view, the less specific it is. For example it is not possible to predict five years in advance the need for specific types of textile material, but only the general demand for textiles. It is not possible to estimate 15 years ahead the demand for textiles, but only the rough ratio between the trends in clothing and the trends in food consumption.

The result of all this is that the economic processes that are outlined in general for a long period ahead must be made more concrete and precise for the shorter periods, with regard to the more and more concrete and known relationships. For this reason, it is necessary to distinguish between the long-term and the short-term plans and at the same time perceive their inseparable unity.

But what actually is "long-term" and what "short-term"? This cannot be defined absolutely, but only in relative terms. A plan for fifteen years is a long-range plan compared with a five-year plan. A five-year plan is long-range compared with an annual plan, and a yearly is long-range when set against a monthly or daily plan. But it is impossible to set up plans for each individual time interval, nor is it necessary. If, for example, we should make a plan for six years into the future it would not differ much from a plan we have set up for five years, and therefore it would make no sense. But, in addition to the longest plan that we are able to set up reliably (today, e.g., we are trying to establish plans for the next fifteen years), we must also make plans for some periods that are enough shorter to make a difference. The time intervals are chosen so that the shorter-term plans can enable us really to look ahead in a more concrete way than in the longer. The difference, that is to say, is primarily one of degree of concreteness.

If the long-range plans were to have the same number of detailed indicators as the short-term, then the latter would not be necessary at all. It is wrong to think that the difference between the short-term and the long-term plan is that the short-term plan sets up essentially different tasks, a different trend, that it is fundamentally a different plan than the long-term. If that were so, the long-term plan would have no significance. For this reason it is not possible for the short-term plans to change some of the indicators radically and leave others as they are contained in the long-range plan. This would inevitably result in a growth of contradictions. The difference between the long-range and the short-range plans cannot be that one radically changes the other. On the contrary, they must agree basically. The difference consists in the degree of concreteness.

Of course, if there are any serious, unforeseen circumstances that make impossible the development according to the long-term plan and compel a radical change, then it is naturally necessary to make this change in both the short-term and the long-term plan. Without such substantial changes the long-term plan would cease to be a plan.

This has tremendous practical significance. The various short-comings in our previous planning consisted, among other things, in an insufficient clarification of the interrelationship of the long-range and the short-range plan. The five-year plans had almost the same number of equally detailed indicators as the yearly plans. Then when many of them could not be fulfilled in a specific year, the targets in the yearly plan were simply changed. When they were changed in one year, they had to be changed even more in the next year, of course, as compared with the targets set up in the five-year plan. In this way, economic development actually was controlled more and more by yearly plans which differed more and more with the five-year plan. The five-year plan lost the character of a plan and thereby the per-spectives for long-range economic development disappeared. This development without sufficient perspective, oriented in fact only by annual plans, inevitably exhibited all the shortcomings we have been speaking of. Various important relationships could not be ensured in time, because, in the space of a year's time, it was not possible to coordinate some related activities that should have been thought of much earlier. If, for example, in a certain year there was a great shortage of refrigerators and the plan had not forecast sufficiently the change in structure of consumer demand, this shortage (aside from foreign trade) could not be made up in the course of one year, because any substantial expansion in the production of refrigerators, and all that went with it in the way of auxiliary production, would require a longer period.

Without a longer term plan, unforeseen contradictions are bound to develop. This has been our experience in the last few years and it makes necessary certain changes in planning practice. In the first place is the necessity for the longest possible forecasts, longer than given by a five-year plan. Not even a five-year plan can assure that various projects can be started in time for the period when they will be found essential. Five years, for example, is too short a time to assure widespread and complex automation of production. The con-ditions for introducing it must be created and a vast amount of auto-mation equipment, regulatory apparatus, automatic computers, etc., must be produced, and special enterprises must be set up to produce them. Preceding this, there must be a huge amount of research and designing, the training of highly qualified personnel, etc. Of course, some of these are tasks that require more than five years. In order to make an essential change in technology and structure of production, we need a longer perspective and must therefore draw up longer-term plans for a period of, say, fifteen years.

At the same time we have had the experience that longer-term plans must always contain the more general indicators which are essential for a prompt inauguration of all necessary economic activities. The more general in nature and the smaller in number the indicators of a long-term plan, the more stable the plan. These more general processes and a limited number of general processes can be scientifically predicted. If we increase the stability of the longer-term plans, the long-term plans need not be redone and changed so many times to conform to changes in the short-term plan. Then the short-term plans can be really concretized without changing the fundamental trend of development that has been outlined in general.

Increasing the stability of the five-year plans requires the organization of constant, uninterrupted work on these plans (in special bodies set up solely for this purpose). This creative activity must mean a continual projection of unforeseen and unforeseeable concrete circumstances (both negative and positive) into the five-year plans, in such a way that, while they remain living and real plans (not just a totalling of dead figures that have been passed up by actual developments), there is as little disturbance as possible of the basic processes and connections, which are the most important for the national economy. On the one hand, the planning body must try to help create reserves, in a purposeful and effective way, to prevent any great disturbance of the five-year plan by unforeseen occurrences. On the other hand, where a chain reaction from such events cannot be entirely prevented because of insufficient reserves, it must seek and calculate solutions that will least disturb the general perspective that has been adopted for the economy as a whole. The planning body must constantly and in a creative way, work toward the projection of the concrete, actual economic trends into the five-year plans, and toward the planned use of newly discovered possibilities for efficient development.

It is important to keep in mind, in regard to all plans, their inner unity, their general, basic unity and gradual concretization. If we are planning a five-year trend of basic investments, that is, the production capacities of different branches, then the general nature of these tasks does not mean that the basic investments could be determined by non-obligatory estimates. Just as erroneous is the idea that we can make substantial changes in the annual plans of the basic planned investments of the five-year plans. The five-year plan would not have the necessary stability and this would leave the enterprises without perspective. The general nature consists in the fact that the investments of the different branches show only roughly what will be their actual production in the next few years. If we establish a certain production capacity by building or expanding certain enterprises, we do not thereby determine in which year and in what specific amounts the concrete types of product will be manufactured. The production capacity provides only the basic conditions for production, which can then in any given year be a little higher or lower and, in particular, can be met by producing different specific types or a range of products. The volume of production can, therefore, be expressed only by a very approximate or orientational indicator, and must then be made more specific in the yearly plans.

The general proportions which we set for five years in advance must be the result of scientific study of the necessary trends in production and demand of a general group of products. Of course, only this development of *general* groups of products can be dependably forecast and, on the basis of this forecast, decisions made on investment. These must be investments that will make possible, by means of machinery and equipment prepared for in the long-range plan, to produce various specific types of products for which a demand will arise in the current year. If, for instance, we decide to invest in the knitting-goods industry, it is neither possible nor necessary to know what will be the specific demand for certain types of knitted textiles, because the knitting machines can produce a range of goods. In determining the investments we must, of course, have a rough knowledge of the demand for "knitted goods" in general and to make sure of this general group of products requires that certain investments be assured.

On the basis of more stable five-year plans, more stable relationships among the enterprises and between customers and suppliers can develop. And this was previously lacking. On the basis of more stable supplier-customer relationships more concrete plans can be set up from below, from the enterprises. Why? Because each enterprise has its plan for five years, for what will be the rate and direction of its development; it knows what the investment possibilities are, as well as the approximate amount of man-power on which it can count. On the basis of this, it can in turn tell its suppliers what it will need in rough terms, what amounts and what types of product. Then, methods of setting up the annual plans can be changed in the sense that they will be set up by the enterprises themselves or by the directorship for a group of enterprises, merely with the help of the central economic body which must primarily delimit the relations between foreign trade and domestic production. The central body need not then, by the aid of a vast amount of indicators, issue directives for planning the production of the enterprises, but restricts itself to checking on the consistency of annual plans of the enterprises or of associations of enterprises with the state five-year plans. According to the actual conditions in production and on the market the enterprises must plan their annual production programmes in harmony with their long-range plans which are a part of the state plans.

Since the enterprises and the factories must determine their activity in the most concrete way, annual plans are not sufficient, they must have still shorter-term plans. On the other hand, in the centre where there never will be, nor can there be, such concrete direction as in the enterprise, it is enough to continue to renew the five-year plans, assuring their concretization for each year and their annual confrontation with the year's plans of the enterprises.

It follows from the preceding that, in demanding the greatest possible concreteness in management, we must realize there are various stages of concreteness relating to the plan's period and scope. Failure to understand this leads to errors in management, to formalistic direction without knowledge of the matter. For example, an attempt to guide from the centre or to plan ahead for a longer or shorter period of time as concretely as must be done in production itself usually means management without knowing the relationships and therefore mistaken management. The result must be a growth in contradictions.

The relationship between the general and the particular, and between the long-term and the short-term is not sufficiently understood by some non-Marxist economists who have not mastered the dialectic method. Therefore, they do not understand the possibility of planning the coordination between the development of production and the trends in society's demands. They reject our concept of planning, saying that only the production of some goods that have a concentrated market — which means those purchased by a few large enterprises — can be planned. They have in mind the production of machinery and equipment which are purchased in turn by large production enterprises. According to them, one cannot plan the production of consumer goods because the market is dispersed. They point out that goods are bought by a huge number of trade outlets and a still greater mass of individual consumers. Therefore, they say, there are tremendous changes in demand for different products and their production cannot be planned.

Some fundamental errors appear in these views, the chief of which we shall list.

In the first place: unless we plan production of consumer goods we cannot plan the production of means of production. For, after all, the means of production serve to produce consumer goods. Without a knowledge of the demand for consumer goods, planning production of means of production must result necessarily in surplus productive capacity in some fields of production and a shortage of productive capacity in others. This, of course, will be seen only in the actual demand for consumer goods on the market. Then will be seen how much a given expansion of production of means of production established the preconditions to satisfy the demand for consumer goods.

But such "planning" of means of production is not planning because it is not based on a knowledge of trends in demand for these means of production. The founding and expansion of enterprises without any knowledge of final consumption is seen under capitalism primarily in the fact that too much and, later, unused capacities arise, in a premature closing of enterprises run by the weaker capitalists, etc. The shortage of production capacities in other fields connected with this does not appear so visibly under capitalism, because these shortages of certain products can appear in the short run to be balanced by rising prices. Therefore we cannot call it planning when the production of consumer goods is not planned and the trend in purchasing power is not forecast.

155

In the second place: the objection that production of consumer goods is designed for a dispersed market (having in mind primarily the small trade outlets) does not apply to socialism because the trade outlets are not dispersed. There is not a huge number of private tradesmen who act independently one of the other and against each other, as is true under capitalism. Trade under socialism is actually a unified nationalized trade that, without completely excluding a certain healthy competition between the different trade enterprises, makes possible a uniform organization and concentration in the relationship between trade and production, as well as a uniform price policy.

This actually assures a uniform market research and forecasting of trends in demand for the whole state. On the basis of a statistical study of long-term trends of development in demands for very general groups of products, and, in harmony with a knowledge of the development of real income into the future, it is possible to make a unified forecast of the trends in the *basic* structure of demand, and in accord with this to plan the production of consumer goods and carry out concrete contractual negotiations between trade and producers for deliveries of goods. There is no doubt that this is a great advantage compared with the separate negotiations between private traders and private producers.

Of course there still are many shortcomings in our planning of trade. In the first place, these are an expression of the general shortcomings connected with the old system of administrative planning of production and trade. Based on insufficient analyses, the annual plans of retail trade turnover, drawn up by administrative methods in the central planning bodies, do not arouse sufficient interest on the part of the trade bodies and the workers in better satisfaction of the needs of consumers. Retailers, with the relative surplus of purchasing power, in most cases fulfill their plans of retail trade without exerting any special effort in regard to changes in the range of goods, in demanding better and more modern products, in assuring that all sizes are in stock, all styles, etc. Instead there is an interest in selling the products that make up the largest (physical or price) proportion of their turnover and which can be used to fulfill the plan most rapidly, rather than in fuller satisfaction of a demand for a varied and even relatively inexpensive range of goods.

156

In the field of trade, therefore, it would be necessary to set up the annual plans of trade activity in accordance with the long-term economic plans, only in the trade enterprises, and after changes in the material interest of trade. The trade enterprises can be interested in the fullest possible satisfaction of consumer demand and thereby in a concretization of long-range plans of production and sale of consumer goods that would assure not only the fullest detailed harmony of supply and demand, but would also assure that consumer demand would be stimulated, when they are offered new and better use values. (This we shall speak of later.)

Summary

In conclusion we may sum up by saying: the main expression of socializing of labour, socialist national cooperation, is generally the direct social orientation of labour. We have seen that the labour of all members of a socialist society, if it is to develop in harmony with their social needs, must be managed by a unified plan within the limits of society as a whole. Uniformed planned management must be carried out by means of a whole system of purposefully interrelated management bodies, which by means of plans and other instruments of management must assure a coordinated development of all economic activities which are basically related. We have shown the intrinsic complexity in such a system of national management and the necessity of a conscious respecting especially of the dialectic relationships between the general and the specific, universal and the individual, as well as the long-term and short-term in planned management, if this is not to turn into an administrative bureaucratic system which is alien to socialism.

It is tremendously important to understand the relation between the long-term and short-term in planned management, in which the relationships between the general and the specific reappears in a specific way. These relations must be applied purposefully if scientific management is not to become erroneous subjective management. It is precisely the insufficiency of perspective that results from a lack of generalization of the individual findings and insufficient study of the general reasons for certain individual phenomena that are in essence the same, that makes impossible a timely forecast of various trends into the future and the timely acting on the necessary fundamental measures. We often change too many individual details without completely solving them, because we try to do away with shortcomings only after they appear, instead of changing promptly their common fundamental causes.

We cannot solve each individual shortcoming separately and isolated from the others as they come into the open. In planned management it is necessary to constantly generalize the development that has taken place and, on the basis of this, forecast the generally necessary trend of development into the future. We must reveal the essential connections among whole broad groups of phenomena and coordinate their basic development in time and thus avoid the growth of fundamental contradictions among them. It is only on the basis of this that we can solve individual and partial contradictions and during a short period change individual activities in detail. In this way it is necessary to consciously respect socialist planned management, the dialectics of the general and the individual, of the long term and the short term.

In the entire foregoing explanation even though we showed the necessity of relatively independent decision-making by the lower specific bodies of management, we came to these conclusions more or less from the standpoint of cognition. It recognizes the impossibility of deciding in the central body on all economic activities in the whole of society, and the necessity for the existence of a certain division of labour between the central and the peripheral bodies, certain mutual relationships between all managing bodies and the different cognition and method in these different bodies. We have more or less assumed the existence of a unified general interest of all governing bodies and we have abstracted this from any sort of conflict of interest.

In fact, however, there is no management that does not have definite specific interests. The general social interest is abstract, expressing the essence of all peoples' interest under socialism, carried into effect by means of a large number of specific and individual interests whose general unity cannot be absolutized. There are definite non-antagonistic conflicts of interest between the concrete interests of people, which will necessarily be projected, in this way, into the specific decisions by various management bodies. Unless there is an analysis of these conflicts of interest, unless their causes are revealed, as well as the way they show themselves and the form of solution — in other words, unless certain mutually contradictory relations between people are disclosed — any description of a socialist system of planned management must remain one-sided and incorrect.

Precisely because socialist economic theory formerly absolutized the unified planned cooperation of people under socialism and did not disclose the intrinsic contradictions in this cooperation, it did not contribute sufficiently to overcoming subjective methods of planned management. Instead it supported subjectivistic and teleological concepts. We shall therefore proceed now to clarify these contradictions, to give their reasons and the necessary way of solving them, trying not to fall into the other extreme of not seeing that these contradictions developed within socialist planned cooperation, within the cooperation of society as a whole.

2   The Necessity for Socialist Market Relationships

a   The Necessity for an Optimum Development of Socialist Production and Market Relationships

Socialist labour is a complex of objectively necessary economic relationships. It cannot develop according to arbitrary, subjective desires of individuals, because then it could not be recognized as social labour. Only by harmonizing the specific types of work performed with a certain objectively necessary development of labour, i.e., a development according to which necessary economic relations prevail, will labour have the character of social labour.

We have tried earlier to formulate the most general economic laws determining characteristics of the objectively necessary development of productive labour. If labour is to have the character of social labour, it must assure the production of use values in the proper proportions, must constantly increase its own productivity, with the full use of potential sources for production, and must assure a steady final consumption as rapidly as possible.

The optimum harmony of all these necessary aspects of development of social labour results in socially necessary labour. One cannot make sure, of course, that all labour expended will be fully in harmony and thereby a necessary development of social labour. Why can this not be directly assured? In the first place, because there are difficulties in discovering all the specific economic relationships under changing economic conditions and the specific forms of labour they necessitate which express the socially necessary labour. There are great obstacles to the discovery of objectively necessary development of labour, especially in the initial period of socialist development. In the second place, there are conflicts of interest that are specific to socialism and this impedes the use of labour in a socially necessary manner. These conflicts cannot yet be eliminated at the present stage of development of productive forces.

We shall not analyse in more detail the difficulties of cognition, but shall briefly summarize and not go beyond the bounds of the problems we are discussing. The difficulties are roughly as follows:

a) All aspects of the necessary development of labour, as well as the conditions for it to be socially necessary labour, cannot be ascertained at a single centre, as we have shown in the foregoing. This fact is not a subjective statement, but is because economic movement is the most complicated movement of matter.

The intrinsic relations of social production are very complex, especially when we are ascertaining specific phenomena or making a decision on which use values, with what equipment and in what interval of time, etc., we are to produce. To make a decision we must discover all the technical aspects of production, all possibilities of division and combination of labour, all possibilities of alternative consumption, and therefore the substitution of some use values by others, all possibilities of combining aspects of production. That involves combining the development of use values, their proportional production, most economical production, etc. As we have said, this cannot be fully worked out from a single centre; there must also be a great number of specific, peripheral management bodies.

b) At the beginning, the links between the management bodies are inevitably imperfect. This is true especially in the initial difficulties in collecting information, in regard to coordination, gathering and releasing information. which is always cumbersome in the beginning stages of any new organization. The management orders are then based on insufficient base material, on distorted, irrelevant or even inconsistent information, etc.

c) Processing information is also primitive, connected with the fact that in organizing socialist production there are always difficulties because new methods, forms and means of managing a socialist economy arise. These cannot be rigid and unchanging, but must adapt to the rapid changes accompanying the building of a new social order. Inevitably there will be errors in theory and method, in the personnel skills and in the way they carry out the fundamentals of present problems, etc.

Thus contradictions must arise between the plans and the guiding directives, on the one hand, and the objectively necessary development of labour and production on the other. The nub of the matter is that some of the economists, especially those in economic practice, try to explain contradictions between the specific development of labour and its objectively necessary development by pointing to the cognitive difficulties and thus explain all economic difficulties in general. At the same time — also from the point of view of these cognitive difficulties — they refuse to recognize any significance in socialist market relations for solving the contradictions within social labour. In other words, every deviation of actual expenditure of labour from what is socially necessary they interpret as a demonstration of insufficient knowledge. Therefore, they seek the solution only in an improvement in knowledge, increasing the qualifications of the governing personnel, improving techniques and technical instruments of management, making information more precise, etc.

Although such efforts to improve cognition and technique of management are essential, this is a tremendous oversimplification of the whole problem, if the reason for any contradiction between the necessary and the concrete development of labour is sought only in the field of insufficient knowledge on the part of governing personnel, and if the role of interests in the management, the mutual relationships of interests and cognition and concrete economic activity in general, are ignored. It is an old Marxist thesis that the direct stimuli of people's interests are so strong that they lead in some cases even to actions that are contrary to their rational knowledge — in fact, they will not even admit to such knowledge if it runs counter to their interests, and they deny it to other people if they have the power to do so.

We may also say that insufficient economic interest in the socially necessary development of labour will always be one of the main reasons for the retardation of the development of the process of cognition itself, and thereby the improvement in economic management. Every economic system must create the corresponding economic interests and incentives for the socially necessary development of labour. A society which has only a sort of superstructural, political, moral, etc., stimulus for performing socially necessary labour, and therefore for examining and finding out about the necessary forms of development, while the direct, immediate, economic incentives are lacking or even work in reverse (against the socially necessary development of labour), must perish sooner or later.

We cannot, therefore, leave aside the investigation of interests and their influence on management and on the actual economic activity of people, even in studying socialist management and socialist economic activities, especially the specific, productive work of the people. We must investigate how much a specific development of socially unnecessary labour, is the result merely of certain short-comings in cognition and how much it is affected by immediate interests that do not fully correspond with social interests. We must discover how far these interests hamper a correct cognition or are a stronger stimulus to action than any sort of rational knowledge. And, finally, to what extent can we speak of social cognition of the necessary development of each individual concrete labour and fail to see that social cognition will always be only the knowledge of a generally necessary development, and not each individual concrete form of it. In deciding on the concrete development, there will always appear direct stimuli that no one can confront directly, but only over a longer period, with the social interests.

A metaphysician always absolutizes the relation between the general and the individual, fails to see the necessity for their intrinsic contradictions and believes that a finding on the general, objectively necessary development of labour is at the same time an absolute finding on the necessary form of specific individual labour. And it never occurs to him that under conditions where one social centre cannot determine each use of labour and where this labour is primarily dependent on the work incentives of those who more directly decide, its development, the study of these incentives, and a search for ways of controlling them over a long period, is of prime importance for assuring the socially necessary development of labour.

Even the best possible social recognition of economic relationships cannot take the place of making detailed changes, on the basis of specific information, by a huge number of individual, specific management bodies, into which will always be projected certain economic interests as direct stimuli to decision and action. But if we examine these economic stimuli, we find that they do not develop in absolute harmony. On the contrary, they arouse conflicts between the different managing bodies and therefore also bring about conflicting economic activity.

Of course, the previous economic stimuli to this conflict in activity between different management bodies (branch or enterprise) were caused chiefly by the present system of administrative management. Under this system, all the attention of the management bodies was, by means of the system of planning indicators, one-sidedly aimed mainly at the quantitative aspect of production, and willy nilly led to a neglect of the qualitative side of production and development of use value.

The central planning and managing bodies could, with all the indicators, direct only the volume of production, either in very general groups of products or a small number of selected products. Even the so-called "quality" indicators are, from the economic standpoint, again merely quantitative indicators, because they set mainly the development of certain volumes of production (either in terms of value or in physical units), recalculated per unit of manpower (productivity of labour), or in other quantitative terms for the development of production and labour expended (indicator of production cost trends, number of workers, basic means of production, etc.). Except for an insignificant number of centrally designated features of technical development, all these indicators could not determine the improvement, replacement, technical and technological method of production of the actual use values, etc. The development of the actual qualitative aspect of production, by which the needs of society are satisfied and stimulated had to be left mainly to the enterprise and factory managements, who were alone capable of assuring this, because of their direct contact with production, and through this with research and development.

But this qualitative development of use values, as well as their proportional production (which, again — except for a small number of selected tasks — cannot be assured from the centre), is inseparably linked with the quantitative side of production. There is a dialectical, intrinsically contradictory relationship between them. Labour must develop both quantitatively and qualitatively to assure not only the growing amount of various use values, but also new and better use values. At the same time a certain growth in the quantity of labour and its product is a condition for qualitative development. Every disproportionate growth of one or the other aspect must appear sooner or later at the expense of development of the other that is in the long run its own condition.

For a certain period there can be a development — for example in quantity production — at the expense of the necessary improvement of the use values produced and a replacement of old by more progressive ones. But at a certain moment there must appear an inadequate development of use values which, of course, also means an inadequate development of the technical features and productive capacities of the means of production as the main hindrance and obstacle to a further increase in volume of production (either absolutely or calculated in relation to manpower). Where, in brief, there are not enough new, technically better means of production, there cannot be a sufficient rise in quantity of production. The same is true in regard to the reverse type of one-sidedness, even though there has been, so far, no practical form of this. A disproportionate amount of labour expended on perfecting the products, too frequent changes in the production programs, etc. would needlessly retard the growth in volume of production. Only the best harmonized development of all aspects of production will assure the most rapid and constant growth of consumption.

As we have already said, the assurance of such an optimum development of production in each individual branch of production — and in social production as a whole — is very difficult, merely from the standpoint of cognition. The completely random nature of optimum development, however, means that those who are directly managing production (especially directing the enterprises), as well as those directly engaged economically (productive and sales workers), have no interest in the optimum development of production. On the contrary, they have an interest in a one-sided development of production.

The enterprises were impelled toward just such one-sided, mainly quantitative, development by the old administrative method of management. The way the centre year after year rather mechanically increased the quantitative targets, without sufficient economic justification, by means of the corresponding planning indicators, increasing controls on the fulfilment of these one-sided indicators, and, finally, the linking of all material rewards to these quantitative indicators — with only general, political and moral appeals to improve the technique and the quality of production — had to bring about a disproportionately quantitative development, at the expense of the quality of use values, commodities and service and new technical production. Each enterprise necessarily concentrated on the fulfilment and over-fulfilment of the annual planned volume indicators (either volume of gross production, of commodity production, net production, gross production per worker, etc.) and avoided everything that slowed them up or made more difficult this fulfilment of the plan. This means that they avoided technical changes, the improvement of products, the introduction of new products (in fact, they often silently permitted a deterioration in the quality of the products), etc.

This system of providing one-sided incentives can not be transformed into a system that stimulates optimum development by an expansion of the number of centrally planned and controlled indicators. All practical attempts in this respect must fail and all similar theoretical considerations remain empty, general and unrealizable abstractions. No one could or can say how general central indicators can be a substitute for creative research, developmental, constructive, blue-printing, technical activity in the enterprises, which is the basis for qualitative development of production and which can be, as a result of certain existing economic incentives in the enterprises, either more or less suppressed or more or less developed. Nor has anyone imagined how the central indicators can assure all detailed proportions, the production of each individual type and range of goods always in amounts corresponding to changes in demand.

If it is necessary for the management bodies directly connected with production — mainly the enterprise managements — to have an interest in the general optimum development of production, the question then arises, how can this interest be constantly aroused. The idea that it suffices to set some special rewards for technical development, for improving products, for producing all the necessary range of goods, etc., is just as abstract and empty as the idea of centralized specific determination of all production aspects in all the enterprises. If the central body cannot determine this concrete development of use values, it cannot then link the material rewards with anything but what the enterprise management itself determines. If the higher body cannot judge for the enterprise how it should change and improve the products, what new products to introduce, how to change the technique and technology of production, etc., then it cannot do anything but set up some special rewards (premiums, etc.) to be paid if the enterprise generally demonstrates any sort of development of use values.

The control of development is necessarily very superficial, administrative, and cannot prevent rewards being given for the development of use values that do not correspond to the trends in demand, that take either the wrong course or an ineffective one. The development of use values is primarily dependent on the interest that prevails in the enterprise. Such an administrative setting of rewards, linked in differing amounts to various indicators (without the possibility of calculating from above the optimum harmony of these indicators and therefore the optimum mutual relationship between the rewards) must give rise to insoluble contradictions among the rewards themselves. The decisions of the enterprises about rewards are usually not the best ones; instead the rewards will be highest completely as a matter of chance — most will be for one-sided production decisions. That is to say, if fulfilment and over-fulfilment of the volume indicators bring greater reward, together with political and administrative control on fulfilling the plan to increase volume of production, then premiums for the development and improvement of use values will be ineffective or of little effect.

Since the best decisions cannot be made by the enterprises on the basis of centralized planning indicators, economic conditions must be formed that will provide incentives for qualitative development of use values. At the same time, they cannot be allowed to put their narrow interest as producers ahead of those of consumers. There must be checks and controls to smooth out the contradictory interests of producers and consumers that still must necessarily arise.

If certain special economic relationships had no effect on people, there would appear at the given stage of development a general tendency to expend as little labour as possible, to expend as little skilled labour, as little capital, and not to develop labour any further (either the quantitative or the qualitative aspect). On the other hand, there would be a tendency to consume as large a quantity as possible of new, better and frequently changing use values. In the first case, as producers they would act at the expense of the second tendency, and as consumers (either of personal or production consumption) the second tendency would prevail at the expense of the first. For this reason, only a mutual inter-action of both tendencies, a constant confrontation and balancing out, can make social interests come into effect, i.e., the general interests of people as producers (as workers) and as consumers — and this will be the interest in an optimum development of production.

Only if people as consumers feel directly every decision they have made on production, i.e., if they realize continually that when the one-sided, narrow interests as producers dictate the decisions made in production this will *directly* reduce their own consumption, whereas optimum decisions will result in better consumption, will they have an incentive to influence an optimum decision on production. There must, therefore, be economic relationships among the producers that will continually force them to take account of the consumers' interests, as they make decisions on production. Here, any producer, who makes a one-sided decision at the expense of consumers, should feel the negative effect on himself as consumer, just as the optimum decision should bring a positive effect. And economic relationships where there is a constant confrontation and direct mutual balancing of people's interests as producers and as consumers, furthering a socially necessary expenditure of labour — these relationships are what we mean by *socialist commodity-money relationships.*

These are relationships, by means of which (under given socialist working conditions and consumption patterns, still containing the unavoidable one-sided direct tendencies of producers and consumers) the interests of people as consumers can constantly influence the interests of people as producers and provide economic stimulus to develop production in an optimum way. These relationships cannot eliminate the narrow production or consumption tendencies that are always cropping up, but they can help to overcome them in a rapid and flexible way, because each worker can quickly see, by

167

his own consumption, the production decisions or work that has not developed in harmony with the socially necessary expenditures of labour.

The reason for the existence of socialist commodity relationships does not, therefore, consist, as some economists think,[1] in the fact that there are still relatively independent decisions made in the socialist enterprises.

Relatively independent decisions of specific management bodies, particularly in the enterprises, the necessity for which was explained in the first chapter, are only the objective condition for the existence of these commodity relations, because even then one-sided socially undesirable decisions can be made about production, contradictions can arise between producer and consumers (and among producers themselves as well).

The condition for the existence of such economic contradictions is, however, not their cause, for the possibility that such contradictions may arise does not mean that they must necessarily come about. The necessity for these economic contradictions and therefore the necessity for the existence of socialist commodity relations as a special form of these relationships, without which these contradictions could not always be overcome at the given stage of development, must be derived from the objective, intrinsically contradictory work and consumption conditions, under which there must appear limited, direct

---

[1] For instance, J. Vejvoda says, "Under the rule of state socialist ownership of means of production commodity production is a consequence of the objective existence of the operative economic independence of individual state socialist enterprises in the form of an operative administration of means of production. The relations among these enterprises, although they were of a centralized planned nature, took on the form of production and exchange among themselves. Commodity production arises where division of social labour links in one economic whole producers who are economically independent of one another. This economic independence asserts itself in its historical development, first in the various forms of ownership and later in the form of operative administration of state socialist ownerships, which is its final historical form. When the operative administration disappears, i.e. the operatively economic independence of enterprises, commodity production in the state socialist sector will also disappear, within the framework of a state-wide ownership of means of production."
Jaroslav Vejvoda, "Všeobecné základy zbožní výroby v rámci státního socialistického sektoru" (General Principles of Commodity Production within the Framework of the State Socialist Sector), *Politická ekonomie*, No 6/1958, p. 534.

tendencies of material interest, influencing the specific expenditure of labour.

The theory that only confirms the existence of certain relatively independent operative "managers" and derives from these the fact that commodity-money relations must exist, will end up where it should have begun. It does not explain *why* there are these "managers", what are their economic characteristics and their interests, what economic contradictions there are between the "independently managed enterprises" and why commodity-money relationships are an essential form for solving these contradictions.

Socialist commodity relationships are, therefore, a necessary form that helps to solve the contradictions between concrete labour expended and the socially necessary expenditure of labour. These are contradictions that still appear under the given work and consumption conditions as a direct result of certain tendencies of limited material interest.

We could formulate in brief the contradiction giving rise to the socialist commodity-money (market) relationships and which are at the same time the necessary form for solving it, as follows:

It is a contradiction between socialist labour or socialist cooperation of all society, which appears in the general, direct, planned social orientation of labour (without being able to assure full harmony between the concrete development of labour and its socially necessary development), on the one hand, and the socialist character of labour and of consumption which, to a certain degree, still gives rise to limited individual or group material stimuli to work, causing a deviation of the concrete labour expended from the socially necessary development.

In our subsequent treatment of the subject we shall need to concentrate primarily on a clarification of the more detailed connections between socialist work and consumption conditions, on the one hand, and the emerging production and consumption interests and production decisions in the socialist enterprises on the other. At the same time, we shall need to point out in more detail why the market relationships are leading production enterprises, through their own material interests, to an optimum or socially necessary development of production. We shall speak of these relationships as they would develop with regard to the recognized economic contradictions, abstracting the treatment from the fact that at present they do not develop in our society in this way. Therefore, even the exposition of the consequences of the really consistent utilization of socialist market relationships will necessarily be an exposition of theoretical conclusions arising out of the recognized economic contradictions that grow up when there is insufficient use of market relations, with one-sided economic stimuli and administrative management. Finally, we shall attempt to show why there cannot be really optimum development of production by socialist enterprises only by means of superstructural, political or moral incentives and why the fundamental stimulus must be material, arising from socialist commodity-money relationships.

b The Character of Labour, Consumption and Commodity Relations

We have already shown that socialist associated labour arouses a stimulus to work throughout society. The labour of all people under socialism is no longer exploited, there are no antagonistic contradictions between labour and capital, no parasitic consumption by capitalists, the results of social labour are distributed according to socialist principles among the members of society (making sure that the incapacitated are also consumers). In other words, there is a socialist appropriation of nature by all of society, no longer divided into antagonistic classes.

This appears in the decisions made by society on the expenditure of labour in such a way that society voluntarily subordinated itself to the guiding directives of social organizations. The effort to assure the greatest possible satisfaction of social needs at a high and constantly rising qualitative and quantitative level is the prime incentive for setting up plans for society as a whole. Harmonized with this stimulus or interest of society are the interests of all the production units and all the people.

This is an abstract picture of the general essence of the interests of all people. But previously this general coincidence of interests of all was absolutized. The essential agreement, the unity, is not absolute identity. Within this unity there necessarily remain non-antagonistic contradictions. These are not random contradictions, resulting only from errors in management, but necessary contradictions that are

170

constantly arising from the objective conditions of expenditure of labour under socialism.

The present level of development of productive forces is characterized primarily by mechanical and factory production where a relatively great deal of manual labour must still be expended; moreover, this labour is more and more an appendage to the machine rather than creative human labour. The automation of production is only an exceptional occurrence, and it will be a long time before it is so widespread in industry as to become a general, characteristic feature of production that absolutely prevails.[1]

Labour in production, therefore, is not yet an activity that in the main permits man to use his intellectual capacities, his deep theoretical knowledge and practical experience to solve new tasks arising such as those arising in maintenance, changing the range of goods, or improving and repairing automatic production, in which man would be the real creative ruler over the productive mechanisms.[2]

---

[1] "The characterization given above of the state of mechanization and automation in engineering (in Czechoslovakia — O. Š.), similar to that in other branches, shows that, on the whole, automation is now only in the initial stages of development. Although some positive results were attained where conditions were created, we must emphasize the fact that these results are not yet typical for the present state of our economy and do not express the level of technique attained in the different branches, but are actually the first swallows of the spring; the advanced technique is not yet very widespread."
Auerhan, Balda, Dráb, Říha, *Základní problémy automatizace* (Basic Problems of Automation), Prague 1963, p. 205.

[2] "Automation is not only the thorough-going culmination of man's liberation from heavy physical labour and from working in an unpleasant environment harmful to the health, but also more and more frees man from standardized monotonous, repetitive, stereotyped jobs in the sphere of mental work; thus man is more and more released for his own special interests in work, for creative work that requires extensive knowledge and a full utilization of the huge possibilities of the human brain, and at the same time is itself the fundamental condition for full and all-around development of the human personality. From the standpoint of the position of man in the process of material production, this appears in the gradual shifting of the focal point of man's participation in production from direct servicing of machines in the shop to the sphere of over-all management of extensive automatic systems of machinery, their maintenance and repairs, and especially to the field of research, development, improvement and creation of automatic equipment and technological regimes." *Ibid.*, p. 188.

In analysing all sorts of specific labour we find that, under the given technical conditions, there still is, not only very much arduous physical labour, but also, in particular, a great amount of monotonous labour that is spiritually exhausting.

In order that labour may become a vital need it must be creative work, that is, work that permits a certain spiritual soaring of man's capacity, the development of his initiative and his over-all talent. Of course, such labour does exist on a certain level (scientists, technicians, artists, etc.). But the prevailing part of labour does not yet have this character and cannot at the present level of development.

The problem of creative, interesting, satisfying work cannot be simplified only to the relation between physical and mental (muscular and rational) work. If we divide labour into physical and mental, it cannot, in the first place, be a question exclusively of work done by muscular exertion or of work that is exclusively rational. After all, it is merely a question of expressing the main character of the work, according to which aspect is prevalent. In the second place, one cannot say that mental work is always interesting and physical always monotonous. The work of a clerk keeping accounts of materials can, for example, be one-sided, monotonous, tiring and generally uninteresting. It is repetitive and unending and goes on constantly, without any great change, every month, every year.

Creative and interesting work is mainly in fields of creative research, inventing (the work of scientists, inventors, designers, technicians, architects, etc.), and, further, work where the muscular and rational meet, supplement each other and constantly change. So one cannot even say that the same profession has a constant proportion of muscular and rational labour. For example, an analysis of the work of chauffeurs showed that in driving on highways, the mental effort is 35.1 per cent, whereas driving the car in town require 61 per cent mental effort. One cannot say that driving a car in town gives the driver greater satisfaction just because he must use his mental faculties to a greater extent, must think more, recognize and process mentally the traffic signs, solve traffic situations, etc. The truth might be just the opposite. The drive outside city limits would probably be more interesting (except for other disturbing factors, such as being a long time away from home, difficulties in obtaining meals), because on such a trip he can exercise his initiative (speed of driving, etc.) and is not so tied down by external conditions on which he has no influence.

Quite different is the relationship in the work of a lathe operator, where it has been found that mental effort in manual cutting of an external thread is 13.5 per cent, cutting a thread on a lathe 23 per cent, whereas it is 41.3 per cent in assembling a pump model. The endeavour of a worker to be transferred to assembly work on models can be explained not only by the fact that the work is better paid, but also that it is more varied, more interesting and the worker can show more initiative and has much greater satisfaction from the results of his work. At the present time, however, there are not many such jobs.

Another important factor is that at the present stage of development there is low productivity of labour which results in a relatively long work week, which in turn affects the possibility of getting an education, of gaining knowledge for performing other work. A spot investigation made in 1960 on the daily utilization of a non-agricultural worker's time shows the distribution given in the following table, in minutes, with a total fund of time of 1440 minutes (p. 174).

These conditions make it considerably more difficult to improve the skills of workers, either in their own field of activity, or in other spheres. With this state of affairs, one cannot judge very well whether most of the workers would gain further skills, enabling them to shift to another type of work or alternate jobs or perform various auxiliary jobs.[1]

There is at the present level of development a rigid division of labour and great differences between the individual types of work. People are tied down to a certain kind of work, performing it in various alternatives practically throughout their productive life. It is

---

[1] "Division of labour, already undermined by the machine, which makes of one man a farmer, of another a shoemaker, of a third a factory worker, of a fourth a stock broker, will completely disappear. Education will enable young people to go rapidly through the whole system of production, enable them gradually to go from one branch of production to another, according to how the needs of society lead them to this or through their own inclinations. Education relieves them of the monotony that is impressed on every individual by today's division of labour. Thus a communistically organized society will give its members the opportunity to apply their talents in every way."
Friedrich Engels, "The Principle of Communism", tr. from Czech ed., *Writings*, Vol. 4, pp. 340–341.

TABLE 13   *Daily Utilization of Time by Workers (in minutes)*

	Men	Women
Time at work, including travel to work	554	487
Care for self, home and children	196	405
Self-education, active and passive amusement	209	101
Sleep and rest	481	447

Source: *Statistická ročenka ČSSR* (Statistical Yearbook of the ČSSR), Prague 1962, pp. 376, 377.

true that there is mobility of labour and changes in occupation occur, but this concerns only a smaller group of workers or only a certain period of structural changes in the economy, such as a shift from agriculture to industry, a transfer (and re-training) to newly built heavy industry, mines, mills, etc. For most people, in particular the specialists, a transition to another occupation or profession is barred by the loss of skills and experiences acquired in their present occupation, meaning that a change in occupation would lead in many cases to lower earnings. A stimulus to fluctuation is the attempt to find better earnings or working conditions, which most workers can achieve by better use of their previous skills and experiences. Therefore much the greater part of the workers remain practically throughout their productive years in roughly the same occupation, even though they do not, of course, perform the same specific work. (For example, may be first a lathe operator, then an assembly worker or foreman, controller or trainer of apprentices, etc.)

Under these technical conditions of labour and with the rather rigid social division of labour, most workers cannot do creative work, their work cannot correspond to their natural human capacity for development, nor to their own particular and chief life interest.[1]

[1] "...But how rapidly this development will proceed, how soon it will reach the point of breaking away from the division of labour, of doing away with the antithesis between mental and physical labour, of transforming labour into the 'prime necessity of life' — we do not and *cannot* know...

"...It will become possible for the state to wither away completely when society adopts the rule: 'From each according to his ability, to each according to his needs'

Satisfaction cannot therefore be a stimulus to performance of this work — on the contrary, work performance must have other less direct stimuli growing out of the objective stage of development of productive forces.

It would be a considerable over-simplification of the whole problem if we were to conclude that economic interests of people and their impulses to work were derived only from the character of the work. Even if production, and thereby people's labour, is the decisive point in general economic relations, labour itself develops, in turn, under the diverse influence of the other economic processes. Processes like the distribution of means of production and consumption goods, exchange and consumption, are not just passive reflections of production, but have a certain relative independence of development and considerable influence on the development of production.[1]

Even if the technical level of labour in itself and the method of division or cooperation of labour, determining the character of people's labour at every stage of development, have decisive influence on the attitude taken by people towards labour, especially to the stimuli to work, we must not overlook the substantial effect of the distribution and consumption process on these work incentives.

In brief, the interest (or lack of interest) of people in work, in certain types and methods of work, the definite force and development of this interest — all this is not dependent merely on the character of the work itself (even though this plays a decisive role), but on other economic processes also. So, *the general attitude* of people to work is an expression of a complex cognitive and psychic process, in

i.e., when people have become so accustomed to observing the fundamental rules of social intercourse and when their labour becomes so productive that they will voluntarily work *according to their ability*. 'The narrow horizon of bourgeois right', which compels one to calculate with the coldheartedness of a Shylock whether one has not worked half an hour more than somebody else, whether one is not getting less pay than somebody else — this narrow horizon will then be crossed. There will then be no need for society to regulate the quantity of products to be received by each; each will take freely 'according to his needs' ''. V. I. Lenin, "The State and Revolution", in *Selected Works*, Vol. II, Part 1, p. 299–300, Foreign Languages Publishing House, Moscow 1951.

[1] Cf., the fuller clarification of this relation in my work *Ekonomika, zájmy, politika* (Economics, Interests, Politics), Prague 1962.

which is reflected primarily the character of labour itself, directly determined by the level of development of productive forces; furthermore, the existing methods of distribution, exchange and consumption of material goods, and finally, various non-economic processes (moral, ideological, political, etc.) act on this with different force.

If we leave aside this entire cognitive and psychic process, we can, of course, say in simplified fashion that the development of labour is determined in a decisive way by the development of productive forces and division of labour, and also considerably by the development of other economic, distribution, exchange and consumption processes, and indirectly by other non-economic processes and relationships. It must be clear to every Marxist economist that this is an extremely abstract expression of some of the most fundamental relations within social development that do help to understand its essence, but are completely insufficient to influence it or consciously direct it. Among other things, the whole complex cognitive and psychic process going on in the heads of people and reflecting all the social relationships, and thus bringing about a certain development in human labour itself — all this is abstracted.

Anyone who wants to understand really concretely the connections determining the development of labour in social production and consciously act on this development, must make a careful study of work incentives and of the influence of the distribution and consumption processes — together with the decisive effect of productive forces and of the character of labour — on the development of these work incentives. For purposes of actual management, of course, it is not enough to learn only about the generally prevailing relations at the socialist level of development, although we must be content with this for the present.

This requires detailed knowledge of the various social strata and groups within the economic relations determining the specific development of their economic interests and work incentives.

For example, there may be some kinds of work in a socialist society (of some scientists, inventors, etc.) that are so creative that they arouse enthusiasm to such an extent that the distribution and consumption processes will have only minimum effect on their work incentives — they will tend to perform their work without regard to the development of renumeration, prices, consumption, etc. But it is evident that these are exceptional cases and that initiative of most people (and of most scientists, artists, etc.) is considerably affected by the development of social relations in distribution, exchange and consumption.

A necessary result of the present state of productive forces is still a relative shortage of consumption good . Expropriation of the capitalists did away with class distribution of consumption goods and a further rise in production made possible a substantial increase in the workers' average personal consumption. At the present stage the consumption of foods, is, in the main, sufficient, as can be seen in the following table:

TABLE 14   *Trends of Per-Capita Food Consumption in Czechoslovakia*

	1936	1955	1965
Annual meat consumption, in kg	34	44.8	61.7
Annual fat consumption, in kg	14.1	16.6	20.2
Annual sugar consumption, in kg	23.2	33.7	37.5
Annual vegetable consumption, in kg	65.5	85.2	76.9
Annual number of eggs consumed	138	164	227

Source: *Statistické ročenky ČSSR* (Statistical Yearbooks of the ČSSR), 1963, 1965.

According to the calculations of health workers, a person needs an average of about 3100 calories daily. One sees, therefore, that foodstuffs are sufficient in regard to caloric value but this does not mean we should ignore the fact that there still are great differences in the nourishment of different social strata of the workers. Over-all average figures do not disclose all human needs, such as the demands for better quality, more varied and more healthful foods (there are shortcomings in supplies of some types of foodstuffs, such as vegetables, legumes, fruit, better quality and more varied semi-prepared foods and preserved goods, tropical fruits, etc.), and also in consumption of meat and meat products a rising trend for the nutritionally correct foods should be envisaged.

Quite different is the situation in regard to satisfying needs for durable consumer goods, where, it is true, the needs of the people in regard to clothing and other basic goods are substantially covered, but the present development of production does not make it possible to satisfy many other consumer wants, and cannot yet do away with the great differences in consumption of different social strata.

After the Second World War the satisfaction of the workers' needs increased rapidly. But today's purchasing power (and the much higher demand that would arise if the purchasing power were not limited) is far from being satisfied. At present, for example the demand for wireless sets is fully covered, for since 1955 almost every family owns one, every third family a television set, every sixth family a refrigerator, and for the remaining worker families the television sets, refrigerators and other electrical equipment is, in view of income and price levels, out of their reach. The demand for housing has not been met in the case of a large proportion of the population and a relatively small proportion has been able to satisfy their demand for automobiles, cottages, expensive holiday trips abroad or in Czechoslovakia. This is completely leaving aside the question, to what degree one family or another, appearing in the statistical survey as owner of certain use values, (radio, refrigerators, etc.), would need new and better use values.

At the current stage there is not a large enough quantity of consumer goods to be able to provide everyone with them according to his needs. In general, personal material needs are constantly higher than the possibility of satisfying them and this will have to be reckoned with for a relatively long period. Only with a relative surplus of all basic material consumer goods, can we build communism. Not until there are the technical and production conditions where an absolute majority of people will no longer consider the performance of socially useful work as a necessary evil, but as their own, primary interest, can a socialist society change to a communist one. Or when the personal interest of people in certain creative activity will be essentially connected with the social needs for this work, and at the same time, when a surplus of all basic consumer goods will do away with the need for socially differentiated distribution in which certain people doing very arduous work according to their abilities cannot obtain consumer goods in the amount or of as high quality as other people can, meaning that economically differentiated social strata arise — all these conditions must disappear before a socialist society can change into a communist one.

Until that time the need to regulate consumption by a social distribution of consumer goods (which means, of course, the inadequate satisfaction of the material needs of a large number of people) makes it impossible still to overcome the situation where the satisfaction of these needs is a regular, immediate interest of these people. The direct interest of most people is for their material consumption to be as high as possible, for their growing needs to be gradually met. The increase in consumption, however, does not depend essentially on changes in method of distribution, but on the growth and the structure of social production, on social expenditure of labour. Therefore it is necessary to link consumption of individuals with the results of their work, which is part of society's work. In other words, it is from this relationship that the need for distribution according to work performed arises.

At a given level of productive forces, having a decisive influence on the character of labour and the level of consumption, most people do not yet perform this work for its own sake, but as an unavoidable condition for assuring their consumption. If there were not such a link between consumption and their participation in the work of society (except for some special cases), most people would probably not perform the type of work they do.

The objection that people have not only material needs, but also cultural and other social needs, is indeed correct, but it ignores, in the first place, the inevitable hierarchy in people's needs that appears as a certain generally valid average development of human needs. Not until we have reached a higher level of satisfying the basic material needs, can there be a more rapid general rise in the cultural needs of people, which are constantly developing in an inseparable relationship with their material needs.

In the second place, what is still more important is the fact that even the satisfaction of cultural needs at a given level of development is conditioned by material consumption, either directly (e.g., a passenger car as a means for becoming acquainted with historic places, a way for rural inhabitants to take part in cultural projects, etc.) or indirectly, i.e. by paying for cultural programs, which actually means that the productive workers leave a certain material consumption to the cultural workers, etc. The interest in either immediate or indirect material cultural consumption is therefore the main direct incentive for performing work for society.

The simplified interpretation of distribution according to work performed, consisted, however, in speaking only about distribution according to quantity, quality and social importance of the work. This, in practice, oriented only on the expenditure of labour in certain fields and professions according to conditions and indicators delimiting the amount of labour (by time or number of products) and their quality in the narrower sense of the word (carrying out certain pre-scribed tasks, technical parameters of the products, etc.). Even if labour is expended according to these criteria, this still does not mean that it will be socially necessary labour.

Rewarding labour only from these aspects corresponds to the old administrative system of planning and management, where it is assumed that carrying out a plan set from above automatically means to expend socially useful labour. Connected with this is the adminis-trative scheduling of wage funds from top on down and linking them with the fulfilment of the enterprise's planning indicators. Within the enterprises, then, the important thing is the differences between occupations (this is how quality of labour is understood, too,) as complex labour determined by certain skills, in carrying out rules, on work routine and the quantity of the work results.

In this way labour is not evaluated according to whether use values were produced in the necessary proportions or whether new and better techniques were introduced into production, etc. The reward is simply not linked with whether labour approaches socially necessary labour or not or whether it develops in harmony with the laws of de-velopment of social labour. It is assumed that the enterprise always assures the socially necessary expenditure of labour. Within the enter-prise it is then enough to reward in such a way that all the necessary occupations and work performance will be carried out, as well as assuring the planned productivity of labour in the enterprise.

Of course, under socialism — that is to say, under conditions where attaining an increase in consumption is a direct stimulus to the ex-penditure of labour, the work will generally be performed in a way to gain the highest consumption. This means that, according to the method of distributing consumer goods and its linking with the ex-penditure of labour, labour itself will primarily develop.

180

In general there is a tendency to expend as little as possible of labour that is not yet in the actual social interest, or to acquire the maximum quantity of use values for the minimum expenditure of labour. There will be an effort to expend as little as possible on difficult, complex, physically or mentally tiring labour, an effort to prevent the increase in amount or complexity of labour, together with a tendency to change one's previous labour and work tasks to more difficult or more complex work only inasmuch as there is higher reward and consumption.

This is a tendency that exists not only among individuals, but also in whole production groups. The interests of individuals join in the common interest of those groups who, by their specific expenditure of labour can have substantial influence on the over-all level of remuneration or the consumption of a given collective. This means that the collectives that, through their specific management bodies can decide with relative independence on the expenditure of their labour (on production), will decide to expend this labour within certain limits and, when it is possible to choose between different methods, in a way that will assure them the highest possible consumption.[1]

It is important to recall again the relation between the management organizations, which was analy ed as a condition for the existence of commodity relations. At the level of a certain degree of division and cooperation of labour — in certain production units — there is a general fund of material rewards dependent on the work expended in that unit. Here the method of deciding on the labour, in relation to the reward for the given collective, becomes decisive.

Someone might object that the fund of rewards is scheduled from the top on down, and the dependence on fulfilling the plan from the

---

[1] "The relative independence of individual socialist enterprises to a certain degree conditions the particular interests of the enterprises's collectives as production units, upon whose work the income of the collectives and their members depends. The contradiction in the dual form of interests of producers appears here as a non-antagonistic contradiction between the unity of state ownership and the organization into more or less independent enterprises. This is one of the special features of society's ownership under socialism that distinguishes it from society's ownership under communism. P. Erdös, "Commodity Production and Value Categories under Socialism," *Voprosy ekonomiki*, No. 5, 1959, p. 103.

bottom on up, and that at every level of cooperation and management there is a clash between rewards and decisions on the work (e.g., in the departments or ministries, in the associations of enterprises, in the enterprise or factory, etc.). This is true, but only if we understand this as a simple administrative scheduling of rewards from the top on down. Only at a given level of cooperation and management is the fund of material rewards realistic, where there is an exchange of product of some branches for products from others. At a given level of cooperation all workers will be linked by a common interest (all will get a reward for the results of their joint work) in relation to how they decided concretely on their joint work and in relation to how much use value they will obtain for their work results from other units. This is the cooperation that we call an enterprise.

The enterprise, then, is an economic production unit, which is linked not only with a certain common specific production and which decides with relative independence all aspects of this production, but also obtains a certain share of society's consumption (goods and services) in relation to its production. Therefore, it enters into certain exchange relationships with other economic production units, from which it obtains certain necessary use values in return for the results of its own work. An enterprise is a unit that has certain specific, material interests in common which act as direct incentive the labour of this unit for expending on production.

Let us return briefly to the way these questions are posed and solved by the distribution theory. According to this theory, the plan always assures a socially useful expenditure of labour, it is always in harmony with society's needs. From this assumption there arises a theoretical explanation of commodity production which reads as follows: value grows out of the necessity for converting heterogeneous work (differing in complexity) to a common denominator and for calculating the amount of this work. This is necessary in order that every enterprise might receive the same amount of labour from others in return from a certain amount of labour expended (value) — in other words, merely to ensure equivalence. In accordance with this, there must be also a direct tying of the wage funds from the top on down, only in proportion to the over-all planned amount of labour of the enterprises (number of workers multiplied by the working time multiplied by the average wages for different categories). So value is, in this theory, only a method of determining and balancing a certain quantity of heterogeneous labour. In this concept, money is only an accounting unit — a certificate for a certain time unit.

But this is an intolerable simplification of the facts. In this concept commodity relations do not result from contradictions within social production, as a form of necessary solution of these social contradictions, but only as a form of keeping records of labour expended and of assuring an equivalent exchange. In reality, it cannot be a question of simple equivalence. The enterprises cannot obtain an equivalent value only for the actually expended labour. That would be the case only if the labour of all the enterprises is socially necessary labour. If there is really a consistent utilization of socialist commodity relations the enterprises can receive only the equivalent value corresponding to their value-forming socially necessary labour. If there is a difference between the actually expended labour of the enterprise and the objectively necessary labour, there must inevitably arise losses or gains in labour for the enterprise.

The contradiction between the concretely expended and the objectively necessary labour means either that the labour does not have socially necessary productivity, or does not accord with the consumer needs, or that better, newer use values are not produced, etc. The basis for this contradiction is not only a lack of knowledge of the objectively necessary labour, but also one-sided production tendencies (not increasing productivity, not producing the whole necessary range of goods, not changing the quantity and quality of use values produced, etc).

"But, after all, each enterprise is compelled to fulfill the society's plan, the director is appointed by the social governing bodies and is responsible to them for fulfilling the plan — how can such a tendency appear?" — this is the immediate response of every defender of the previous administrative methods of planning. But it is precisely *because* each enterprise, each director, is trying to fulfill the plan, for which he is not only responsible to the governing bodies, but also the fulfillment of which is a condition for using all the funds of rewards of the enterprise (wage fund, premiums and bonuses, etc.). Precisely for the reason that there is no compelling interest in an optimum development of production, but in fulfilling and over-fulfilling the plan, there must necessarily be a one-sided development of production and an increase in the one-sided tendencies we have listed.

As we have already shown, no central or departmental planning and management agency can determine specifically all the complex, inter-related aspects of the development of labour in the different enterprises in a way that they will be coordinated and therefore the optimum relationships. In particular, they cannot determine the actual qualitative content of production, the development of use values and the detailed proportions of production. The qualitative content of the production, that is, the production of the whole necessary range of goods of the necessary quality, the technical development, the improvement of the use values produced, etc., must be assured by the enterprise itself on its own initiative. No indicators set from above can be a substitute for this initiative.

The enterprise's initiative, however, is inevitably restricted by administrative plans from the centre. The administrative determining of annual plans without sufficient technical economic analyses and under considerable influence of the subjective wishes for high rates of growth and a mechanical, absolute disaggregation of the central figures to the enterprises, must not only restrict the qualitative development of production in the enterprises, but often make it literally impossible. The introduction of new products into production, the improvement of technique and technology of production, the expansion of types of goods produced, etc., temporarily cuts down on the increase in volume of production and thereby retards the fulfilment and over-fulfilment of volume targets in the plans. Therefore, most enterprises simply avoid all this. In fact — in the drive to carry out the plans, the enterprises are forced to cut down on their range of goods, to choose the type of product that requires the most material (in gross production), to expand needless interchange that does not increase productivity, to allow quality of product to deteriorate, to lower the effectiveness of investments and of labour, etc.

Thus, under conditions of essentially one-sided, quite subjective annual administrative plans sent down from the top, with the responsibility and material interest of the enterprises directed toward the fulfilment of these plans, there must inevitably arise the above-described, one-sided tendencies toward socially useless production.

Of course, even when the plan does not literally force the enterprise to engage in such one-sided activity, under the given conditions of directive planning, there arises a material interest in one-sided quantitative development of production, rather than the genuinely best. Under such conditions, no enterprise is compelled by the market, by the consumer needs,[1] to improve products, but there is always more of an effort to fulfill and, as far as possible, over-fulfill the quantitative plan. The enterprise receives not only higher material reward, but also more moral recognition for a quantitative over-fulfilment of the plan than for introducing some new and better products for the consumer at the price of non-fulfilment of a quantitative plan.

On the assumption that there will be certain basic changes in setting up plans and especially in doing away with the one-sided administrative annual plans sent from above to the enterprises, it will be necessary to create the economic conditions under which their own material interests will compel enterprises to assure the optimum development of production. These must be relations under which the funds for rewards will be reduced in proportion as they expend their labour in a socially unnecessary manner and, on the other hand, rewards will be enlarged whenever the labour approaches the socially necessary labour or optimum production. These relationships are socialist commodity-money relations, market relations.

What are market relations?[2] Their external form is the *exchange*

---

[1] "The logic of a centralistic model excludes in principle the possibility of correcting by direct horizontal contact between supplier and customer, without the participation of the central elements (or other elements of the economic administration, if the matter is of lesser importance), because the fundamental criterion of the correct procedure in the enterprise and the criterion for utilizing material supplies is the degree to which the orders contained in the higher plan are carried out, and not the extent of satisfaction of the actual needs that appear in effective demand."
W. Brus, *Modely socialistického hospodářství* (Models of a Socialist Economy), Prague 1964, p. 218.

[2] We must emphasize that here we are discussing abstract market relations. We know very well that equality of sellers and buyers in the capitalist market is limited. The market cannot always act smoothly under all conditions to optimize social welfare and even under socialism the functioning of the market will not be perfect. We discuss these limitations in other chapters. Here we are concerned only with the abstract concept of the market.

of use values with relatively free decisions and an equal position of seller and buyer. This means that neither the one nor the other is compelled by law (by the exercise of power) but only by economic motives to buy and sell. What is the essence of these relationships? It is the exchange of use values in definite relationships (by means of money, that is, prices), where value will prevail as the most general basis for exchange relations, and contradictions between labour expended and the needs of society are solved. Market relations help to assure that the labour expended in the enterprise tends to be socially necessary.

In such a method of exchange we call the exchange relations, realized by means of money, the prices. Price is the money form of the socially necessary quantity of materialized and living labour expended on the exchanged commodity (value) in which, at the same time, the level of satisfaction of society's needs is reflected by a given use value.[1] The movement of prices is a form of solving the contradictions between value and use value.

This is the determining characteristic of market relations. It is not simply a mutual exchange of use values, but an exchange on the basis of value. It is a relationship, in which the contradiction between value and use value is solved and the concretely expended labour tends to be the socially necessary labour. With these relationships, prices are formed and changed in such a way that the interests of society in objectively necessary expenditure of labour will incessantly prevail, against the narrow interests of producers (suppliers) in a one-sided expenditure of labour at the expense of consumption. But, on the other hand, the one-sided interest of consumers (purchasers) in maximum and new consumption without regard to labour expended, is also corrected.

The interests of the enterprise collective are affected by the direct dependence of the income trends (rewards) of the individual members of these collectives on the income trends of the whole enterprise. In selling goods to the customers, the enterprise realizes its value,

---

[1] "Price is the expression of the law of value. Value is the law of prices, i.e., the generalized expression of the phenomenon of price."
V. I. Lenin, "Once Again the Overthrow of Socialism", *Writings*, Czech ed., Vol. 20, p. 446.

made up of the transferred old value (value of the used up means of production) and the new value created by the actual work of the enterprise collective and forming its gross income. This newly created value is no longer divided between the value of variable capital and surplus value, as under capitalism. Instead it is entirely appropriated in a socialist way. By means of planned orientation of prices (which will be discussed in more detail later) and specific planned distribution processes, part of the newly created realized value (gross income) is drawn off from the enterprises to the centralized social funds, or others above the enterprise level (e.g. partly to the directorship over the enterprises, etc.). From the gross income the enterprises must also cover all their other obligations to society (interest and loan payments, etc.).

The remainder forms the actual income of the enterprises and goes mainly for personal income (reward for labour) of the members of the enterprise. According to the needs of society, part of the actual income of the enterprises can be used also for expanding their production funds, as the enterprises decide. The part of the income of the enterprises designed for the personal incomes of the workers (fund for rewards) makes them interested in the development of the entire gross income of the enterprise. Whether the fund for rewards is set as a percentage of the gross income of the enterprise or of the remainder after the payments are made by the enterprise from its gross income to society, there is an interest on the part of all the workers in the enterprise in the realization of as high a gross income as possible and in its rapid growth.

The realization of the value of goods produced by socialist enterprises goes on within the cooperation and the limits of the planned development of all society. The enterprises do not own the realized values and have only partial independence in making decisions in the planned creation of these values, their realization, distribution and consumption. It is inseparably connected with the relatively independent planning and management role of the socialist enterprises in regard to all reproduction processes within the general planned management in society as a whole. In other words, the whole process of formation, realization, distribution and consumption of value by socialist enterprises is one of the processes of the over-all planned development of the constantly reproducing process of appropriation of nature by socialist society, in which each enterprise collective has its own essential, relatively independent economic role to play.

The interest of all members of the enterprise collective in realizing as high as possible a gross income for the enterprise arises because the fund for rewards is formed from the realized returns of the enterprise. The larger the actual income of the enterprise, the larger the fund for rewards, distributed according to work performed, among the individuals. This means distributing it according to how much each individual contributed to the formation of the realized value and thereby to the gross income and the fund for rewards in the enterprise. The individual workers, however, are not members of an enterprise that is independently owned, but are members of enterprises that are relatively independent appropriating elements within the appropriation of all society. They are, therefore, members of socialist enterprise cooperatives, and thereby also members of broader socialist cooperation for society as a whole. Their labour as the labour of individuals is not directed merely by the enterprise management, but also in broader aspects by the central management body for society as a whole. This fact is of decisive effect in remuneration and thereby also in the consumption of these individuals, creating their actual interest in performing socially necessary labour.

This is the distinguishing feature of our concept of socialist enterprise. Others conceive of socialist enterprises as independent owners rather than as elements in society's system of ownership (appropriation). In actual fact it is only under certain definite conditions that enterprises cannot be considered elements in a unified social cooperation, where the very concept of social cooperation has no justification. These conditions exist where (as specific production-technical and economic units) the enterprises can arise and disappear independent of the conscious decision of the social (central) bodies, where these central bodies have no fundamental influence on the main direction of the production and distribution activity in the enterprises and where the workers are not guaranteed a certain basic share of the national income (when specific centrally established conditions are met). When there is social cooperation, however, the remuneration of individual workers must *to a certain extent* depend directly on the work results of this social cooperation (as an established share).

The reward going to individuals for work performed within the cooperation of society as a whole, and according to basic general management directives of the central management (which, at the present stage of development must still be a state body) must be assured also *basically* by the central body. This shows in a marked way that all the workers are members of the society's cooperation, voluntarily linking their work and subordinating it to the planned management for all of society, in order to assure the material consumption that corresponds to a decisive extent to the labour performed. In relation to quantity and complexity of labour performed in any production element (unit) of this cooperation, the individuals just receive a certain coorresponding basic wage, legally set and guaranteed by the state central body, while the payment of this, of course, depends on certain work conditions that have been established (generally) by the centre.

The basic wage guaranteed by the state is not enough to assure that there be the necessary interest on the part of each individual member of a relatively independent enterprise in making decisons about production (hence about labour) and its development in the enterprise which would correspond most consistently to the optimum development of production. There must also be a certain share in the enterprise's fund for rewards, directly corresponding to the trends in gross income (either in the form of special premiums or special percentage added to the basic wage, etc.). The over-all remuneration of the individual (wage plus the special reward) thus increases in proportion as the actual returns of the enterprise increase, and declines if they decline. But the basic wage of an individual must not decline below the level guaranteed by the state, even if the economically inadequate activity of the enterprise (especially of its management) does not assure the returns and a fund of rewards that would suffice to pay the basic wages.

In exceptional cases when the enterprise has a completely negative development and its fund for rewards diminishes relatively (the sources for paying the special rewards are lost), so that there is a threat that not even the necessary means for paying the basic wages guaranteed by the state will be created, the socialist state must analyse what are the reasons for this trend and take the necessary measures to make a change for the better (either technical measures or changes in management of the enterprise, etc., according to the reasons found), assuring the essential basic wages guaranteed to the workers of the enterprise. Thus, among other things, the existence of socialist society-wide cooperation is shown and the chief conditions for a constant reproduction of the basic social interests of all members of this cooperation. At the same time, an interest arises on the part of all workers of the enterprise in the optimum development of its gross income and hence the optimum development of its production.

The development of gross income is the most synthetic reflection of the trends in labour activity in the enterprise in its relation to socially necessary labour. The gross income grows, when there are genuine market relations among the socialist enterprises, most rapidly when there is optimum development of production activity in the enterprises. On the one hand, it reflects the over-all rise in production and in social productivity of labour, and, on the other, the proportionality of production and the development of use value. The better harmonized the development of all these aspects of production, the more rapid the rise in gross income and thereby the more rapid the growth in earnings of all members of the enterprise collective. Thus there arises an interest on the part of the entire collective in the enterprise in the optimum development of its production and in exerting the necessary pressure on the management of the enterprise to orient the production activity in this direction.

But, in order for the trends in gross income to actually reflect more or less harmony between the labour expended and socially necessary labour, there must prevail a mutual relation and mutual influencing of the interests of the enterprises as producers (suppliers) and as consumers (purchasers), so that by this clash of interests the social interest will emerge. This must be done by genuine market relations and an economic movement of prices.

By means of the inter-action of the interests of producers and consumers, and the economic movement of prices, social interests will prevail. Prices change in such a way that producers will suffer losses when they produce at a lower productivity of labour than the average for society in general, or if they produce more of certain use values than corresponds to trends in demand, or if they produce outdated use values of worse quality, and so on. At the same time there are advantages (profit) for the producer when he produces at higher productivity of labour than the social average, when he adapts flexibly and speedily to demand or produces new use value of better quality, etc.

This movement of prices, therefore, results in continual surmounting of contradictions between the narrow interests of producers and the narrow interests of consumers. There is a continual harmonizing of these one-sided partial interests with the social interests. The point is — in a socialist system of management of production, inasmuch as the central or departmental bodies cannot represent the consumer interest, the consumer should be allowed to judge directly the use value and its effectiveness and to actively influence its production. This is what these higher management bodies can never do for the consumer, even at the present stage of development of socialism.

This means that only the purchaser, and not the higher organization, can evaluate concretely in detail some means of production that has been produced, whether it can help to lower production costs, to produce more efficiently better products, etc.

The purchasers can also judge whether the use values have been produced in quantities needed and whether they have the needed features, with the given costs of production, and whether they will help in efficiency. If the products do not have these qualities, if they do not answer the needs of the purchaser, they are either not purchased or are bought at a reduced price. Here it is no longer a question of the external form of commodity relations, but of the essence. It is a question of creating the material interest in the producers for expending socially necessary labour because of a higher or lower income (profit or loss) expectations. The price movement that specifically creates the exchange relations is an important instrument in distribution of products and regulating the concrete expenditure of labour in the direction of socially necessary expenditure, by using the people's own material interests.

Only in such movement and interaction of the interests of suppliers and purchasers can the optimum development of production in each branch of production and each enterprise be attained. In each branch there will be at one moment or another a complex quantitative relation among all the main developmental aspects of production which might be called the optimum differentiated relation. In a certain branch of production, for example, it may be necessary in a given period to introduce a relatively large amount of new products, even at the price of a slower increase in over-all volume of production and in productivity of labour, because the new products (say, means of production) bring larger returns to the purchasers. On the other hand, another branch might at the same time follow optimum development by a rapid extension of the range of goods produced, in accord with the needs of purchasers, and might have a general — though differentiated — rise in volume of production without introducing new products, etc.

This process of optimum solutions would be achieved concretely in all the enterprises with quite different quantitative relations among all the mutually causal aspects of production. These quantitative relations would change very rapidly on the basis of the evolving conditions of production and consumption. Only the enterprises that are in direct market connection with their customers and, if prices have a real economic function, can find detailed optimum relations in their production and can be led by material interests to realize them. It is because the enterprise under conditions of market relationships has the highest income when its production is at an optimum, that it has an interest in assuring and calculating the greatest return.

Some economists accept the necessity for, and role of, market relationships under socialism, but do not believe that this applies to the production of means of production. They believe that in this sphere the socialization of labour has gone so far that there can be direct central management of production and distribution of products, causing the market mechanism to lose its function.

This, again, is an extremely over-simplified view which reflects realistically neither the present level of development of productive forces nor the tendencies of the next phase of development of productive forces. Except for a few quite unusual instances (power, oil production, mining of coal, etc.), all branches of production develop, not towards an absolute specialization in one product which essentially remains unchanged, but toward a wide range of products that are continually changing and being replaced by new ones. This requires constant calculation and reflection on the optimum development of such products.

In most branches that produce means of production there can be no automatic central management of the enterprises, but there must be specific, relatively independent economic decisions made by the enterprises for a rather long period in the future. As long as in this sphere also the same conditions of labour and consumption affect the workers, there can be no assumption that the management bodies of the enterprise could make decisions without taking into account its highest economic advantage and without assuring the full material interest. In order that the producers' standpoint will not have one-sided influence on the production decisions and the trends in production of means of production, contrary to the trends of consumer needs, there must also be market relationships to correct the one-si..ed interests of the producers.

Economists who simply speak about the fact that market relationships are conditioned by the development of productive forces and from this derive the notion that market relations can be done away with in the production of means of production, are understanding this relation in an absolutely abstract way. They do not realize that the level of development of productive forces, while forming the general conditions of labour and consumption, acts on the character of labour and consumption and thereby on their economic interests and the way economic decisions are made in the enterprises.

The necessity for market relations arises from the conflicts of interest objectively caused by the development of productive forces.

c   **Relation between Material and Moral Incentives**

It is particularly necessary to deal with the question of material interests and their special features under socialism, because the opponents of a consistent use of socialist market relations are always ready to argue that market relations actually make people have non-socialist material interests and these then come in conflict with socialist morality.

People's material interests are always a reflection of the prevailing mode of production, that is to say society's way of appropriating the material use values. It is always the economic relationships that determine the fundamental material interests and not the reverse. It is true that these interests do develop relatively independently,

193

and therefore affect in turn the concrete forms of development of economic relationships. But in their essence they are always dependent on the material position of people, on the existing economic relations. Under all modes of production that have hitherto existed, the basic feature of material interests in gaining material use values, was an activity that — with the given mode of production and with the given position of the subject in the prevailing social relations — made it possible to obtain these necessary use values.[1]

To understand material interests it is not enough to give general definitions, because they always have specific forms under different modes of production and for different social classes, strata and individuals. In the case of capitalists, for example, it is an interest in profit, an interest in expanding value by capitalist enterprise. Contrary to this, the workers under capitalism have an interest in increasing their earnings by wage labour and in reducing capitalist profits to obtain higher wages and thereby higher consumption.

The qualitative difference in the socialist mode of appropriation, as compared with the capitalist, appears also in the particular qualitative features of the material interest of members of a socialist society. In the forefront there still is an interest in increasing material and cultural consumption. Under socialist conditions it is not immoral if the workers try to increase their consumption by performing labour that is required by society. Society requires of individual workers, however, labour that is planned and checked on, and decides on the method of rewarding various types of work. It corresponds completely to the socialist stage of development, if a worker performs his work in harmony with what society demands. The direct form of this social demand appears to him as working orders with a corresponding material reward.

Naturally, this does not mean at all that people are lazy by nature, that they would not work if they did not need to, etc. Not at all; man is a thinking and creative being and decidedly has a desire to work. But if he could choose his work according to his interests and

---

[1] I make a distinction between economic and material interests. Economic interests are a broader concept than material interests (including interest in work, interest in the status of man, in economic relationships, etc.). I have attempted a more detailed treatment of this question in my book *Ekonomika, zájmy, politika* (Economics, Interests, Politics).

wishes, he would choose creative work, would have an interest in changing work at certain intervals, would not over-exert himself with the amount and intensity of labour, etc. He decidedly would not derive satisfaction in standing at one and the same machine day after day for eight hours, without any change in the stereotyped, repetitive movements in serving the machine.

The material interests of socialist citizens, must, however, be distinguished from the remnants of exploitative material interests that tend to linger on, to some degree, even in a socialist society. But they appear as alien interests and in anti-social behaviour of some people (e.g., in an effort to get an income without labour, by cheating, by writing down labour and hours that were not worked, by cutting down on quality, stealing, speculation, etc.).

The basic feature of material interests of members of a socialist society is not the capitalist interest in acquiring an unearned income, in enriching oneself at the expense of others, in subjecting and ruling over other people, arbitrarily deciding on the labour of others, etc.

The actual remnants of capitalist interests in the consciousness of different people must be fought by the socialist society, because they conflict with socialist morality. But we must carefully distinguish — and this we often fail to do — between these alien interests and the material interests that completely correspond to the socialist stage of development. These socialist material interests cannot differ from the old non-socialist interests only by the aim of obtaining as much material use values as possible, but by the method of obtaining them.

In a socialist society, the workers have an objective interest in the kind of work society needs. At the same time this is a prerequisite for the highest consumption of individuals and the highest social consumption. This is also the determining feature of their interests. It applies, as well, to workers whose subjective aim for the time being is only to attain the highest direct individual income and who usually do not understand the long-range dependence of the development of their own consumption on the development of the labour of all members of society. When they attempt to increase their own individual income by actually performing labour in socialist enterprises, doing work that is required and rewarded, their material interest completely coincides with the given stage of development.

Of course there are under socialism material interests that ar

195

direct and individual, and there are material interests of a long-range social nature. If the individual's direct interest is to attain the highest possible personal earnings at one or another job required by society (and this, as we have said, cannot be called unsocialist), then the long-range social interest is that there be a constant, rapid and optimum growth of socialist production to assure a constant, rapid growth in consumption of each and all. This development will create as rapidly as possible the conditions for the transition to communism. In essence these short-term and long-term interests develop in harmony and someone who is following only his own immediate interests does not always act against the long-range interests. On the other hand, we must not absolutize this harmony and fail to see that temporary contradictions must necessarily arise.

If a system of creating personal incomes existed that would always stimulate everyone only to do socially necessary labour, the direct personal interests would always lead everyone to perform labour corresponding also to the long-range social interests. But actually there must arise again and again certain contradictions between the socially directed method of rewards and the socially necessary development of labour. As soon as there is a type of remuneration that does not completely orient the workers on the socially necessary labour, giving, e.g., relatively higher earnings for a one-sided development of labour, increasing quantity at the expense of quality, more for producing goods with higher consumption of material than vice versa, not penalizing sufficiently the rejects, etc., the workers, following their own direct interests, will act quite unconsciously against their long-term interests. It is obvious that expending labour contrary to the long-range social interests must become widespread under conditions of administrative planning and of suppressing socialist market relations.

To suppose that socialist interests are held only by people who have recognized and become aware of the existence of long-range social interests is typical sectarianism. It mixes the categories of "conscious long-term interests of socialists trained in Marxism" and of "direct interests of the majority of people arising from their experiences with the socialist mode of production." It would be absolute idealism and an unMarxist over-estimation of the role of the superstructure in relation to the base to believe that all the population could, in the relatively short time that socialism has existed, pull itself up with its economic and other social knowledge, to the level of the socialist vanguard, and understand fully the relation between their direct and their long-term interests on the level of the socialist vanguard. It is quite nonsense, however, to expect at all that most people would be able to act in accordance with their long-range interest against their immediate direct interest (against higher earnings at the price of lowering receipts, etc.) when there is a conflict between the method of remuneration and the socially necessary expenditure of labour.

Another over-simplified idea is that people either have only long-term, social interests or only direct, personal interests. People's interests are always intrinsically contradictory, and different individuals have weaker or stronger interests in different situations and under different conditions. Communists, as the conscious socialist vanguard, should be the first to understand and to put into effect the long-range social interests (this is not to say that this is always so). This, furthermore, gives them absolutely no right to a sectarian disdain for the generally prevailing direct material interests of the workers, which result from a given mode of production.

On the other hand, we should not under-estimate the Marxist-Leninist education of workers which speeds up the understanding of the basic social relationships, speeds up the recognition of the long-term fundamental interests of people and leads people to act in harmony with them. If there are temporary conflicts between the direct and the long-range interests, genuinely socially-conscious people give priority to behaviour that corresponds to their long-term interests. Socialist education helps in the recognition of these long-term interests, and thereby toward a more consistent social orientation of man's activity, a more consistent overcoming of the direct, personal behaviour that pursues only momentary gain.

A profound understanding of the changed social character of labour under socialism does not mean, however, anything other than the understanding of the need for and significance of a certain optimum performance of labour for society, the necessary social distribution and use of the results of labour, etc. But labour itself does not change in the sense that for socially conscious people stereotyped and uninteresting or very intense work would be their main need and

197

interest. These people have only deeply comprehended the social superiority of these over the capitalist type of labour, and therefore will consciously defend the socialist economy against any attempt to restore capitalist economic conditions. Their general incentives for the regular performance of labour will, however, be no different than for the great majority of the other people.

Social cognition, or consciousness, cannot create or transform by itself the objective direct material interest of people. If the socialist economy should generally and for a long period arouse growing contradictions between the direct and the long-term interests of people, if workers, on the basis of repeated experience, should become convinced that it is more advantageous for them to act according to their direct interests, because when they did the reverse they would have a palpable cut in earnings and consumption, no education or awareness would help, but would merely become empty phrases.

The factor that has decisive effect on forming interests is people's own experiences. It is through experience that economic relationships enter directly into people's consciousness. The ideological and moral influence can only speed up knowledge that matures on the basis of their empirical findings, the essential and intrinsic relationships of phenomena that they had only sensed and accumulated. But no ideological influence can form people's consciousness for long, if it runs counter to the experiences that have accumulated over a period of time and which help them to realize gradually the knowledge about and the position of every individual and his relationship to other people, which also has an effect on their direct interests. The very best explanation of, say, the socialist principle of remuneration according to labour performed would be ineffective if the workers were not convinced by their own experiences that the actual differences in reward express the differences in the quantity and complexity of labour expended, or that an increase in productivity of labour leads also to a rise in their real wages, etc.

If consumption appears as the chief goal of people's interests and socialist labour as the chief way to attain it, then the importance of proper distribution comes emphatically to the fore, lying much closer to consumption than to production and therefore coming much more directly in the thoughts of people as a condition for consumption than the more remote production. And it is precisely the purposeful linking of distribution and the necessary productive activity (which is the real basic condition for consumption), a linking that is carried out by people who are able to recognize even these profoundest economic relations and who orient the interests of all on the socially necessary production activity. The reward, in which each individual has direct interest, tied up with the type, method and development of labour that society needs, arouses an interest in performing socially necessary labour, that is to say, arouses the socially oriented material interest. A socialist distribution according to labour performed, as the essential socialist economic relationship, assures harmony between the direct personal interests and the long-term social interests.

The more thorough-going the socialist distribution processes (on which the development of consumption depends and therefore the development of people's interests), developing in harmony with the social need for the labour expended, the more rapidly the socially beneficial expenditure of labour by every individual will spread, even if there has been no previous stimulus by direct reward in individual cases. Experiences will multiply, showing that every improvement in work, increasing the productivity of labour, etc., will lead in the final analysis to an increase in consumption, even if this is in various forms and at different times. This experience then forms the fertile ground for all educational processes, for a more rapid understanding of the more hidden and complex distribution processes throughout the national economy (processes of distributing the national income, etc.) and vice versa for even more socially conscious labour without regard to the immediate material advantage (but with the conviction that it will appear later for society).

And on the other hand, the less consistent the distribution in accordance with the social benefit of labour expended, the more often it happens, for example, that an actual rise in productivity of labour or improvement of quality of products etc., will not result in as rapid reward as there might be elsewhere with a slower rise in productivity or quality, the slower will be the development of consciously social expenditure of labour. On the contrary, in fact, it will mean an expansion of practices of expending labour only to get the largest immediate reward and the socialist process of education will lose in effectiveness. Such uneconomic distribution will not only directly retard higher quality or more productive expenditure of labour, but will also hamper the development of effective socialist education and consciousness.

The past development has shown that only distributing according to work performed within the socialist enterprises cannot assure a really socially necessary expenditure of labour, if the old administrative method of planning prevails and socialist market relations are not utilized. We have seen that the opposite is true — the old system led to one-sided socially undesirable production and unsocial expenditure of labour. A more consistent use of market relations, however, assures a more thorough social orientation of labour expended. It is not the market relations, then, but suppression of them, not using them, that arouses unsocial interests, and has hampered the process of realizing the long-range social interests, having as result a growth of conflicts between concrete work and socially necessary labour.

The material interests of socialist producers cannot be understood as unchanging and valid for all times. On the contrary, the immediate material interest of each person is formed constantly anew, especially in connection with the way his material reward tends to develop and particularly what it is offered for. The social utilization of material interest, therefore, means a constant socially conscious orientation of the interests of groups of people and of individuals by concrete forms of material rewards, mainly by tying these rewards to the labour performance needed by society.

The ideal situation would be one where the real content and relation between rewards could be constantly aimed at the direct material interests of people in assuring the optimum development of production. Even if we never fully attain this ideal state, one of the conditions for approaching it is a more consistent use of socialist market relations among enterprises. It is the utilization of these relations that will bring out, much more consistently than before, the interests of enterprises in an optimum development of production, which will then lead the enterprise management to remunerate the individuals within the enterprise in a way that will interest them in performing work that is necessary to assure optimum production.

In addition to the material interest, there are, of course, other stimuli to expend socially necessary labour: moral stimuli (social recognition, awards, socialist competition, etc.), the understanding of the social significance of certain work and a profound feeling of social responsibility, love for certain creative work, etc.

The moral stimuli have a decisive effect also on the performance of various special socially beneficial and usually unpaid work, such as "brigades" and other social campaigns. In them we see most evidently people's understanding of certain social needs and interests, and the subordination of direct personal interest to these long-term social interests.

We must see that under certain conditions there can arise real work enthusiasm among people, even if they do not realize all the profound economic relations and changes. This enthusiasm cannot be identified with conscious socialist labour and even less with a communist relation toward labour.

In the initial post-revolutionary period there was work enthusiasm and a realization of certain great social and political changes that entered into the consciousness of most people through direct, surface phenomena, such as eliminating capitalists and their hirelings from the factories, such as changes in the leadership and a rapid increase in the number of people holding leading positions who have come directly from the ranks of the workers. In addition, the rapid elimination of such social phenomena as pauperization, unemployment, fear of old age, of sickness, etc., all had effect on the upsurge of the initial work enthusiasm.

Most of these people did not realize what the real economic changes were or the complexity of the socialist economic development, nor was labour the actual prime life necessity for these people.

People did not need to know, and the absolute majority still do not know, what has changed in the distribution of national income, how the surplus product is distributed and used, etc. They had genuine work enthusiasm, but in time the most evident changes in the character of labour, in its management, which aroused the enthusiasm, disappear from memory, people become accustomed and the work becomes an everyday matter. This is especially true of the new generation that did not live through the actual course of the changes and even makes very superficial comparisons (often on the basis of superficial and distorted information) of their life and labour, with life and labour in various industrially advanced capitalist countries.

201

The consequence is that they cannot feel the post-revolutionary labour enthusiasm if the work does not attract or satisfy them. It is not at all by chance that this labour enthusiasm can be kept alive longest for some special campaigns (some of the brigades, etc.). But these campaigns must not be formally required, and people must really be aware of their importance and need.

It would be a mistake not to see that such voluntary unpaid work can be only occasional, exceptional work. It is needed for some special collective needs, but cannot be used to assure all the necessary personal consumer goods. In these unpaid work campaigns there usually are no great differences in quantity and complexity of labour performed — or, if so, only for a short time. When work is performed over a long period of time to obtain the necessary and growing quantity of personal consumer goods, it would not be possible to assure continued differentiation in work performed by individuals unless the consumption rewards were differentiated. For this reason, the endeavour to attain differentiated rewards for different work performed over a longer period for society, and rewards that increase in proportional to the labour for society, is in the general interest under socialism and is completely in harmony with socialist morality.

We should realize that morality and all the moral incentives reflect the essence of social interests, and social interests are decisive for morality, even if morality and moral incentives do have relative independence of movement. If contradictions do not grow up in the economic base — and, therefore, there are none within the interests that directly reflect this base — that is to say, as long as personal interests are in harmony with social interests, morality has an objective basis for development in harmony with the interests of individuals and will actively help in constantly forming this harmony. But when contradictions in interest come about, either in the interests of individuals and those of enterprises, or between enterprises and society, between direct interests of individuals or groups and the long-term interests of society, these must always be resolved economically. An attempt to solve them only by means of moral appeals, contests, etc., would not lead to the goal, because such isolated attempts at moral incentives could not change the material interests of the workers and the economic processes which bring them about.

If contradictions arise between the direct material interests of people and their social interests, because of erroneous economic management, especially the system of wage and salary payments, people will generally act according to their immediate interests, and the moral appeals to combat these immediate personal interests will not be very effective. In other words, if behaviour in harmony with long-term interests requires substantial and lastingly different labour of most people from that which bring them directly higher personal income, or if social interests demand work from people that will bring them considerable material loss, only because of the erroneous system of planned management, because socialist market relations are insufficiently utilized, labour is incorrectly rewarded, etc., this has the final effect that people will act to attain directly the highest possible material reward, even at the expense of long-term social interests. If, instead of rapidly doing away with these economic mistakes, the desire is to solve everything only by means of general moral appeals, it will end in fiasco, as every sectarian solution must.

The situation is quite different, of course, when people are willing, in order to further their long-term economic and political interests, to give up their immediate advantages or even to go to their death, if they know that there can be no long-term improvement in their general living conditions unless there is a fundamental change in the political and economic situation, in some cases by force of arms. But only a dogmatic person could confuse or identify these political interests of workers, that arise under exploitation and oppression, with the long-range economic interests of workers under socialism. In a socialist country an armed struggle is no longer a way to put through the long-term material interests of the workers of the country and if the workers lose thought of long-term interests (despite all the propaganda), and especially if there are growing contradictions between the immediate personal material interests of people and the possibilities of carrying them out, this will be primarily an expression of a directed economic development in the country. Contradictions that have been growing for a long period of time among the different economic interests (the social and the group or individual) under socialism must essentially be evidence of mistakes and shortcomings in the economic management because in a socialist system all economic processes (bringing about the economic interests) are a part of planned management.

Furthermore, these economic mistakes and shortcomings could not be solved by general moral appeals or by people renouncing the consumption to which they have a right, over a long period of time.[1]

We do not want to deprecate the importance of moral stimuli in building a socialist society. On the contrary, it is a matter of defining the place, the possibilities and the significance of this morality. As Lenin said, "Not directly relying on enthusiasm, but aided by the enthusiasm engendered by the great revolution, and on the basis of personal interest, personal incentive and business principles, we must first set to work in this small-peasant country to build solid roadways to Socialism by way of state capitalism. Otherwise we shall never get to Communism; we shall never bring these scores of millions of people to Communism. That is what experience, what the objective course of development of the revolution has taught us."[2]

d Socialist Cooperative Labour and Market Relationships

We have shown that the reasons for socialist commodity production lie in the intrinsic contradictions of socialist labour, which cannot be surmounted either by direct, planned orientation of labour or by socialist rewards to individuals. Instead, there must be special commodity exchange relationships that help toward a social orientation of the interests of producers and consumers and thereby a harmonizing of production and consumption. This is the case at the present stage of development of society where the social character of labour has made socialist appropriation necessary, as well as the direct social orientation of labour. At the same time, labour and consumption are such that the main, direct incentive for individuals to do work, strongly influencing also their work as definite work collectives — the

---

[1] "Disdaining the material needs of workers, and emphasizing mainly enthusiasm and social consciousness, social and moral forms of incentives and reward, hampered the development of production and of raising living standards of the workers. This had negative results in internal politics and in international politics..." N. S. Khrushchov, "For New Victories of the World Communist Movement", *World Marxists Review* No 1, 1961.

[2] Lenin, "Fourth Anniversary of October Revolution", *Selected Works*, Vol. II, Part 2, p. 601, Foreign Languages Publishing House, Moscow 1952.

enterprises — is the material reward. At this stage of development, special market relations still have an important social function.

Clarification of this profound, objectively determined reason for commodity production under socialism is also positive refutation of the theory explaining it by the existence of two forms of socialist ownership, for this relies on secondary, superficial phenomena. Instead of explaining the special socialist form of appropriation of nature by men, which is carried out, among other ways, by means of commodity exchange relations, this theory is based on an *a priori* establishment of the ownership by certain groups of people, without being able to explain why it appears again and again, how it originated and the reason for it. This theory leaves aside the explanation of the general essence of exchange relations in all socialist production, and between all socialist state and cooperative enterprises as well. The ownership theory begins where it should end and ends where it should begin.

Socialist cooperative enterprises do indeed have their own specific historical origin in the remnants of medieval small-scale production in the capitalist economy. But this specific historical origin is not, and cannot, be the main reason why they are retained for a long period within socialist production. If the socialist economy did not retain for a certain period definite qualities of one type of labour or another (especially in agriculture), to which corresponds a relatively more cooperative socialist form of production than does the state socialist form, this special form of production would have disappeared long ago or would have changed into the state socialist production form. The main reason it was retained is not merely or even primarily some sort of psychic survival in the minds of former small producers, not to speak of the fact that in the USSR, for instance, a whole generation has succeeded the original cooperative farmers. Instead it is the particular character of the labour that requires something in the nature of cooperative social production which, in turn, evokes and reproduces a psychic reflection (especially in regard to interests) in the cooperative producers.

What is the main particular feature of the cooperative form of socialist production (especially in agriculture, where it carries the most social weight) in comparison with the state form? What is the essential difference between state and cooperative enterprise under socialism? It is not the purpose of this study to make a detailed analysis of these particularities, but only to give a brief enumeration to bring out some of the most fundamental characteristics that are important for an exposition of socialist market relationships.

A cooperative enterprise usually has a relatively small number of workers and a lower level of development of productive forces, therefore a lower degree of social labour than the prevailing majority of socialist industrial enterprises. This is seen primarily in the relatively low technical equipment of cooperative enterprises, in which there is a much higher proportion of living labour in relation to embodied labour than in the great majority of industrial enterprises. These are less specialized and in the main have small-scale technology. The level of division of labour or the labour specialization within the cooperative enterprises is relatively much lower than in industry.

We shall not examine the degree to which these qualities of labour are caused by the natural conditions of agricultural production (for example, doing repair work where the cooperatives are relatively dispersed), nor how far or how fast these particular features can be changed. We shall merely consider them as a definite, relatively long-term fact under socialism, which must necessarily affect the relation of people to their own work, to each other at work, to their work results and towards the conditions for reproduction of the mode of production with which they are linked.

There can be no argument that labour itself is relatively even less a vital need and interest for people in agriculture than in industry at the present time, that people do the work as something essential to earn a living. At the same time several factors make rather difficult a detailed social delimitation of the work of individuals and a social control of the results of their work. In the first place, there is the fact that the jobs are not as specialized as in industry and must be considerably changed according to actual experiences and decisions made by a worker in relation to rapidly and constantly changing work conditions. In the second place, most of the work results do not show their quality or their extent immediately after work is finished, and the results of various individuals' work cannot be exactly distinguished because they tend to merge. And, finally, the same expenditure of labour, the same quantity of labour gives quite different and unpredictable results, especially for different natural reasons and their constant changes.

Under these conditions, the actual cooperation of people must have a certain specific form, must have a specific system of planned management and, finally, requires certain special work incentives and inducements to obtain and use new means of production. All these special main characteristics are most evident in the social form of production we call the socialist cooperative form, although this does not mean that it must take this form, with all the secondary characteristics. One might easily imagine a social form of production, with somewhat different features in its details, but with the above-listed main characteristics, and that this could be the corresponding social form of production under given work conditions.

Under the given conditions of labour there must be economic relations and social incentives that will induce people to perform the best quality of work with the necessary intensity and productivity of labour and in the socially necessary quantity, both as planned by society and according to the best experience and knowledge of each individual. This, despite the fact that they must quite often change their workplace, change the partial cooperation, and that each is forced to rely on the work of another that is difficult to check on directly. Here we see primarily the necessity for very close ties between the earnings of each individual, with strict checks, and the social income of the entire cooperative. Even though it is necessary within this collective to control the quantity and quality of the work of each individual as strictly as possible, and to give different rewards for different kinds of work, nevertheless the actual reward should be closely connected with the real social result and the social income that is realized.

The earnings of individuals must change relatively fast, in relation to the changing social productivity of labour of the whole cooperative, while frequent differences in this productivity of labour (especially as a result of changing natural and other conditions of labour) bring considerable differences in individual rewards. Of course there is no remuneration in the cooperatives that is guaranteed by the state and the development of each individual income is fully dependent on the trends in income of the whole cooperative.

Such close connections between the incomes of individuals with the actual results of their labour and the income of the whole collective form relatively favourable conditions for the socially necessary expenditure of labour. The direct dependence of the earnings of individuals on the gross income of the whole collective also creates greater interest in the efficient use of all means of production, because the relatively lower the consumption of means of production in relation to the over-all receipts of the cooperative the relatively higher the gross income which is the basis for individual incomes.

Any material interest can be nullified by many types of circumstances, of course. These do not alter the fundamental correctness of the above-described intrinsic economic relations, but they can prevent them from being applied — they can arouse contradictions between the social interest and the individual interests of cooperative farmers. For example, the cooperative's possibility for efficient farming, with a view to local natural and economic conditions, can be strait-jacketed with administrative plans. Or there can be a disproportionately low reward for work in the cooperative, in comparison with work of the same quality, quantity and intensity in industry. When there is a possibility to shift over to industry, there is not enough interest on the part of some cooperative farmers to work on any farm. Or certain administrative measures can reduce or completely separate rewards paid individuals from the actual cooperative income attained. Or a completely insufficient check on labour, slack record-keeping, work norms, etc., or lack of records on the effect of means of production on income trends, can undermine an interest in the socially necessary labour and an effective use of means of production. Or the practice of financing investments without requiring payment, or writing off the interest due, or loans unpaid, can erode the interest in effective use of investment means and basic capital. All these possibilities, however, mean only that the economic relations are not sufficiently respected, not that they do not exist. Even though there can be such shortcomings in the economic policy of a socialist state or in the management of some cooperatives, thus undermining the effect of this special economic form of cooperation on the socially necessary work performance, this does not mean that this special form of socialist cooperation has no general validity.

Under the working conditions explained above, the importance of certain special features in the planned management of cooperative production come to the fore. In the first place, there is need for relatively more independence in expenditure of labour, in view of production, and in view of the small amount of specialization and the low level of development of technique. The cooperative must have a relatively large possibility to make independent decisions in regard to its specific production with certain, very general social orientation of this production, taking account of the changing social need for agricultural products. At the same time — and precisely because the earnings of each individual are dependent on the collective earnings — all members of the cooperative must be able to take direct part — and also through elected, collective bodies — in important decisions in regard to production, distribution and other economic matters of the entire cooperative. Each cooperative member can — and this is because there is more or less small-scale technology — easily get an idea of the work done by the whole cooperative and have substantial influence on its development. This, in turn, strengthens the social interest and the interest of each individual in the socially necessary orientation of the work and of the joint production. Whenever detailed administrative planning of production by higher state bodies restricts and ties down the initiative of the cooperative members and compels, perhaps, some economically less advantageous production activity, their socially oriented interests are undermined and narrowly individualistic, direct interests grow up.

It is quite clear that cooperatives must be linked even more than the state socialist enterprises by market relations to their customers, whether these are state enterprises or other cooperatives. For this reason, the decisive direct incentive to production, under conditions of relatively greater independence in management and decision-making, is in obtaining the highest possible income for the cooperative. The development of this income must depend on the actual sale of goods. The customers must have the possibility of rejecting products. The cooperatives must be compelled by the realization of the value of the goods to try to expend labour in a socially necessary way. This must be done through market relationships with socially necessary expenditure of labour which will continually help to overcome the one-sided decisions taken on production, which conflict with social interests.

Price relations and trends are of special importance in cooperative production. They have even stronger influence on the concrete proportions of agricultural cooperative production than in industrial production. Of course, the fact is that the administrative measures in setting inflexible purchase prices of agricultural products bring out more disproportions that cannot be completely overcome by the best detailed administrative planning of agricultural production from above, than there would be if price trends were economically based and the administrative hindrances to agricultural production were removed. Especially in the commodity relations between state and cooperative enterprises the prices should be formed as much as possible to orient production and supplies on types of farm products for which there is greater demand.

We are not interested in analysing in detail this specific problem, but only in showing that commodity production in socialist cooperatives has the same fundamental reasons for existence as in state socialist enterprises, and, moreover, they appear here in much more striking form. Again it is the character of labour and consumption that arouses direct work incentives of entire cooperative units striving to obtain as high earnings as possible within certain limits imposed by a socialist society. But if these direct social limits are still more general and skeletal and the work of individuals is still more directly linked with the income of the enterprise, the workers having relatively more influence on the management of the enterprise, the necessity for market relations between cooperative enterprises is still more marked.

Whereas the socialist cooperative form of production has appeared as a special form of socialist production in some branches, especially in agriculture, as a result of the low level of development of forces of production and of the social character of labour taken over from capitalism (as the socialist economy was taking shape), this form persists for a long period during socialist development, for the lag in development of productive forces in these branches limps behind the others. The above-described production and working conditions require a relatively more independent role for the individual cooperatives in the socialist appropriation of nature, than have the socialist state enterprises. The socialist cooperatives appear not only in the economic sense as more independent production and ownership collectives than the state enterprises, but this fact also has its legal expression and gives rise to certain psychic attitudes, especially in regard to the interests of cooperative members.

Socialist cooperative members know that their individual income (and consumption) is fundamentally dependent on the cooperative's income and is not guaranteed by anyone else, that is, not even by the socialist state. If the cooperative form of production is properly used and managed, it arouses a very strong direct interest on the part of the cooperative members in using their initiative to perform work that contributes the most toward bringing in the greatest income to the whole cooperative. Whenever economic processes, especially price movements, do not aim at the socially necessary expenditure of labour but at a one-sided development, these group interests in the cooperative lead to a one-sided, socially less necessary expenditure of labour. But it is a serious mistake for the socialist state bodies to react to this by taking certain administrative measures instead of ensuring the economically necessary changes in the incentives (price changes, etc.).

Socialist cooperatives themselves voluntarily submit to general planned direction of their production by the socialist state, especially in order to assure sales of their produce. This means that these group-owned collectives join in the socialist cooperation of the entire society and expend their group labour in harmony with the planned needs of society as a whole. But as soon as this general planned direction by the state, where market relations are purposefully used and, with them, related financial measures (setting prices and price limits, credit, subventions, taxes, etc,) change into detailed and administrative regulation of the cooperation, tying down their initiative and making little use of market relationships, the special features of the cooperative form of production are weakened and lose their specific importance in stimulating the development of production within the cooperatives. The cooperative workers lose their initiative and have no interest in expending socially necessary labour (many times they lack even the possibility for this, because of administrative, one-sided, detailed plans and regulations), and contradictions between the concretely expended and the socially necessary labour will grow up.

The socialist cooperative enterprises require socialist market relations even more emphatically than do the state enterprises. Within very general, skeletal state plans, these market relations must help in a decisive way to overcome the contradictions between concrete expenditure of labour in the cooperatives and the socially necessary labour. This does not mean to deny the general fundamentals of market relations, either between the cooperatives and the state enterprises or between the state enterprises themselves. In both these socialist forms of cooperation there are basically the same internal contradictions in labour and the same conditions in consumption, and not only in the cooperatives, but also in the state enterprises the effect of direct material interests of the workers is felt in the specific production decisions taken by these enterprises, even though not to the same extent as in the farm cooperatives. The contradiction does, however, compel commodity exchange between the state enterprises themselves and between them and the cooperatives.

The magnifying of differences between cooperative and state socialist enterprises in the recent past, and the theoretical concept that cooperative production is the sole reason for commodity production, led to a denial that commodity exchange relations exist within state socialist production. At the same time, it led to an administrative separation of the material interests of workers in state enterprises from the social results of labour in these enterprises. These administrative forms of management, which also suppressed the commodity nature of socialist state production, made the difference between state and cooperative production appear to be even greater.

Full recognition of the commodity character of production in state socialist enterprises and a more thoroughgoing connection of trends in personal income of the workers in these enterprises and the income of the enterprises themselves on the one hand, and, on the other hand, the strengthening of the industrial character of agricultural production, as well as the gradual change of personal income payments to cooperative members to remuneration resembling wages (together with other changes) will mean in the future a diminishing of the economic differences between socialist state and cooperative production. At the same time, however, it will disclose much more emphatically the existence of deeper, more general reasons for socialist commodity production than those propounded by the defenders of the ownership theory.

212

Summary

Socialist economic relations must ensure that concretely expended productive labour should always be socially necessary labour. Such a development of the various kinds of social labour performed in the huge number of specific production economic units (enterprises), must be ensured by a complex socialist system of management bodies built up in hierarchical fashion. The enterprise management bodies cannot act in absolute unity, not only because of inadequate cognition, but also because of certain objective non-antagonistic conflicts of interest between them. And these cannot be entirely overcome by the social plans.

The conflicting stimuli for the activity of the enterprises result from the fact that under socialism people's work cannot yet be their chief interest and most people perform it in order to get as much material consumption as possible and the cultural advantages based on it. This direct incentive for the work of individuals is felt in the relatively independent decisions taken by the collectives, where the specific economic decisions and the method of expending labour in the enterprise have decisive influence on the size of the enterprise's fund for personal reward and on trends of consumption among the workers of the enterprise. Even though these decisions are taken within the framework of the state plans and other central directives, there will always be a certain choice between one or another variant in the specific line of production, which has a large number of interrelated and conflicting aspects of development and the decisions will always be affected by the existing conditions for obtaining the greatest funds for rewards.

Under conditions where the specific production decisions are directly influenced by the material interests, there must necessarily be special market relations, by means of which the interests of consumers can constantly exert economic pressure on producers and impel them towards an optimum development of production.

When there are market relations between socialist enterprises, the development of the fund for rewards will depend on trends in the enterprise's gross income. Gross income of the enterprises will rise most rapidly when there is optimum development of the production activity of the enterprises, with a genuine economic movement of prices and interaction of the interests of suppliers and customers by means of which social interests are effectuated. With such mutual harmonizing of interests, socialist market relations will contribute to the socially necessary orientation of the labour of enterprises.

The unsocial one-sided tendencies in interests cannot be explained as manifestations of the existence of market relationships. Leaving aside explicit survivals of exploitative interests in the consciousness of various individuals, one-sided interests in attaining the highest material consumption by wrongly oriented labour (in conflict with the socially necessary labour) arise, on the contrary, from insufficient use of market relations and erroneous remuneration procedures. This unsocial development of labour in the enterprises and of individuals cannot be overcome by general moral influence, but only by rectifying the mistakes and shortcomings in the economic management. The moral and educational influence does, of course, enlarge the ranks of those workers who, on the basis of a knowledge of the long-term social interests, are able to act with a social conscience in harmony with the long-term interests and at the same time to battle for economic solutions to the growing contradictions.

The contradictions rooted in the character of labour and consumption existing under socialism arise in a relatively more marked way in some sectors of a socialist economy, where for a long period a relatively low level of development of productive forces persists (especially in agriculture, repair services, etc.). In these sectors there must necessarily exist, for a time, forms of socialist relations that we call in our country socialist cooperative forms. Cooperative production was for a long time designated as the reason for commodity production under socialism. Actually, however, the cooperative enterprises are socialist enterprises that produce and exchange goods with approximately the same intrinsic contradictions of labour as exist in the labour of socialist state enterprises, but in a sharper and more striking way. Socialist commodity production results from the conditions of labour and consumption; while they prevail throughout all of socialist production, the intrinsic contradictions of labour and their effect on management decisions appear in somewhat sharper form in some special economic sectors and here require the socialist cooperative form of commodity production.

214

3 Special Features of Socialist Market Relationships

a The Development of the Relation between Value and Use Value

As we have already shown, private-property and socialist commodity-money relations have one basic root in common. Labour is expended in separate group cooperations under conditions of developed division of labour; labour is not a vital need but the necessary prerequisite for obtaining commodities from others. It is social labour, but is not always socially necessary labour, since there are certain mutually conflicting special interests. There must be, therefore, exchange relationships between the producing units that compel them to try continually to produce as much as possible, with the greatest productivity, to produce new goods of better quality, always harmonizing the proportions of production with trends of demand.

These general common traits of the existing systems of commodity production do not mean that private-property and socialist commodity production are identical. We must also perceive the specific features that cause them to differ and which are so fundamental that we can speak of two special *types* of commodity production.

The basic feature of socialist commodity production which differentiates it from the private property system is the fact that it develops within a socialist cooperation of society as a whole and its relatively independent agents are socialist enterprises which are only parts of the total socialist society. There is no such purchase and sale of commodities that would endanger the existence of socialist cooperation in the society as a whole. It is impossible for means of production to be sold to private persons, in a way that could lead to private production or which would threaten socialist cooperation of society.

This cooperation is expressed in the direct social orientation of labour under socialism and is primarily characterized by the fact that the basic proportions of production are *a priori* subordinated by long-term plans to the envisaged structure of needs of all society. Before production activity can act as an immediate individual or group incentive, it has a broader general aim established by the central bodies and designed to satisfy the needs of all members of society. Although the former theoretical absolutizing of this fact was incorrect, for it lost sight of the immediate, narrower stimuli and goals

215

of production activity of individuals and production cooperations, it is impossible not to see that direct social orientation of labour is of main determining importance under socialism.

Under capitalism private labour is of decisive importance. This means that the determining factor for expending labour is to bring in the greatest private income. The contradiction between labour expended according to private decisions and socially necessary labour arises not just because of lack of knowledge, and insufficient private recognition of socially necessary labour, but is the necessary consequence of private interests that are decisive for the performance of any labour, regardless of the interests of other people. Under these conditions labour is to a larger degree only indirectly social labour, realized as social labour only by means of the market. Therefore it is indirect social or abstract labour that is realized by means of the value of commodities.

Under socialism, labour is oriented directly, in a planned way, and mainly in harmony with the socially necessary labour. Of course, not even here is the expenditure of labour fully rid of certain individual or group stimuli and it cannot be completely social labour. If we were to set up such sharply delimited boundaries of the expenditure of social labour and did not admit the actually existing stepping stones or merging of the two, we should be acting metaphysically and not dialectically. Only the metaphysician absolutizes always with his "yes" or "no". He asserts that labour is either directly social labour and therefore cannot be abstract labour, or that it is private labour and this excludes its social aspect.

In reality, of course, there is no such absolute contradiction, or absolute harmony, absolute identity. With the rise of socialism the basic nature of administration and expenditure of labour changed, but no absolute harmony arose between the concretely expended labour and socially necessary labour. An absolutely social character of labour would mean that the concretely expended labour would always be identical with the objective, socially necessary labour. But we have shown that under socialism there still exist certain tendencies toward an unsocial expenditure of labour and therefore contradictions between the specific and the socially necessary labour must necessarily arise again and again. This is not to deny the general, planned harmony of the two aspects of labour.

The contradictions that grow up between socialist enterprises are not of an antagonistic character. It is not a case of putting through the basic interests of some enterprises in conflict with the different basic interests of other enterprises. The enterprises do not oppose each other with fundamentally contradictory interests, as do the private capitalist enterprises. But still there are necessarily some non-antagonistic contradictions in the interests of the different socialist enterprises.

Social planning and control alone cannot surmount the one-sided tendencies of interest of the enterprises. Thoroughgoing utilization of market relationships is needed also, as we have already shown, helping to overcome the contradictions between specific and socially necessary labour; these relationships will motivate the enterprises economically to expend labour more consistently in accord with socially necessary labour.

Under socialism the direct social orientation of labour is of decisive importance in regard to the individual and group incentives to work. This is shown by the fact that these limited market stimuli do not determine the development of the basic structure and the basic proportions of production and that all these basic, macroeconomic processes need not arise spontaneously as they do under capitalism.

Even though the great capitalist monopolies must today plan the development of their production basis a long way ahead, and at the same time try to predict market trends, they cannot plan the direction of the movement of factors that determine the development of these markets (unemployment, the real wages of the workers, etc.) throughout the national economy and cannot be led by any other interest than profit. A narrow private interest predetermines even their long-term investments. This must divert them from any activity that would be socially beneficial but would not bring them profit. A typical example is the gradual depopulation of southern Italy. Private capital does not flow into this area, although it would undoubtedly be advantageous for society, from the standpoint of using local manpower and the immensely favourable climatic conditions, assuming that great investments are made in water conservancy projects, etc. From the standpoint of private capital, however, these are long-term investments without any quick return, and therefore the investments

217

are made in other countries if they cannot be favourably made in northern Italy.

Conditions exist under socialism making it possible for society, on the basis of calculations of optimum variants, to plan the future system and development of basic production. In accord with studies of the trends of development of the basic structure of needs of the population, the basic proportions of future production of consumer goods can be established. All changes in these production proportions require that there first be changes in the proportions of production of means of production. Changes in the latter proportions are, of course, set not only by changes in the production of consumer goods, but also and primarily by changes in the techniques and technology of all production. These technical changes call for changes in the extent of consumption in production, i.e., the consumption of various means of production. At the same time it is apparent that different technologies of production in various inter-related branches of production consume for the same (or similar, inter-changeable) final products, not only different types of means of production, but different quantities. This also means that with different quantities of social labour, using different technology, the same quantity of the final products (similar or inter-changeable) can be produced. This, in the final analysis, makes possible the satisfaction of the anticipated needs of the consumers.

In setting up long-term plans, the basis must be all-round analyses of the given situation in the economy and of the various possibilities of technical development, both in the individual branches of production and in the whole national economy. In calculating the social production costs (on the basis of the production prices of the products, which we shall deal with later), necessary for the final products using various technical variants and after their mutual comparison, it is necessary to choose the most efficient variant — the one having the relatively lowest expenditure of social labour to obtain the relatively greatest quantity of the necessary use values. In making these calculations, the most modern methods of investigation and the most advanced computer techniques and input-output analysis should be used in planning the intersectoral relations. By means of the methods of aggregation and disaggregation, which we described earlier and by the system of successive stages (gradual approxima-

218

tions) the aggregated findings on the inter-sectoral relations must be transferred, using one or another variant of development, from the enterprises to the centre and vice versa until the evaluation of all inter-sectoral costs leads to a finding of the most effective over-all economic variant.

The optimum variant for economic development that has been arrived at by this method of investigation and consumption is even more complicated when the calculations must include changes occurring because of foreign trade (especially in countries that rely to a large extent on foreign trade, as Czechoslovakia does). Here we must include in calculations of the rate of growth of the different branches of production not only the domestic consumption but also the most effective imports and exports.

This is how the ideas on the possibilities of growth of the most effective production in different branches or chief groups of products must come about, not only in regard to domestic needs, but also the market possibilities in foreign trade and the necessity to import products and raw materials to assure the most effective domestic production and other needs. Not until such preliminary concepts are worked out can there be a basis for negotiation on economic cooperation between socialist countries and additional trade agreements. Only a well-thought-out and calculated concept based on several variants can be a foundation for successful negotiations between socialist states, for this makes possible negotiations with profound and long-range knowledge of the conditions of one's own country's effective development and the possible changes that can be made on the basis of mutually advantageous negotiations between partners.

The long-term plans that are prepared in this way, which must contain the necessary economic reserves and should be continually renewed by permanent planning, can become relatively realistic and stable plans. By this type of planning, the relation between use value and value can indeed become the consciously applied relation in the sphere of macroeconomic planning. This can consciously put in effect the fullest satisfaction of needs with the relatively lowest expenditure of social labour.

Under the old directive system of planning, the rational relation between use value and value was lost. Although the standpoint of use value was held up as the absolute antithesis of the capitalist value criteria, in actual fact, the understanding of use value was tremendously simplified in that it was declared to be a matter only of the quantity of use values. There was a complete neglect of the conditions of development of use values and the significance of assuring the huge number of detailed proportions for a genuine satisfaction of needs. Together with this, the underestimation of the importance of real value and simplified understanding of trends in global prices only as units for record-keeping, expressing the quantity of production, led to a setting up of plans that, while they did assure the rapid growth of globally expressed production, did not at the same time assure the most effective economic development. The real result of such plans had to be, on the one hand, a retardation of technical development (the development of use values). The formation of a less effective basic structure of production and thereby a slower formation of conditions for a continuous rise in social productivity of labour (for a more rapid transition from extensive to intensive growth in production). And, on the other hand, it resulted in a less adequate satisfaction of the population's needs than would have been assured by a more effective structure and development. This type of planning corresponding to the simplified, one-sided and absolutized theory of maximum satisfaction of the needs of society, actually brought about a relatively inadequate satisfaction of these needs and a partial negation of use value.

Only a system of planning that takes account of the relation between use value and real value, with the aim of assuring an optimal economic development, can be called socialist planning. Under these conditions, the chase after the greatest increase in over-all gross production ceases to be the basic criterion of the plan's correctness and a genuine, planned ensurance of the basic production conditions for optimum development of production becomes decisive. The chief production condition, then, is the necessary production capacity, its proportional expansion, with the optimum raising of its technical level.

In harmony with the technical and economic concepts that have been adopted concerning the different branches of production and the entire national economy, there must be a planned development of investments that renew and expand production capacity. One enormous advantage of a socialist economy is the fact that it can channel

220

into the desired projects all major investment funds in a unified and planned way and so assure in the macrostructure the proportional and optimum development of social production. But, for this investment to be effective, there must be a real material interest on the part of the enterprises in making the best use of all investment means and all production funds. The enterprises must also have at their disposal their own or borrowed investment funds about which they can make their own decisions, because all investment possibilities cannot be decided most effectively at the centre.

In the same way the basic processes of distribution and redistribution of manpower must be planned in accordance with the technical and economic development and in the necessary basic proportions. According to the envisaged needs for manpower in the different branches of production and in the main occupations, with regard to the character of labour in these branches and occupations, and the interest the workers have in these branches and occupations, the social organizations must purposefully orient the wage policy and various other material prerequisites, such as housing construction, etc., as well as the occupational training of the workers and young people just beginning work, so that the planned distribution of manpower will be carried out as much as possible by economic means. Thus, by means of a planned distribution of manpower and of investments, the decisive production conditions are achieved for assuring a socially necessary development of production.

The real material interest of all enterprises in the most effective possible use of investment funds and of all production assets can be achieved by giving investment credits to the enterprises which would be repaid completely or in part, with interest, by the enterprises from their gross income. Interest will also be charged on all basic production assets and increments in circulation funds. Assuring the direct relationship between the development of these credits and interest paid out of the gross income, and the development of wages and bonuses, also paid from gross income, can arouse sufficient concern for the most effective use of all investments and all production funds. The enterprises must, at the same time, have the possibility of selling to each other the means of production they do not need.

Under socialism, then, there are conditions for a planned orientation of the development of the production base and of the basic proportions of production in harmony with the fundamental long-range needs of society, together with the conditions for the most effective development. This means a conscious application of the concept of use value in its relation to value.

In other words, there should, in the future, also be the necessary productive capacity (although not a surplus) in all branches of production, in order that all the necessary use values might be produced with the lowest possible social costs of production and with technical modes of production that assure the highest effect. Such an economical and highly efficient *long-range* development can never be assured by the market mechanism alone and it is precisely the scientific examination of the trends of the *basic* structure of needs, the calculation of the *most effective* possibilities for utilizing investment funds and a planned channelling of the distribution of the *basic* sources for production, that make up for the inadequacies of the market mechanism. In this sense, society regulates production in a planned way and thereby limits the spontaneous regulating of production by the law of value. But this does not mean that society can ignore in planning the value of commodities (costs of production) and their long-range development. Value in a certain altered form (as will be shown later) still has also an unplanned effect on the determination of specific production programs in the enterprises (types and range of products) within the planned framework of development of production conditions.

Under these conditions, labour can no longer be simply abstract labour, though economists who always want an unambiguous answer to the question of whether labour is or is not abstract will not be content with this. The fact that the basic conditions of labour and its fundamental, general trend of development are directed by society in harmony with the development of society's needs, causes labour to be expended in a direct social way. Since, however, society cannot assure that each specific expenditure of labour will be in full accord with the needs of society, nor prevent the specific production programs set up in the enterprises — i.e., the concrete utilization of the planned production capacities — from following narrow interests, the genuine social nature of labour must still be tested by the market which is itself limited by society. In this sense, labour under socialism still is, to a certain degree, abstract in nature.

222

Furthermore, the question whether the law of value is or is not a regulator of production under socialism cannot be given a straightforward answer of yes or no. The entire *planned* direction and management is aimed at developing use value as much as possible in harmony with real value. After all, this is the way to assure optimum development and is the aim of the socially planned orientation of the basic proportions and the basic production conditions (capacity, manpower, etc.). This is why a socialist society can carry much further the *a priori* coordination of these two basic aspects of production than can a capitalist society.

Many Marxist economists, when they use the formulations "the regulating role of the law of value," "market mechanism," "self-regulating mechanism," etc., do so in a sort of shamefaced way, considering this process to be incompatible with socialism, or even inimical to the working people. If we leave aside all unscientific, moralizing or emotional outbursts, and take a sober look at the basic nature of the process, we shall see that it is an objectively necessary one, ensuring the long-term coordination of use value and of the value of commodities under conditions where the development of these two aspects of social production cannot be planned in advance by society. It is this mechanism that forces private producers, whose paramount aim in deciding on concrete production is to get the greatest possible private income (or of realizing the greatest value and, especially, surplus value), to produce goods with high productivity of labour and to develop and produce use values in the necessary proportions (without being able to check in advance with other producers).

Naturally, this mechanism is put in motion spontaneously under private production and therefore the necessary harmony between use value and value can prevail only on a long-term basis, as average trends underlying the constant disharmony and contradictions. It would be a tremendous oversimplification, of course, if we failed to see that under contemporary capitalism the conditions and instruments for a certain degree of planned regulation (by monopolies and some bourgeois states), of the development of the structure and the basic proportions of production, have already developed. This is not to deny the general spontaneous nature of the capitalist economy, but it does mean that a conscious effort is made to restrict this.

With the origin of socialism there came about the qualitative leap to conditions for socially planned direction of the over-all social production in accord with the forecasts of social needs. A dogmatic absolutizing of this harmony under social planning led to ideas that value relations and the influence of value in deciding on socialist production had been absolutely suppressed. Any view that a certain market mechanism and automatic responses could be used, even if only where planning could not fully ensure that labour would be socially expended, was dogmatically impugned. In reality, despite all dogmatism, the automatic influence of value in the direct production decisions of the enterprises came to the fore, though the practice corresponding to dogmatic notions, emphasized only the negative effects of value on production, preventing the positive action of the market that would force the producer to take account of consumer needs and to develop use value.

The fact that prices were established rigidly by directive, not harmonizing the interests of producers and consumers but arousing the producers' direct interest in realizing as much income as possible (bound up one-sidedly with gross production or productivity of labour, etc.), brought about in the same way one-sided immediate decisions by producers, increasing the contradictions between value and use value. Precisely because gross production (or productivity of labour calculated on gross production) had to be calculated by means of the prices of production, there arose an interest in having as great a volume of gross production as possible, an interest in making products which had the most advantageous price in relation to living labour expended on the product, without regard to the real needs of the consumer. Therefore prices did, willy nilly, have an effect on production. But the directively established prices, not based on economic considerations, necessarily had a distorting effect and caused a growth in contradictions between production and consumption.

The practice that developed according to dogmatic ideas did not have the strength to eliminate the objectively necessary effect of value, or of the prices, by making the income of producers depend directly on their production decisions. But the fact that it prevented a genuine economic movement of prices meant that it did not force the producer to take account of the trends of demand in making his decisions, or to harmonize value with use value. On the contrary, it led more and more toward production that diverged from the real needs of the consumers and that did not develop use value further.

If prices are really to fulfill their economic function, the contradictions between value and use value will not, it is true, be eliminated, but they will not be so sharp or long-lasting. When one-sided decisions are made by producers at the expense of consumer needs, there will be a rapid change in prices and thereby a change in the direct income of the producer in such a way that he will be forced to take more notice of the interests of consumers and to harmonize value with use value. Thus price trends will have a substantial influence on the immediate decision-making of enterprises within the framework of a socially planned harmonizing of value and use value and, in this additional way, contribute to a more thorough-going harmony of these factors.

At the same time, the long-term trend in value, which must be respected in the plans, will determine the development of proportional production. The basic proportions must be assured by means of long-term plans in such a way that all types of goods will be produced in the future in quantities that correspond to forecasts of future demand, without the necessity of deviations of price from value in the long run (or from production prices or trade prices, as we shall show later). This requires studies and predictions not only of the future trends in demand, but also of the future development of production costs of different types or groups of goods, and the effect of these trends on the development of the structure of demand, so that all types of goods might be sold over a long period of time at prices that correspond to value (production or trade prices), and so that demand is fully covered.

This means the planned observance of the law of value also in regard to a long-term assurance of the basic proportions of production. Of course, there is no sense in quarreling over a word, trying to decide whether this does or does not recognize the regulating role of the law of value, even in relation to the basic proportions of production under socialism. If this means the elementary role of value in regard to private capital, where capital flows over, on the basis of private (socially uncoordinated and unplanned) decisions, into the branches of production where the socially necessary proportions were incorrectly forecast, that is, where only the market-induced price trends caused capital to flow into branches where prices and profits were on the rise — in this sense we cannot speak of the regulating role of the law of value under socialism. But it does mean we must take note in socially planned allocation of investments of the future trends of value, and change investment plans if it is found that errors have been made in the basic proportions (if certain types of goods cannot, with the existing production capacity, cover demand and must over a longer period be sold at prices that are above the value or are higher than the production or the trade prices) — in this sense it is not incorrect to speak of the regulating role of value under socialism. But it can be more precisely expressed as the necessity for observing the law of value in planning the basic proportions of production.

We may then say that the chief significance in expenditure of labour under socialism is in the gaining of use values, but that this must develop as much as possible in harmony with value. But to assure the reproduction process — in view of the contradictions mentioned above — value is still a necessity, showing by commodity exchange if labour is expended as socially necessary labour. If the greatest amount of use values is to be produced, there must be a constant and rapid decline in value. If they are to be produced proportionately, they must be produced in such a way that the basis for the movement of their market prices could be their value (production or trade price), with long-term harmony of supply and demand of all goods. There are tendencies in the enterprises to expend labour in a way that will bring in the greatest income, without regard to the use value. But the whole system of planned management with socialist market relationships ensures the optimum development of the enterprises' incomes, with the most productive and fullest satisfaction and stimulating of consumer demand. Of decisive importance is the direction and expenditure of labour that corresponds most closely to the socially necessary labour, where use value and value develop in harmony.

Most difficult of all is the first central analytical study of the future possibilities of growth of production (expansion and qualitative changes in material input) throughout all of society, these possibilities furnishing the base for a rise in national income and the basic distribution of national income into accumulation and consumption. The analysis of future development of consumption (both personal and social) affords the basis for studying the fundamental changes in the structure of personal market demand and, connected with this, the main changes in the needs for means of production (structure of production of means of production).

But changes in the structure of production cannot be decided only by the envisaged changes in demand. Comparative studies of the effectiveness of development of different branches of production — i.e., the most effective use of investment funds — have a decisive role. This cannot be accomplished without using the credit system, the rates of interest, price analyses, all of which are important instruments in selecting the most effective possibilities of using investment funds.

Selection of the most effective variant of a schedule of investments for long-range plans is based, therefore, on fundamental considerations in planning the necessary future structure of production, but at the same time it is essential to take account of the development of production yielding the highest return. Necessary here are the proposals from enterprises which are compelled by financial instruments, when making their proposals, to take note of future market developments as well as of sales possibilities, recoupment periods and return of different credit possibilities. Unless market relations are utilized, as well as the financial, price, credit, foreign-trade and other instruments that are connected with them, the most effective variant cannot be selected for the future development of the national economy. Only these fundamental investment projects can be included in a long-range economic plan that correspond not only to the trend of development of market demand (on both domestic and foreign markets) but also assure the greatest effectiveness, rapid return of credit, payments of regulated interest, etc., of which we shall speak in more detail in the section on money.

At the same time, however, the acceptance of selected investment proposals in the long-range plan assures that they will be given a priori coordination, prompt handling of the investments selected and negotiated, and in general a preliminary finding of all causal factors that would make it easier to carry out all investment aims: e.g., training personnel in advance, timely designing and blue-printing, long-range orientation in foreign trade, etc.

Only in this way can planning by the whole of society (formerly considered to be only a question of balancing out the proportions, without regard to return on investment) be linked with the principle of the highest effectiveness and the market orientation of production. This, in turn, cannot be assured without a purposeful use of the market under socialism and of all the commodity-money instruments connected with this.

b   Special Features of Commodity Reproduction

It follows from the foregoing that under socialism the appropriation of nature by all of society takes place by a direct process. The different enterprises have a relatively dependent role in this appropriation. They do not own the means of production and therefore are not the owners of the values realized.

The method of distributing the means of production has done away with private decision-making on how to use them. Social bodies decide the general nature of the basic proportions of distribution in the interest of all the workers. Of course, the specific forms of this decision-making are effectuated by means of market relationships. The fact that there is social decision-making on the division of the social product, means that the basic distribution of the values realized is also socially determined.

All products are commodities, but enterprises do not receive the whole realized value for their own disposal. The fact that the enterprises must realize the value (by means of the market, that is, in connection with the satisfaction of the real consumer needs) and the fact that they can decide about the disposition of part of the new value — the gross income, with a certain dependence of the size of gross income on volume and use of means of production, means that the producers (the enterprises) have the necessary interest in a socially necessary expenditure of labour.

It is not essential for the enterprises to decide the use of all the realized value. On the contrary, we see here again the progress represented by a socialist society. The renewal and expansion of production conditions in the different branches of production do not depend solely on the incomes realized in these branches or enterprises, but develop, relatively independent of them. The distribution and re-distribution of manpower and of fixed assets, mainly by means of value instruments is made by social bodies in accord with recognized basic trends in the objectively necessary development of social labour.

This is where the superiority lies in the planned social process of reproduction over the former essentially spontaneous development. But the central bodies of government cannot foresee in detail all the changes in personal and production needs or the conditions for production. Even less possible are detailed forecasts of the inter-relationships in production between all the branches and the conditions connected with these changes.

The government bodies cannot determine the necessary changes in all the individual production proportions. But they can and must, on the basis of scientific analyses and generalizations, with the help of the necessary aggregations and disaggregations in planned co-operation with enterprises, forecast the trends in needs for broad groups of products (both personal and production needs) and the necessary changes in the main conditions for production. They can, therefore, forecast the *general* (macro-) proportions of production and the necessary basic distribution processes.

In accordance with this, the governing bodies can not only orient the development of these proportions in a planned way, but also partially assure the material means for it by drawing off a part of the realized value from the enterprises. Long-range forecasting of the trends in proportions and technology of production make it possible also to foresee the rate of growth, not only of the national income as a whole, but also the gross incomes in the different branches. Together with this, the government bodies can make long-range determination of the payments by the enterprises in the different branches to the state budget from their gross income.

When part of the enterprise's gross income is drawn off for the State, there must be definite long-term rates set, on which the enterprises can count. They should not be considered a regular tax, for they are also an instrument of planning by which the state actually influences the size of the part of the gross income remaining at the disposal of the enterprises and thus influences their further development (reproduction). But, at the same time, these payments must not be set individually by the State, from one case to another, because this would lay the ground for subjectivism on the part of the administrative bodies and for haggling and noneconomic behaviour between these organizations and the enterprises. Therefore, they must always set valid long-term rules and regulations in determining these payments from gross income. The enterprises must be able to count on these before they take part in setting up the long-range plans.

As long as there are general production prices (which we shall speak of later), there can also be uniform rates of payments by the enterprises. This would mean that the state body would set the payments for a longer period of time, as a uniform percentage of the gross income of the enterprises. Only in the branches of production where the working conditions are not attractive enough (e.g., in the mines) wage preferentials must be intentionally assured and in this case the enterprises concerned might make lower payments from their gross income.

Some managers fear that if the payments are uniform there would be too great differences in the income trends per worker in the various branches of production, because the growth in productivity of labour differs (equally rapid technical development and growth in productivity of labour cannot be assured everywhere). But this does not take account of the condition emphasized: the uniform construction of *production prices* which assumes that they change together with the development of social *production costs*. If there is a rapid growth in productivity of labour in a certain branch of production, i.e., a rapid reduction of production costs of the commodities, with a balanced supply and demand, there will automatically be a proportional reduction in the production price. This will again cut down on the disproportionately large income. Assuming such a movement of prices, there can also be uniform percentile payments from the gross income, exceptions being made for the branches of production with preferential wage rates. The level of these payments depend on the system of prices, which we shall discuss later, on need for redistribution of the investment funds between the branches and on the existence of other payments to be made from gross income.

In the first place, there must also be a special kind of payment from gross income, which we could call a payment for use of fixed assets. In Czechoslovakia this payment is six per cent of the value or cost price of fixed assets after amortization, but paid from the gross income. This means that it also has a direct connection with the level of the income that remains for the enterprise to pay wages and bonuses, and thus it creates a material interest in the most effective use of fixed assets in the enterprise. The better the use made of the

230

fixed assets, the greater their effectiveness — the higher the gross income created in relation to the value of the fixed assets — the relatively lower the payment from gross income and the more remains for the enterprise to use for wages and other purposes.

Finally, a tax on wages can also be applied according to need, whether this is a definite percentage of the different wage categories or of the total amount of wages, or of increments in wage costs. This tax should create an interest on the part of the enterprise in making relatively higher savings on wages in relation to production and, on the other hand, the State is assured a sum proportionate to the rise in wages in production. This must not, of course, do away with the enterprise's most immediate interest in raising average per-worker wage, though it should lead to rational considerations and calculations, especially if this tax is a progressive one.

In addition to these three types of payments from the gross income, assuring that the enterprises have the necessary interest in the most effective use of the main factor inputs, the enterprise must pay out of its gross income all debts, interest, and fines and penalties. All investments in production including those in long-range central plans, by means of which the state assures the future most effective structure of production, will be financed mainly from the enterprise's own funds, with the help of the credit system. Enterprises that decide to invest and which have their proposal accepted for the long-range plan — we are speaking of large-scale investments — will not at first have sufficient means of their own and therefore will have to rely on credit. The terms for the credit must be set by the bank, on the basis of the planned return of the given investment. During the set term the enterprises must make payments on the loan, plus interest paid partly from amortization and partly from gross income obtained from the new capital assets. If the enterprise does not keep to the term set it will pay higher interest. It will therefore have an incentive not only in planning the most effective investments, but also in putting the capital assets into operation as soon as possible.

In addition to these investment loans, the enterprises can also obtain circulating capital on credit. They must pay interest on these loans. Therefore they will be concerned to utilize as economically as possible all means of production.

The part of the gross income remaining after paying all the enterprise's obligations (payments into the budget, installments on loans, interest payments, penalties, etc.) is fully at the disposal of the enterprise, which decides on its use. Part of the income is used by the enterprise to create a fund for technical development (research and development, etc.), a reserve fund, a social and cultural fund. The remainder serves as a wage and bonus fund which again consists of two parts: (1) a basic wage fund, (2) a fund for enterprise bonuses and special rewards.

The basic wage fund consists of the sums paid by the enterprise for regular wages according to certain general wage scales (basic time and piece wages). The enterprise bonuses and the special rewards are paid out according to its own decision. Workers in the enterprise must be able to participate in such a way that the entire personnel will be interested in economizing, but, on the other hand, the rewards must be differentiated so that those who deserve most credit for a growth in the enterprise income will receive the largest rewards. The more the enterprise economizes on manpower and work time, the greater the remuneration per capita.

To illustrate, we present a simple outline (p. 233) of the distribution of the enterprise's gross income, showing the relation between the enterprise and government bodies, as well as the way the material interest of the enterprise arises.

The outline clearly shows that the enterprise will have a larger wage and bonus fund and larger per-capita wage, when:

1. It has larger total cash receipts (which means, with a rational economic movement of prices, if it produces and sells more, if it manufactures better and more modern products).
2. It saves more on material costs and makes better use of its fixed assets.
3. It invests more effectively and achieves higher gross income in relation to investment costs.
4. It assures a more progressive technical development, a rise in productivity of labour and savings in manpower.

It is natural that there will arise a differentiation in income of the enterprises, according to how economical their operations are and how much initiative they show. But such differentiation is inevitable because it provides the genuine and necessary stimuli for the most effective, the optimal economic development. At the same time, this will give real, objective criteria for judging the abilities of the heads of enterprises and for selecting the most capable and adept leaders in the enterprises. Under the system of administrative management this was not possible.

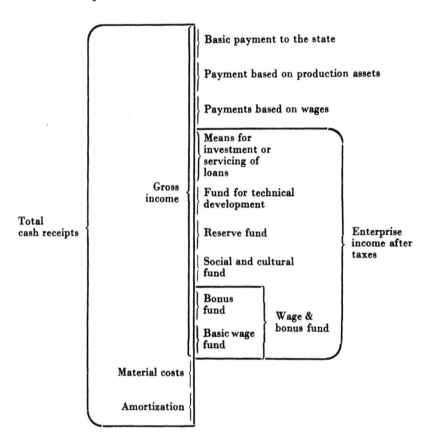

If the enterprise gets into a bad economic situation, this will appear first in the diminishing reserve funds (because it must pay first its obligations to society — the government). If it continues to operate badly, the fund for bonuses and premiums will begin to disappear. When the reserve fund sinks, this is already a signal for the supervisory bodies to make an analysis of the enterprise and discover the reasons for the unhealthy development. If it has come about because the enterprise leadership lacks ability, the necessary personnel changes must be made. Moreover, if there is a serious decline in the enterprise income, the state — as mentioned before — guarantees the workers' basic wages.

Those who fear that an uneven development of per-capita income of the workers will cause an uneconomic fluctuation in jobs, are not taking account of all circumstances. The progressive enterprises will not hire superfluous manpower, because this would decrease per-capita income. They will hire only if they really need the manpower, if they are sure of a market for the increased production and if they will not thereby reduce productivity of labour. Under these conditions growth of employment would be economically desirable. Naturally the workers will tend to leave the worst enterprises. In such cases, there are two possibilities: if society needs these enterprises it is up to society to see that their management improves (technical measures or personnel changes, etc.); if society does not need them, if they are not worth rebuilding, and so on, then it is a good thing if the workers leave the enterprise and it is gradually closed up, or liquidated all at once.

It is decidedly necessary to overcome the non-economic prejudices against a certain necessary movement of manpower from one branch to another or one enterprise to another. This prejudice arose in the period of non-economic directive management. Since there is unequal technical development and trends in demand change, workers will always have to transfer from some branches of production to others.

If this necessity is insufficiently respected in economic practice, this leads to superfluous, unutilized manpower in some branches, and a shortage of manpower working overtime in others. This in itself represents great economic loss. But if, on top of that, some enterprises are continuing to produce unsalable products, just in order to employ the surplus manpower, as has been too often the case in our economy, this is an unbearable waste of not only present living labour, but also past, materialized labour. Moreover, consumers do not get some needed products because there is a shortage of manpower and material in other enterprises.

A socialist society can and must distribute and redistribute manpower in a different way than under capitalism, where the entire process proceeds in an anarchic way and usually with shorter or longer periods of unemployment for part of the workers. Under socialism all the main and quantitatively important processes of distribution and redistribution of manpower must be forecast and planned on a long-term basis. By means of long-range ten- to fifteen-year plans of development in the different branches of production, and with population analyses, it is possible to assure timely orientation of schools and professional training, to accord with the planned economic development. In the five-year plans, by means of which technical development and rates of growth are planned in the different branches, there must also be forecasts of manpower needs and therefore of all the main processes of distribution and redistribution of manpower.

The primary way to assure these planned processes is by the most effective economic stimuli. This means that, in addition to the usual recruiting by the enterprises, and the recommendations of the schools, there must be a properly differentiated wage policy, the necessary housing construction, etc., to arouse an interest among the workers in those branches of production and occupations that harmonize with the social interest. Shortcomings in these economic stimuli, insufficient wage differentials, the lag in housing construction, etc., compelled the use of administrative measures to obtain manpower for various less attractive branches of production. These can only be emergency measures, not something that is inherent in a socialist society.

A serious obstacle to redistributing manpower among the branches are the legal provisions making it difficult to release workers. They demonstrate a rather over-simplified interpretation of the advantages of socialism. Naturally, a socialist society cannot and need not solve shifting of manpower from some branches to others by unemployment, but such shifts must be made possible. Otherwise all workers suffer intolerable and substantial losses. Therefore there must be a possibility of releasing manpower from branches where there is a surplus. The transitions must be made in a way that will cause the workers who are changing employment the least possible damage (preparation of impending changes over a longer period of time, help given by the enterprises in finding new jobs, material compensation, retraining, etc.). The release of manpower — also in cases where this has not been anticipated and planned over a longer period (minor changes, etc.) — makes it possible to allocate manpower to the branches of production where there is a shortage of workers.

In this way, under a socialist system by planning of education, vocational guidance and economic levers, and by means of relatively independent disposition of part of the newly created and realized value and their use by the enterprises for economic stimuli for the workers, a proportional and effective distribution of manpower can be assured. For this it is necessary that the enterprises are not tied down too much by directives in the matter of hiring and releasing workers, in deciding on wages and bonuses. Moreover, the distribution of value, guided into proper channels by the whole of society, though realized within the enterprises must make it possible to arouse the necessary interest of the workers in a proportional and effective development of the process of production.

Of course, redistribution of the value realized in the enterprises is considerably influenced by the organization of the enterprises within the socialist economy. With the increasing concentration of production and the forming of larger enterprises, there is less value to be drawn off for simple and extended reproduction of material assets and relatively higher value of this reproduction is covered from the enterprise's own means. In forming large socialist concerns in a certain branch of production, headed by a branch directorship, substantially all investments will be covered from value realized by these concerns. Redistribution of value for production purposes, between the branches, should be made under these conditions essentially by the credit system. This socialist self-financing of large branch concerns must be assured by the formation of socialist production prices, of which we shall speak later.

But before we come to the problem of production prices we must briefly explain why we consider it necessary to create interest on the part of the enterprises in gross income and not in net returns (profit), and why this interest is not contrary to the interest in net returns or to a system of production prices.

For this purpose we must first clarify the concept of profit, or net returns. In Marxist theory profits (sometimes also the net income) are usually called the money form of that part of surplus value that the enterprise realizes by selling its goods. That is, that part of the value of the commodities which exceeds the costs of production.[1] At the same time we can call this the gross profit, as distinct from net profit that remains for the enterprise after paying all its obligations to the State. To simplify the explanation let us again consider the outline given earlier about the distribution of all the value realized

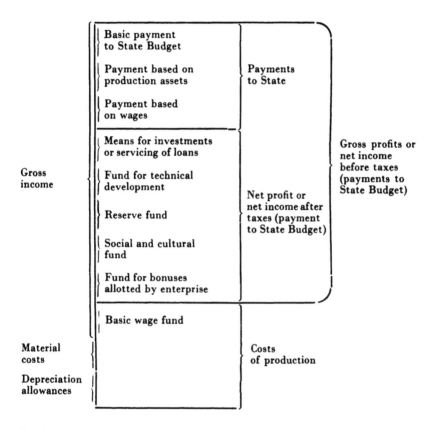

by the enterprise and let us also show here what is called profit — or rather gross profit (net income) and net profit.

If we proceed from the assumption that the people in the enterprise

---

[1] Ed. note: "Costs of production" include material and labour inputs and depreciation charges, but not interest. Not to be confused with production *price* which normally includes an average rate of profit.

have the greatest interest in the size of the basic wage fund and of the fund for enterprise bonuses and both these funds are part of gross income, while only one is part of gross (and net) profits; and if we proceed from the further assumption, that the enterprise also has an interest (even if not so direct) in the size of all the other funds that in one way or another benefit the personnel in the factory, or the general development of the factory funds (social and cultural fund, reserve fund, fund of technical development, of means for investments) that are part of gross (and net) profit, we come to the following conclusions:

1. Under the given assumptions, the enterprise's first interest is in the total volume of gross income, on which depend the funds in which the enterprise has direct interest.

2. Interest in gross income does not conflict with interest in gross profit, because the greater the income, the relatively greater is gross profit. Maximizing gross income does not require minimizing gross profit and even if the enterprise has no interest in increasing profit at the expense of the basic wage fund, it will — at a given basic wage — have an interest in increasing gross profit, and within it the net profit.

3. The interests of the enterprise in different parts of gross income are of differing degree, ranging from the most direct interest to the very indirect and remote interests, with some parts not coming at all into the field of enterprise interest (in the true sense of the word). The most immediate interest is that in the fund for basic wages and, next, the fund for bonuses. The most remote and therefore the weakest stimulus relatively speaking is the interest in funds for investment. Generally the interest in gross income will be stronger than in gross profit (from which the basic wages do not come) and in net profit greater than in gross profit.

4. Payments into the State Budget, both the basic payment and the payment from fixed assets and from wages do not appear to be in the interest of the enterprise — on the contrary, the interest is in making them as small as possible. In this sense one might speak of certain non-antagonistic contradictions between the long-term social interest in maximizing these payments and the direct interest of the enterprise in making them a minimum, or in maximizing net profit within the given gross profit.

Dogmatically-minded economists try to deny these non-antagonistic conflicts of interest, most of them giving as argument the socialist consciousness of workers, etc. But experience in socialist practice shows that this contradiction cannot be denied unless we hide reality with subjective wishes and ideas. The enterprises have always fought with every means for increasing as much as possible the funds that serve directly to satisfy their material interests or the development of the enterprise, even at the price of a relative reduction in all payments, taxes, etc., going into the State treasury. This is so, even though there does exist socialist consciousness of a small part of the workers, understanding the necessity to cover also various social needs by a part of value created and realized in production. Not to take account of this fact and not to reckon with a situation where most enterprises will to one degree or another attempt to achieve their own immediate interests — especially at the expense of obligations that are not their own specific interests — means to err grossly in planned managing of a socialist economy.

In view of this, the payments to the State should be created and channelled in such a way that this conflict will not be needlessly sharpened — will, on the contrary, be moderated — and, furthermore, that the interes tof the enterprise will not run directly counter to that of society as a whole, that there is no economically unjustified enlargement of enterprise funds. Instead there should be conditions conducive to their optimum development. For this purpose it is not correct to determine payments to the State on the basis of gross profit, as some economists have suggested (with the incorrect designation of this method as creating an "interest of the enterprises in making profits"), but from gross income.

If the payments are determined as a certain percentage of gross profits, there necessarily arises a too strong interest in minimizing gross profit and maximizing the basic wage fund, and, connected with this, there is a possibility for the enterprises to reduce relatively the payments to the state by increasing the regular wage payments, in a way difficult to check on. (The central bodies, for instance, cannot determine the level of the performance norms in all enterprises and prevent the enterprise from "softening the norms.") In order to prevent such an undesirable wage drift, the proponents of this method of management propose directively setting a controle of the volume of wage funds by central bodies. This, however, would intolerably perpetuate the administrative determination of wage trends. This always comes into conflict with optimum wage trends and inspires the enterprises to act in an uneconomic way.

Under the old directive planning of wage funds, it was never possible to limit *absolutely* the volume of these funds, from the centre, but an attempt was made to tie volume of wage payments in a certain ratio to volume of production or growth in productivity of labour, etc. On the one hand, these plans were always influenced to a certain extent by subjective judgments, because the central body was necessarily dependent on distorted information from the enterprises which it simply tried to adjust on the basis of its empirical planning experience to a more real basis and, on the other hand, created in this way only the one-sided interest of the enterprise in maximizing "gross production" or "productivity of living labour," etc., but not at all in economically desirable, internally harmonized development of all aspects of production — in optimizing production itself.

It is not correct, therefore, to base the payments to the state from the enterprises on profit, but on gross income, for then the enterprise cannot gain by exaggerating wages (assuming objective prices — of which we shall speak later). Furthermore, this somewhat moderates the contradiction between the State and the enterprises, because if payments are set as a certain part of the whole gross income, calculated in an objective manner, it does not pay for the enterprises to increase disproportionately either the wages or the net income. The important thing is to set these payments, as far as possible, according to uniform criteria, so that backward enterprises will have no advantages over the progressive ones. It is also necessary to establish the rates of payment for as long a period as possible in advance (three to five years), and before the enterprises begin to work on their long-range plans, so they will know what obligations they have toward the State and according to this seek the most favourable investments, and in general conditions for maximizing their gross income, their basic wages and their net profits.

The prerequisite for this development is, however, a genuinely economic development of prices under socialism.

240

Summary

The special features of socialist commodity production are, first of all, that it is production of socialist enterprise collectives, developing within a socialist cooperation of the whole society, i.e., within the framework of a socially planned orientation of the development of production. Direct social orientation of production (by governmental bodies) has decisive importance in regard to the still existing individual and group incentives for work. The main importance of socially planned orientation of labour is that it determines the basic structure and the basic proportions of production and all basic conditions for production to promote this development. On the other hand, the kind of incentives arising from narrower interests that are seeking immediate income (value) advantages, and sometimes are developing in contradiction to the interests of society, can essentially affect only the concrete use of the conditions of production in setting specific individual and group proportions of production. At the same time, however, the market relationships themselves are again and again compelling corrections of non-social production decisions, even if embodied in the plan, and thus help to assure the socially necessary expenditure of labour.

Under such conditions, labour has generally and essentially a direct social character. Of course it is also to a certain degree still abstract labour, in that the *a priori* planned social nature of every specifically expended amount of labour must in the end be tested and corrected by the market. Even though the basic development of production follows use value, according to plan, it must also assure the most harmonious development of use value and of value. Price trends still have substantial influence on the development of specific decisions made by the enterprises and as long as prices can really fulfil their economic function, they help, within the planned limits, in optimizing the production decisions made by the enterprises.

Socialist market relationships are also revealed by the fact that decisions on the basic distribution of the realized value are made either directly (through payments to the State Budget), or indirectly (by financial policy), chiefly by bodies representing society in such a way that the planned national economic development is materially assured. They can orient the distribution and use of part of the value controlled by the enterprises, and provide suitable stimuli for creating an interest in the enterprises in the most effective use of all production funds and of manpower. Under the given conditions socialist enterprises have an interest in maximizing gross income and, within this category, making basic wages and net profits as high as possible.

The chief particularities of socialist commodity production are to be found in the sphere of price formation and we shall, therefore, devote a special section to this question.

III SPECIAL FEATURES OF SOCIALIST PRICE FORMATION

1 Basic Construction of Prices

Even under socialism prices are primarily a form of expressing value. But merely recognizing this basic relation between value and price is not enough. It does, it is true, disclose the basic and determining relationship, but on too abstract a level. In its concrete expression, the relation between the magnitude of value and of price can be very different, and still price remains the expression of its basis — value. Therefore, ascertaining in an abstract way that price is a form of expressing value is only part of the answer and must be followed by finding out the ways to overcome the contradiction between value and use value, of other relationships determining the development of prices.

In analysing prices it must always be kept in mind that there are certain processes by which a society based on commodity production distributes in an *indirect way* the values created, and hence certain quantities of goods between economic units (that sell and purchase the commodities) or among the general public that purchases the goods. Of course, under socialism this indirect distribution takes place within a general, directly oriented framework and, furthermore, is supplemented and corrected by a number of other direct distribution processes. Prices still remain, however, one of the chief factors in distributing the created production, because it is impossible to distribute directly by social agencies the huge amount of concrete use values, without, at this stage of development, undermining the economic stimuli. At the same time, it is not possible without using prices to orient even the general macroeconomic distribution processes, nor even to effectuate other direct distribution processes.

In connection with this basic function of prices, on the one hand, the significance of prices for the development of economic interests of the enterprises (the units for selling and for purchasing commodities) and all workers is brought out, and, on the other hand, their importance for planning production and distribution on a macroeconomic scale. It is from these two standpoints that one must judge the construction, formation and development of prices under socialism, and study the best way to achieve the necessary development of economic interests and an optimum planned orientation of macroeconomic development.

First let us analyse on this basis the question of the basic construction of prices under socialism, and then the method of forming them and the main forms of development in various areas of exchange.

We must differentiate the basic construction of prices for selling products by one socialist enterprise to another (whether this is one production enterprises to another, or to a trade enterprise), from the construction of prices at which enterprises will sell to the general public. In this first part, we shall deal with the construction of the "inter-enterprise" prices which are called in practice wholesale prices. We must also keep constantly in mind that this is the *basic construction* of these wholesale prices, and not the actual prices which must always diverge somewhat from the basic construction. The type of price we shall choose as a method of construction of wholesale prices will always express only a certain long-term base for their specific, flexible movement — the construction is the core of their oscillations.

The question is discussed whether price should generally approach the actual magnitude of the value of the goods, or $c + v + s$ (c = value of means of production transferred to the commodity, v = value of labour paid, s = value of surplus product). In a positive sense this would mean that we would need to calculate, as part of the price, the magnitude s in a certain ratio to the magnitude v, because, as we know, only labour power is the creator of new value, both of the value created by necessary labour and the value created by surplus labour.

244

If we calculate that labour of a certain complexity creates not only value paid out to the workers directly (v), but also the value of the surplus product (s), and assume that the relation between the labour paid for and the surplus labour is the same for all workers, this means that the ratio between magnitude s and magnitude v will be the same, in the case of all types of goods.

We could then allocate total s, created in the whole society (part of the national income above the value paid directly in the enterprises for productive labour) in a certain ratio to the amount of paid labour, to the prices of the different types of goods. This would mean distributing s in relation to v and thus, roughly, would be the way value-based prices would be constructed.

The usual argument to justify this or that type of price under socialism is that the type of interest of the enterprises enforces a corresponding type of price. Using the gross income as the basis of the enterprise's economic interest is alleged to correspond to the value-based prices, whereas the interest in profit corresponds to the production prices. But this is a very simplified view, one which does not describe the whole complexity of the entire relationship and, in particular, it oversimplifies the very concept of material interest of the enterprise.

Only from a very simplified concept of the "interest in wages" and bonuses or shares in the income for workers of the enterprise, could one call the most advantageous type of price, the value–based type. With it the enterprise would have — in producing any type of goods — an income proportionate to the amount of living labour expended on a given type of goods. In other words, the more labour expended, the larger the gross income, and vice versa. The material interest would be for producing any type of necessary goods whatsoever.

But if an enterprise is forced to cover the payments to the State from gross income, calculated, for example, as a percentage of the value of production or capital assets, and must, in addition, cover investments from gross income, the value-based type of price would not be the most advantageous type.

When prices are constructed on the basis of value, it is impossible to arouse interest in the most effective use of production assets (C) or in accumulating means for investment (I), without evoking an anti-social interest on the part of producers in producing goods demanding greater amounts of living labour and lower expenditures on plant and material, and vice versa — a lack of interest in producing goods requiring large expenditures on plant and material.

If the payments to the State are calculated on the basis of production assets (OC) and if investments are financed from the enterprise's own income (with interest payments, if the financing is done on credit), it is more advantageous for the enterprises to achieve in relation to the total amount of paid labour (v) the highest possible gross income, out of which — after payment to the State based on production assets, investment expenditures and interest changes — there remains for the enterprise the relatively highest income. If the enterprise would preferentially produce goods with a relative high proportion of v and a proportionate share of s, by means of a certain volume of C, it will definitely have a larger income for its own use than if, with the same volume of C, it produced goods with a smaller share of v and s. In both the first and the second case, the same high volume of C, I and I' would have to be paid, but in the second case from a smaller s than in the first.

Of course the enterprise cannot arbitrarily determine its production program and must take account of the structure of demand, but it still can — under conditions of considerable monopoly in production and especially if there is a sellers' market — to a large extent force the customers to take its products. Therefore we must seek a construction of prices where the interest of the producers will least conflict with the interest of consumers.

We shall show later that, in the same way, the value-based construction of prices is not advantageous from the standpoint of a planned optimum of macroeconomic processes.

But it is not true either that if the enterprise's interest is in profit, the most adequate base for price formation is the production price — the price in which the value of the surplus product is calculated in proportion to the value of production assets or *to a decisive extent* in proportion to the value of production assets.

Under the assumption that here would be only the interest of employees in bonuses or in profit-sharing, or an interest in the amount of profit, purely from the standpoint of getting as much as possible extra personal reward, the enterprises should, in the case of production prices, have prior interest in manufacturing the types of products that have high material costs and fixed assets. The greater the consumption of production assets (both circulating and fixed capital), the greater the profit calculated in the commodity prices, and hence the greater the extra rewards for the workers in the enterprise. Under these conditions there arises even a socially uneconomic interest: the enterprises may even have an interest in *avoiding* the production of goods with relatively low consumption of production funds, and therefore are not interested in producing all the socially necessary types of goods. Again there arises a contradiction between the interests of producers and those of the consumers.

Again it is found that the method of enterprise incentives under socialism cannot be chosen arbitrarily, that there must necessarily be an over-all interest in the enterprises in the most economical use of all production factors (manpower, as well as capital assets), with fullest satisfaction of the needs of society — in other words, an interest in the optimum development of production. The enterprise must not only have an interest in attaining the highest remuneration for its workers, but also in the most effective use of all capital assets, both on the basis of their obligation to expand them out of their gross income and to make certain payments to the State, in proportion to the value of capital assets. With this kind of incentives for enterprises, the best price type is the production price.[1]

At the same time, of course, the difference between interest in gross income and in profit (as part of the gross income that exceeds the value of wages) disappears. This difference can be artifically maintained only by a directive linking of wages with other factors (by governing bodies above the enterprise level) rather than with gross income. This sort of directive linking of wages is again, however only a remnant of the old administrative method of managing the enterprises and would evoke further uneconomic orientation of interests of the enterprises. Therefore, it is necessary to link the enterprise's interest in wages (without administrative measures) with its interest in maximizing gross income.

If the enterprise has an interest in making gross income as large

---

[1] I consider the so-called "two-channel price" as one of the forms of production prices.

as possible, not just to attain as high wages, bonuses and other remuneration as possible, but also to assure the necessary funds for investment and for making payments (taxes) from production funds, there must also be a system of socialist production prices that correspond to this type of material interest. It is, however, incorrect to consider the production price as a price whereby the value of the surplus product is allocated *only* in proportion to the value of production assets and not at all in proportion to the value of the wage funds. This would not fit Marx's conception either.

For a long period under capitalism, prices took the form of *production prices*. They were, of course, brought about by the necessity for developing private capital and this was because every private capitalist had to get surplus value in proportion to total capital invested, without regard to its internal composition — that is, without regard to the relative amount of v that creates s. If there were not under capitalism a method of distributing the surplus value by means of production prices, the development of production would not be assured in branches with a high composition of capital, and the essential long-term and proportionate development of production would not be assured.

The construction of production prices no longer corresponds to the present conditions of development of capitalism, when the category of monopoly prices has arisen. The huge monopoly capital organizations, by means of monopoly prices, appropriate the surplus value created not only in their own production but also in others — at the expense of non-monopolist private enterprises — and thus create favourable conditions for their own growth.

Marx's theory shows that the capitalist production price, assuming competition, must assure in every branch of production essentially the same rate of profit in relation to the total capital (constant and variable) necessary for its annual production of commodities, without regard to its organic composition. The rate of profit is therefore measured as a magnitude in relation to total capital used (not only that used up in production, but also the value of the fixed capital that did not go into the value of the commodities). Regardless of the rate of turnover of capital the annual rate of return on total capital is the test. The decisive factor for capitalists is the total fixed and circulating capital necessary for annual production, and this must approximate the return in every other branch of production.

Naturally the production price is in reality created spontaneously only as an average, constantly deviating tendency within the capitalist competitive struggle. But if we have as our point of departure a purely theoretical concept of production price, this would mean that every unit of capital would, regardless of its organic composition and rate of turnover, bring the same annual rate of profit, or a socially average rate of profit.

On the assumption that capital has a yearly turnover, the cost price of realized commodities would equal the value of capital used and the rate of profit contained in each individual commodity would be the same as the real, average rate of profit calculated on the total social capital. In case the capital has a more rapid than annual turnover, the cost price of realized commodities would be higher than the capital used and the rate of profit contained in the individual commodities would be lower than the actual capital rate of profit. On the other hand, with a slower than annual turnover, the ·cost price would be lower than the used capital and the rate of profit contained in the commodities higher than the actual rate of profit.[1]

Under socialism it is not a question of appreciating private capitalist property and the rate of profit cannot arise within a competitive struggle as a magnitude expressing the appreciation of capital. A socially planned procedure must, however, be assured, in order that in socialist enterprises there might arise the necessary interest in the most effective possible use of all production factors, or in a constant assurance of the relatively lowest reproduction costs in producing commodities. Socialist enterprises must have an interest in the largest quantity of socially necessary commodities being produced using the relatively lowest volume of fixed and circulating production funds, and the lowest labour costs. If the enterprises increase the quantity of produced and realized commodities, they will proportionately increase not only gross profit, but also that part of gross income that remains at their disposal for remunerating workers.

---

[1] "This again shows how important it is in capitalist production to regard individual commodities, or the commodity-product, of a certain period, as products of advanced capital and in relation to the total capital which produces them, rather than in isolation, by themselves, as mere commodities." Karl Marx, *Capital*, Vol. III/1, p. 224.

At the same time, every individual enterprise that has lower production costs than other enterprises producing the same types of goods, or that reduces its costs of production in relation to the existing socially necessary costs, should have a correspondingly higher share of the gross income at its disposal.

This can be achieved if production prices of the individual types of commodities are constutited, on the one hand, from the socially necessary production costs, and on the other hand from the profit, calculated as the profit element of the price per unit, by means of socially determined rules for price formation. This profit element in the price per unit is derived by means of socially established coefficients (expressed as percentages) of the value of fixed and circulating production funds, as well as from the value of wage funds.

The formula for a production price can be expressed as follows:

$$P_j = \frac{C_j}{Q_j} + z_j,$$

$$\text{when } z_j = \frac{F_j(z)\,\varrho_1 + F_j\ ^{(0)}\varrho_2 + v_j\,\mu}{Q_j}$$

where

P_j ... is the production price of the "j"th type of product

C_j ... is the cost ($c + v$) of producing amount Q_j of the "j"th type of product

C_j ... is $A_{ij} + V_j$

A_{ij} ... is the material cost of the "i"th type necessary to produce the Q_j amount of the "j" type of goods (i.e., including amortization)

V_j ... is the wage cost for producing Q_j amount of the "j"th type of goods

Q_j ... is the amount of the "j"th type of goods (in material units) produced in a given unit of time

Z_j ... is the profit rate in the price for a unit of the "j"th commodity

$F_j^{(z)}$ ... is the value of fixed assets after amortization necessary to produce Q_j of the "j"th type of goods in a given unit of time

$F_j^{(0)}$ ... is the value of circulating assets necessary for producing Q_j of "j"th type of goods in a given unit of time

V_j ... is the wage payment needed for production

250

ϱ_1 ... is the coefficient (percentage) established by society expressing the dependence of part of the profit rate in the price on the value of fixed assets

ϱ_2 ... is the coefficient established by society which expresses the dependence of another part of the profit item on the value of circulating assets

μ ... is the coefficient established by society expressing the dependence of a third part of the profit item on the value of wage costs.

The above-described construction of a production price corresponds to the necessary system of distribution of gross income among the enterprises and the state by the system of payments from gross income which we mentioned earlier. The enterprises share the gross income (and therefore the whole increment of gross income) with the state by paying in a certain percentage of gross income calculated in relation to the value of capital assets, and also a certain uniform percentage from gross income after deducting the payments from capital assets — and then, perhaps, another percentage calculated in relation to the value of wages paid. Under the assumption that the base for the uniform payments will be harmonized with the basic calculations of production prices, i.e., by centrally established percentages of the individual profit elements, conditions can arise where it would be advantageous for the enterprises to produce quite different types of products from the standpoint of composition of reproduction costs. The advantages of products with high unit labour costs or high unit material costs would entirely disappear. The profit established in the basic calculation of production prices both in relation to capital assets and to wage funds will be paid for the main part to the state in the first and second types of payments. It will be important that the part of the profit remaining to the enterprise for its own use will be, in case of products with high unit costs for plant and material, higher in relation to commodities with lower unit costs only to such an extent, as the production of the former requires higher investment outlays than the production of the latter. The structure of production should actually have no effect on the extra rewards paid to the workers (bonuses or share in gross income). That is, there should be extra reward for producing some types of goods in proportion to the actual labour input in the production of each type.

It is understandable that this cannot be *fully* achieved by any centrally established construction of prices, by any centrally established system of payments by the enterprises into the State Budget, and always in the concrete conditions of the different enterprises there will be differences in the advantages of producing the various types of goods. Regardless of this, there will be in each enterprise, the very next day after any price reform an immediate differentiated reaction between prices and production costs for the various types of goods. Therefore it is necessary to understand the significance of a certain basic construction of prices or a concept of a type of price, only from the standpoint of overcoming, by a change across the board, the intolerable system of non-economic prices that remains from the directive system of management and endeavouring to do away with the *essential* differences in return in the individual branches of production or groups of products.

Socially undesirable differences in profitability of different types of products or, on the contrary, socially desirable differences in the profitability of others can be adjusted only by continual price movements with competition on the market, as we shall demonstrate later.

Therefore, the type of price should be understood on the one hand as the basic construction determining the main criteria for unique price reforms in shifting from the directive to an economic system of management and, on the other hand, as a *fundamental tendency* of development of wholesale prices that could be accomplished over a long period within the more flexible price movements and fluctuations. This fundamental tendency of development of wholesale prices of certain aggregate price groups, which is actually an abstraction from the detailed deviations and movement of prices of the specific products, could even be forecast in a central price board and serve for purposes of planning of which we shall talk later.

So far we have shown that the type of production price of the construction we have described corresponds, better than does the value-based price, to the economic interest of socialist enterprises in using most effectively all production factors. This type of price really does assure a method of distributing the surplus product by means of wholesale prices between the branches and types of goods, one which does not induce the enterprises to attempt *a priori* to produce — in order to attain as large an income as possible — goods that are not in the consumers' interests. In going over to a greater extent to production of goods with relatively high capital inputs, the enterprise will gain correspondingly in higher returns, so that not only does it not slow up the steady technical development and an increase in capital intensity of production, but the enterprise creates also the necessary higher volume of investment means (or means for repaying loans and interest) necessary to assure relatively larger volumes of capital assets. This construction of wholesale prices also permits any necessary shift to products that require relatively more labour inputs because in essence they are as advantageous in bringing extra rewards to the workers of an enterprise as the production with lower unit labour inputs.

But production prices are also a more favourable type of price than one that is value-based, for optimizing macroeconomic development, for a planned selection of the most effective variant of development of the macrostructure of production.

In deciding on the basic proportions of production and distribution of the factors of production, the main difficulties arise in the sphere of cognition (although even here interests play a certain role, which we shall discuss later). The difficulty is in obtaining the most exact knowledge of the most effective economic development, as well as the actual contribution of the preferential development of a certain branch of production or the production of a certain group of products. Production cannot be expanded without limit. There is always a definite limitation to the possibility of a growth of production in a specific number of branches and within them a specific number of groups of product or, finally, of individual types of products. The quantitative limitation is given by the existing resources for growth at the given stage of development, by means of which society can attain a certain rate of growth — in other words, a greater amount of products.

Of course, the resources for production differ in quality (here quality is taken to mean capacity to produce at a certain rate of growth). Manpower and means of production of differing quality not only produce use values by different methods, but also have the capacity — in mutual combination — to increase social productivity of labour at different rates. For example, by means of a given technology and with manpower of certain skills, the volume of production can be increased in a given period only by one per cent annually, but with technology and manpower of another quality production in the same period might increase the same or similar, interchangeable use values by, say, five per cent annually.

In determining its future economic development, society cannot simply examine the future development of qualitatively different needs and distribute the existing resources for production in such a way that the production will develop proportionally and in harmony with the needs. The governing bodies must also examine the various alternatives in order to discover how to multiply as rapidly as possible their resources for production, by means of what kind of technology, and with what skills to achieve the greatest possible growth of use values in a certain period.

At the same time, of course, the final qualitative result, i.e., consumption goods for the general public toward the end of the planned period, need not be *completely* the same (by means of different technology we can also produce qualitatively different products). But these must be use values that satisfy the future needs of the population and, in some cases, must be able in some ways to replace the demand for different goods that have hitherto been consumed. In practice, the number of possible variants increases enormously if we do not merely follow the possible trend in production in accordance with the existing trend in domestic demand, but in harmony with the development on world markets and the possibility of future exports and imports.

It is, therefore, a question of calculating and choosing the most effective, or optimum of a great number of variants of economic development. It is precisely for these calculations that the basic construction of prices is of extraordinary significance.

In these calculations, it is, first of all, necessary continually to compare the envisaged trend in production costs for certain necessary final products. On the one hand, by means of the price expression of certain broad groups (aggregates) of products, we obtain a picture of the trend in production costs necessary to produce a certain amount of final products and, on the other hand, we are able to survey the relationship between these costs and the envisaged *amount* of final products.

Moreover, a socialist society must have an interest in producing every individual type of goods at the lowest possible costs of reproduction. Or, in other words, the greatest volume of necessary use values must be obtained with a given cost of production. If we study the final amount of use values after a long-term trend of production, in relation to the pre-supposed costs (e.g., the amount of cotton cloth obtained after five years in relation to over-all costs of reproduction, which will be necessary to produce them in the fifth year), it is not so much a question of calculating the surplus product or the income obtained by society , but of expressing the effect, i.e., the masses of use values obtained by certain costs of production (including the values of fixed assets necessary for this production).

Included in these calculations are the costs society had to lay out (investment, material and wage cost) for the production (assuming a specific technology) of the necessary amount of final products after a given period. This effect is compared with the effect in the base year. The difference, which shows us the trend in effectivness, can be compared with other variants in trend of production (using different technology), in order to ascertain the most effective development.

Entering into the sphere of material inputs in production of the final products is, first of all, the volume of fixed assets in the given branch of production and newly created by investment in the period studied. Since, with the given calculations, it is not a question of determining the value of the final products, but of determining the effectiveness of future development, we are not interested here in the calculation of value of fixed assets which actually remain in the given branch (after depreciation), but in finding out the total value of fixed assets that must shift from other branches to the branch that is being studied and which produce in the final instance the final product we are considering. Therefore the planned volume of fixed assets is counted in with the procurement price.

Next, there are the circulating funds (raw material, fuel, power, etc.) that enter into the field of consumption in production of the branch in question, either at each moment of development as stocks of raw material and semi-finished material, as a certain value in unfinished and finished products, or as the corresponding value in the form of money.

Finally, at every moment, certain wage funds are necessary in the production of the goods in question; these funds represent mainly a certain value of consumer goods. These are necessary in turn, in order that society might have the final products. At the same time they take the form (together with the circulating funds), as part of the circulating means, either as value contained in the product or in money form.

This summed-up procurement price of the anticipated fixed assets and the value of the anticipated means of circulation represent the total anticipated costs of production that must be expended by society to obtain a necessary final product. The difference between these costs and the final amount of use values (at fixed prices of base year) does not express the value of the surplus product, because during the planning period the prices can — and probably will — be reduced on the final product, as the cost of production diminishes. Or the prices of the raw materials used may decline, etc. It would, therefore, be a mistake to equate the endeavour to attain the greatest effect (which we are calculating) with an effort to attain the highest surplus product.

In these complicated calculations, prices take the form of magnitudes that should make it possible to compare the costs of reproduction expended on the production of one or another final product. These prices will always express the total expenditures (value of fixed assets, circulating production funds, and wage funds) in the production branch for the specific final products.

On the other hand, prices serve in these calculations also as the expression of the development of a *certain amount of the product in question.* We mentally freeze the price movements for a moment, abstract them from their dependence on the changing expenditures of labour, and use them as unchanging prices. An over-all price increase of a certain product, then, does not express the increased expenditure of labour for its production, but only the increased total amount of the given product (while the actual expenditures of labour could even decline).

For example, the statement that the production of silk fabrics has increased from 10 million crowns to 15 million crowns, tells us nothing about the trends in actual costs of production for the given product, but only that the total amount of silk fabrics produced increased by 50 per cent.

256

When prices are fixed in this way and used only as magnitudes for the purpose of keeping records, to show changes in the quantity of large groups of products, the basic construction of prices is not important. In these calculations actual units in kind cannot be used as indicators (units, metres, kilograms, etc.), because it is often necessary to compare the quantitative development of heterogeneous use values. Whether the price expresses the actual value of the product or the production price, or a price arrived at by quite different construction, is at the moment not at all important.

But in calculating the effectiveness of *development*, the role of price is constantly alternating — it is used alternatively for both purposes: to express quantity of products and quantity of social labour expended. For these reasons the basic construction of prices is of extraor dinary significance. Different constructions can give quite different pictures of the development in effectiveness of production. A certain construction can greatly distort the analysis of effectiveness.

In comparing the difference in how effective a development is in the case of two diverse technologies of production, often linked with basic divergencies in the structure of social production and with completely different development of relations between branches, the decisive criterion for judging the effectiveness will always be the final amount of the interchangeable products and the total costs of reproduction necessary with the given technology of production. This is true, for instance, when comparing the efficiency of production of wool and cotton fabrics with the production of synthetics.

With the help of constant prices (base price of the final product in question) we express the anticipated growth in production at the end of the period under study with one or another technology of production. We must project into the envisaged growth in *quantity* of production the growth in costs of reproduction by means of prices that are actually anticipated, which would express these costs of reproduction in a comparable way for diverse variants. In a given amount of social labour that must be expended in producing certain use values and which, in the final stage of production (the final link in the social division of labour), appears as paid costs of reproduction, the effect is projected in the form of a certain amount of final product. The character and function of the price or the costs of reproduction are quite different in this comparison from those of the price of the final product.

As a result of very complicated calculations, different costs of reproduction, necessary when different technologies of production are used, must appear as they are projected into the final year in their relation to the volume of final product, expressed in constant prices. The difference between these two resultant relations will be one of the most important, if not the sole, indicator of effectiveness of one or another variant of technological development. The greater the difference, the higher the effect shown by the calculation. Society can in one way or another increase consumption with the given inputs or can save on the expenditure of labour if this amount of use values is not needed.

These calculations of effectiveness of diverse variants of development should, of course, be made not only at the centre, but also by each enterprise or branch management. To put it in another way: it is only on the basis of calculations of effectiveness of different specific variants of development, in the various branches of production that the planning centre can compare the effectiveness of development of broader, branch or industry variants.

Also in calculating the effectiveness of development of various intra-branch variants of development in the enterprises, it is necessary to project in advance the anticipated growth of production in constant prices against the anticipated costs of reproduction. Because it is difficult to foresee the future situation on domestic or foreign markets and the resulting price movements of certain types of goods, it is necessary to study and forecast the anticipated relation between the growth of production in constant prices and the increase in costs of reproduction in actual development and, on this basis, study also the future possibilities for actual price trends of the products in question and their effect in the development of market demand. The greater the effect shown by a certain variant of development in constant prices, the greater hopes there are of marketing these products at relatively reduced prices (or if there is a general inflationary situation with rising prices, this could be a slower rise in the price of this one product). At the same time, the most effective variants assure that there is a rapid return of credit obtained for investment, thus giving hopes of winning out in the competition for further investment, after the portion of the enterprise income allotted to additional wage payments has been assured.

If all these calculations of effectiveness of development by the enterprises and the central bodies are to be distorted as little as possible by prices, the most advantageous type of price must be sought, from this point of view. In comparing the value-based and the production prices, it is found again that the production price is better, since it distorts less the reproduction costs that are being compared for the different variants of development. The basic construction of prices corresponding to the actual value of the commodities $(c + v + s)$ causes serious distortion in the calculation of effectiveness. When prices are constructed in this way, the total costs of reproduction do not appear sufficiently in the prices and a large part of the value of fixed assets may often be lost, hidden in one production or another because the amount of profit actually reflects wage costs only.

Let us take as our example a branch where there is the alternative of producing a certain final product M, either by technology "a" in which the use of material X prevails, a material that is produced with relatively low fixed capital inputs, or technology "b", in which material X can be replaced by material Y which has a high fixed capital input for its production and requires large investments. To simplify the example, let us assume that the production concerned must be 10,000 tons annually, either of material X or of Y, and that both these amounts will have the same costs of production, but with different composition of the costs:

TABLE 15   *Comparative Costs of Production*

	10 000 tons of X annual costs of production, simplified composition	10 000 tons of Y annual costs of production, simplified composition
wages	400 000 Kčs	300 000 Kčs
circulating funds	90 000 Kčs	150 000 Kčs
amortization	10 000 Kčs	50 000 Kčs
total	500 000 Kčs	500 000 Kčs

If value-based prices are used, profit will be proportionate only to wages. Let us assume that $S : V$ is $1 : 2$, then the value-based price for X and Y is:

TABLE 16   *Value Based Prices*

	Material X	Material Y
costs of production	500 000 Kčs	500 000 Kčs
profit (50 % of the wages)	200 000 Kčs	150 000 Kčs
value-based price	700 000 Kčs	650 000 Kčs

When there are value-based prices, the enterprises producing M will naturally have an interest only in the cheaper material Y and the demand for material X will be minimal. Furthermore, they will have no interest in the fact that, for instance, expanding the production of material Y makes the intermediary costs higher. Nor will they care that the economic effectiveness of product M is actually lower when technology b is used then with technology a. The branch producing Y will itself try to get the necessary investments and even the central planning body would not, with the given price relationships — and with the huge number of such buyer-seller relationships in the national economy — find out how ineffective this type of production would be.

The situation looks different when production prices are used.

Let us assume that amortization is one tenth of the value of fixed assets and that profit in the production price is composed of 5 per cent of the value of total fixed assets and 8 per cent of the value of wage funds. Table 17 shows the composition of production prices.

The example clearly shows that with production prices there is greater demand for material X and society saves on the investment costs connected with the increase of production of material Y. Of course, this is merely a simplified example. Furthermore, it is not a question of bolstering our arguments by this example, but merely of making clear a fact that cannot be refuted. This is that value-based prices do not and cannot express sufficiently the costs of investment, either direct or induced, connected with one or another type of production — or only in quite insufficient degree through the level of

260

TABLE 17   *Composition of Production Prices*

	Material X	Material Y
1. Value of fixed assets	100 000 Kčs	500 000 Kčs
2. Value of circulating funds	90 000 Kčs	150 000 Kčs
(1) + (2)	190 000 Kčs	650 000 Kčs
3. 5 %	9 500 Kčs	32 500 Kčs
wage payments	400 000 Kčs	300 000 Kčs
4. 8 %	32 000 Kčs	24 000 Kčs
composition of profit 5% of fixed assets plus circulating funds	9 500 Kčs	32 500 Kčs
8 % of wage payments	32 000 Kčs	24 000 Kčs
total profit	41 500 Kčs	56 500 Kčs
cost of production	500 000 Kčs	500 000 Kčs
production price	541 500 Kčs	556 500 Kčs

amortization. In such a way all calculations of effectiveness of production will be tremendously distorted.

On the contrary, the production prices express much more strikingly the total production costs and improve the enterprise's — and the central body's — calculations of effectiveness of production and investment.

Thus the system of production prices appears to be the more advantageous, both from the standpoint of over-all interest on the part of the enterprises and from the standpoint of all considerations in planning the most effective economic development.

The socialist production price differs generally from the former capitalist production price in that:

a) it does not arise through spontaneous development in the course of competition (clash of interests of different capitalist units), but in a socially planned procedure;

b) it is not formed only as a result of the past development of production costs and a class distribution of the created value, but in harmony with the future planned development of production and the socially necessary distribution of the created value;

c) it is not formed as an expression of the necessity to appreciate private ownership of capital and to achieve the general level of profit in relation to capital employed, but as an expression of the calculation of the general social need for gross profit in relation to the individual components of the socially necessary costs of reproduction;

d) the profit contained in the production price is no longer appropriated by private owners of the means of production, but is distributed in a planned way by means of certain long-range economic instruments between the state and the enterprises and is used both for the satisfaction of the social needs of the workers and for direct additional remuneration of the enterprises's workers.

The most difficult problem is that of the transition from an administrative price system, where many price relations were set by subjective decision, to a system based on the construction of production prices. It is not just a technically difficult problem (the enormous number of specific prices — about 1.5 million in Czechoslovakia), but it is also an economic problem. The production price can actually form only the basic construction, while the specific prices at which goods will be sold from one enterprise to another, must be equilibrium market prices. That means that a great number of specific prices will deviate from their basic construction, will be either higher or lower than their production price (they will temporarily have higher or lower levels of profit than the average).

Both the technical difficulties and the fact that each individual price need not equal the production price, should be taken into consideration in going over to a system of production prices. This means that it is enough for the centre to adjust the *macroeconomic* price relationships (between a certain number of large, aggregated price groups), without trying to set each individual price and its relation to all the others. This facilitates the central calculations for an across-the-board price reform, when the central bodies change — instead of 1.5 million individual prices — about 25,000 price groups. Moreover, this will immediately allow the branch enterprises to determine — in the framework of these amended price groups — the specific individual prices, not just by trying to calculate their production price, but also by taking account of the market situation and by trying to form equilibrium prices. The problems of equilibrium prices will be discussed in greater detail later. Here we shall only briefly mention the main problems of a total price reform without trying to analyse the technical aspect of the problem.

The proportion of the different components in the costs of reproduction used for calculating profit must be set by the planning centre in a way that during a relatively long-term planning period (say, five years), the total volume of realized gross profit will suffice to cover at least the total value of planned accumulation. In case there is a greater volume of profit (which could in addition cover part of social consumption) this would not create any great economic problem. The specific volume of gross profit to be realized in the global production price, i.e., in realizing all wholesale prices in a certain planning period, will always be affected by practical economic considerations (the necessary volume of payments from gross income into the state budget in relation to other payments such as tax on turnover; the necessary weight of the enterprise payments to the state from gross income, in order that the pressure on enterprises to economize be sufficient; the necessary price rises to establish essentially uniform, objective payments from all branches of production to the state, etc.).

We need not especially emphasize that, with the above-described basic change in price construction, there is not only the difficulty in getting central documentation on the socially necessary production costs for producing the different groups of commodities, but especially a calculation of the effect of changes in every individual price group on the production costs of other price groups' products. These relationships — taking into account the immense feed-back effect, can be calculated in a short time only with the use of modern computer technique. At the same time it is of paramount importance to aggregate properly the different prices in price groups and to ascertain the specific weight of each price group of means of production in the production consumption of other products (price groups).

It is, therefore, a question of finding out, for each price group, the cost of production $(c + v)$ plus the calculation of the centrally fixed percentage of the value of fixed assets necessary for the production of a given group of products (e.g. 5 or 6 per cent), plus the percentage of the value of circulating funds and, finally, adding a fixed percentage from wage costs. By computing these magnitudes, the production price for a given group is obtained and the coefficient expresses the deviation from the old price of the given group of products. Using these coefficients in calculating all complicated inter-group connections and in projecting all price changes gradually in the cost and profit changes of all groups, we arrive at new production prices of the different aggregated groups of products.

A special economic problem, connected with this calculation is the attempt to influence in some cases the socially necessary cost of production toward the lower world costs for producing the group products in question. This means — in some obvious instances — not just to register passively the data about costs of production, but to reduce the calculated production prices at the start and thus to put pressure to lower domestic costs. This would be the case where there is not only a considerable difference between domestic and world production costs (the latter being lower), but also where there are some as yet undisclosed hidden production reserves which were in the enterprises' interest. This is a method which could be applied only in a few obvious cases in a price reform which must be carried out in a relatively short period of time, but not as a regular procedure. It will be a matter for the further development of wholesale prices to achieve by means of the pressure of competition and foreign trade — which we shall deal with later — a closer equality between domestic production costs and those of world costs and prices.

We must now proceed from problems of basic construction of wholesale prices to a treatment of the specific formation and movement of wholesale prices in the system of economic management of a socialist economy.

2 Economic Formation of Wholesale Prices and their Trends

Specific wholesale prices paid for products by socialist production enterprises or by other economic units in production (associations of enterprises, branch directorships, etc.) will deviate more or less from production prices conceived as the basic construction of prices.

The exchange of goods among socialist enterprises is carried out by means of wholesale prices. (Enterprises are here conceived of in the sense we have explained earlier and we are leaving aside other possible economic units in production.) That means that the absolute and relative level of these prices has considerable effect on the amount of money receipts of the enterprises and on their utilization in purchasing material, etc., that is to say, on the economic result that stimulates directly the production efforts of the enterprises.

The specific level of prices always acts on the interests of the enterprises as sellers and buyers of commodities.

As suppliers or sellers, the enterprises are interested in having the goods sold bring in, by means of prices, as large a gross income as possible for the labour expended. If all products could be constantly and invariably sold at the real production prices, enterprises would have a substantially equal interest in producing and selling all the necessary types and ranges of goods (on the assumption that there are no difficulties in obtaining the production factors, such as equipment, raw materials, skilled manpower, etc.). With these pre-suppositions the proportional production of all necessary goods would realize the highest income — the enterprises would sell all products and an appropriate share of this income would be left at their disposal.

Actually, however, other circumstances always enter in, preventing a constant and absolute harmony of wholesale prices with the production prices; quite the contrary, they compel constant divergences from them, so that production prices can appear only as a long-term average basis or tendency within the movement of wholesale prices.

It is primarily a question of different relationships between the use values and prices. So far we have taken note of the basic connection between value (socially necessary production costs) and price, and have explained the need for shifting from value-based prices to socialist production prices, if we want to be able to calculate and plan the optimum basic structure of production. Socialist production prices are actually a transformation (merely by redistributing part of the value of the surplus product) of the value of commodities and they change as value changes. But the real wholesale prices must deviate from this basis which forms the production prices, because in a certain connection, the use value of the goods necessarily also has an effect on them.

The relationship between use value and price appears primarily in the development of the interests of the buyers and of their demand for individual types of goods. The structure of demand constantly changes: the absolute and the relative demand for one kind of use value will grow and for others decline. (The same is true of changes in demands of consumers for consumption goods, but we shall speak of this later.) Changes in demand are caused either by changes in production (through price changes caused by changes in value, through changes in use values — new products and the like) or they have relative independence of movement, regardless of changes in production. If the proportions of production of individual use values could change completely in accordance with changes in structure of demand, the specific wholesale prices would also move in harmony with production prices. Actually, however, the proportions of production cannot change absolutely in accord with the changes in structure of demand, nor, therefore, can selling prices develop absolutely in harmony with production prices.

Let us abstract for the time being the difficulties of recognizing and foreseeing the detailed trends in structure of demand and therefore also the necessary detailed proportions of production. Even assuming that the trends in structure of demand can be known, proportions in production cannot always change immediately and fully in accord with these changes in structure of demand. We cannot always assure the necessary changes in conditions of production (equipment and capacities, skilled manpower, deliveries of raw material, foreign trade deliveries, etc.) and these changes cannot always be covered by reserves in production, although they do play an important role in solving these difficulties. There will always be shorter- or longer-term contradictions between the amount of use values delivered and the size of demand for these use values.

We must realize that use values are often inter-changeable which means that in consumption certain specific use values can be replaced by other similar use values. There is even a certain comparable gradation among use values, so that a product with given technical and other properties can have relatively higher or lower use value in comparison with another product, and can satisfy therefore the need of a specific qualitative type in a more or less adequate way. In the case of means of production the lower or higher use value of two interchangeable products will appear mainly in the lower or higher effect obtained by the buyer: the higher use value of a means of production enables the buyer to achieve a relatively greater growth in gross income than would the lower use value. From this standpoint each enterprise as purchaser can judge the use value of interchangeable means of production.

For this reason the trends in demand for a certain type of means of production must necessarily appear in the trends in demand for other means of production. The growth in demand for a product with a given use value will have as its result a decline in demand for a similar product, which has lower use value. These shifts in demand will be influenced to a *decisive* degree by the relations of prices for these interchangeable products.

On the assumption that the products would be sold for production prices, this shift in demand from a product with a lower use value, to one with a higher, would be dependent on the mutual price relationship of the two products. If the product with a higher use value had the same or even a lower production price than the one with a lower use value, there would be a clear shift of demand from the second to the first. Each enterprise needing the given use value would try to buy the product with the higher use value. But if the production price of the product with higher use value were higher than for the product with lower use value, the shift of demand to the first product would be unequivocal only on the part of these customers whose income would be increased by the use of the equipment or material with higher use value (even if bought at a relatively higher price). But since the use of a certain means of production is not the same for all purchasers and not all will have the same return from its use, the shift of demand to the means of production with the relatively higher use value will only be partial. The relatively higher the production price of such a product, the relatively lower the demand for it, so that at a certain price level there will be no shift of demand from the product with lower use value to the one with the higher.

In this mutual interchangeability and differing levels of use value of two or more types of means of production lies the first reason why sales prices must deviate from production prices. If it were possible always and immediately to adapt the extent of production of each commodity to the extent of demand for it at its production price, the wholesale prices could equal — if we abstract other relationships — the production price. Actually this is not possible. It is not always possible to produce a certain new product with relatively higher use value in amounts adequate to cover fully the extent of demand, if it were sold at the production price. Nor is it even possible to immediately reduce production of a substitute product with lower use value in proportion as demand declines (or in some cases to stop production at once), not to speak of the fact that there are often stocks on hand.

For these reasons, wholesale prices must always be created with anticipated trends of demand and supply in mind (dependent on temporary possibilities of making progressive production changes) for products with mutually interchangeable use values. The wholesale price of a product with higher use value can be set lower than the price of a product with lower use value or at the same level, only if production can immediately cover the anticipated demand, and if production of the product with a lower use value can be cut at the same time or completely stopped (assuming there are no stocks on hand). If this possibility does not exist, the wholesale price of the product with higher use value must be set higher than that with the lower, at a ratio that would balance out the anticipated demand and supply for all interchangeable products. The same can be achieved by lowering the wholesale price of the older products with lower use value (in order to restrict temporarily the shift of demand from this product). Or there could be a combination of both.

Wholesale prices should diverge only temporarily from production prices, however. The conditions and proportions of production must be deliberately changed to make it possible fully to satisfy demand for each product at wholesale prices more or less equal to production prices. Production of goods with higher use value must be expanded as rapidly as possible and in the necessary amount, so that it will not be necessary to restrict demand by setting a wholesale price higher than the production price. And vice versa, production of goods with lower use value must be cut or stopped, so that it will not be necessary to maintain a demand for it by reducing the wholesale price below the production price.

From the standpoint of the effect of price on the purchaser, sales prices should be raised above production prices only if the higher demand cannot be satisfied, for objective reasons, over a relatively long period of time (shortage of raw materials, production capacities, etc.) or if the demand for the new product could not be sufficiently anticipated and the production (or stocks) of the old interchangeable product reduced or stopped. In the latter case, it is always easier to lower these increased sales prices of the new product subsequently than to raise them.

It should not be permitted to increase sales prices in cases where the production of scarce goods can be quickly increased or where there are no objective difficulties. Nor should it be allowed at all if the producing or trading enterprise merely wants to get a higher income in this way. It is not, therefore, a question of reducing demand for a certain product by increasing the wholesale price above the production price for making speculative gains, but only to respect certain objective and temporarily inescapable reasons. But this is only expressing the social interest which would usually remain only a pious wish if there were no way to compel the enterprises by economic factors to respect it. We shall speak of this later.

In the above connection we have been observing, first, the effect of use value on wholesale price trends.

Another important relationship between use value and price should be the effect of their inter-action on the producer. We have shown that the actual production price (assuming equal conditions of production) would create equal interest of producers in the production of all necessary types of product, but in reality the wholesale price must deviate from the production price, even from the standpoint of its effect on the buyer. Each deviation acts in a certain way also on the seller.

We may generally say that increasing wholesale prices of a certain commodity will also increase the interest of the producer in making it, for this will increase his earnings, and yield higher income in relation to labour expended on the product. The reverse is true when the price is reduced.

Each increase in wholesale price over the production price, carried out for the purpose of restricting demand, will arouse a corresponding interest on the part of the producers — the sellers — in speeding up the increased production of certain goods. Thus the trends in sales prices have an influence in gradually expanding production of the goods in question and in balancing supply and demand, creating the conditions for wholesale prices and production prices to come closer together or to balance.

If the price of a new product is raised above the production price, the producer will quickly try to expand production. If the usual practice is to raise prices for new products with higher use values, this causes the producers to have the material conditions (covering higher initial costs, etc.) and the necessary interest in constantly improving and expanding use values in accord with the customers' interest.

If sales prices are raised for a product which cannot be produced for the time being in larger quantities because of objective difficulties and therefore the entire demand cannot be covered, there are two possible approaches. Either the production difficulties and then the increased price of the product will induce the producer to expand production. Or it may not be in the power of the producer to help expand production of this commodity, or it is not even desirable for the producer to have greater interest in its production (e.g., if there is a shortage of raw materials, etc.). In that case a system of dual prices must be used (one for the buyer and one for the seller), which we shall discuss in somewhat more detail later.

The reverse is true if the wholesale price must be reduced below the production price in order to sell a product for which the demand has fallen. The relative decline of the sales price makes the producer less interested in producing this commodity and he will reduce or stop production. In this way after a certain time the relative reduction in price disappears altogether.

It is a question, then, of cases where a certain movement of wholesale prices brings a harmonious development of interests of buyers and sellers and acts to overcome gradually the conflicts between production and consumption or to reconcile them.

There are, of course — as we have shown — cases where one cannot harmonize the interests of buyers and sellers, or production and consumption, by a movement of sales prices. In these instances the single movement of wholesale prices must be divided into two opposite movements. These are exceptional cases, where it is necessary temporarily to limit demand for certain goods, and at the same time the interest of producers in making such goods is also to be restricted. These are, for instance, commodities made of raw materials imported with great difficulties or of materials hard to obtain, etc., and the situation cannot be solved by raising the price of the raw material. In such a case, the price should not be raised for the producer (seller), but reduced, although it is to be raised to the buyer. The solution for this contradiction is the system of dual prices: relatively lower prices for the producer and relatively higher prices for the buyer. The difference goes to the state in the form of a special tax.

From the standpoint of mutual relationships of use value of types of goods of different grades, the use value and its influence on trends in demand will again and again come in conflict temporarily with the trends in supply, and therefore a temporary deviation of wholesale prices from production prices is found to be necessary. This should be in a ratio that will give rise to an *equilibrium price* which, by deviating from production price, harmonizes demand and supply, first of all because it restricts or increases demand. But this disturbs the proportionality, which also disturbs the equivalence of exchange, and consumption is one-sidedly deformed. This is, therefore, only a provisional necessity that must sooner or later be balanced by a development of production in a way that will again overcome the deviation of sales prices from production price (at a relatively lower price a restriction or stopping of production of the commodities, at a relatively higher price an expansion of production).

There arises in this connection one of the fundamental questions, most often discussed in socialist economic theory: how are equilibrium prices to be formed and how can they be constantly returned to the level of production prices by changing the proportions of production? In a broader connection, this is again a question of the relation of the market mechanism and socially planned procedure, in assuring the proportional development of socialist production.

Until now the market mechanism has been considered incompatible with socialism for the two following reasons:

1) It means an *a posteriori* adapting of production to the situation on the market, which, it is alleged, would mean great losses and production would not be subordinated to social priorities;

2) Under conditions of considerable monopoly in production, it would enable the producers to increase prices for speculative reasons by cutting down on production (supply) as compared with demand and thus to get monopoly profits.

The first reason arises from a considerably over-simplified concept both of the market mechanism and of socialist planning. In the discussion up to this point I have shown that, even under conditions of capitalist production, the private enterprises cannot decide on their future development merely on the basis of the past development of the market, but must try — especially in deciding on investment — to foresee future development. Of course, they cannot forecast changes in market demand with enough reliability, and therefore their decisions will always need to be corrected by the actual market trends. The market forces them to make — especially on a micro-economic level — decisions that will often come in conflict with their former basic and long-term economic decisions. This will be true particularly in the sphere of investments, if the capacity is not properly prepared and therefore insufficiently utilized, or if expensive adaptations have to be made, if there are failures and bankruptcies of the individual entrepreneurs, etc.

But even under socialism — although there are more favourable objective conditions here for long-range, planned economic decisions — it is not possible to foresee everything correctly, and therefore there must be a continual correction of basic economic decisions made in the past. Under an administrative system of management, the market could not be, and in fact was not, a corrector of erroneous planning decisions. As a result, contradictions between demand and supply increased to a greater and greater extent, doing constantly greater harm, and the demand not only of socialist enterprises, but even more so of the consumers, was relatively worse and worse satisfied.

Even under socialism it is therefore essential for a real market to function as a continual criterion and corrector of erroneous decisions in planning. The less often supply comes into conflict with demand, the less often will sales prices have to deviate from production prices; the less often additional corrections must be made in the production decisions, the better for socialist planning and the more automatically will the role of the market mechanism diminish. This will be a healthy, economic negation of the role of the market mechanism and not a negation that is made in an administrative way from purely ideological reasons to the harm of the workers!

If, then, the need to subordinate production to society's priorities is used as an argument against the market under socialism, this is justified only under special conditions, when the economic stand-point must be explicitly and temporarily subordinated to serious political purposes. These might be, for instance a rapid increase in defence measures, a policy of independence from hostile states, etc. Then we can imagine laying down production or investment tasks that not only take no account, for the time being, of market demand, but also involve directive setting of prices for whole economic branch-es and consequently a non-equivalent exchange for the benefit of one branch at the expense of another – e.g., rapid industrialization at the expense of agriculture, etc.

But if it is debatable how long any serious disturbance of balance can speed up economic growth, it is absolutely clear that social prio-rity should not lead to arbitrary, long-term restriction or deforming of the market or denial of the law of value. A long period of priority development of some branches of production and some products at the expense of other necessary branches and products, together with long-term price deformation must sooner or later cause an insoluble conflict between production and consumption, between the interests of the producers and of the consumers, and disturb the smooth course of the reproduction process and growth.

When we are speaking of short-term, limited preference given to some types of production (e.g., for certain types of social [public] consumption, to introduce new production facilities in an undeveloped region, to assure a politically important, but less profitable kind of exports or imports, etc.) even then, such activity must not be al-lowed to conflict with the basic task of production to satisfy the pur-chasing power of the consumers, developing as a result of certain planned, fundamental distribution processes — of planning macro-proportions in the distributing of the national income. Of course, even in such cases, society must not only know what this priority is costing them, how much is the intentionally made deviation in price as compared with the socially necessary costs, and how long it can permit such priority to continue, but it must also make sure that any loss incurred by an enterprise that is compelled to carry out priority orders will be compensated. Otherwise it would violate the principle of material interest of enterprises.

The second argument concerns the danger of speculative, monopoly price rises. This does not refute the fundamental need for creating equilibrium prices, solving the contradiction between supply and demand. It only brings up the subordinate question of how to solve the problem of equilibrium price in connection with the producers' one-sided interest in raising prices.

At one time Oscar Lange[1] tried to solve this question. Fearing the one-sided effect on prices by monopoly producers, he pointed out the necessity for a parametric type of price, a price that cannot be subjectively influenced by leading executives in production, but will be formed by objectively arising processes. At the same time, he saw the need for equilibrium prices as indispensable data for production, as data on the exchange relationships of various alternative types of goods, without which production could not develop in harmony with demand, and as the most effective way of doing this.

Lange's approach was an advance because he was quite clearly aware of the impossibility of a central, detailed, directive determination of the production of different types of products in advanced industrial countries under a socialist economy. He saw the problem of equilibrium prices and their influence on the economic decisions made by the enterprises in accordance with the trends of market demand. On the other hand, he feared the result of violating the necessary parametric nature of prices under highly monopolized socialist conditions of production. So he proposed that equilibrium prices, particularly for means of production, should be created by the central planning body, which would in some way substitute for the market. But he believed that it would be enough for directors of socialist enterprises to have centrally established rules and regulations, according to which they were to minimize their costs in relation to the prices set, and decide on the production programs in such a way that their costs would enter into the established prices, etc.

While Lange's approach is noteworthy as the first attempt to link planning and market under socialism and thereby a form of criticism of the way the role of prices was neglected in the administrative system of management, we find his solution inadequate in the light of today's experiences. In the first place, it has been found that not even all means of production can have prices set by a central body in

---

[1] Oscar Lange, *Pisma Ekonomiczne i Spoleczne*, 1930–1960, Selected Writings, Warsaw 1961.

a way that would always make them equilibrium prices. Secondly, it is not enough to outline for the directors of enterprises only the general rules for making decisions and to overlook the fact that they will have to act under the pressure of the economic interests of the enterprise's workers. The entire proposal cannot assure a solution of the basic clashes of interest between the enterprise's advantage and that of society, between producers' and consumers' interests, and, in the final analysis, it will lead logically to an administrative, uneconomic solution.

Under pressure of the enterprise workers' interests to have higher wages, the directors will try to raise prices, to choose the most advan, tageous structure of production from the producer's point of view- to restrict the qualitative development of production — all this at the expense of the consumer. The central price body is, in the end, forced to rely on reports from the producing enterprises, and with the immensely broad range in type of product, it cannot check on the actual social need for the costs of production listed, the real possibilities to reduce them, or in general on the social need for the products, the ways to improve them, etc. Without documentation from the enterprises, market prices, equilibrium prices, cannot be set, because the central body cannot judge whether these prices will mean a loss or too much profit for the producer. Moreover, it does not have even the knowledge or experience of the consumers. Only for a very narrow group of the most important types of product could the centre perhaps substitute for the function of consumer in making these judgments. It cannot study the need for products only by the movement of inventories, because the monopoly position of the producers forces the consumers to buy even products that do not really want, just because there are no others.

The central body can react to a market situation only with a delay, and each price change, carried out by the centre in a much less sensitive way than by the market mechanism, calls for shifts in production and new disproportions. It, therefore, cannot prevent speculative moves by producers, unjustified rewards in some enterprises (independent of the degree to which they satisfy social needs on the level of efficiency), growing contradictions between production and consumption, and a lag in technical and qualitative development.

It is impossible to avoid direct clashes between the interests of producers and consumers on the market, and the creation of specific equilibrium prices for a large mass of goods, affected by this. In order to limit the one-sided advantage going to the producers, it is necessary even under socialism to restrict unjustified monopoly and to develop all forms of market competition among the enterprises, using measures by the central economic body to cut down on the speculative moves by the producers. But, at the same time, the economic, relatively free, formation of prices should not be prevented.

It is chiefly through pressure of the market, with the threat that unsuitable goods will not be sold and that there will be economic difficulties, that bonuses cannot be paid, nor shares received of the enterprise's income — this is the economic pressure that will make the individual enterprises really try to produce what is demanded by the market, to assure the genuine needs of the consumers, to improve production and introduce new products, lowering production costs and prices. No administrative control (which cannot discover the real possibilities and the reserves in the enterprises), no general rules, no general moral and political appeals can compel an enterprise to abandon a tried and tested type of production that brings large earnings, and go over to producing completely new goods, changing the technology of production. The centre cannot induce enterprises to reduce prices if it is not in their interest to do so, to seek new production possibilities if the plant is working at full capacity, etc.

In brief, as long as the earnings of producers are dependent on their work for society, and as long as no one outside the production collective can judge the possibilities for development and the concrete appearance of this labour, just so long will it be unavoidable to have, to a certain extent, action of the market mechanism and market competition. Otherwise it would be impossible to prevent a serious qualitative lag in socialist production.

The most important instruments to use against monopolistic, speculative price increases are — in addition to competition on the market — state financial instruments like credit, interest, taxes, foreign-trade measures, etc. We shall speak of these in connection with anti-inflation policy. A socialist state cannot even abandon certain administrative measures, drawing off the obvious speculative profits and lowering prices when price and quality control point to such speculation. For a limited number of the most important goods, having decisive influence on the reproduction process and on living standards, and where the central body has the knowledge of the matter to determine the economic movement of prices, it will then be possible and necessary to continue administering prices centrally. But the basis for fixing prices should be not only a harmonizing of use values of these types of goods and their effect on demand trends, but primarily it should be the socially necessary development of production costs (value or production prices) that is the basis for the price and the influence of the relation between supply and demand (the influence of use value at a given value) on the deviations of sales prices from production prices.

The constantly progressing mathematical methods trying to make exact calculations of these complex and mutually contradictory relationships between use value of goods and their price, were for a long time — and sometimes still are — rejected by dogmatic Marxist economists as un-Marxist. If these methods proceed from the value base of the price (or socialist production prices) and calculate only the quantitative magnitude of price deviations from their value base, caused by comparative use values, and their relation with a certain trend in supply and demand, then they have a correct scientific theoretical basis. But if they ignore the long-range determining relation between value or rather, production price and the specific sales price, if they try to make use value the *determining* or even the *sole* factor in regard to prices, then these prices rest on unscientific ground. This theory is unscientific because it ignores the decisive and long-term determining relationship between value and price, it does not see the need for fluctuations of specific prices around this value basis and observes only the surface (external) relation (although it is also an essential and important one) between use value and price. Some Marxist economists have dogmatically ignored the correct findings on the surface relationship between use value and prices which were arrived at by mathematical methods, by some non-Marxist economist, although they may not have recognized the Marxist theory of value. Most dogmatic Marxist economists narrowed down their interpretation of price movements to a theory of the relationship of value and price of commodities and failed to see the relationship between use value and prices. Although the relation of value to price is the determining feature, still the theory explaining *only* this relation (usually in a simplified way, not treating the specific socialist transformations of this relationship) can have no practical significance for socialist price formation.

In the case of means of production or aggregated groups of production means, one can approach not only a central price management by *a posteriori* observance of the development of production costs, but also on the basis of scientific predictions of all fundamental economic relationships determining the movement of sales prices (trends in costs of production, use values, interchangeable use values, etc.) *plan* the necessary development of sales prices of these groups of production means.

This involves determining in advance the trends of sales prices so as to correspond to the trends in production prices, i. e., ascertaining the average profits and having the sales prices decline in proportion to the possible and realistic forecast of a decline in production costs of different products. But, at the same time, in planning the trend of sales prices, their movement should be determined so as to respect the necessary deviations of sales prices from production prices, from the standpoint of their relation to use values or to interchangeable use values.

It is no easy matter to carry out this type of planning, for it requires very complex comparisons. A special method of calculation is necessary to express their various effects for the consumer and to foresee possible changes in the proportions of production. The most realistic method is the use for those basic means of production, where the use value is simpler and it can be approached more easily (by means of a limited number of technical parametres).

Those sales prices that are to be reduced in a planned way on the basis of a calculation of a possible declining trend in production costs give the producer an incentive to cut production costs as rapidly as possible and so at the same time to create the conditions for increasing per-capita income in the enterprise. But, at the same time, tying planned sales price to the use value, and to parametres bringing improvement, enables the producer at a certain moment to achieve relatively more favourable prices for a new product with higher use value, stimulate the enterprises to constantly introduce newer and better products.

278

This way of setting price trends in a planned way, respecting all essential relationships that determine them, would be a scientific, non-bureaucratic guidance by society of optimal development and of the individual proportions in production. The price trends, especially for aggregated groups, would be of a more general nature than the detailed administrative determination of the quantity of production of different types of product and would enable the enterprises to make independent decisions on their production programs. They could be worked out in the form of expert recommendations of scientific research institutions and taken over by the higher governing bodies. Finally, and this is the most important feature, this would orient the interests of the enterprises in the direction of social interests and would not compel them to act against their interests, as was the case in most of the old administrative production commands.

But in those cases in which society is unable to foresee the possible development of production costs for most products, and, especially, if it cannot calculate the level of comparable use values of interchangeable products; if it cannot foresee the trends of demand for products with different but interchangeable use value, because of the tremendous complexity of this use value, then it must allow, also under socialism, relatively free price formation, even if, in some cases, only within certain limits. This is especially true of consumer goods, but also of many types of means of production.

When a socialist society does not make possible a relatively free price movement and, at the same time, cannot assure a rapid and flexible reaction to changing conditions of production or of demand, when — that is to say — it maintains prices by directive, there will necessarily be contradictions between production and consumption. Either the enterprises have relatively less interest in producing certain goods, as opposed to a relatively higher demand for these goods, or — on the contrary — there is a relatively greater interest in producing goods for which there is less demand. One way or another, this rigid, administrative price formation ignores complex relationships which influence the development of prices, and causes growing clashes of interest that are distinctly contrary to the loudly proclaimed social interest which is often pointed to as a justification of the directive method of price formation.

3   Construction of Trade Prices

Trade prices are the basic construction for *retail prices* of consumer goods sold by socialist trade organizations to the public. They differ from the construction of wholesale prices in that, firstly, their absolute and relative level has a decisive effect on consumption — through them the exchange of different amounts of specific labour actually ends in consumption by the workers. Secondly, the difference between trade prices and wholesale prices is that the former include another part of the value of the surplus product that exceeds the average profit (in the form of turnover tax and trade margin), so that through them the value delimiting all personal (both individual and collective) consumption by society is realized. They also help to determine the distribution of this value among different strata of society.

From the first fact follows that the relations among prices of consumer goods cannot deviate for a long time from the value base, that is, from socialist production prices that are the transformed expression of the development of the value of different types of goods. *Long-term* relations among trade prices of consumer goods must correspond fundamentally to the relations of these production prices, even though on another absolute level. Only in this way can the general and long-term equivalent exchange among various groups of workers be assured. Only in this way can we make sure that workers who produce, say, shoes, and expend a certain amount of labour on their manufacture, will receive on the average and over a long period of time the same amount of expended labour back (after deductions have been made for the benefit of society) in other consumer goods they purchase. They should receive an equivalent amount of labour even if, during a period of time, the productivity of labour has risen unevenly in the production of the other goods they buy.

From the second circumstance we find that when the values of consumer goods are realized, the total value of the surplus product for covering all final consumption (individual and collective) must also be realized. This includes the consumption exceeding that of the productively employed, secured by their direct remuneration for labour. The share that these productive workers have in the total personal consumption will depend essentially on the difference between the total volume of prices of consumer goods and the volume of direct remuneration of workers in production. Later we shall simplify this and speak of this remuneration as wages, although it includes all forms of remuneration in production (bonuses, etc.), and similarly for the cash payments and payments in kind for cooperative producers.

The larger the difference between the total price of consumer goods and the sum of the wages of the productively employed, the relatively smaller the share these workers obtain from the national income and vice versa. In this sense, wages and prices are the basic instruments for distributing the national income and for covering certain social needs. If the total average profit included in the production prices represents the money form of part of the surplus product, then the other part has the money form of the turnover tax and the trade margin — the difference between the total production price of consumer goods and its total trade price.

The construction of a production price is such that the combined producers in the different enterprises will not receive directly back for their disposal the total value created by their labour, from the sale of goods by the enterprise. By means of the system of trade prices and of certain planned distribution processes, part of the surplus product is realized for the benefit of society and is used independent of its creators and without being first appropriated by them. This is also done for the benefit of the producers, for it assures certain social needs that are essential for the producers themselves. The producers must always be informed about the use of the surplus product and must have a broad direct and indirect participation in the decisions on how it should be used.

The question arises whether it is useful to *do away with* the turnover tax or any similar tax that is taken only in prices of consumer goods, and put the whole value of the surplus product in the form of profit into the wholesale price, and, in that case, whether the consumption of the entire surplus product could be assured. The problem, as is known, consists in the fact that the volume of social consumption and non-production net investments, covered by the surplus product, is considerably larger than the volume of production net investment, also covered by the surplus product. A much greater part of the surplus product must, therefore, be consumed in the form of consumer goods and if there is an even distribution of the value of the surplus product in the prices of the means of production and of consumer goods, there will also be a larger part of this value of the surplus product realized in the sale of the means of production.

Theoretically one could easily imagine the elimination of the turn-over tax without causing insurmountable obstacles in realizing the values of the surplus product. By doing away with the two price levels and bringing the wholesale and retail price levels closer it is intended to facilitate making optimum calculations to achieve better planning methods. It is not the purpose of this work to deal in any more detail with this complex problem. In connection with our exposition of the problems of retail prices, we need only point out here the conditions for realizing the production at retail prices, whether they contain a special tax or not.

Even if, in the course of further economic discussion, the idea should prevail that it is necessary to keep a special tax that should be realized only in retail prices and not in wholesale prices, this tax would, on the one hand, have to be lowered considerably, because an increase of the level of wholesale prices became necessary and, on the other hand, it must change in comparison with the turnover tax as now practiced. Without regard to the theoretical discussion, this tax is today a real fact and the price reform being prepared does not reckon with eliminating it completely. The economic system of management requires, however, that it be fundamentally changed in character. We shall return to this question later. First we must show what are the conditions for realizing the social production that arises in connection with the different modes of realizing the entire value of the surplus product — with or without the special tax in the prices of consumer goods.

We should recall first one of the fundamental Marxist findings in the sphere of socially extended reproduction. In commodity exchange the condition for smooth running of the reproduction process, if we abstract this from the changes caused by foreign trade, is to make the aggregate price of the means of production (Department I) equal the aggregate money cost designed for the purchase of means of production. These money costs are essentially created by the total value of used-up means of production contained in the social product (c) and the total value of accumulation of fixed assets (nc). We can only realize in the aggregate price what is finally destined for production consumption. As soon as the aggregate price of means of production becomes greater, over a relatively lengthy period of time, than the aggregate price of production consumption, part of the means of production would not be sold and not consumed. And vice versa, the price of production consumption cannot be greater than the aggregate price of means of production, because there would be no way of obtaining the means of production in such a case. Naturally, foreign trade could change these relations, but our previous experience shows that one cannot have for long any excessive difference between the value of exported and the value of imported means of production, so in practice foreign trade cannot change these basic relations very much.

If we abstract foreign trade from our account, the first condition for a smooth extension of reproduction is for the aggregate price of means of production to equal the aggregate price of material input. If we then count on realizing the social average profit in prices of means of production -- i.e., if we calculate at production prices and abstract the temporary deviations of sales prices from production prices we obtain this equation:

a) $Ic + v + z = (Ic + nc) + (IIc + nc)$

where I = Department producing means of production
II = Department producing consumption goods
c = money form of production consumption (amortization +
+ material costs)
v = wages paid in production to productive labour
z = gross profit
nc = increment in production assets (fixed assets and inventories) covered by surplus product

The aggregate price of means of production must equal the aggregate price of means of production used in both groups plus the price of accumulation in means of production in both groups.

Another condition is that the aggregate price of consumer goods must equal the aggregate price of non-production (final) consumption. Non-production consumption is personal consumption of productive labour corresponding essentially to the wages (abstracting from non-material consumption and the increment in savings), the personal consumption of non-productive labour and of the disabled, and all remaining social consumption of non-production institutions, non-production accumulation, trade costs, etc.). Again leaving aside foreign trade, the following equation applies:

b) $IIc + v + z + d = Iv + nv + IIv + nv + sp$

where d = the money form of surplus product exceeding profit =
= turnover tax + trade margin;

nv = increment in wages in production (in Department I and II) covered by surplus product,

sp = total non-production consumption exceeding the personal consumption of productive labour (exceeding $v + nv$).

As Marxists know, the resultant of these two equations is a certain necessary value relationship between the two groups. Any part of Department I can be designed to cover the value of non-production consumption only if it is realized in exchange for commodities of Department II, i.e., for consumer goods. (Because non-production consumption cannot be covered in physical form by means of production.) Department II can buy the means of production only at the price at which it consumed the means of production (c) and at which the production assets are to be extended. But in order for Department II to be able to buy the means of production at this price, it must again sell consumer goods at this price to Department I. As we know the transfer of money between Departments I and II is carried out only for the mutual exchange of means of production and consumer goods, if there is not to be on the one side or the other an unrealizable surplus of money and if the smooth running of the reproduction process is not to be disturbed. Nothing in this fundamental necessity is changed, whether the exchange is made directly between the individual socialist enterprises of both Departments or through the state (state budget, etc.). It would seem, then, that we could use Marx's formulation of a third equation expressing the mutual value relation between Departments I and II and furnishing conditions for the smooth running of expended reproduction, but with the small modification that personal consumption of capitalists should be considered as non-production consumption:

c) $Iv + nv + r = IIc + nc$

$r =$ the part of value, according to Marx, that is designed for personal consumption of capitalists of Department I or for consumption they allow for non-productive labour.

Actually, however, this equation essentially corresponds only to conditions of private commodity production, where more or less every Department (private enterprises) can use only that *part of the value* for the consumption of their group, which it has itself realized (that is, it cannot shift any part of the value from one private enterprise to another). Enterprises in Department I can use for the consumption of the capitalists and the workers essentially only the part of the value which they have themselves realized, just as enterprises in Department II can use for production consumption (consumption of means of production) only the part of the value they have themselves realized (leaving credit out of consideration).

But a new possibility arises under socialism. A socialist state can draw off part of the value realized by the sale of goods of one or the other department and assign it to use outside that department. For example, it can take the part of the value realized in the sales of consumer goods and use it for accumulation in enterprises of Department I. Or, on the contrary, it could take part of the value realized by sales of means of production and use this to cover social consumption. But even these shifts are conditioned on the one hand, by a certain objective relation between the two Departments and on the other hand, a shift from the one to another excludes the reverse movement. Over a longer period of time there can be either a shift from Department II to Department I or the reverse, never both at the same time. Even under socialism there is a certain objectively conditioned relationship between Department I and II, that prevents an arbitrary value transaction by the state, even if there are certain essential modifications reflecting the socialist economic relationships.

The socialist differs from the capitalist relationship primarily by the fact that the consumption by capitalists is absent. In the reproduction relationship, however, this is not an essential peculiarity and in place of the value part destined for the consumption by capitalist (r) we must reckon the value part destined for the consumption of non-productive labour and for social consumption in general (sp).

But if we take into account the essential features of socialist reproduction relationships, i.e., the possibilities of value shifts made by the socialist state, from one Department to the other, then we must express the third equation in three possible variants. Firstly, as a variant without any values shifts, which is theoretically the easiest to understand and therefore we shall start the exposition with it. But in practice such an equality in value would be only a chance exception. Secondly, the variant could be a value shift from Department I to Department II. Finally the variant would make possible a value shift from Department II to Department I (a variant that was most often found in the old wholesale prices which did not cover even the need for production accumulation).

Let us begin with the exceptional value equality of two reciprocally exchanged parts between Department I and II.

a) $Iv + nv = IIc + nc$

This is an equation expressing the variant of the value relationship between Department I and Department II making possible a smooth extension of reproduction. With this relationship, Department I sells the means of production to Department II at the exact price it needs for paying wages to its workers and Department II sells the consumer goods to the workers of Department I at the exact price it needs to purchase the means of production for its production consumption (inputs). Under these conditions each group can without difficulty assure extended reproduction. Department I has wages covered by consumer goods not only for its previous workers (v), but also the wages of further necessary manpower (nv). Department II has covered the value needed to renew and extend its production assets ($c + nc$) by buying means of production.

The second possible variant is a surplus of value of production consumption of Department II ($IIc + nc$) above the value destined for wages in Department I. In this case Department I sells the means of production to Group II at a price Department II needs ($IIc + nc$) and from the realized value pays its wages ($Iv + nv$) and still has a surplus of value remaining (dsp). The state must draw off this part and expend it on social consumption, such as the wages of nonproductive workers, etc. For this sum the non-productive workers or institutions purchase consumer goods which had not — in the given value portion — been bought by workers of Department I. This is expressed by the equation:

b) $Iv + nv + dsp = IIc + nc$

$dsp =$ the part of the value of the surplus product drawn off from Department I (either by tax, or by percentage payment from profit, etc.) expended on social consumption.

With a general rise in the level of wholesale prices and lowering of tax on turnover, i.e., under conditions where also in the prices of means of production part of the surplus product designed to cover social consumption will be realized, in practice the relation between Department I and Department II will usually be expressed by the second variant of the equation. Then, of course, value $IIc + nc$ is larger than $Iv + nv$ by the value of dsp. This surplus of the value of means of production destined for Department II over $Iv + nv$ must be drawn off in money form by means of dsp and through the non-productive manpower and institutions (their consumption) shift over to Department II. From there this portion is again expended on the purchase of means of production and so on and on.

If there is a substantial rise in the level of wholesale prices of both departments, where in wholesale prices of means of production a greater value is realized than would correspond to the needs for means of production of both departments, then part of the means of production must be transformed by means of foreign trade into consumption goods. This means that in cases where $IIc + nc$ does not grow as rapidly as $Iv + nv + dsp$, it would be necessary to export a certain amount of the means of production (exceeding in value the needs of Department II) and import for this amount consumer goods in order that $Iv + nv + dsp$ might be fully covered by consumer goods. But if this transformation of part of the means of production, exceeding domestic needs, and realized by exchange in foreign trade, should run into difficulties, than production of Department I would need to be restricted and the production of Department II extended so that at the given prices there should be harmony between production and consumption.

The larger the part of the value of the surplus product that is realized directly in wholesale prices (and therefore also in prices of means of production — on the assumption that there should be the same rate of profit in both groups), the greater the need to draw off part of the value of surplus product by the state from Department I in the form of certain percentage payments from incomes (dsp) and the need for equality of value between $Iv + nv + dsp$ and $IIc + nc$. Only the exchange in foreign trade, which has an important and ever larger role in the structural harmonizing of specific sources and needs, can make it possible — given this system of wholesale prices — for $IIc + nc$ to be less than $Iv + nv + dsp$.

Whereas in the future the second variant described above will tend to prevail in the exchange between Department I and Department II, in the past the third variant predominated. For its theoretical interest we shall give this in more detail.

It is a variant in which the value of means of production corresponding to the wages in Department I $(v + nv)$ is greater than the value of the production consumption in Department II. This means that Department II sells as much consumer goods to the workers of Department I as they can purchase for their wages. At the same time Department II realizes the value corresponding to its production inputs $(IIc + no)$ for which it can purchase means of production from Department I and in addition realizes a certain portion of the value (da) which it does not need for its production input. This portion of the value (da) is drawn off by the state and distributed to the enterprises in Group I for investment which they use to purchase means of production from one another. This actually extends the production accumulation in Department I as compared with the production accumulation covered from the profit of Department I. The enterprises can use the value they have thus realized by selling each other their means of production and which in general equals the portion of the value which they received from the state for investment (da), in order to pay out wages. Through these wages it (da) again goes to Department II through the purchase of consumer goods, where the state again draws it off, etc.

The equation of the third variant is:

c) $Iv + nv = IIc + nc + da$

where $da =$ the portion of the value drawn off from the value of realized consumer goods by the state (turnover tax, etc.) and expended on accumulation in Department I.

If we should illustrate the matter by substituting numerical magnitudes for the symbols, the over-all schema of socialist extended reproduction would look as follows, if the third variant is used:

$$I = c + v + \underset{\substack{nv \quad nc}}{\overset{}{\diagup z \diagdown}} = \text{aggregate price}$$

$$550 + 450 + 50 + 200 = 1250$$

$$II = c + v + \underset{\substack{nv \quad nc}}{\overset{}{\diagup z \diagdown}} + d = \text{aggregate price}$$

$$300 + 100 + 20 + 80 + 300 = 800$$

$$II \diagdown \underset{20}{\overset{dnc}{\diagup}} \underset{100}{\overset{da}{\diagdown}} \underset{180}{\overset{sp}{\diagdown}}$$

The tax exacted on the realization of consumer goods (d) would be divided in our case into the part by which production accumulation in Department II is extended ($IInc = 80\ znc + 20\ dnc = 100\ nc$), i.e., it is a matter of redistributing the surplus product among the enterprises of Department II; furthermore into the part that is being shifted to Department I for the extension of production accumulation (da); and, finally, into the part that goes to social consumption. Under these conditions, the entire social consumption, whose value is — not only in our example, but also in the whole of previous socialist experience — much greater than the value of all the production accumulation, is fully covered from the surplus product realized by the sales of consumer goods and drawn off in the form of a turnover tax.

This is how all three equations of the third variant would look if numbers were substituted:

a)
$$Ic + v + z = Ic + \underset{\substack{z \quad da}}{\overset{}{\diagup nc \diagdown}} + IIc + \underset{\substack{z \quad d}}{\overset{}{\diagup nc \diagdown}}$$

$$550 + 450 + 250 = 550 + 200\ 100 + 300 \quad 80\ 20$$

$$\underbrace{\qquad\qquad}_{1250} \qquad \underbrace{\qquad\qquad\qquad\qquad}_{1250}$$

b)
$$IIc + v + z + d = Iv\ nv\ IIv + nv\ sp$$

$$300 + 100 + 100 + 300 = 450\ 50\ 100 + 20\ 180$$

$$\underbrace{\qquad\qquad}_{800} \qquad \underbrace{\qquad\qquad\qquad}_{800}$$

c) $Iv + nv = IIc + nc \quad da$

$$450 + 50 = \underbrace{300 + 100 \; 100}$$
$$\underbrace{500} \qquad \underbrace{500}$$

The previous practice has been to draw off the major part of value of surplus product in retail prices of consumer goods. As a result there came to be a big spread between the level of wholesale and retail prices and almost the entire surplus product was distributed through the state budget. Not only did this make difficult any manipulation of prices and various calculations for comparison and for optimization, but furthermore this needlessly expanded the redistribution role of the state budget and separated the decision-making on the use of a part of the national income from the sphere where it was created and was to be used again (chiefly in connection with production accumulation). This considerably disturbed the principle of direct material interest and responsibility of the enterprises.

With a considerable reduction in turnover tax and increase in volume of profit realized in the wholesale prices, this undesirable state of affairs will be done away with and the production accumulation will be essentially covered by the profit realized in wholesale prices. Nonetheless the turnover tax will not yet completely disappear and part of the value of surplus product will be realized in this special form, not to speak of the fact that the trade margin is also a certain form of realizing part of the value of surplus product.

Under the old system of management, however, the turnover tax was set in a rather subjective way and its level completely differed from one type of goods to another. The rather high turnover tax in the prices of some types of goods unjustifiably increased their price and cut down demand and consumption. This was so even in many cases where it would have been advantageous to expand production, for the raw materials were available, and thus demand could have increased. This was, however, prevented by the high turnover tax, fixed by directive.

From what we have said it follows that it would be most advantageous if the tax, the total revenue from which must be calculated according to social need, were to be distributed as part of the trade price of each type of consumer goods, in proportion to the production price. The trade price must, then, as the basic construction for the price of consumer goods, first of all assure the realization of the necessary total volume of the turnover tax which must be calculated for each planning period and be divided among the different types of goods in a uniform way.

This will mean a shift from the subjectively differentiated turnover tax to a uniform tax rate, where the total amount of tax would be a uniform percentage distributed among all retail prices. In this way, the foundation would be laid for retail prices to give a true picture of demand and to signal to production the consumer demand trends. Naturally this transition cannot be carried out all at once, for it requires considerable changes in the structure of retail prices, and it brings great shifts in demand which it would be impossible to satisfy by immediate changes in production. There must, therefore, be a very cautious approach, and the whole process of going over to a uniform tax rate considered as a long-term procedure taking place in several stages. But from the very beginning this transition will assure that movements in retail prices corresponding to market relations act directly on the movement of wholesale prices, even if the tax rate will not be uniform at the start for all groups of commodities.

Similarly, the trade margin must be included in trade prices at a certain percentage — that is, the part of the value that must cover all trade costs. This is primarily the material costs of trade of all types, the wage costs for workers in trade, overhead expenses and, finally, a certain value reserve which is — as we shall show later — essential in trade. The over-all trade margin globally determined by the total trade costs for a certain planning period (changing with the extent of trade activity) will be essentially a uniform percentage included in the trade prices. At the same time it would be useful to set a relatively higher level of the margin for inexpensive goods. Since the level of wages in the trade sector will also depend on the level of gross income attained by the trade enterprises, and this income will, in turn, depend on the level of over-all realized trade margin, the employees in trade will not only have an interest in increasing the over-all trade turnover, but also a greater interest in selling inexpensive goods.

The trade price, then, will be composed of the wholesale price (fluctuating around the production price), a certain tax rate and the retail margin, both fixed more or less uniformly as a percentage added to the wholesale price.

4 Market or Retail Prices

The trade price was described as the basic construction for the sales price of consumer goods. The specific price at which these goods are actually sold is called the market price or, more usually, the retail price. The relationship is similar to that between the production price and the wholesale price. The trade price also represents the basic construction chiefly from the standpoint of value, i.e., the price expression of the way value is realized in order to assure the basic and necessary processes of its distribution in society. The actual price — as we have already said — can never be based only on value, but is always affected by the use value, and the contradiction between value and use value. It is from the standpoint of these relationships that there must again occur a temporary deviation of the specific selling or market price of consumer goods from the trade price. The market price, therefore, moves under the influence of certain relationships of use value around the prevailing trade price as a special form of the value of consumer goods.

Unlike most means of production, consumer goods are difficult to price because of the tremendous complexity of the use value. While the use value of basic means of production can be relatively easily approached and compared by means of a limited number of technical parameters and even expressed in a synthesis by means of the effect it brings in the production inputs (increase in productivity, in gross income, etc., for the purchaser), it is very hard to do the same for consumer goods.

Most consumer goods cannot be adequately described only by the technical aspects. A very important feature of use value is the aesthetic appearance of the products that have a strong — and very diverse — effect on consumer demand. The great number of different aspects of use values, including the aesthetic, and the still greater number of possibilities that one or the other aspect will prevail in the evaluation by different social strata of consumers, makes it very difficult to forecast the general evaluation and comparison of use values by the

292

consumers. In the case of consumer goods there are, furthermore, much more interchangeable and comparable use values than for means of production.

At the same time, such an objective comparison of use values is constantly being made by consumers. If every product were sold at its trade price, it would inevitably follow that the consumers would constantly compare the interchangeable products as regards price, and use value. Demand would, of course, rapidly increase for the products with relatively lower price and relatively higher use value, whereas the demand for other products would decline. Consumers do not, as a matter of fact, compare only interchangeable use values, but weigh, evaluate and compare all available use values and, according to their purchasing power and at the given prices, set up a certain scale of necessary use values. It is not a question of individual evaluation of use values, but of evaluation by broad social strata and, finally, by the whole population. If we should assume that all products were to be sold at trade prices, there would be different hierarchical groupings of the demand for certain products among social strata having different levels of purchasing power. Therefore there always is, at a given stage of development, a certain over-all social demand for different types of goods.

It would seem, then, the best way would be to sell consumer goods at trade prices and ascertain, thereby, the extent of social demand for different types of goods at these prices, and then adapt the proportions of production to this extent. But these are precisely the simplified, metaphysical ideas, misunderstanding the actual development and the necessity that contradictions will grow up and be solved, between use value and value, also under socialist commodity production. It was these simplified ideas that were, and still are, reflected in the endeavours to have centrally established, relatively unchanging prices for each individual type of goods, and in insufficient appreciation or a misunderstanding of the role of prices in solving contradictions between use value and value.

Using modern statistical and mathematical methods, a socialist society can roughly forecast the basic structure of demand, i.e., the demand for the main groups of products at certain prices and with a given purchasing power. It will be able to calculate very roughly the income or price elasticities — that is, the quantitative changes that will come about in the structure of demand, with a quantitative change in income of certain strata or of all the population, or if prices change in this or that large group of commodities. In fact, a more extensive use of these methods will make it possible to foresee in the future, with deeper knowledge of the matter, changes in the structure of demand for general groups of commodities.

It is, however, absolutely impossible to predict reliably the detailed changes in the structure of demand, changes in demand for different types or even ranges of goods which are caused by a great number of different relationships. It is impossible to foresee how, when a new product appears on the market, demand will develop for this product or for others, how demand will develop if one or another product is changed or if there are income changes for small groups of people, and what is caused by non-economic influence, etc. As a result of all the unpredictable relationships (assuming inflexible prices) some types of goods are sold out and completely disappear from shops and storehouses, while other kinds pile up for months and years as unsalable goods, and gradually deteriorate.

It is naturally of decisive importance that there be reserves of commodities, and that production react rapidly to changes in demand. But if prices do not fulfil their genuine economic function, there must be, firstly, large reserves, to prevent complete selling out of various types of goods. This would be great and needless loss to society (labour tied up in inventories, in the needlessly big storage facilities, freezing capacities, etc.). Secondly, this would not solve the problem of surpluses of unsalable and useless products and the losses to society connected with this. Thirdly, and most important, it takes no account of the fact that there are clashes of interest between the consumers on the one hand and the workers in trade and in production on the other — conflicts that result from a system of planning where directive management is linked with the deadening of the economic function of prices. And just these conflicts hinder a more rapid adaptation of the production proportions to detailed changes in the structure of demand.

If prices are set as fixed and unchangeable and if the fact that they are determined in detail by central bodies prevents consideration of the effect of use values on trends of demand (even when the price-fixing officials at the centre tried to compare the use value of products, they were unable to predict the detailed trends in demand), then to a certain extent a contradiction of interest between the buyers (or consumers) and the sellers (trade and primarily production) must develop. The consequences of unchangeable and considerably subjective setting of prices were the great and unforeseeable changes in demand, to which production could not continually adapt, taking into account its minimal production cycles, its inter-sectoral relations, etc. Furthermore, this ran into contradictory interests of trade and production.

The interest of employees in trade to fulfil the planned trade turnover did not compel them to study and take account of the detailed pattern of consumer demand. It did require planning in advance a turnover which could be fulfilled by covering certain more or less constantly growing over-all items in demand. Respecting the minor items in demand, changes in demand, etc., would mean only more work and worry, but it would be no conspicuous contribution toward plan fulfilment. In this way, workers in trade had an interest contrary to that of the consumers.

Production, in turn, was interested only in fulfilling the quantity plans of production (gross production, commodity production, etc.) and connected with this were the endeavours to produce a selected range of goods which would help easily to fulfil the given volume targets, to leave the product price relatively unchanged, to neglect quality of production and development of use values, etc. If the trade organizations tried to convey, when ordering from the production enterprises, the consumer demand, they usually clashed with the opposing interests and often met with real difficulties in production (unrealistically high volume plans), which was unable to react to the detailed demand trends. It is precisely in these growing contradictions and losses in the sphere of trade that we see most clearly the objective necessity to put in effect the economic function of prices.

Market prices must, by their relatively free movement around trade prices (or, at least their potentially free movement), contribute to the solution of the constantly re-appearing contradictions between value and use value. It is exactly because the government price bodies cannot predict in detail the demand trends, nor even assure that production may react immediately to every detailed change in demand — if there are not to be growing social losses — that prices must to a certain degree change flexibly in harmony with the actual changes in relations of demand and supply. This means that the market prices must, within certain limits, rise above trade prices in the case of goods where demand has suddenly increased over supply and — on the contrary — must decline when there has been an unanticipated drop in demand.

Of course, the only *fundamental* solution for these contradictions are changes in production, expanding the production of some products and reducing or eliminating the production of others. A dogmatist believes, however, that some social or governing body must order such a change in production. This is an over-simplified reaction that has no connection with reality. If we realize that, for example, in Czechoslovakia, there are roughly one and a half million types of products that must, furthermore, be constantly changed and developed — by the introduction of new products and scrapping of outdated ones — we understand why no central or ministerial supervisory body can constantly study and command the detailed production changes, the expansion of production of some types or ranges of goods where demand has grown and reduction in production of less desired products, etc. Quite the contrary, this centrally bound, detailed decision-making brings a very inflexible, delayed reaction, if there are any changes made at all.

It is, therefore, necessary to assure that minor changes in production programs are made flexibly by the enterprises themselves, even if they must change somewhat their short-term production plans, and they should not be prevented from doing this by detailed directive planning.[1]

But at the same time, these changes should be stimulated by a flexible price movement that contributes toward a more rapid overcoming of temporary minor contradictions. A temporary rise in mar-

---

[1] "The decentralized model makes possible a direct response by the supplier to the wishes of the customer. The dependence of the enterprises on the market resulting from the setting up of indicators and material incentives based on return from sales, and the possibility of freely determining the extent and structure of production, leads to a sensitive reaction of supply to demand, even when the program is being set up, and also while it is being carried out."
W. Brus, *Modely socialistického hospodářství* (Models of Socialist Economy), Prague 1964, p. 218.

ket price for goods whose set price was found to be too low, in view of the relatively higher use value of the given product (compared with other use values) and where supply could not cover demand, restricts for a time the rise in demand and prevents the commodities from being completely sold out. But this price movement is also a stimulus both for the workers in trade and for the producers to expand production and sale of this commodity. The relatively limited rise in market prices which is then projected into wholesale prices enables the production enterprise to cover possible production losses connected with the sudden and unanticipated expansion of production or a transition from one type of production to another. The reverse process calls for a decline in market prices.

There must be a direct connection between the delimited movement of market and wholesale prices. In practice one can assure that every movement of the specific market price is projected into the corresponding movement of trade margin and wholesale price, so that every reduction in market price of certain goods will to a certain degree lower the trade margin (and therefore there must be a certain reserve — the risk fund — covered by this margin) and the wholesale price, while a rise in market price would cause a reverse movement. This would either lower the interest of the trade organizations, and the producers in selling and producing the goods in question, or, in the contrary instance, would increase it. Rises in market price would mean the necessary expansion of production and supply of the commodity and would form the prerequisites for a gradual reduction in price to the level of trade price, with a concomitant increase in consumption.

When the market price reaches the level of the trade price, with complete balance of supply and demand, the optimum amount of production of the given type of goods would be attained. At that level, the orders put in by trade organizations and the production of the goods should no longer be increased (or only as much as demand increased). If there were insufficient foresight and the trade orders and production were to increase disproportionately, there would be a reverse movement -- supply would exceed demand and the market price would decline below the level of trade price.

Here again the principle would apply that there should be only exceptional increases in price of regularly produced commodities (as compared with newly introduced products), even if done within set limits. This should be done only if the producers cannot, for some objective reason, rapidly increase production. Even in such cases, where the rise in demand for a certain commodity was not foreseen in time, the trade organizations, before a rise in market price is permitted, should see to it that production and deliveries of this product are rapidly expanded, even if it might have to pay an additional percentage on the wholesale price from its own reserve funds, if this involves a change that would cause extra production costs. Only where this is not possible, or if producers cannot deliver the goods in a short space of time, should there be a temporary rise in market price.

This limited regulatory effect of price movement on detailed proportions of production cannot be completely excluded under socialism, if society is not to suffer large, unnecessary losses in material and labour, as well as inadequate satisfaction of the needs of consumers. This is true in a phase where the governing bodies cannot predict the individual demand patterns in detail, cannot maintain huge reserve capacities and stocks of material and goods that would balance out every unanticipated growth in demand (not to speak of the above-mentioned repeated and needless losses on unsold goods, the disproportionately large stocks of goods in the storehouses, etc.), and, finally, cannot yet do away with individual non-antagonistic conflicts of interest that appear in the detailed decisions made on production and sales of goods under socialism. Under these conditions a certain free movement of prices means much less social loss and therefore corresponds much more to the social interest of the workers than does a system of rigid, centrally established prices, which necessarily are subjectively determined.

We need not again refute the distorted view of dogmatists on the socially determined and limited influence of market prices in determining minor proportions, alleging that they negate the socialist principle of planning and introduce the regulatory role of the law of value into production. Actually a socialist society can and must, by means of the plans for society, determine the development of production in accord with the trends in social needs. It can, and must, do so to the degree it can actually assure harmony between production and consumption. But as soon as it determines the development by detailed directive plans, in contradiction to the trend in specific consumer needs, plans actually come in conflict with the interests of the population, even if they carried out the very best subjective intentions of the administrative bodies of society. Planning is not a socialist process that is an end in itself, but an essential instrument for harmonizing socialist production with the needs of a socialist society as fully as possible. To the degree that it is not possible to predict detailed demand patterns, and where a limited regulatory effect of the market on production can help to adapt more rapidly the detailed production programs to this demand (that is, to contribute to a really optimal use of the planned branch capacities), to that degree a socialist society must utilize this socialist market mechanism. Any dogmatism in this field causes a socialist economy irreplaceable material harm, and damages the prestige of socialism in the eyes of a large number of workers.

It is understandable that, together with any freer movement of prices, even if it is within constantly controlled limits, market competition has to be used as well, exerting economic pressure on the individual enterprises. Especially under conditions of socialism, where there is considerable concentration of production and, in most branches, even an explicit monopoly position of the branch directorship (management), the danger has arisen that the enterprises will misuse the system of free prices for speculative purposes. Therefore, together with a relative free formation of prices, all possible anti-monopoly measures must be applied, as well as measures that will encourage market competition for all production.

The principle of market competition must have as much weight for the central administrative bodies as the principle of concentration and specialization of production, and both must be constantly observed in their inter-relationships. Concentration and specialization of production makes possible a considerable increase in mass production, which lowers production costs. But this should not be merely an administratively created concentration that leaves actual production dispersed. Moreover, specialization of production has not the same value and importance in all branches of production.

If a monopoly is formed in a certain branch of production by purely organizational means, while production remains divided among a large number of individual enterprises producing the same kind of goods, the conditions exist for making the larger enterprises independent and thus overcome the monopoly situation created merely by organizational measures. This also provides the conditions for market competition among these enterprises and an inter-acting pressure on the development of quality of products and reduction of prices. Together with this, attention must be constantly given from the governing centre to this branch of production and effective action taken against any tendency toward monopoly agreements and procedures.

In some branches of production, especially in the consumer goods industry, specialization of production is not so important, because here there is a continual need to produce many types of goods on a smaller scale, which have to be constantly modified to stimulate market demand. In such branches any sort of monopoly organization of production comes into conflict with the requirement to increase the influence of the market on the development of production. In these branches it will be necessary to assure permanent market competition between some independent enterprises for the benefit of the consumer interests.

Even in those branches where concentration and specialization of production is inevitably of great importance and where the world level of production (for instance, in engineering, metallurgy, etc.) cannot be assured without considerable monopoly in production (especially in the economy of a small state like Czechoslovakia) the pressure of market competition must be applied through foreign trade. In such highly specialized branches of production, usually, exports also have great importance, so that the direct pressure of world markets and the direct impact of prices on the exporting enterprises can form a sufficiently strong instrument against monopoly speculations. Similarly, the purposeful use of imports of both consumer goods and means of production exerts the necessary economic pressure on domestic producers, whether they do or do not have a monopoly position. We shall speak later of the application of these instruments in connection with financial policy.

From the standpoint of price development, we see that foreign trade must have decisive influence in gradually bringing nearer the level and relations of domestic prices to the prices on the main world markets. These are the markets that are typical and determinative for the type of goods in question, where prices are influenced by broad world competition and there is rather less monopolist speculation.

The policy of gradually increasing the pressure of these prices on domestic prices will limit in an economic way the price speculation in this country without having to restrict their movement by directives.

This is not to say that it will be necessary or possible simply to adapt all domestic price relationships to world prices. Prices here must always express primarily the actual production costs and the market relationships at home. The pressure on our products exerted by world prices for exports or imports of goods will be primarily a pressure to cut production costs in this country more rapidly and to improve the quality and modernity of our goods, as well as being a healthy obstacle to monopoly tendencies. In this way the conditions of production and prices will be gradually adapted to world prices in all cases where domestic products lag behind. This must be done in a progressive way, stimulated and accelerated by the economic policy of the state.

Although the application of a system of market competition is of prime importance as the most suitable instrument against monopolistic abuse of the relatively free movement of market prices, a socialist system cannot completely abandon some administrative restrictions of price movements of the larger price groups. And, of course, it must set by central directives the most important, key prices. Especially in the initial period when there are great disproportions and market competition cannot yet function sufficiently, there will need to be a certain limitation of the movement of larger price groups. This limitation on the extent of price movement must not, however, prevent the signalling to producers by price changes the trends in market demand and the creating of an economic interest in the production enterprises in making the necessary changes in production.

Furthermore, the centrally fixed prices of the most important products should not be understood as rigid, unchanging prices. They must change gradually as the production and market conditions change. It will be mainly a question of setting obligatory or maximum prices of basic types of the consumers' vital needs, staple foods, basic raw material, fuel, energy, etc., and, perhaps, introducing obligatory or minimum purchase prices for the basic agricultural products. The central administration of these prices must not be bureaucratic but must rely on continual market analyses and the production situation. It is understandable, however, that these basic and economically decisive prices — even though there must be some movement — will be steadier than prices that are not centrally administered.

It can be taken for granted that in this price system there must be some control on price movements at a high qualitative level, which should be connected with a continual analysis of price movements. In case of obvious price speculation — if there is intentional creation of scarcity on the market, by underutilization of available capacities, raw materials, and other production possibilities — the central bodies must have the authority to draw off the speculative profits by setting special additional charges.

We can expect that this will be only an exceptional case, and, after all, the socialist society will always have enough means of doing away with such speculation, if there really are evidences of unsocial interests, of remnants of private interest tendencies to profiteer. Therefore, the fact that such isolated cases can appear should not mean that we reject the use of any socialist market relations and dogmatically insist that socialist planning is incompatible with a limited regulatory use of the law of value.

The greater and the better the level of utilization of all exact methods of studying the movement of inventories in trade, of collecting and rapidly, automatically conveying information to producers by means of the most modern record-keeping, calculating and communication technique, the more rapidly and flexibly such information will get from trade to the producers and the more consistently all production reserves (capacity, material, etc.) will be utilized, the more rapid and flexible will be the reaction of production to detailed (even daily) changes in the stocks of goods and the narrower will be the fluctuations of market prices. At this stage of development a more important condition will be the possibility of relatively free movement of market prices, linked with the use of market competition.

Summary

In general, we may sum up as follows: even under socialism the basis of prices is value, and the movement of prices must permanently solve the contradictions that arise between value and use value. This objectively necessary essence and function of prices is an expression of the fact that the exchange relationships among all types of enterprises (in the above-described economic concept) are still essentially market relations. But, at the same time, one must see the special socialist character of these market relations and the decisive significance of direct social orientation of the development of total social labour, which appears also in the special character and price movement as the main form of expressing market relationships.

Value under socialism must be necessarily transformed into socialist *production price*, which is the condition for the optimum development of the social extended reproduction process. Production price appears as a long-term logical tendency within the actual movement of wholesale prices, by means of which goods are exchanged between socialist enterprises (in production and trade). The movement of *wholesale prices* contributes toward the flexible solution of the non-antagonistic contradictions that arise between socialist enterprises (between seller and buyer, producer and consumer).

Production prices are the base for *trade prices* — that is, the basic construction of prices of consumer goods. The sale of goods to the public is the concluding phase of a renewing process of exchanging the results of the different work activities between the relatively independent socialist collectives of workers (in the economic and even non-economic sphere). The trade prices assure the equivalence of these exchanges, assure each working member of society consumption at a value that corresponds — after certain deductions are made for society as a whole — to the amount of socially necessary labour he has expended for society. They also assure the realization of a part of surplus product used to cover some of the social consumption.

Trade prices express the necessary prevailing long-term tendency within the short-term movements of *market prices*. Market prices of consumer goods, by their specific movement, contribute to the solution of the contradictions between value and use value which arise in the production of consumer goods. The relatively free movement of market prices contributes towards a faster and more flexible adaptation of production and supply to demand for individual types of goods, to the extent that society cannot directly assure this harmony of supply and demand in detail and in advance.

IV MONEY UNDER SOCIALISM

1 Previous Concepts of Money under Socialism

When there is commodity production there must also be money.
A well–developed commodity production and market cannot do
without money. Money is the general equivalent, expressing the
value of all kinds of goods, and is, furthermore, the means that makes
possible the circulation of goods.

Without a general equivalent it would not be possible to express
the value of different goods in developed commodity production. It
is enough to imagine what it would mean if the value of each good
had to be expressed over and over again in terms of every other commodity for which it was bartered. In developed commodity production, the direct barter of goods for other goods is unthinkable.
Nor can socialist commodity production, as highly developed commodity production, do without real money which performs functions that are universally needed for commodity production in
general.

We are not concerned in this work to solve all complicated specific
problems connected with the functioning of money under socialism.
Other theoretical works are needed to elaborate such questions as
the development of the purchasing power of money, the role of the
state in administering the circulation of money, assuring its stability,
circulation by currency and bank transactions, convertibility of cur-

rency under socialism, controlling and utilizing financial processes, etc. Here we are interested in carrying forward the theoretical conclusions about the existence of commodity production and market relationships, derived from certain intrinsic contradictions of a socialist economy, to the field of money. We must show that money under socialism is actual money, arising from the same contradictions that give birth to commodity production and to bring up the problems that exist in present money practice and which must be solved in the near future, theoretically and practically in most socialist countries.

Every timeworn practice and theory which tried to suppress or formalize commodity relations under socialism regarded money as mere accounting units that fill certain technical functions for accounting and record-keeping, but no longer serve to solve economic and therefore social contradictions. Even though most official theories in the Soviet Union and other socialist countries spoke of money as actual money, they were content to make a formal enumeration of its functions as a measure of value, means of circulation, of payment, etc., without showing that these functions are a necessary expression and form of solution of certain economic and interest contradictions also under socialism. Even though some of these theories admit the existence of contradictions between use value and value of commodities and a certain role for money in the solution of this contradiction (cf. the latest edition of the Soviet textbook, *Political Economy*, Moscow 1963), firstly, they do not explain this contradiction as a necessary expression of the contradiction arising from the very character of labour at the socialist stage of development of production forces, reflected also as a non-antagonistic contradiction between group (enterprise) and society's interests[1], and, se-

---

[1] They admit only the contradiction between the concrete expenditure of labour and the socially necessary labour from the standpoint that there are different social-economic sectors (state and co-operative) and, therefore, differing stages of socialization of labour, which is simply a repetition of the Stalinist theoretical explanation of socialist commodity production. They attach to this the explanation of the contradiction between use value and value as an expression of the active "contradiction between the achieved value of production and the growing needs of society and its members" (*Political Economy*, 4th ed., Czech translation 1963, p. 520). But this is merely an abstract formulation that evades the actual solution of the problem. It does not say what gave rise to this contradiction in a situation when production was to be constantly harmonized in a planned way with the

condly, they believe that this contradiction can be solved merely by conscious planning by the state, centrally administering every single price and money transaction. This is a purely superficial concept of the economic contradictions under socialism.

This superficial and simplified concept of commodity and money relations, using theories that do not formally deny the existence of these relationships, does not actually differ much from the theories that consistently reject the possibility of having real commodity-money relationships under socialism. That is, even if in the essence of the answer to the question whether commodity-money relations do or do not exist under socialism we come up to an evident contradiction between these two theoretical trends, this remains only a formal contradictory assertion. Neither the proponents of the first nor those of the second demand in their conclusions anything that would require a fundamental change in the present economic practice prevailing in socialist countries and agree essentially with the conclusions that, with the aid of the most modern computer technique, we must begin to calculate the value of products, or, rather, the socially necessary amount of labour expended on each product.

Although it is stated in the above-mentioned textbook of political economy that, for example, not even a direct calculation and recording of social labour makes it possible to eliminate commodity-money relations under socialism, it fails to emphasize the ways in which money and price, their function and movements, differ from the so-called exact expression of social labour by certain money units

trends in demand and tacitly present this contradiction as a mere expression of the impossibility of *fully* planning this harmony. But even this inability is evidently conceived of as a difficulty in cognition and they completely ignore the existence of conflicts of interest. This theory avoids answering the questions whether the solution of this contradiction is or is not the necessary price movement, whether the level and movement of prices has an influence on the interests and the decisions of the production enterprises or not, whether the existence of a given price system stimulates or retards the introduction of new products and better satisfaction of needs, whether conflicts arise between the interests of state enterprises as producers and as consumers, or not, whether prices and money have a definite function in solving these contradictions, etc. Evading all these questions, this theory ignores the essence of the problem and remains an eclectic heap of various abstract and superficially specific, dogmatic and empirical assertions.

(rubles, etc.), as envisaged, for example, by I. S. Malyshev, one of the typical proponents of the second group of ideas.

To quote from his views: "In order to transform all the different kinds of concrete labour in one type of social labour of the same quality, a socialist society expresses all these kinds of labour in a standard (unchanging) price valuation, and thus expresses a unit of social labour in a certain amount of money."[1]

Or, further: "A certain sum of money is, under socialism, nothing other than evidence of a certain amount of social labour, i.e., a certain number of products. We say so and so many rubles, and we have in mind a certain amount of social labour, or vice versa, we have in view the labour expended and express it in rubles. The social method of expressing labour in money terms is fundamentally different from the method of expressing these costs in commodity production. There it is done in an elemental way and here it is an organized process. There they are expressing one kind of human relationships, here we are expressing others. This is the essence of the matter."[2]

These ideas roughly reflect the notions concerning the direct distributive function of money in regard to the expended amount of labour in society, as held by the petty bourgeois ideologist Proudhon in his day (even if they are based on completely different economic premises). Proudhon wanted under capitalism to introduce something in the nature of "labour money". He thought it sufficed to calculate how many hours of labour must be expended on the production of the different products and, according to the total number of labour hours contained in all the individual products, to issue paper stamps, say, in the ratio of one stamp to one hour -- with the total number of one-hour stamps figured according to the total number of hours contained in the consumer goods. These views, in certain interpretations, admit that there are different qualities of labour. That is, they say, all jobs must be classified by complexity and quality in various groups and converted, using a certain key, to simple labour hours. For example, labour in Group IV, carried out in one hour

---

[1] I. S. Malyshev, *Obshchestvenny uchet truda i tsena pri socializme* (General Calculation of Labour and Price under Socialism), Moscow 1960, p. 92.
[2] *Ibid.*, p. 93.

would equal two hours of labour in Group I. In this way all the different kinds of labour, contained in the commodities, are converted to simple labour and the total amount of labour is then expressed by the total amount of simple labour hours.

The different members of society, then, should get an amount of labour money that would correspond to the hours they have worked in terms of simple labour. And for this labour money they have received, for this work, people would obtain products containing the same number of labour hours.

It is, therefore, essentially the "theory" of Proudhon's labour money, saying that under socialism today it is feasible, because labour is now directly social labour. Of course, this view is no less idealistic than it was in Proudhon's time. It is true it has as its point of departure the correct statement that, under socialism, labour is *directly* oriented social labour and that consumer goods are distributed according to work performed. It ignores, however, the fact that there is far from full harmony between the specifically expended labour and the socially necessary labour and that within the general development of social labour marked out by plan there still arise contradictory tendencies in the specific expenditure of labour, which compels the existence of commodity relationships. This view, that is to say, ignores the fact that socialist production is still necessarily commodity production. It does not comprehend that, while commodity relations help to overcome the contradictions within social labour, they cannot eliminate them. It is complete underestimation of the intrinsic contradictions of commodity production and their objective causes. From this it follows further, that those who hold these ideas consider money under socialism only as a means of distributing income according to labour, and not that it is an expression of contradiction in commodity production, not as a necessary means of solving the contradiction within the commodity.

It is true that money under socialism is used so that part of the products are distributed among the different workers according to work performed. But the necessity for this is not the reason for the existence of money or for the existence of value. If, for example, there were no commodity production, but there still was a necessity to distribute according to work performed (and one could imagine this), then there would still need to be some labour money or stamps to distribute according to work performed, probably in the form we have spoken of. But anyone who identifies the exchange of goods with the distribution according to work performed fails to understand the essence of production and exchange of goods.

When goods are sold, the producer does not receive stamps for work performed, but value in the form of money in return for value in the form of goods. This is quite a different concept. Wherein lies the difference?

a) First of all, the individual labour of the producer of the goods does not decide how much money he will receive — which would be the case if the distribution were made according to work performed. The decisive matter is the value of the type of goods he sells. But that is determined, not by the individual labour, but by the socially necessary labour. He could receive more — or less — than his individual labour time amounted to.

b) In some cases the producer of the goods does not even receive the value represented by the money equivalent to the value of his goods, but a smaller, or sometimes greater value (that is, a lower or higher price than the value). The deviation of specific prices from the value or the production or the trade price is the expression of disproportions in production. As the process of realizing the income of the production collective in relation to the degree of social worth of the work they performed, it is also an important stimulus to increase or decrease the production of certain goods.

c) Finally, the producer of the goods need not get the equivalent for his goods in money. He has expended the labour, but he has not been able to sell the goods. He will not receive the equivalent of his labour, because it did not count as social labour. This is also possible under socialism in isolated cases. Here also it can appear as expression of the contradictions in commodity production that some goods are not sold at all. Socialist producers can have great losses in income after they have expended the labour, whether they are producers' cooperatives or state enterprises.

Here money is not a system of mere stamps, by means of which society carries out some sort of distribution, but represents value as an expression of general social labour — they are its embodiment. When collective producers receive money for their goods, they get a certain value represented by the money. This means that their

310

labour, expended on the production of certain goods asserted itself as a part of the general social labour (which cannot be ascertained in advance, directly — the expression of this is the existence of commodity production). A given collective always receives the value of a certain magnitude, a certain amount of money, but it is probable that this value (in this whole section on money I abstract the argument from the transformation of value into production and trade prices) represents a smaller or, it may be, a greater amount of labour than was actually expended on the production of the goods. But this is not evidence of an incorrect application of remuneration according to work performed, but, on the contrary, a necessary expression of the contradictions in commodity production. Either it is an expression of the fact that socially necessary labour is different from that expended by a certain enterprise, or of the fact that all the collectives (enterprises) producing the same goods expended together more — or less — work on goods of the same type than society needs.

That is to say, money represents a certain value, independent of the values of all other types of goods, which the producers receive in a certain quantitative ratio to the value of their own goods, while in this ratio there appear rather more complex relationships than a simple, direct social distribution according to work performed.

Economists who believe that money under socialism is merely "labour" money — obviously do not understand the fundamentals of a general equivalent and the necessity for it in commodity production. It is the underestimation of the objective reasons for commodity production and of its contradictions that gives rise to the idea that there already exist conditions for simply calculating time expended on the production of goods and for each individual to receive a corresponding share according to his individual working time. They do not understand that there are not yet the objective conditions for such a calculation of time, and that even such "calculation" would not eliminate the contradictions of commodity production. The inability to calculate the work time is not, therefore, merely a matter of incorrect cognition, but mainly an expression of the objective reasons for commodity production.

If the socialist character of labour changes, if the internal contradiction of labour that is typical of present-day labour and commodity production ceases to exist, then the objective conditions for expressing

311

the amount of labour expended on all products directly in terms of time could be brought about (for planning and similar purposes). Until that time arrives, however, value and price cannot be replaced by a direct calculation of all kinds of social labour in time equivalents, but value must be expressed by money which is the general equivalent of the value of all goods.

The economists who pronounce in the above-mentioned textbook that money is actual money under socialism go no farther than this meaningless assertion in differing from those who would essentially like to reduce money to record-keeping stamps. Precisely because they speak of all the functions of money as functions that can, under socialism, be used *only* in a planned way and consciously by the state, they show that they do not comprehend, or do not want to, the character of economic contradictions under socialism and that they absolutize the planning and conscious direction of socialist economic management. This is why — though they disclaim it — they reduce money finally to mere calculating units that the state uses to express, measure and keep records of the quantity of production and distribute it among institutions and individuals.

As long as the idea exists that all contradictions between use value and value can be solved *only* by planned intervention by the central governing body or by general moral and political appeals to the enterprises; that, furthermore, the central body can find out not only the value of each individual commodity, but also necessary deviations of price from value for assuring harmony of supply and demand; and that any change in price can be made *only* by a central directive — until that time the idea will prevail of an over-simplified and formalized relation, rather than an actual socialist commodity-money relationship. Although those who hold these ideas know that no central governing body can replace the direct relation of interest between producers and consumers in selling and buying millions of types of goods, and that they cannot know all about the constantly changing concrete, detailed needs of the consumers, the detailed production and sales conditions; although they know that in no sphere is there so much subjective judgment as in the sphere of practical price formation, which is the reason for a constant piling up on the one hand of unsalable goods that are spoiling and losing their usefulness, while on the other hand consumers cannot obtain many kinds of scarce goods — despite all this, these economists insist on a price formation where money does not in fact either express value or help to solve, in its function as means of circulation and payment, the contradictions of commodity production.

These economists well know, for example, that under the old system the loans made to the enterprises are not genuine credit, because its repayment does not affect the material interest of the enterprises. The credit obtained by the enterprises for various production purposes is mechanically counted in the costs of production and, just as mechanically, is paid from the account of these costs. Whether the loan is used more or less effectively, whether it is paid off in a shorter or longer period of time, has no substantial influence on the level of material remuneration of the workers of the enterprise. The relative savings in economizing on credit cannot be used for paying wages. Even if the producing enterprise uses credit to produce goods that remain unsold in the storehouses, or are sold at great loss on the domestic of foreign market, this inefficient use of credit does not endanger the material interest of the enterprise as long as it fulfills the plan. Therefore, credit does not act as material stimulus for more efficient management and economizing on means of production. Money functions in this case only formally as a means of payment and does not help actually to solve the economic contradictions. Nevertheless, the authors of the above-mentioned textbook are not bothered by this fact when they formally enumerate the functions of money under socialism.

The formal statement made by these economists that money under socialism fulfills the function of a general equivalent and the other functions that were generally discovered by Marx has no theoretical significance so long as it is not bolstered by a study of why these functions *actually are not performed* in socialist practice as known hitherto or why there is such a conflict between the abstract theoretical statement and the economic reality. It does not help to solve the economic contradictions that are actually growing up, nor can it refute the completely idealistic speculations that deny the necessity for commodity-money relations under socialism. Only if we realize that there are certain economic conflicts of interest that cannot be solved in a socialist society without money and if we have the courage to change fundamentally economic practice so that commodity-

313

money relations can *actually* help to solve these contradictions, can we begin to do away with the conflict between general theoretical assertions and the actual functioning of money in socialist economic practice.

2   The Function of Money under Socialism

a   Internal and External Conditions for the Value Base of Money

When we speak of money, we have in mind primarily a definite object which functions as a general measure or representative of value, as a means of circulation or of payment and retainer of exchange value.

But if gold can be successfully replaced by paper money for the internal circulation in capitalist countries, and thus the convertibility of this paper money for gold done away with, it is even the more likely that a monetary system can be assured within socialist countries where private economic interests can no longer take the upper hand over social needs and violate the socially managed circulation of money. There are ways and means of assuring the relative stability of the price level or of preventing it from developing spontaneously. We shall discuss these instruments later. This ensures that paper money is used (either by individuals or by economic or other institutions) not only as a circulating medium and means of payment, but also as a retainer of exchange value with various forms of saving or of temporary postponement of monetary expenditures.

Not even under socialism can paper money serve as a measure of value, because it has no value in itself (or the insignificant value of the paper), but only indirectly expresses a certain value. From the standpoint of purely internal functions of money within socialist countries, it would not be necessary to have a gold basis at all. In setting the prices of individual types of goods, they are not compared with the value of gold, as we have shown in the preceding chapter. Fundamentally the basic price calculations arise from certain cost prices or reproduction costs, and with one system or another of forming the specific price relationships. There is a price continuity in which not only the continual quantitative changes in price relations, but also more thorough-going, across-the-board changes in price level (price reforms) are caused by various circumstances and follow out various economic or political aims. But always the old, accepted prices are worked with, converted in different ways (either increasing or decreasing) to change the over-all price level or the price pattern.

All these over-all, more thorough-going changes in the price level are not caused essentially by some *a priori* spontaneous change in the amount of circulating medium, but on the contrary, a purposefully determined change in level of income and prices, and thereby in the sum of prices of goods and services, compels changes in the amount of money, with a given function of money as a measure of price (usually a traditional, historical one). With a system of central price formation and with the old administrative system of management, prices of different types of goods had to deviate more and more from the value of goods (in a very different, arbitrary way), and money, therefore, lost *de facto* its function as a measure of value.

Under the new *economic* system of management, a production price can assert itself as the basic trend of its developmental motion, within the relatively free, market formation of most prices, whereby a constant mutual comparison of reproduction costs and production prices of the different types and groups of products, mainly by the production enterprises themselves, will be made.

In this system one cannot, of course, say that the price of each individual type of goods expresses its value. Nevertheless, that value forms the most general, though modified, basis for prices (the socialist production price), is revealed in the fact, that sooner or later, each change in overall socially necessary amount of labour expended on the production of a certain type of goods appears in the commensurate direction of change in price. The total sum of prices of all goods, then, must represent the *total value* expressed by a historically originating amount of money.

Without free convertibility of currency for gold and without a purposeful alteration of the gold content of a monetary unit by the state when the value of gold changes (in some cases without altering the prices of all goods as a result of the change in value of gold, retaining the nominal content of a monetary unit), there is actually no longer any comparison of the value of goods, by means of money, with the value of gold. There is only an approximate *mutual* comparison of the value of individual types of goods by comparing their production costs or production prices. Value as the amount of materialized socially necessary abstract labour expressed by money, can be only roughly represented quantitatively by means of the total price of a certain large, selected group of various kinds of products, where one could assume that deviations of their production prices from value will balance each other out. A certain sum of money, thus, represents always a certain general value appearing, with greater or less deviation, by means of the price of various types of goods and as a general representative of value, and can also fulfil the function of circulating medium, means of payment and retainer of exchange value.

But not even under socialism can money be completely severed from its gold basis, as long as there is foreign trade (or any other foreign financial transaction), especially between socialist and capitalist states. With such inter-state exchange there is no sole international currency, nor can there be at present (not even among socialist countries, as long as there is a substantially unequal level of production costs). Prices must be recalculated in the currency of one country into prices expressed in the currency of the other. There is, therefore, a need to fix reciprocal rates of currency exchange (between socialist countries as well), which would assure the equivalence of the exchange of use values, i.e., a ratio between the units of exchange of the two states where the fixed volume of currency would express roughly the same purchasing power.

Although it is possible — as we have shown — to determine these reciprocal rates of exchange by using as point of departure the comparison of prices of certain selected, representative goods (which, of course assumes that there are similar price relations among the basic types of goods and services), which to a certain degree already occurs among capitalist countries, this cannot prevent an unequal development of purchasing power of different currencies or of the balance of payments of the different countries. To assure relative stability of the reciprocal rates of exchange and an increased assurance of the sellers and buyers in international exchange transactions, gold must remain the basis of all currencies. Or it could be a currency that has relatively stable gold coverage and an international gold convertibility.

Let us, for the time being, leave aside the currency problem in relations among socialist countries and first observe this problem from the standpoint of the need for foreign-trade and other value relations between socialist and capitalist countries. Socialist countries do not get along without foreign trade with capitalist and developing countries. This is especially true of such countries as Czechoslovakia, which, by no insignificant part of its national income is commercially linked with these countries. Both the increasing foreign trade and the inevitable growth in tourist trade necessitate setting a certain rate of foreign exchange between the socialist state and capitalist states, and together with this, the expression of gold parity of the socialist country's currency.

In relations among capitalist states the gold standard has been replaced by a "monetary gold standard" where the price of gold is determined *de facto* in a monopolist way (a long-range artificially maintained gold parity in relation to the dollar, for example, regardless of the real exchange value or the supply of gold on the market) and, by means of special international agreements and funds, keep the rates of exchange fairly high among the signers of the agreement. As a consequence, the socialist countries are compelled to express the gold parity of their currency when they trade or have other economic contacts with capitalist countries. Of course they base this on the price of gold, set in a monopolist way and expressed, e.g., by the gold parity of the dollar and its actual purchasing power. When they sell their goods on capitalist markets they convert the prices obtained on these markets to prices in domestic currencies, by using officially established gold parities of their currencies and foreign rates of exchange set on this basis.

The question arises whether the fixing of these rates of exchange and of gold parity of socialist currencies are of significance only in foreign trade or have even only a technical accounting significance in converting foreign exchanges made in world prices to domestic prices, or if there must be direct economic links between the foreign trade and domestic prices; whether, therefore, there is a connection between rates of foreign exchange, gold parity and the internal purchasing power of the socialist currency.

Under the old administrative system of management the prices were formed within a socialist country without any relation whatsoever to world prices, the domestic market is completely severed from foreign markets and trade and the actual internal purchasing power of the currency is not tested in foreign trade transactions. The export of the socialist currency beyond the borders of the country, as well as its sale for foreign currency is forbidden to private persons as well as to all institutions and organizations. It is the exclusive prerogative of the appropriate state body (state bank or an empowered exchange office) to exchange, for visitors from abroad, foreign currency at an established rate into the local currency. Foreign trade is carried on without the use of the domestic currency at prices set on foreign markets. Payments coming from the trade operations are realized in the usual world payment media.

Under this practice, the gold parity is set for the domestic currency by the socialist state (e.g., the present equivalent is one crown = 0.123426 grams of pure gold), but this has no real significance except in bookkeeping and for keeping records of foreign trade and foreign payments, within the state and as a basis of comparison in setting the exchange rates. It has no relation to prices on the domestic market. Determining the gold content of the crown means also establishing its official rate of exchange in regard to other world currencies (i.e., one dollar = 7.20 crowns, etc.). Through this crown of gold parity the domestic wholesale prices are converted to the prices actually obtained for goods exported on world markets and, vice versa, prices paid for imported goods are converted into the domestic wholesale prices. For example, one exported lathe of a certain type has a domestic wholesale price of 20,000 crowns and its world dollar price is 1,388.9 dollars; at the above-described gold parity and in the official dollar rate of exchange for the crown, the price in crowns of gold parity, the so-called trade parity, is 1,388.9 times 7.2 or about 10,000 crowns.

The gold parity of the crown set in this way does not express the relation of this crown to the goods sold on the domestic market, and therefore has no relation to the prices that are valid on the domestic market in regard to prices obtained on world markets. The price set in the crown of trade parity differs considerably from the price in the domestic market crown. The export at 10,000 crowns of trade parity cannot be covered by goods that cost 10,000 crowns on the domestic market, because the prices on the domestic market are completely different prices, expressed in different crowns than the prices prevailing in foreign trade and recalculated in trade parity. This is not changed by the fact that, for example, some exceptional commodity could by chance have a domestic price identical with price in trade parity. Therefore our foreign trade enterprises must constantly convert the domestic prices of exported goods into prices in trade parity and vice versa.

Characteristic of this situation is the existence of several different rates of conversion of domestic currency to foreign, with different methods of exchange (e.g., the rate for tourist who come to this country, for trips made by people in this country to foreign countries, for various non-commodity transactions, etc.). This is necessary because the gold parity of the crown does not reflect the real purchasing power of the crown on the domestic market, determined in domestic prices. If, for example, 100 dollars are exchanged for 720 crowns in accordance with the gold parities of the two currencies, one cannot buy for these 720 crowns the amount and types of goods on our internal market that one could on world markets for 100 dollars or that would compare with our exports for 720 crowns at trade parity.

According to the old, over-simplified concept of commodity-money relations under socialism, this economic practice was accepted as unchangeable, and therefore it was noted even theoretically that the determination of the gold content of the monetary unit follows two different, unconnected, purposes or rather purposes artificially divided by practice. One of them was to determine the parity of domestic currency for foreign-trade calculations and the other to fix a certain nominal value of the domestic monetary unit to assure its function as a measure of value.[1]

---

[1] This, for example, is how the expression of the value of goods within a country by the value of gold by nominally determining the gold content of the ruble is explained in the Soviet textbook of *Political Economy*, Moscow 1963, Czech translation:

"As we know, the function of measure of value can be fulfilled only by a monetary commodity having value itself. This monetary commodity is gold. In the Soviet Union and in other countries of the Socialist camp, gold has the role of general equivalent." (p. 523).

"Since the ruble has gold content, the planning bodies that plan the costs of production and set the prices of goods, that is, compare the value of goods with money, express in this way this value in gold." (p. 524).

With this concept of value, any connection between world and domestic prices was considered superfluous, and the gold content of the monetary unit was, from the standpoint of setting domestic prices, considered only as the fixing of the value of money without comparing in reality the value of the goods sold on the internal market with the value of gold. Prices of commodities or their mutual relationships were not, in fact, affected by changes in the value of gold and did not express — as we have shown — even the actual value of the different goods and their reciprocal value relationship. Although the domestic value of goods actually was not expressed in money, and the prices were formed in a very subjective way, some economists considered this state of affairs only as an expression of imperfect technique, record-keeping or skills in calculating value and did not demand more in their abstract theory than a more precise expression of the domestic value of money.

Despite this discrepancy between the theory about the function of gold as a domestic measure of value and the economic practice no account is taken in this concept of the great and fundamental influence of foreign trade (and in recent years the tourist trade, etc.) on the development of the home economy. It overlooks the fact that it is not feasible to create such artificial barriers between the domestic and the world prices, as well as between the money serving the home market and that used in foreign trade transactions, as has been done hitherto. The greater the weight and significance of foreign trade for the development of a certain socialist economic entity, the less it is possible to sever its internal value relationships from the foreign. (Of course, even in the case of countries where foreign trade has no such economic weight, the lag in development of values on the home market behind the world development is an expression of general economic backwardness).

When this is the practice, not only is there no pressure of world markets on the development of home production, with a constantly increasing lag behind world development, but also a growing part of the domestic value is gradually transformed, through foreign trade, into a relatively diminishing value realized on foreign markets and for this a relatively smaller amount of use values is imported, without these losses being counted or recorded, not to speak of bearing material responsibility. In this situation foreign trade does not serve

320

as it usually does — to increase the national income of the country taking into account comparative advantage (comparative costs). On the contrary, there is a gradual loss of national income that considerably increases the above-mentioned contradictions within the social reproduction process. At the same time, it becomes quite evident that no country can with impunity sever its internal value relationships for a long period and to a substantial extent, allowing these to lag behind world value relationships.

Another consequence of this finding is that the internal function of monetary units as representative of value cannot be mechanically separated from their functions as representatives of value in foreign-trade exchanges. That is, one cannot create something like special monetary units for foreign transactions, functioning only as an artificial measure of prices without the function of representing the value of goods on the home market. On the contrary we must see the inseparable connection of all internal and external functions of money, and, therefore, also of money under socialism, if it is conceived of as actual money.

Among other things, this means that the monetary unit expressing the value of a commodity, both as it is sold at home and as exported goods, must also for purposes of foreign trade express the value of an amount of gold (representing a certain exchange value on an international scale with a certain international purchasing power), which could be used on the home market with roughly the same exchange value (for a given amount of the monetary units representing it, crowns for instance, the usual international volume of use values can be bought on the home market). In other words, it is a question of making it possible to buy, for the amount of domestic currency expended on a certain amount of typical and comparable types of goods and representing for the purposes of international trade a certain amount of gold when exchanged according to the official gold parity for a certain amount of foreign monetary units, roughly the same amount of goods on foreign markets.

Let us clarify this complicated affair with a quite simplified example. If a certain amount of very diversified types of goods costs on the home market 10,000 crowns and the same amount of essentially the same type of goods on world markets has the price expressed in an amount of foreign currency that represents 100 grams of gold, then these 10,000 crowns should also roughly represent 100 grams of gold. The accounting unit of the domestic currency, in our case one crown, would then represent 0.01 gram of gold. Then the higher the domestic price, the less gold the monetary unit would represent and vice versa. Assuming that the given amount of goods cost 20,000 crowns on the home market, one crown could represent only 0.005 grams of gold, so that one could obtain, in turn, 100 grams of gold or foreign currency (e.g. dollars) representing 100 grams of gold, which would again correspond to the price of roughly the same amount of goods on foreign markets.

When this is the practice — that the official gold parity of the currency is altered with a great change in price of a certain, selected, representative group of goods (and services) on the home market, or if there is a marked change in the international price of gold (if, for example, there is a cumulative change in gold parity of foreign currencies, such as a mass devaluation), it becomes possible to express the value of commodities not only by means of the domestic currency on the home market, but also to compare this value immediately and constantly with the value of the same goods on foreign markets. In this situation the function of money as representing the value of domestic goods is no longer severed from its function as a calculating unit (measure of price) in converting domestic currency to foreign. Furthermore, this does not separate the function of money at home, as the representative of value, from the world general equivalent function as a measure of value. This makes it possible to constantly compare the domestic value with international value which prevails on world markets.

The gold parity of the monetary unit, by means of which this currency can be compared with foreign currencies (serving to express the value of the goods in international trade) therefore makes it possible to compare directly the value of a certain quantity of domestic commodities with the value of goods on world markets.

The money, representing in this instance the actual amount of general, abstract social labour (appearing on an international scale as the necessary amount of labour to produce a certain amount of gold), makes possible the comparison of the social productivity of labour on an international scale with the social productivity of labour on a national scale. In this way, the untenable contradiction growing up in the practice of socialist economies between the function of money within the country and its function in international terms, is disappearing.

Naturally, the greatest practical difficulty lies mainly in the choice of the group of commodities whose domestic price is to have a decisive effect on the setting of the gold parity of the monetary unit (considering the international exchange value of gold). In practice the states usually must proceed from the objective prices and price relations and then, with regard to the price level of a certain selected group of commodities, establish gold parity of the currency as well as the rate of exchange to foreign currencies.

It must be seen that among *national* values (production costs) of different types of goods there are always certain differences. This is especially true of the national values of commodities in socialist countries, which had for many years been completely isolated from the movement of world values as a result of the administrative system of management. These differ considerably from the level of national values of goods in coutries where the internal markets develop under substantial influence of international competition. Despite the fact that in all countries of the world some specific price relationships are formed ever anew as an expression of specific changes in production costs of one or another type of goods within the country, a basic tendency is also constantly felt, bringing closer together the production costs of the predominant part of the goods produced, as a result of international competition. For this reason, there is a natural base in most countries of the world for determining the gold parity of the currency in the form of prices of a quite broad sphere of basic types of commodities, the reciprocal relations of which do not greatly differ from the price pattern among the same types of goods in another country. This shows the effect of international competition on the formations of a world value (average world costs of production) for a quite broad group of basic types of commodities. Greater divergencies of production costs of individual types of goods from the world average are, in countries where the influence of international competition is not closed off, more the exception and certainly smaller in extent than in countries that have strongly isolated the internal production and the internal market from this international influence.

In the development of the different national economies it is essential that in certain periods the production of some types of goods be protected even if this production is for a time less productive than in other countries (who are able to export them). In such cases the need is to protect these specific home products by means of various state measures (duties, quotas or bans on import etc.). Under special conditions, determined not only by economic, but also by political and other social factors (a period of national liberation, social economic revolution, the struggle for independence, etc.), some countries may feel the need for strict protection of the development of the entire industrial production that is not yet able to stand up to international competition (especially in the initial period of industrialization), or may even need to protect the entire domestic production (for example, the whole socialized and not yet consolidated production). Under these special conditions, one can understand the need even for such a monopoly of international trade and for such a complete isolation of domestic production and the market from the effect of international competition that national value will for a short period of time, develop quite independently from the development of world value. But if such isolation lasts too long and becomes actually an instrument retarding economic growth, the development of productivity of labour in national production, as compared with the international productivity with the consequent needless losses in national income and in final consumption incurred in international trade (as was shown clearly in the analysis of the economic development of Czechoslovakia), then it must be done away with, as must all other local restrictions that hamper the development of productive forces.

There will, of course, be great difficulty connected with the transition from such conditions of complete isolation of domestic production and of the home market to conditions of substantial broadening of international competition to domestic production. It can be done only as a purposefully directed process.

Let us briefly show what problems arise in the transition to the new and economically desirable conditions, although we shall not try to exhaust these problems or examine them in detail.

As we have stated, the greatest difficulty in the sphere of monetary measures will be to determine the group of commodities, the price of which could serve as basis for establishing the economically based gold parity of the monetary unit. Precisely because such divergent levels of value and price relationships arose during the long period of isolation of Czechoslovak production and market — to take this as example — the number of specific domestic prices differing from the world prices will be relatively great, much greater than in any country that developed without this isolation. Moreover, we must realize that the whole set of problems is made more difficult by the substantial differences between wholesale and market (retail) prices within the country, with quite different relations among wholesale prices themselves and among market prices.

If, for example, the change of the gold parity of the currency were to be carried out from the standpoint of expanding the tourist trade and of eliminating some divergent rates of exchange, it would be necessary first of all to make account of the market prices of the large majority of goods and services purchased mainly by foreign tourists. The purchasing power of the domestic currency on the home market (expressed in internal retail prices) would, in this way, be compared with the purchasing power of foreign currencies on the home markets of those foreign states, and establishing an approximate equivalence would in this way form the necessary exchange basis for expanding tourist trade.

But, since as a result of the long period of uneconomic, directive price formation in our country, too great a difference has arisen not only between the wholesale price level and that of retail prices, but also often between the respective price patterns, gold parity of the crown established on the basis of retail prices cannot suit the purposes of foreign trade. The basis for calculating prices in selling commodities by the enterprises abroad is the domestic wholesale price, which must be continually compared with the corresponding prices obtained on world markets. Not only that: quite different collections of goods (different types and groups of commodities) are present in foreign-trade exchanges than in the retail sales of goods and services to tourists.

Establishing gold parity for the crown for the purspose of facilitating foreign trade transactions and comparing domestic and world value in the exportation and importation of goods requires that we proceed from a correlation of domestic and world wholesale prices for the most frequently traded types of goods. Practice has shown that the completely different relations within our domestic wholesale prices, as compared with the world relations, lead to completely different results (different conclusions on the gold parity of the crown), according to what kind of commodities are chosen for comparison. In comparing the average domestic wholesale prices of A, B, C, D types of goods with the average *world* price of these commodities, it is found that the gold content of the crown must be set at X grams, but comparing E, F, G, H bring us to the conclusion that the gold content of the crown must be Y grams. Whatever type of goods is chosen for comparison, whatever the size of the collection of goods (the average prices) compared as a basis for establishing the gold parity of the crown and thereby its rate of exchange with foreign currencies, the actual domestic wholesale prices of many types of goods will always differ from the world prices of the same types of goods. This cannot be prevented, because it is an expression of many years of differing development of our domestic production costs (values) of the individual types of goods from the development of world production costs (values) of the same types.

It will be a matter for practical solution to choose a group of commodity representatives, for comparing the purchasing power of the home and foreign currencies, such that the *relatively* greatest number of exported commodities — converted by means of the established gold parity of the crown — will roughly correspond to world prices of these types of goods (on typical world markets), and the relatively smallest number of exported types of commodities will diverge from world prices. At the same time we must, of course, take into consideration the group and prices of the imported goods. On the basis of the gold parity of home currency thus established, we may compare the development of value (price) of goods produced in this country and their world value (price), we may ascertain the differences and especially the *degree of difference* between the domestic values of various types of goods and their world values. In this way also, at every moment of the development, certain types or groups of goods are found to have a domestic value (necessary costs of production) that is higher than the world value, and therefore their export at a price set by world value is disadvantageous. In the case of other types of goods it is the reverse and export is profitable. The reverse in each case applies to imports.

The economic system of management will compel production to find ways of maintaining a foreign market by decreasing production costs for the goods not advantageous to export, or ways of replacing them with more profitable types of goods. But when this transition to more efficient technology or to producing other goods requires a longer period of time, during which it will not be possible, from the standpoint of the interest in maintaining the market connections, to cease exporting the unsuitable production, it will be up to the production enterprise to make careful consideration, in the framework of the enterprise's over-all economy, of what are its possibilities. In an extreme case it will be necessary for the state to give assistance in the form of temporary tax-relief or by other means. In the imports of goods some home products with a value (cost of production) that may be higher than the world value, there can also be temporary protection in the form of customs duties and similar instruments. But all such protective measures that actually make up the losses resulting from backwardness of productivity of labour in home production and from high production costs, must be exceptional measures for a limited period of time, so that they will not become a harmful protection of general, long term economic backwardness.

These are, however, problems of foreign trade and payments policy, the analysis of which does not concern us at this point. We wished only to indicate the way to gradually overcome the untenable barriers between the functions of money within a socialist economy and its functions on an international scale, connecting especially their functions as representative of value of domestic commodities with the function of measuring value of goods traded on the world markets, and the actual economic determination of gold parity of the home currency and of the foreign exchange rates related to it.

In a situation where there are great differences between the relations of wholesale and retail prices within a socialist economy, it may be unavoidable for a certain period to establish even a special rate of exchange for purposes of the tourist trade (tourist rates). As we have already said, in such a case the purchasing power of the home currency is compared with foreign currency on the basis of domestic *retail* prices and usually of different collections of goods and services. From these comparisons the need for somewhat different exchange relationships than those prevailing in foreign trade relationships may arise. The need for these special tourist rates disappears as soon as the level and pattern of retail (market) prices begins to approximate the level and relation of wholesale prices, as is the case in most capitalist countries.

The question arises whether it would not be possible to do without the gold base for currencies in exchange relations among socialist countries.

If the division of labour and cooperation among socialist countries and their mutual trade relations are to develop successfully and rapidly, there must, first of all, be assured such mutual exchange rates as would assure a genuine equivalence of exchange in the sense described above. Under conditions of a gold standard, gold is the direct measure of value in relation to which the representative value of money is generally expressed, and on this basis its reciprocal exchange rates. The system of the gold-exchange standard means an attempt — given the monopolistically determined price of gold — to assure the equivalence of exchange by means of an agreed fixing of reciprocal rates of exchange, taking into account comparable purchasing power of the different currencies. Capitalist states set the gold parity or the different currencies by comparing the internal purchasing power of their own currency (according to internal prices) with the purchasing power of the currency determining the monopoly price of gold and its gold parity. Would it not be possible to fix the reciprocal rates of exchange for the currencies of the socialist states by mutual agreement, directly on the basis of calculation and constant study of their internal purchasing power, without expressing their gold parity?

It would seem that such a possibility is taking shape as the guiding system for facilitating the foreign trade transactions between socialist states, even though no small difficulties must be surmounted. In the first place, it would require solving the method for a realistic way of expressing and comparing purchasing power of socialist currencies. This is extraordinarily difficult for states that have a very different economic level and price relationship. It will be necessary to select representative and determining sets of the types of goods that every state needs, that every state produces and that is roughly the same in regard to use value. According to an over-all price for the sets of commodities thus selected, it will be possible to determine the internal purchasing power of the different currencies and therefore their reciprocal rates of exchange as well. The real exchange rates would have to be influenced to a large extent by the balance of payments of each country, and therefore by its level of production and its position in the international division of labour.

Precisely this selection of a set of commodities and the constant study of their irregular price changes and, on this basis, the purposeful determination of the reciprocal rates of exchange and changes in them, will be a very difficult problem. Solving it, however, would provide the conditions for a proper establishment of rates of exchange under conditions where gold would be no longer the general basis for currencies (because there is a shortage of gold in most countries) and none the less the equivalence of inter-state exchange could be assured. The fact that there are no such realistically grounded reciprocal rates of exchange retards the development of international socialist division of labour and cooperation, which could be even more rapid and successful. Creating a unified measure of purchasing power for socialist currencies is the prerequisite for the equivalence of exchange between them and of an objective basis for all value transactions. The possibility of such a solution will be speeded up commensurately as the shift to real economic systems of management and to systems of production and market prices within the different socialist states develops.

At the same time, this system does not conflict with the determination of rates of exchange with capitalist states, where, of course, with normal market relations in mutual agreements on foreign exchange rates, the economic strength of a country, and of its gold reserves, and its position in the international division of labour will prevail. In relations with capitalist states the value of each currency of socialist countries must be expressed and secured by a certain gold basis or a monetary reserve of the currency functioning as a general equivalent (dollar, pound).

A well drawn up system of exchange rates among socialist countries could not differ from their rates of exchange resulting from equivalent relations to capitalist currencies (e.g., to the dollar). In case of failure — either for gnoseological reasons or because of conflicts of interest — to assure, by the above-described method, the economically necessary exchange rates, assuring equivalency of exchange of use values, there would be no other way than to determine these rates of exchange on the basis of real gold parity of currencies of the socialist countries and under the influence of mutual trade relations.

Whichever way the reciprocal rates of exchange are determined, it is never merely a process of calculation, but requires also the necessary material assurance of the value of each currency that is reciprocally compared, and the influence of mutual trade relations be taken into account. Each of the states concerned must have the possibility of receiving in exchange not only the goods of the second state (for they do not always answer its needs), but also the currency of any other state whose goods it does need. It must, moreover, be assured that it will incur no loss in corresponding purchasing power.

Not only should economically realistic rates of exchange be purposefully set (through international agreement), but there must also be assured a free reciprocal convertibility of the different currencies, so that each state may receive, for its exports (including the planned amounts) to a certain country, goods from still another country (again this may be within the limits of the planned and previously agreed imports).

Here immediately arises a need to set up some sort of international monetary fund that would assure a relative stability of the rates of exchange that have been agreed on and the realization of reciprocal currency conversions by means of a fund guaranteeing value. This could be either in the form of a gold fund or a currency fund that could at any time be converted to other currencies. All participating states would contribute to this fund and each would be guaranteed the necessary currency of other participating states for its claims on any one state.

It is not our purpose in this work to solve the whole complex problem of forming and assuring economically realistic, but also relatively stable, rates of exchange among socialist countries. And we do not intend at all to solve at one stroke the question that arises concerning the relation of such inter-socialist monetary agreements to the already existing international monetary agreements and funds (Bretton Woods agreements and the related International Monetary Fund) to which most socialist states do not belong. These are tremendously intricate economic problems requiring special research studies for their solution. It is a question of pointing to the existence of real money within the socialist economies, internal functions of which can no longer be separated from their international monetary functions. Every postponement of theoretical or practical solution of these important economic problems means a delay in a potentially much more rapid and successful international economic cooperation.

b   Media of Circulation and of Payment

Money under socialism carries out the function of circulating medium. That is, it serves as means for making possible the circulation of goods.

Circulation is smooth-running, if the money received for goods sold is immediately spent on the purchase of goods, if it stays only a relatively short while in the hands of individuals and is continually changing place. The producers of goods and all those who receive money in ready cash do not, in this case, want to retain value in the form of money for a longer period, but do wish to spend it on other use values. This is why paper money can act as a symbol to replace real value in circulation. When people accept paper money, they believe it represents the value that it nominally expresses — at that moment they are not at all interested in some sort of abstract value, but in the specific use value they can get in the amount represented by the value of their money.

Paper money or coins of less precious metals act as circulating medium and replace the actual value which every seller on the market imagines in the form of a whole set of diverse goods which he will be able then to buy with the money. The fact that it fulfills a transitory function as medium of circulation, serves only for the purchase of goods, changes place and replaces goods, means that money can appear as a symbol, a sign representing real value.

The seller receives as medium of circulation a paper symbol that represents the general value and he can either receive or give this value for a larger or smaller amount of labour expended on the production of the specific goods exchanged than the socially necessary amount of labour represented by the money (not being aware of the divergence of production price from value, but of the more apparent divergence of market price from production price). It is by this

331

possibility of non-equivalent exchange realized by money and caused mainly by a divergence of the market price from the production price that money helps to overcome the contradictions of commodity production. Money can thoroughly carry out this function of circulating medium, that is the transitory exchange of a certain representative of relatively stabilized value for goods, the price of which fluctuates, only if the value represented by every monetary unit does not change too rapidly.

Wherever the immediate transfer of money from the hands of the buyer to the hands of the seller is a condition for the transfer of goods in the opposite direction, money acts as medium of circulation. In exchanges where payment is made after the transfer, money is not a medium of circulation but of payment. Therefore, the amount of ready cash acting as medium of circulation will depend primarily on the amount of commodities, or, rather on the total price of goods sold at a certain period directly for money.

Under socialism, too, the economic law discovered by Marx still applies: it expresses the reciprocal relation between the total price of goods, the velocity of circulation of money and the amount of money functioning as medium of circulation. The total price of goods sold divided by the average turnover of money gives the total amount of money needed to function as circulatory medium. This economic law must be respected even in a socialist economy.

Here it becomes clear that actually paper money merely represents a certain value and under only certain conditions can take its place in circulation. The producers must receive for their goods of a certain value money that represents a certain relatively stable value. They are willing to accept mere symbols, paper devices, on the assumption that they will receive in return goods for them of approximately the same value. As long as the amount of paper money that comes into circulation is of an amount and of a total nominal value that is necessary, other things being equal, for full-value money, then it does not matter whether the money is made of paper or iron or gold. But as soon as more paper money comes into circulation, or its total nominal value begin to exceed the total optimum need for full-value money, there would be a surplus of money which, under certain circumstances, could become a general depreciation of money and a rapid inflationary process.

For this reason, economic regulation of the circulation of money by the state is of paramount importance.

The circulation of money is, however, inseparably connected with its function as means of payment. Moreover, any excessive expansion of media of circulation is always linked with an excessive extension of means of payment and vice versa. For this reason one cannot explain the possibility of inflation without taking account also of the function of money as means of payment.

Wherever money is used to pay for goods sold on credit — that is, goods that have already been delivered or are being paid in advance — it is used as means of payment. Money can shift in a certain directions without goods moving at the same time in a contrary direction.

Money serves as means of payment also in remunerating for labour, paying for services, taxes, etc.

These payments bring about the need for further money, if they are not carried out by means of money that also is functioning in a given period as medium of circulation (some money functions alternately as circulatory medium and as payment). But experience shows that not all payments can be made during a certain period by means of money functioning as circulatory medium. This does not mean that the same sums of money must be added as the sum of the payments from which we have deducted those covered by the money also functioning as circulatory medium. The means of payment can in a certain period serve several times over — which means it can have several turnovers. This commensurately lessens the need for means of payment.

Even under socialism it is true that the necessary amount of money functioning as circulatory medium and as means of payment can be expressed by the fraction:

$$\frac{\text{total price} \atop \text{of goods sold} \quad - \quad {\text{total price of goods} \atop \text{sold on credit}} \quad + \quad {\text{sum of all kinds} \atop \text{of payment}}}{\text{average turnover of homogeneous money (functioning both as medium of circulation and of payment)}}$$

When there is economic regulation of the amount of money functioning as circulating means and as payment, not only the total price of goods on the market must be observed (fund of goods), but also all the other necessary payments realized in ready cash by other transactions, and with a given velocity of turnover of money, must also be watched to see that the amount of money does not exceed essentially the optimum amount needed.

A change in the amount of functioning money and therefore the withdrawal or emission of new money by the State Bank, on the assumption that it does not exceed the necessary amount and that it assures the stability of money, is linked mainly with the rates of economic growth. The State Bank can affect the amount of functioning money in accordance with the given situation of economic development mainly by regulating the credit system (in addition to other instruments which we shall speak later of, in a general way).

In the administrative system of management, credit was afforded the socialist enterprises actually only through rather formal loans, because obtaining credit and using it did not substantially affect the material interests of the enterprises. They did not feel the difference whether they obtained the money to cover costs of production by financial grants which they did not need to repay or by credits. The interest payments were simply added to the planned costs of production and as long as they carried out the plan, they received the means for paying planned wages and premiums. The fact that a clear majority of the enterprises always fulfilled the plans and went beyond them, despite the fact that the general development of production costs was often unfavourable and uneconomical, was only a particular sign of the limitations of the directive method of planning and management.

Under the new economic system of management, every loan will be repaid by the enterprises, both by returning the cost items and also by payments from the gross income, in order to speed up repayment. The interest payments will also come out of income. The higher the cost of production and the more that must be taken from the income to repay loans and interest, the less remains for the remuneration of all the workers and the other needs of the enterprise, and vice versa.

Under these conditions, credit will begin to fill its real economic function. The rate of interest and the period of repayment of loans (especially those for investments) will cause calculations to be made of the minimum necessary rate of effectiveness of investments, assuring not only enough growth in income for the enterprise to be able to repay the loan and make interest payments, but also assure a rise in remuneration (bonuses and shares in the enterprise's income) and cover other long-term and for the employees short-term needs. Furthermore, the enterprise will count on receiving interest on all its monetary means deposited in the bank and may for a period of time give up its own investment activity.

The bank can then influence the development of investment activity by the interest rate and setting the time for repaying loans, in accordance with the need for economic development. Raising the rate of interest and shortening the repayment time limits will restrict the investment activity of enterprises, and will, at the same time, induce the enterprises to increase their own deposits. When interest rates are reduced and longer time limits are set for repayment of loans, the enterprises will, on the contrary, find it advantageous to use their own financial means for production and, furthermore, to request and utilize advantageous credits. According to the given economic situation, the bank will be able to make it profitable to invest in projects requiring less capital and with rapid repayment, or vice versa.

When interest rates are lowered and with a general growth in investment activity, there will also be an increase in the need for money, not only as means of payment, but also as circulating medium, and therefore the emission of money will increase, there will be a rise in the interest rate, a slackening off of investment activity and increased deposits, and a smaller volume of money will be functioning.

3   Management of Financial Processes in the New System

A very important feature in the economic system of management is the central orientation or stimulation of all financial processes, assuring their differentiated mutual effect and their utilization to achieve various economic-political purposes. These are processes carried out by means of money, achieving a certain distribution or redistribution of income among the various institutions, collectives or individuals and by which the development of economic activity of individuals or economic units can be very sharply changed.

It is a question of directing such processes as credit and interest, payments from enterprise income and taxes, prices, wages, state investments and subventions, tariffs, issuing of money, establishing gold parity and rates of exchange, etc. The management of these processes usually causes certain changes in the purchasing power of money, in its influence on the development of economic figures and activity.

Although the achievement of a balanced and smooth development of the economy may be set as the goal of the whole economic policy, in general and over a longer period of time, where there will be rapid growth of production and consumption, both developing in harmony, as will supply and demand, and accumulation and consumption, and where moreover the currency will also be stabilized, this abstract goal will not be able to cope with the various specific economic conditions. It is necessary to carry out a different economic policy and a different direction of financial processes under conditions of stagnation of production or depression than under boom conditions. There must be a different policy to cope with a shortage of manpower from that applied where there is unemployment: one for a situation of surplus production and general marketing difficulties and another where it is a sellers' market; one for conditions of deflation and another for an inflationary situation. Only on the basis of well-rounded economic analyses is it possible to determine also the concrete economic-political goals and the management of all processes, especially the financial processes that can be used to bring the desired equilibrium and smooth economic development nearer.

At one time the idea prevailed in socialist countries that the best way to assure a rapid and continuous economic growth was by central planning of the economy by directives. This idea was found to be wrong. Not only was the goal itself of achieving as rapid and continuous a growth of production as possible viewed in an oversimplified way, leading to an extensive, priority development showing up many negative sides, but at a certain moment not even this goal could be realized in Czechoslovakia and a characteristic interruption in the growth of production and economic stagnation occurred. The transition from administrative planning by directive to an economic system of management, in which — together with new, more scientific methods of long-range, macroeconomic planning — great significance

336

is given to central direction of financial processes, is therefore carried out under special economic conditions, where specific economic-political goals must be observed and the corresponding control and direction of financial processes carried out.

Here it is not a question of analysing all these economic policies, but merely of showing — in connection with the new interpretations of the role of money in a socialist economy — their utilization under the above-described special economic conditions. These are conditions that arise as a result of the old administrative methods of management, conditions that will arise sooner or later in all socialist countries and therefore the interpretations of this special — now necessary in Czechoslovakia — economic policy has general significance. Moreover, it will be possible to comment on the repeated argument that the transition to the new system of management and the relative freeing of price formation will bring about inflation; this argument is used by the opponents of these changes to try to prevent their realization.

Let us briefly summarize again the economic conditions that have arisen as a result of the old administrative system of management.

In most branches of production, technology of production has lagged more or less behind the progressive world development and in many branches production equipment is outdated (not only obsolescent, but also physically outworn). Employment is very high and there is a relative shortage of manpower (in relation to demand). There is little differentiation in the remuneration of the workers between the highly skilled and the unskilled, thus undermining the incentive to perform work of high quality. The continuing extensive growth of production, with its disproportions, creates tension in the supply and demand relations and substantially greater demand for capital investments than the existing supply. The organization of production is characterized by a high degree of monopolization. The demand for consumer goods is satisfied quite unevenly and special shortages are found in some durable goods (autos, housing, construction material, etc.). There is a great lag behind the most advanced world development in some services and in some forms of transportation. Also in the sphere of prices there is not enough differentiation between high-quality and standard goods. The international balance of payments has been passive for several years. There is relative stagnation in the trends of national income.

Under such conditions, changes must be brought about to speed up the technological reconstruction and modernization of production, to raise substantially the economic effectiveness of investments and do away with inefficient use of raw materials and manpower in the unprofitable factories and operations. Changes must be gradually introduced in the methods of production and in its structure that will bring production costs closer to progressive world cost, and make the supply of goods respond more flexibly to market demand. It is necessary gradually to change the relation between total supply and demand in order to create a buyers' market and to stimulate demand with better quality goods and more rapid changes in commodities. There must be a redistribution of manpower in favour of branches and fields where there are shortages. The qualitative development of production, raising the productivity of social labour and making structural changes, should lead to equilibrium in balance of payments and a more rapid growth in national income.

In order to carry out these economic goals, we should begin to introduce an anti-inflationary financial policy, linked with a differentiation in remuneration, greater price differences and equilibrium prices. Without making greater differentiation and a greater spread between the remuneration for simple, unskilled labour and complex highly qualified labour, there is no possibility of creating the necessary premises to speed up the technological and qualitative development of production. But, since wage differentiation can be made only if there is a general, more rapid growth in average wages than has been the case in recent years, rising wage costs and the price differentials in the transition to market equilibrium prices (under conditions of general disproportionality) will act in an inflationary direction. This makes it all the more necessary, of course, in this intrinsically contradictory economic situation, to strengthen other anti-inflationary financial measures.

We must counter the arguments that the economic system of management will cause an inflationary development, by pointing out that in reality a hidden inflationary development has been in force up to now as a result of the administrative system of management, and also that the continuing inflationary pressures are only the result of additional measures to overcome the results of the old system of management. The inflationary development was shown mainly in the growing demand by enterprises for capital investment without genuine material coverage. This tension in the field of investments brought about first of all wide-spread dispersion of investment projects and an extension of the length of time taken for construction, and consequently investments became constantly dearer. But also in the field of consumer goods inflationary pressure made itself felt not only in the moderate rise in average prices of various groups of goods, but also in the lowering of quality, of durability and style of the products, in the public's loss of time spent hunting the needed goods, and in a certain amount of unrealizable purchasing power.

The most important anti-inflationary measure must be a stricter policy in regard to loans to enterprises, especially for capital investments. By setting considerably shorter periods for paying off the loans in relation to the life expectancy of the investment and by using competition in granting the loans for investments, as well as by means of relatively higher interest rates, it is possible to restrict considerably the volume of investments in production. State subsidies for production investments must be cut to the minimum. On the other hand, a certain amount of wage raises in the building industry will contribute to its expansion and increase the supply of housing construction. Increasing the supply in the branches producing capital investments (construction, engineering, etc.) in relation to the lowered demand creates the necessary economic pressure on these branches and speeds up their qualitative development, enhances technological progress, and increases productivity of labour.

By means of relatively high and uniform payments from the enterprises to the state (taxes) a strong economic pressure will be created on the backward enterprises to adapt to the conditions of the leading enterprises. Those enterprises which, even after changes in production programs and other technological and economic changes, do not have enough gross income to pay the uniform charges to the state and still show a profit, must be gradually liquidated. Manpower released in this way can be used by progressive enterprises or in other economic branches without harming the workers' interests (by covering cost of retraining, moving the family, etc.).

The new rate of exchange should be fixed so that there is a possibility of the largest possible volume of exports without subsidy. But if there should be in exceptional cases serious reasons for granting relief in the interest of the state to some exporters, the grants should be gradually reduced in a planned way until they are completely eliminated. In above-average branches of production that would then export with extraordinary profits, the necessary interest and means for expanding exports will be created. Even at the cost of lowering the total volume of credit it will be necessary to leave to them the major part of their extraordinary profits for expanding investments. In this way, heavy pressure is exerted from world markets on all the lagging export enterprises, through the prices realized here, and strong interest is created in exports that bring a high return.

Imports will also be used for competitive pressure on prices and quality of home products. Eliminating the administrative, bureaucratic decisions on imports, doing away with the monopoly position of domestic producers in regard to imports and consumer pressure on imports (by the sale of foreign currency for imports, both to production enterprises and to trade organizations) together will have a strong effect in making domestic production more efficient.

In general, it is necessary to strengthen markedly the antimonopoly measures and create conditions for a very effective market competition between enterprises. All the organizational tendencies in production that create only administratively highly centralized branch monopolies should be done away with. This does not mean abolishing the progressive, genuine concentration of *production* that speeds up technological developments but preventing the purely administrative concentration of organization that undermines competitiveness between the sellers and prevents free choice by buyers. Even where it is advantageous to organize branch trusts, the enterprises within these trusts must have enough economic freedom to compete among themselves for the largest number of orders from customers.

The heightened control of trends in prices and incomes will make it possible to detect incidental, purely speculative monopolistic price raises, maintaining high equilibrium prices of some types of goods by artificially restricting production. In such cases special taxes can readily be used to draw off the economically unjustified profits and thus convince enterprises by exprience that it is useless to increase profits by such speculation.

Even though it probably will not be possible to completely prevent a moderate price rise during the necessary transition to market equilibrium prices, when there must be greater price differentials and wage increases, connected with the process of increasing wage differentials, a purposeful anti-inflationary policy of the state in other fields will exert strong economic pressure to speed up the qualitative and highly profitable development of production. On this basis a more effective development of foreign trade must be achieved, an equilibrium in balance of payments and a more rapid growth in national income. In this way, it will be possible, in turn, to assure a more rapid growth in real wages and living standards of all the inhabitants.

The changed economic conditions, of course, will bring with them a need for corresponding changes in the financial and general economic policy of the state.

4 Using Financial Instruments in Planning

Since the economy of contemporary capitalism has gone beyond the limitations of the market mechanism of early capitalism, with its economic *laissez-faire* theories, it would be naive romanticism to expect that a mere revival of the function of the market mechanism under socialism would assure highly effective and harmonious development of the economy.

The market mechanism by itself never could do away with the contradiction between direct decision-making concerning production in accord with *present* market demand and decision-making preparing for *future* production to satisfy and create future demand. On the contrary, decisions about investments, about technological development, about training manpower, about complex changes in production programs, made on the basis of present market conditions and on dispersed and isolated unscientific considerations by the different enterprises about future marketing possibilities, must give rise to fundamental contradictions with actual market demand in the future.

The harsh, destructive crises and the growing social contradictions led mankind to learn the conditions and methods of conscious community control of preparing future production, as well as distribution processes, in order that future supply might correspond to demand as consistently as possible and, furthermore, that consumption by society as a whole might continually rise. It is the abolition of private ownership of means of production and the introduction of economic planning that provide conditions and instruments of such conscious control of national economic development.

Although the previous development of economic planning in socialist countries has shown that a negation of market relationships undermines the initiative of enterprises in questions of production and technology and obstructs efficiency, the rehabilitation of market relations must not be conceived as a weakening of the principle of planning the economy of society as a whole. Only a rational synthesis of both processes can provide the conditions for a new and higher level of development of the socialist economy.

It is not difficult to link the plan and the market in a theoretical abstraction and demonstrate the necessity of their unity under socialism. It is much more difficult to work out concrete forms of their interaction and integration under specific social-economic conditions. An attempt to clarify this interconnection under conditions of the present-day Czechoslovak economy can, indeed, disclose various generally valid procedures and forms, but as a whole, it can express only one of the specific ways which are so many and varied that only in the future can we take any great step forward in forming a general theory of socialist planned management.

We shall now attempt to make a theoretical sketch of the new system of planning, with the use of the market mechanism, the financial, and — especially — the credit instruments, which could be put in effect in Czechoslovakia. We do not propose, however, to exhaust this theme or to guarantee that it will show exactly how the procedure will be carried out in practice.

One of the most important guarantees that planned management in the ČSSR will be more scientific, are thorough analytical and comparative research studies which will give a theoretically well grounded idea of the long-range possibilities for the most efficient technological development of Czechoslovak production with a view to its internal and external conditions, on the one hand, and, on the

342

other, for long-range trends of consumption and living standards. Furthermore, the studies of possible variants of technological development must be carried out both within the different branches of production and centrally on a country-wide scale, using uniform methodology and coordination. The uniform methodology should make possible a comparison of economic effectiveness of the different variants of technological development, approximately according to the ideas presented in the chapter on prices.

It is only by means of these research studies concerning possible changes in technological development and the main trends of development in consumption that we can provide the foundations for drawing up long-term prognoses of economic development. All attempts to set up *a priori* rates of growth of social product or national income, either by extrapolating the previous development in the ČSSR, taking account of the limiting factors, or by making comparative studies of the rates of development in other countries, are based on purely deductive methods and lack the necessary internal analytical procedure which is especially important when there are qualitative changes in the system of management of the economy.

Long-term prognoses of development, based on analyses of different possibilities of fundamental technological changes and their impact on social production and on social life (concretization of contemporary, abstract, considerations about the scientific-technical revolution) are of fundamental importance in assuring promptly some qualitative changes in the previous economic and social development. Unless such realistic forecasts are made, it is impossible, for instance, to prepare in time a change in the electric power system or a real conversion to automation, a fundamental change in the training of manpower, the necessary specialization in scientific research, and so on. Therefore there can be no serious talk of a planned management of social development, unless these prognoses are made.

Relatively reliable prognoses of the long-range (fifteen- to twenty-year) trends of development of the national economy, together with constant specific studies of the economic phenomena of technological development and trends in market demand (domestic and foreign) make it possible to draw up medium-range (e.g. five-year) plans of economic development. The process of drawing them up can be considered as only a series of approximations, with interaction of the central planning body and the management of the enterprises, aimed at the formation of an optimum plan in accordance with previously defined characteristics.

The central planning body draws up, on the basis of estimates of the possible expansion of productive factors, of basic technical changes, of an increase in the productivity of labour and the growth of different branches of production, the first general consideration of the possible growth of social product and national income. The preliminary distribution of the funds of production accumulation is made among the different branches of production in accord with the first prognosis of price development, the concept of the necessary technological development and expansion of productive capacities, as well as the need to increase personal and social consumption, contemplated change in demand structure, and the effective possibility to export goods.

All these preliminary basic outlines of plans, arrived at on the basis of continuous research of market demand and of the effective possibilities for technological development, plans that enforce structural and proportional changes in production, should be drafted in two or three possible variants. In each variant the economic development considered would have different socio-economic consequences, different rates of growth of the standard of living, different ways of satisfying social needs or different working conditions (hours of work, etc.). On the basis of these different variants of macroeconomic plans the highest political bodies should have the possibility to choose the most suitable variant, which, in turn, will determine the goals for the planning body and so give direction for further work on the plan.

The chosen and elaborated variant of possible development will give the branch management the first macroeconomic orientation on the possible direction of their own development. On the basis of this first macroeconomic variant, the central planning body must draw up for the state bank the preliminary basic conditions for carrying out the policy in investment credits.

In accord with the envisaged trends in capital investments in the construction, engineering and other industries, as well as the expected imports of investment assets, and on the basis of approximate price trends and the effectiveness of investments, a preliminary idea of the total volume of investment credit is obtained. After the central body has outlined the possible and desirable effectiveness of capital investments in the different branches of production, the maximum time limits for repaying the loans and the interest rate for the three investment groups are established: long-term, medium-term and short-term. This maximum time limit must always be considerably shorter than the service life of the investment, so that the loan can be paid from the income created by these investments. If the credit conditions are properly set, this has an accelerating or decelerating effect on the volume of investments, as the need arises. Furthermore it influences their effectiveness and structure.

The bank, on the basis of these credit terms that have been set by central planning bodies, holds a competition for loans provided, during which the applications for loans are made by the enterprises, giving the different variants of investment trends. In order that credit may be used as an instrument of planned orientation of investments, the tax policy must be carried out in such a way that the enterprises must in a certain extent depend on credit for their basic capital investments. At the same time, however, the effect of the investments must be to assure an increase in the enterprise income in order that the workers pay might rise and their interest in development investments will be sufficiently aroused.

In the competition for capital investment projects to be included in the five-year plan, there is the first selection of investment proposals, discarding those that do not come up to the standards set for effectiveness (e.g. the envisaged growth in effect does not guarantee repayment in the time limit). Only those which fulfill all requirements can be accepted for the next round of selection.

In case there is greater demand for credit than available funds in one investment group (e.g. with a short life of the capital investment) and less demand in comparison with supply in another group, the bank can transfer funds from one group to another. If there is a generally higher demand for credit than the planned supply, two possibilities present themselves. Either the conditions set were too lenient and, by maintaining the total volume of credit (hence the financial expression of volume of investment) and making the requirement more strict (hence raising the effectiveness of investments), harmony can be achieved between supply and demand for invest-

345

ments. This would yield greater growth in national income and, within it, a larger absolute and relative fund of consumption, than had been originally planned. Or it might be found necessary to increase the absolute volume of investment funds, without changing the requirements, thus covering the entire demand for credit. In this case, national income will rise more rapidly than was expected, but the share of the national income going to savings need not change.

If there is a lower demand for credit than planned, the reverse is the case — either the requirements for credit application are made easier to increase the demand or the total volume of planned credit is decreased.

Decisions as to which reaction should occur in regard to the relation between supply and demand for credit are to be made by the central planning body. In general it should be kept in mind that the whole round of investment competition is only a second approximation on the path to setting up the optimum plan (the first approximation is the preliminary rough structural idea arrived at in the planning centre). It is a process where the preliminary planned macrostructure meets with the specific proposals and variants from the enterprises that have arisen not only through these preliminary outlines, but also on the basis of much more concrete analysis of the various possibilities of effective investment (technological advance) and of the trends in demand and in future markets.

When the enterprise applies for credit under previously set requirements, it must have a rather more concrete idea of the effectiveness of any one investment project than has the planning centre. It not only feels the pressure of future repayment from income (in case the conditions are not met the enterprise will suffer not only loss in income but also higher interest payments), but also has to have a relative increase in income per employee, so as to assure wage rises in the future. In this way, there can be not only more realistic correction of the ideas in the planning centre on the effectiveness of future investments, but also on various possibilities of development in structure. The central planning body can never discover as many possibilities for technical advance or substitution as the enterprises can.

All proposals for investment and applications for credit which the bank must verify by the usual commercial procedure to discover how realistic they are and how adequate the guarantee, must be gathered in at the planning centre, where the third round of approximation is made. There the over-all relation (macrorelation) between supply of, and demand for, credit is made, with the concomitant macroprocesses. Furthermore, by the use of the most modern balancing methods, a check is made on inter-branch relations for the different investment proposals and the economic effectiveness of the proposed variants of development.

When drawing up its preliminary proposals for investments, a branch enterprise must deal only with its nearest suppliers concerning material needed to cover the probable orders. From them, it can obtain only provisional agreement, conditioned usually, in turn, by their own investment prospects. No branch enterprise can determine by itself all the inter-branch relations and all the resulting investment projects in other branches, the realization of which is the condition of its own investment prospects. It can calculate in advance the effectiveness of investment from its own standpoint, but not the effectiveness for the national economy. It is the business of the planning centre to investigate the total costs of investment to the national economy for the different variants of development in the individual branches of production, the material needed to cover them and their economic effectiveness. Particularly, by analysing the different ways to increase effectiveness of foreign trade, the central body can give preference to some of the many variants that will be highly advantageous from the standpoint of exports as well — and assure the needed materials through more effective imports rather than from domestic production.

In this way the planning centre can in this second round amend its original ideas as to structure and make them more concrete, elaborate more effective variants of economic development and, on this basis, make more precise the bank's general credit requirements. At the same time, of course, it can make recommendations to the bank concerning some of the branch investment plans. If it finds them economically ineffective, it will either demand greater efficiency by making the credit conditions tougher, or strike them out. Thus, the second round of the competition for credit is begun — of course, based on the further research and calculations made concurrently by the enterprises.

347

From these consecutive rounds of competition for credit a collection of proposals for investment emerges that -- unlike the first round -- will be bolstered by the more concrete analyses and will have much less conflict between the point of view of the enterprise and of the general economy. On the basis of these proposals, the central planning body then proceed to the third round of balancing which should result in the macrostructural Five-Year Plan, approaching an optimal plan. If necessary there can be at this point a more precise delimitation of the credit terms, and then the contracts for loans can be concluded between the banks and the enterprises.

This is a planning procedure that combines progressive planning methods and economic analyses and views with the concrete proposals of the enterprises which bear direct material responsibility and income risk for all investment projects and must therefore calculate very carefully and, where necessary, correct the general ideas of the planning centres. Here, of course, the bank not only plays the passive role of intermediary between the planning centre and the enterprises, but is also responsible for the security of the loans and the stability of the currency and therefore must check on the reliability of the enterprises' proposals. Furthermore, by making analyses of the financial state of the economy, of the circulation of money, of monetary liquidity, etc., it should actively collaborate with the planning centre in drawing up an optimum economic plan and in setting the conditions for obtaining credit.

This is a concrete form of combining economic planning and the market. Furthermore, it is not the present market that is to determine future production. The planning body tries to predict future market trends and see to it that the necessary preparations are made at the present time. With specific ideas about the effectiveness of enterprises' investments, the planning centre can forecast future trends in production prices of different groups of products and, in this way, can concretize its market trends and calculate the reverse effect on proportions of production. But it needs the enterprises' responsibility for market results to make them have a real interest in an optimum development and thus help to set up the best possible plans for the national economy.

The Five-Year Plans do not determine the specific volume of output in the different branches of production, nor the production of different kinds or ranges of goods, in other words the micro-structure of production. Only an approximate orientational idea of the probable necessary volume of production of the different branches of production is given by the Five-Year Plan, preparing the necessary production capacity. Actual utilization of these production capacities, or the actual volume of production and its microstructure is a matter for the short-term plans (annual, bi-annual or even shorter periods) of the enterprises. These can arise only from the actual development or from short-term forecasts of market demand or from customers' orders and contracts. These short-term production plans and decisions of the enterprises will deviate more or less from the long-term production plans and must be continually concentrated in the planning centre and compared with the long-term macroeconomic plan.

The contradictions that arise between the short-term and long-term plan can have different causes. Constant analysis is needed to disclose and solve them, both by the planning centre and by the central financial organization. But the main thing is to recognize factors that require changes or amendments in the investment plans and thence corrections of the Five-Year Plan, and situations that, while they lead to changes in macroprocesses and macrorelationships, can be solved by various financial instruments without any substantial change in investment projects.

Changes in investment plans can arise, for example, from substantial unanticipated changes in demand (either foreign or domestic changes), or from new possibilities of highly effective technological changes in some branch of production, sharp price changes in imported products (especially raw materials, etc.), changes in export opportunities, making for better capacity to compete, etc. All such substantial, unexpected changes can also compel changes in investment projects contained in the Five-Year Plan or revision of the whole Five-Year Plan. This is why we must consider work on the medium-range plans as a continual process of analysis, reckoning with unforeseen changes of the main economic processes that may compel even fundamental change in production structure and therefore in investment plans. But this planning must also be creative work in the sense that when changes are necessary it seeks a solution that will disturb as little as possible the fundamental inter-branch relations, leaving most of the investment projects unchanged.

There are unforeseeable changes in macroeconomic processes that can be met either by changes in the production structure within given production capacities (i.e., without changing the investment plans) or by changes in other economic processes that are closely connected, without having to change substantially the structure of production. For example, a more rapid but limited rise in wages than envisaged by the plan can be compensated by a rise in prices without having to change greatly the structure of demand and supply. A more rapid price rise, linked with a corresponding increase in productivity of labour, can be covered by production even if there is a structural change in demand or in foreign trade. And there can be a great many such changes that do not compel a change in investment plans.

It is essential to analyse constantly the contradictions that arise between the short-term production plans or economic reality, on the one hand, and long-term economic plans, on the other. The impact of unforeseen economic processes determines the necessity to assure a balance either by structural changes in production that lead to structural changes in investment or by change in the financial processes that do not require changes in the planned structure of investment. The need to respond to certain economic processes by making purposeful changes in certain financial instruments, or the need to prevent an undesirable development of some economic processes (signaled in time by continual market research), by means of various financial levers, requires that there be a central financial body capable of coordinating or directing the day-to-day development of all financial processes.

The basis for stability in inter-branch relations and in forecasts of future market condition is a relative stability in planning investments, assuring the essential changes to use all possibilities of raising the rate of return on investments. The more precise the forecasts of future markets, the relatively smaller the reserves of production capacities needed and the less the economic loss. For this reason, it is of great economic importance to preserve the stability of the economic investment plan, unless this is done at the price of a loss in effectiveness or by slowing the rate of technological development.

Therefore, developing the future basic structure of investments and production by national economic plans, with the market assuring an interest in high rates of return, is a more progressive way of economic development than is a spontaneous growth of a future production base that is not centrally planned or coordinated.

Summary

Marxist economic theory up till now merely noted the existence of money under socialism and recounted, in a formal way, the monetary functions that had already been discovered by Marx. But it was unable to explain why these general theoretical statements differed from the operation of money in socialist economic practice, nor the reasons for the specific changes in these functions brought about in the present-day economies.

At the present stage of development the functions of money in capitalist countries cannot be severed from the changes caused in the development of money in international exchange. The great concentration of gold supplies in one country with a relative shortage of gold in general, and the great economic strength of that country, led to a monopolist determination of the price of gold by it and to a situation where its currency partly took over the role of general equivalent, in the internationally regulated rates of exchange among states.

In economic links between socialist and capitalist countries, the socialist states are forced to express the gold parity of their currencies as their internationally recognized guarantee of value. If the internal expression of value represented by money (on the basis of the total price of a certain, selected, broad set of commodities), or in other words, the expression of the internal purchasing power of the currency is linked with the determination of its rate of exchange and gold parity on the basis of the comparative purchasing power and the gold parity of other currencies, then the internal and external functions of money are linked and the domestic value can be compared with the value on world markets, making possible equivalent exchange in international transactions.

Within socialist countries, gold ceases to have the function of measure of value, and money expresses the value that is effectuated by means of the prices of a certain collection of diverse commodities, in which the deviations of production prices from value are roughly balanced out. If, by means of the selected sets of commodities, it should become possible to make such a comparison between socialist countries on an international scale, then their reciprocal rates of exchange can be regulated without the need for gold to function as a general measure of value.

As the representative of relatively stable value in the economic regulation of the amount of money by the state, money serves as medium of circulation, means of payment and retainer of value. In the function of means of payment it is utilized for crediting of economic activity, especially of investments, by the socialist enterprises and it stimulates them to achieve the greatest efficiency in credit operations.

Under economic management, the state utilizes the regulation of money and of all financial processes to achieve various economic-political goals. The financial processes by which a certain distribution or redistribution of income among institutions, economic units and individuals is attained, can be variously applied and cause different trends of development in economic activity, chiefly in production, corresponding to the changing economic conditions.

When the socialist state uses financial instruments this does not weaken the planning of the basic production structure, but on the contrary assures the highest effectiveness, while making a planned preparation of production capacities, coordinating them with future market demand.

The enterprises' interest in seeking most effective investments is linked and coordinated with the central plan primarily through the credit mechanism. This is a new way of linking national economic planning with the market mechanism and the pressure of competition.

V   CONCLUSION

The analysis up to this point has shown that socialist economies arc now at a stage of development of productive forces where they cannot yet assure the socially necessary development of labour without using specific market relationships. Market relationships as an expression of certain, so far objectively inescapable, non-antagonistic contradictions of economic interests, reflecting the intrinsic contradictions of social labour, given the existing conditions of labour and of consumption, must develop in the socialist cooperation of society as a whole. They do not permit private appropriation of the means of production and they are an inevitable form by which people working for each other in group cooperation, are again and again compelled to adapt their own relatively independent group economic decisions to social interests. Insufficient use or suppression of these market relationships brings a growth in contradictions between the individual and the group interests, on the one side, and the social interests, on the other, and re-enforces one-sided, unsocial economic decision-making. Socialist market relationships are, therefore, a necessary form of exchanging labour activity among people, helping to overcome rapidly the contradictions that still arise within social labour: they are an essential process, by means of which — leaving asido other processes — people appropriate production in a socialist way.

It would, however, be an over-simplification of the whole matter if the importance of a consistent use of socialist market relationships were to be considered only as a correction of the direct group economic decision-making or as a way of adapting group economic activity *a posteriori* to the requirements of the market. The opponents of socialist market relations try, in this way, to narrow down the concept of utilizing these relationships. The significance of their utilization actually does not lie at all in some *a posteriori* adaptation of production to the market, differing from the planned approach which is interpreted as the antipodes of the market mechanism, primarily because the plan precedes production, while the market comes afterward. The significance of socialist market relations is precisely the fact that they are utilized to harmonize group and social economic interests either at the time decisions are made on the long-range production activity in its relation to a future market, or in deciding on minor, direct changes in production activity in accord with the direct, insufficiently foreseen changes of the market.[1]

After all, even in capitalist production it is not only a question of *a posteriori* production decisions on the basis of the momentary or the past situation on the market, but also the taking of decisions on the basis of estimates of the probable future situation. Naturally, under pre-monopoly capitalism, the estimates of the future market were extremely weak, made as they were by a vast number of individual, dispersed capitalists, and the *a posteriori* correction of these subjectivist production decisions were so frequent and so fundamental that the circumstance of preliminary market estimates was negligible. Much more marked are the market prognoses under monopoly capitalism, and especially so in the era of advanced state monopoly, when a great concentration of production and marketing creates favourable conditions for a quite high level of probability and, furthermore, provides the conditions for partly influencing the development of the markets (especially by state-monopoly intervention) and for very rapid response to the immediate or the early anticipated changes in demand.

The most modern record-keeping and communication methods,

---

[1] "*Ex post* regulation is indeed a feature of an elemental economy without a central body that carries out the goal of society, and the corresponding proportions as expressed by the plan. This does not, however, refer to a planned economy where the market mechanism is used as a form of conscious influencing of the economic process." W. Brus, *op. cit.*, p. 216.

which we have already spoken of, aid the great monopolies to react to each change in commodity inventories (frequently even the stocks of consumer goods (in the large commercial corporations), before the relation of demand to supply can cause a change in price.

But, still, these are only estimates, prognoses (although often carried out by means of the most modern research and mathematical methods and with a relatively high degree of probability), because the instruments for influencing the development of the market by monopolies and by bourgeois states are too weak, and are one-sided from a class point of view. There still occur, therefore, crisis corrections of production decisions (sometimes only minor crises in certain branches), sudden slashes of production, great bankruptcies, monopoly destruction of stocks of diverse goods, non-utilization of production factors (capacities, manpower, etc.), on the one hand, and, on the other hand, sharp price rises in some types of goods, speculating and booms in some branches. This is how capitalist production reacts directly to the contradictions that arise between production and the market. Although these are typical capitalist forms of direct adaptation of production to unanticipated market developments (with the important escape valve of arms production, which should not be overlooked in the analysis), with enrichment of some capitalists and impoverishment of others, and this is, of course, particularly harmful to the working people, it is, after all, only the adaptation of specific production to its objectively necessary development.

Only a socialist economy can create the conditions for qualitatively new harmony of production and the market. It makes possible incomparably greater accuracy in predictions of future trends in structure of demand on the home markets (this cannot be denied, even in view of the past shortcomings in this field, most of them caused by subjective considerations) and, furthermore, it has greater possibilities of regulating the main factors determining the development of these markets (employment, money incomes, prices, etc.) and a unified direction of investment activity. In all these regulatory and governing measures, it is not the interest of one class that prevails, but the general interest of the whole of society.

But for the long-term planned development of socialist production to be actually harmonized in the most thorough way with the trends in demand and to correspond to the socially necessary development

355

of production, so that real social interest would prevail in the long-term planned management of production trends and the market, the reverse influence of the socialist market must affect production; production must be connected with consumption by socialist market relations. The production enterprises, without whose active participation long-term social plans cannot be set up, must at the time the plan is forming already be aware that they have responsibility for planning production that can be sold, and that their income will depend on it. Therefore they will proceed in a quite different way than hitherto in setting up the plans, will investigate quite differently the future production possibilities and the trends in consumer needs, will seek the most effective variants and present quite different planning material to the central bodies.

Under the old administrative planning, the main interest of the enterprises in setting up the plans was to gain as much capital as possible for investment and all the manpower they could, with as low production targets as possible and to this end they subordinated all the required planning data and information. But if there is consistent utilization of market relationships, they will be interested in such investments and future production conditions (capacities, manpower, etc.) that will enable the enterprises to achieve the highest effect with the relatively lowest volume of factor inputs.

Thus, not only through the cooperation of society as a whole, but also — and only — by a consistent use of socialist market relations within this cooperation of society, conditions arise for a qualitatively new long-term harmonizing of production, the market and consumption. Not until these conditions prevail does it become advantageous for the enterprises to produce what is advantageous for society, i.e., the individual and group economic interests are really harmonized with the economic interests of society as a whole. If there should arise an enterprise interest in long-term optimum production activity, there is also naturally an interest in the most rapid *a posteriori* change and adaptation of production activity to the detailed changes in the market that cannot be foreseen and which are recognized only after the event. The unpredictable detailed changes in the market cannot be eliminated even under socialism, and opponents of market relations need not be alarmed at the fact that production responds *a posteriori* to changes in the market. Instead, they should endeavour that as quickly as possible the necessary interest and possibility of such *a posteriori* reaction should arise in a socialist enterprise.[1]

Opponents of market relationships show greatest fears over extending the power to make decisions in the socialist enterprises and they advance arguments that there is a danger that the monopoly position of the enterprises will lead them to abuse this power. It is interesting that this argument was not applied by these same people when the administrative directive methods brought about all the negative aspects of the producers' monopoly position, with their full weight and even against the will of the enterprises.

Against this, the consumers were completely powerless (either as individuals or as enterprises). The producing enterprises were compelled, both by the one-sided directive and unrealistic plans and by their own one-sided interest, to put a brake on technological development and on introduction of new and better products into their production plans, to narrow the range of products and worsen their quality, increase the amount of needless goods that were produced and stored, not being able to cover the growing amount of real needs, etc.

General moral appeals and educational measures, all the external controls and the administrative intervention, could only moderate what the whole system of overcentralized planned management compelled, acting as an objective force in regard to the production enterprises. General moral and political appeals spoke of the necessity to broaden the range of goods, to change and improve the products, while everyday experience made the enterprises realize that such action would threaten the fulfilment of planned volume of production and that this would not only cause a reduction of material reward, but also be a disgrace and, if the situation was repeated, perhaps even lead to changes in the top management. There is nothing more unMarxist than the idea that only by the operation of the ideological

[1] "It would seem that the source of the objections to the decentralized model that by its fundamental nature it is unable to consciously govern the economy *ex ante*, lies again in the identification of the market mechanism in a competitive capitalist economy and the market mechanism in a planned economy. The sound of the word 'market' evidently still arouses unpleasant associations " W. Brus, *op. cit.*, p. 216.

superstructure can experience, which teaches the opposite, be overcome, or that by *a posteriori* external control of the results of production activity we can eliminate something that again and again is caused by the objective conditions of the management of this production activity.

It is not by more and more extension of the controls and the restriction on the enterprise's activity, by expanding the number of indicators, that we can overcome this one-sided production activity and the negative, really monopolistic action of the enterprises. On the contrary, this can be done only by broadening their economic powers within the socialist plans for society and also by concomitantly increasing the economic influence of consumers through the market on the direct long-term decisions taken by the producers. Still a number of other economic measures can be taken to weaken the monopoly tendencies of the socialist production enterprises. Nor will a socialist society relinquish the power to take measures against explicitly anti-social speculation. But why should the danger of such tendencies be raised to oppose proposals for a more consistent utilization of socialist market relations, which would greatly weaken this threat, if these same tendencies appear so strong when socialist market conditions are being suppressed?

For socialist market relationships to act on socialist production enterprises and arouse efforts on the part of the enterprises to satisfy as fully as possible the needs of the consumers, in an optimum development of production, the one-sided administrative management and restrictions on the enterprises must be done away with. Under that system, the quantitative aspect of production was on the ascendent at the expense of the qualitative aspect, and the initiative of the enterprises was undermined. Many who admitted the significance of a more consistent utilization of socialist market relations are not yet able to comprehend that they can be applied only if the one-sided directive forms of management of the enterprises are eliminated. They defend the directive form of management, identify it incorrectly with what they call direct socialist management and counterpose this — again incorrectly — to the "indirect form", considering the former more socialist!

These people are actually scrambling and obscuring concepts in a completely unscientific way, and making difficult any necessary and healthy criticism of administrative forms of planning and management. A system of management that takes quite insufficient account of the objective economic circumstances and, in particular, ignores the fundamental connection between certain distribution processes and the development of production activity through the material interests of people, is what has been called an administrative system by directives. The characteristic feature of this type of management is the issuing of commands in an administrative way to achieve this or that development in economic activity. The will to achieve this desired development does not sufficiently respect the hidden processes and phenomena with which the management of economic activity is fundamentally connected and depending on which a certain desirable development will be fulfilled or not, or the development of which will, on the contrary, be retarded or stopped by the given command.

In criticizing the directive form of management, the point is not whether the development of a certain economic activity is governed directly by means of certain instructions or indirectly by means of certain mediatory instruments. The fact at issue is that it governs without knowledge of some fundamental economic and other social relations and with a faith in the omnipotence of simple administrative management acts of will and law. Precisely because an uneconomic, or insufficiently economic, administrative system of management usually has as a result serious proliferation of economic contradictions, showing that the fundamental economic relationships have not been respected, a socialist society must deal as quickly as possible with it and criticize its non-socialist character.

Of course, rejecting the administrative forms of management does not mean rejecting a so-called direct social management of production. It is no chance matter, on the other hand, that the defenders of the old administrative forms of planned management over-estimate the value of direct commands concerning production and not only under-estimate the indirect, mediated instruments of management, but even consider the indirect forms of management to be unsocialist. There are many reasons for these views. In the first place, they reveal a lack of knowledge when they under-estimate the many complex, interrelated aspects of the development of social production activity and the significance of the initiative and interest of producers

359

in assuring its optimum development. And, furthermore, they over-look the decisive influence of all direct *and* indirect distribution pro-cesses on the development of material interests of the workers, and thereby on the development of their production activity. It is precisely the inability to understand these complex relation-ships that caused the one-sided, over-simplified planning, and the ordering of only some aspects of production and the neglect of other, no less important ones, or the hope that their development would be assured by general moral appeals and stimuli. On the other hand, the one-sided and very detailed scheduling of material rewards from the top on down, which could not correspond to the very diverse and constantly changing conditions of production, rendered impossible the all-round socially necessary development of production activity, not to speak of the fact that this was generally under-estimated as compared with various moral stimuli. Naturally, all this had to end in a complete neglect of the need for indirect distribution processes, carried out by means of commodity exchange, and its considerable influence on the development of production activity.

We may say, in sum, that a socialist society can, and must, utilize both direct and indirect forms of management of production and that the choice between one form or the other must not be subjective or arbitrary, but a purposeful selection of the most suitable one to be used to achieve most effectively the objectively necessary develop-ment of economic activity, which respects all fundamental economic relationships. At the same time, however, it must be realized that the so-called direct forms of management of economic --- especially pro-duction — activity are actually direct management only in the last links in the hierarchy of the administrative system, that is, only at the level of factory management bodies, or even in the workshops. In the management bodies that are more separate from the actual pro-duction activity, the directives in regard to production represent a management form that reaches the actual producers only in a me-diated, and usually changed (by specifications, application to detail, etc.) form. In the case of these management bodies one may speak of direct management of production only in the broader sense of the word, in the sense of delimiting the actual production activity, as distinct from other economic activity, such as wage, price, tax, trade and other aspects.

The central delimitation of the production activity should be carried out only to the extent that the central body can discover reliably enough the necessary future development of this production activity. At the same time, they should recognize its great complexity and diversity, the difference in availability of information concerning the necessary development of each of these aspects, and thereby the need for differentiated methods of central delimitation or orientation of their development.

From the standpoint of the analysed problems, it is important to realize that the development of some aspects of production activity, which the central bodies cannot predict with enough realiability (for lack of information on the premises of development) and which they are even less able to assure by means of obligatory directive indicators, but whose rapid development is desirable, in view of the relation to other processes, these should be indirectly oriented by means of planned material incentives. If the central body cannot, for instance, predict exactly and determine with dependability the long-range development of productivity of labour in some, or all, branches of production, this development can nevertheless be roughly forecast by means of some indicator. They can use this indicator itself or pass it on as an orientation indicator for the enterprises, but, in any case, the socially necessary development of productivity of labour must be indirectly oriented, by means of the material interest on a certain development of gross income (which reflects, among other things, the development of productivity of labour). Whatever the method — by means of certain distribution processes or by these processes linked with commodity exchange processes that the central body can directly determine (radically, at one stroke or relatively stably over a longer period of time) — it is possible to attain a certain socially necessary development of production, or some aspects of the development, with greater reliability and with less growth of economic contradictions in this way than under the directive system of management.

The warnings of various dogmatic theoreticians are completely abstract and remote from reality, when, without any more detailed knowledge or deeper analyses of the development of certain intrinsic contradictions in the socialist economy, they regard any use of socialist market relations in socialist states as a revision of Marxism-Leninism and do not hesitate even to assert without concrete evidence that it means the return of capitalism. They know no other arguments than that market relations arouse profit-seeking attitudes of the managers and private-property tendencies that they allege would finally lead to a revival of capitalism.[1] These are completely speculative, abstract statements that preserve and re-enforce the ideological dogmas that arose in the Stalin era of Marxist thinking and do immense harm to the actual development of socialist economics.

Actually, no capitalist profit-seeking interest can arise under conditions of socialist market relations developing within the socialist cooperation in society as a whole, for there is no private profit and no private person can appropriate the income and make a profit on the exploitation of the labour of others. No one can privately purchase the means of production and transform them into capital. For this reason, there can be no psychosis of private greed and all such tendencies are hang-overs from the past, against which society is fighting. But if it is considered greed for profit if the workers try to expend labour in a way that will assure them as high income as possible, either as individuals or as part of a production collective, then this endeavour is not caused by market relations, but comes from deeper reasons that exist whether market relations are suppressed or are consistently used (of course, when they are suppressed there is a much greater degree of anti-social expenditure of labour to attain the incomes). We can be morally indignant over this fact and roundly curse it, but this does not change the matter.

True Marxists were always distinguished, however, by the fact that they took note of reality, studied its laws of development and acted in accord with the discovered laws. They acted on reality with instruments for speeding up the change in the direction indicated by these laws. But any endeavour to jump over a stage of development and to use moral instruments against economic laws must fail and become empty sermonizing.

If, at a given stage of development, raising the level of material, and thereby the cultural, needs of individuals is still the main direct incentive for performing work and if the socialist market relations

[1] See, for example the lead article in *Monthly Review* (editors Leo Huberman and Paul M. Sweezy) for March 1964, criticizing the ideas of socialist commodity relations and titled, "Peaceful Transition from Socialism to Capitalism?"

are one of the economic processes by which the socially necessary orientation of these incentives can be brought about and which cannot be replaced by any other economic process, then any moralizing must fail, which tries to replace market relations and endeavours by itself to correct the one-sided, anti-social orientation of labour brought about by the one-sided material incentives which arise when market relations are neglected. Moral action will be effective only if it works in harmony with the correctly oriented material incentives, if, in accord with these, it helps toward a socially necessary work performance.

Nor would it help to make a sophistical misrepresentation by opposing various adequate concepts as do some Chinese theoreticians who, on the one hand, recognize the necessity for differentiated rewards for work but, on the other hand, reject the principle of material interest and material incentives for their work.[1] But why should there then be any differentiated rewards or why any material rewards at all for labour, if people are not interested in them, and they are not an incentive for human labour? After all, according to this theory, it would be enough to inspire people with moral appeals to work and then, independent of this, give each one a certain equal amount of necessities of life. But it is clear as day that material consumption cannot yet be severed from the work performance, because it is the chief incentive, and without it social work would disappear. Therefore, differentiated material rewards are necessary in order for people to have the necessary interest in performing different socially necessary labour, and for them to have an incentive to prepare themselves for the kind of work needed — by attaining various complicated training, knowledge and information necessary for different kinds of skilled work. And it is necessary to link these individual rewards with the incomes of the enterprises realized in market relations, in order that there may be incentives for the objectively necessary expenditure of the labour of all for genuine social purposes. Material reward is, therefore, objectively still the specific incentive to work, whether or not this pleases some people.

[1] See, e.g., the speech of the deputy head of the propaganda department of the Central Committee of the Communist Party of China, Chou Yang on Oct. 26, 1963.

The distaste of dogmatists for using economic instruments in orienting the labour of people and their preference for moral stimuli comes, for the major part, from the fact that it is much easier and simpler to pronounce political appeals, slogans, moral entreaties, general criticism, and so on. It is much more difficult to create the proper economic incentives for certain activity or to make complex economic analyses to seek the true reasons for certain negative economic activities and, by changing these economic factors, to eliminate the negative activities. It is only in such action, based on analyses, that there can be really effective political leadership and a planned management of social and economic activity under socialism. General political and moral appeals will not change people's nature or interests, nor will they really overcome economic contradictions.

Of course, in order to successfully overcome socialist economic contradictions, it is not enough just to make more consistent use of socialist market relations, but it is necessary to improve all analyses, the method and technique of planning, methods of record-keeping, collecting and transmitting planning information, etc., as we have already mentioned at the beginning of this work. The reason we are not analysing these problems in more detail is not because they are less important, but because they are beyond the bounds of this work. But we can state flatly that no move toward more scientific planning methods would help — or would actually be scientific — if market relations are not used to solve conflicts of interest and to create a genuine interest in optimum development of production, not only in the central bodies, but also in the enterprises.

Everyone who has at heart the fate of socialist economics and is interested in its triumph in the historic competition with capitalism must, therefore, see that the main danger to it lies not in the system of management based on economics and in the utilization of all socialist economic incentives, but in the distorted, administrative, formal, bureaucratic system. Fighting against this and battling for the new, genuinely economic, form of socialist planned management is the main task of Marxist economic theory and practice.

BIBLIOGRAPHY

1. Auerhan J., Balda, Dráb, Říha, *Základní problémy automatizace* (Basic Problems of Automation), Prague 1963
2. Baran, Paul A., *K ekonomicheskoi teorii obshchestvennogo razvitiya*, Moscow 1960
3. Behrens F., *Arbeitsproduktivität, Lohnentwicklung und Rentabilität*, Berlin 1955
4. Behrens F., *Ware, Wert und Wertgesetz*, Berlin 1961
5. Belkin V. D., *Tseny yedinogo urovnia i ekonomicheskiye izmereniya na ikh osnovye*, Moscow 1963
6. Bettelheim Ch., *Ekonomika Francie po II. světové válce* (France's Economy After World War II), Prague 1958
7. Bettelheim Ch., *Zagadnienia teorii planowania* (Problems of the Theory of Planning), Warszawa 1959
8. Bollhagen P., *Die Dialektik von Produktivkräften und Produktionsverhältnissen als Grundlage der gesellschaftlichen Entwicklung*, Berlin 1960
9. Bor M. Z., *Ocherki po metodologii i metodikye planirovaniya*, Moscow 1964
10. Brus W., "Pienadz v gospodarce socjalistycznej" (Money in a Socialist Economy), Warszawa, *Ekonomista* No. 5/1963
    10.a) Brus W., *Modely socialistického hospodářství* (Models of Socialist Economy), Prague 1964
11. Cole G. D. H., *Principles of Economic Planning*, London 1935
12. Czikos-Nagy, *Problemy cenoobrazovanija i politika cen* (Problems of Creation of Prices and Politics of Prices), Moscow 1960
13. Čípek H., Tesař J., *Sovětští ekonomové o problémech řízení a plánování* (Soviet Economists on the Problems of Management and Planning), Prague 1958
14. Dyashenko V. R., "Sistema tsenoobraznykh faktorov i osnovy ikh klassifikatsii", *Voprosy ekonomiky* No. 2/1963

15. **Dobb M.**, *An Essay on Economic Growth and Planning*, London 1960
16. **Dobb M.**, *Ekonomicheski rast i slaborazvitiye strany*, Moscow 1964
17. **Dobb M., Bettelheim Ch.**, "Socialism and the Market", *Monthly Review* No. 4/1965
18. **Efimov A.**, "Nazrevshiye zadachi sovershenstvovaniya narodnokhoziaistvennogo planirovaniya", *Kommunist* No. 4/1964
19. **Egerland H.**, "Die Auswirkungen der Preistypen auf die Geldbeziehungen", *Deutsche Finanzwirtschaft* No. 11/1965
20. **Engels B.**, *Anti-Dühring*, Prague 1947
21. **Erdös P.**, "Tovarnoye proizvodstvo i stoimostniye kategorii v sotsialisticheskom khoziaistvye", *Voprosy ekonomiki* No. 5/1959
22. *Finantsy i kredit*, *Uchebnik*, Moscow 1962
23. **Fišer D.**, *Zákon plánovitého rozvoje národního hospodářství* (The Law of Planned Development of the National Economy), Prague 1961
24. **Flek J.**, "Počet pracovních sil v československém zemědělství a faktory ovlivňující jejich potřebu" (Size of Manpower in Czechoslovak Agriculture and the Factors Affecting the Need for it), *Zemědělská ekonomika* No. 9/1965
25. **Frisch R.**, "Generalities on Planning", *Industria* 1959
26. **Frisch R.**, *Norské modely finančních proudů* (Norwegian Models of Financial Trends), Economic Institute of ČSAV, Prague 1965
27. **Galbraith J. K.**, *Economic Development*, Cambridge 1964
28. **Gatovskiy L.**, "Rol pribyli v sotsialisticheskom khoziaistvye", *Kommunist* 1962
29. **Grabowski C.**, *Pienadz wspolczesnego kapitalizmu* (Money in a Capitalist Society), Warszawa 1963
30. **Grabowski C.**, *Problemy planowania gospodarczego we Francji* (Problems of Planning the Economy in France), Warszawa 1964
31. **Habr H.**, "Příspěvek k používání matematických metod v podmínkách socialistického plánovaného hospodářství" (On the Use of Mathematical Methods in a Socialist Economy), *Ekonomický časopis* No. 1/1962
32. **Haberler G.**, *Razvitiye i depressiya*, Moscow 1960
33. **Hackett J.**, *Economic Planning in France*, London 1963
34. **Halaxa V.**, *Intenzita práce za socialismu* (Intensity of Labour under Socialism), Prague 1963
35. **Harrod R. F.**, *Teorii ekonomicheskoi dinamiki*, Moscow 1959
36. **Hayek F. A.**, *Collectivist Economic Planning*, London 1935
37. **Heimann E.**, *History of Economic Doctrines: an Introduction to Economic Theory*, New York 1964
38. **Hilferding R.**, *Das Finanzkapital*, Vienna 1920
39. **Horvat B.**, "Drei Definitionen des Sozialprodukts", Belgrade, *Konjunkturpolitik* 1960
40. **Horvat B.**, *Samoupravleniye, tsentralism i planirovaniye*, Belgrade 1964
41. **Janza V.**, "Ceny, plán, řízení" (Prices, Plan, Management), *Nová Mysl*, Prague 1963

42. Jelic B., *Sistem planiranja u jugoslovenskoj privredi* (System of Planning in Yugoslav Industry), Belgrade 1962
43. Johnson H. G., *Money, Trade and Economic Growth*, Cambridge 1962
44. Kalecki M., *Náčrt teorie růstu socialistické ekonomiky* (Outline of the Theory of Growth of a Socialist Economy), Prague 1965
45. Kantorovitch L. V., *O použití soudobých matematických metod při určování ekonomické efektivnosti investic* (Use of Contemporary Mathematical Methods in Determining the Economic Effectiveness of Investments), Prague 1958
46. Karlík J., *Pokrokový charakter peněžního odměňování družstevníků* (The Progressive Nature of Money Wages for Cooperative Farmers), Prague 1961
47. Keynes J. M., *Ein Traktat über Währungsreform*, München 1924
48. Keynes J. M., *Vom Gelde*, München 1932
49. Keynes J. M., *Obecná teorie zaměstnanosti, úroku a peněz* (General Theory of Employment, Interest and Money), Prague 1963
50. Kocanda R., "Plánovité řízení a užitná hodnota" (Planned Management and Use Value), *Nová mysl* No. 8/1963
51. Kocman M., *Výrobní vztahy a řízení ekonomiky* (Production Relations and Management of the Economy), Prague 1963
52. Kodet Z., *Hmotná zainteresovanost v průmyslu ČSSR* (Material Interest in the Industry of the ČSSR), Prague 1963
53. Komenda B., *Ekonomická funkce a působení velkoobchodních cen* (Economic Function and Effect of Wholesale Prices), Prague 1964
54. Kondratshchev D. D., *Tsena i stoimost v sotsialisticheskom khoziaistvye*, Moscow 1963
55. Kornai J., *Overcentralization in Economic Administration*, Oxford 1962
56. Kosolapov N. I., *K voprosu i dialektikye tovara pri sotsialisme*, Moscow 1961
57. Kouba K., "Reálné podmínky pro nutná opatření" (Realistic Conditions for the Necessary Measures), *Hospodářské noviny* No. 11/1964
58. Kouba K., "Vztahy mezi plánovitým řízením, dynamikou a strukturou výroby" (Relations between Planned Management, Dynamics and Structure of Production), *Plánované hospodářství* No. 12/1964
59. Koslow G., *Die Warenproduktion und das Wertgesetz im Sozialismus*, Berlin 1961
60. Kožušník Č., *Vývoj cenové soustavy v ČSSR* (Trends in Price System in the ČSSR), Prague 1963
61. Krelle W., *Preistheorie*, Tübingen 1961
62. Kronrod J., *Peníze v socialistické společnosti* (Money in a Socialist Society), Prague 1956
63. Kronrod J., *O tovarnom proizvodstvye pri sotsialismye*, Moscow 1961
64. Kurskiy A.D., *Ekonomicheskiye osnovy narodnokhoziaistvennogo planirovaniya SSSR*, Moscow 1950
65. Kýn O., Pelikán P., "Kybernetika a řízení národního hospodářství" (Cybernetics and Governing the National Economy), *Plánované hospodářství* No. 16/1963
65a) Kýn O., "Vědecké základy cenové politiky" (Scientific Fundaments of Price Policy), *Nová Mysl* No. 7/1963

66. Lange O., *Pisma ekonomiczne i spoleczne* 1930—1960 (Economic and Social Writings 1930–1960), Warszawa 1961

67. Lange O., *Entwicklungstendenzen der modernen Wirtschaft und Gesellschaft*, Vienna 1964

68. Lenin V. I., *Sebrané spisy* (Collected Writings), Vol. 1–38, Prague

69. Lerner A. P., "Statics and Dynamics in Socialist Economics", *Economic Journal*, June 1937

70. Lerner A. P., *The Principles of Control*, New York 1964

71. Lewis W. A., *The Principles of Economic Planning*, London 1961

72. Liberman E., "Plan, pribyl, premiya", *Ekonomicheskaya Gazeta* No. 46/1962

73. Liberman E., "Plan priamiye sviazy i rentabelnost", *Pravda* No. 325/1965

74. Liberman E., "Rentabelnost sotsialisticheskikh predpriyatii", *Ekonomicheskaya Gazeta* No. 51/1965

75. Filip M., "Nekotoriye voprosy tovaroobrashcheniya SSSR v sovremennom etapye", *Voprosy ekonomiki* No. 11/1959

76. Livšic A., "K otázce dvojakého charakteru práce za socialismu" (On the Question of the Dual Nature of Labour under Socialism), *Politická ekonomie* No. 4/1957

77. Maier W., Mann H., "Zu theoretischen Problemen der Schaffung sozialistischer Weltmarktpreise", *Wissenschaftliche Zeitschrift* No. 4/1964

78. Malischev I. S., *Obshchestvennyi uchet truda i tsena pri sotsializmye*, Moscow 1960

79. Mujzel J., *Stosunki towarowe v gospodarce socjalistycznej* (Commodity Relations in a Socialist Economy), Warszawa 1963

80. Margolin N. S., *Finanční plánování SSSR* (Financial Planning in the USSR), Prague 1963

81. Marshall A., *Money, Credit, Commerce*, New York 1960

82. Marx K., *Grundrisse der Kritik der politischen Ökonomie*, Berlin 1953

83. Marx K., *Kapitál* I, II, III/1,2, Prague

84. Marx K., Engels B., *Sebrané spisy* (Collected Writings), 1–14, Prague

85. Massé P., "The French Plan and Economic Theory", *Econometrica* No. 2/1965

86. Matho F., *Ware-Geld-Beziehungen im neuen ökonomischen System*, Berlin 1965

87. Matviyeyev B., *Organizatsiya planirovaniya narodnogo khoziaistva SSSR*, Moscow 1959

88. Meade J. E., *Planning and the Price Mechanism*, London 1949

89. Meade J. E., *Trade and Welfare*, London 1955

90. Mendelson A., *Stoimost i tsena*, Moscow 1963

91. Mervart J., *K otázce cen na světovém socialistickém trhu* (On the Question of Prices in the World Socialist Market), Prague 1958

92. Milke H., *Planung und Leitung der Volkswirtschaft*, Berlin 1964

93. Minc B., *Úvod do plánování národního hospodářství* (Introduction to the Planning of the National Economy), Prague 1952

94. Minc B., *Politicheskaya ekonomiya sotsializma*, Moscow 1965

95. Mises L., "Die Wirtschaftsrechnung im sozialistischen Gemeinwesen", *Archiv für Sozialwissenschaften*, April 1920

96. Myrdal G., *Mirovaya ekonomika*, Moscow 1958
97. Němčinov V. S., *Ekonomichesko-matematicheskiye metody i modely*, Moscow 1962
98. Němčinov V. S., *O dalším zdokonalování plánování a řízení národního hospodářství* (The Further Improvement of Planning and Management of the National Economy), Prague 1964
99. Němčinov V. S., "Modely narodnokhoziaistvennogo planirovaniya", *Voprosy ekonomiki* No. 7/1964
100. Novoshilov V., "Voprosy razvitiya demokraticheskogo centralizma v upravlenii sotsialisticheskim khoziaistvom", *Raboty kafedr obshchetvennykh nauk* No. 24/1958, Moscow
101. Oliva F., "Zboží za socialismu" (Commodities under Socialism), *Plánované hospodářství* No. 3/1958
102. Oliva F., "Zbožní výroba za socialismu" (Commodity Production under Socialism), *Politická ekonomie* No. 8/1959
103. Ostrovitiyanov K., "Zbožní výroba a zákon hodnoty za socialismu" (Commodity Production and the Law of Value under Socialism), *Politická ekonomie* No. 1/1958
104. Ostrovitiyanov K., "Stroitel'stvo kommunizma i tovarnoye proizvodstvo", *Voprosy ekonomiki* No. 10/1961
105. Pajestka J., *Plánování národního hospodářství* (Planning the National Economy), Prague 1955
106. Petrakov M. I., *Rentabelnost i tsena*, Moscow 1964
107. Petrović M., *Politička ekonomija* (Political Economy), Belgrade 1958
108. Pigon A. C., *Socialism versus Capitalism*, London 1944
109. *Politická ekonomie* (Political Economy), učebnice (textbook), překlad z ruštiny (translated from Russian), Prague 1963
110. Preobrazhensky E., *The New Economics*, Oxford 1965
111. Reinhold O., "O nové ekonomické soustavě plánování a řízení národního hospodářství v NDR" (The Economic System of Planning and Management of the National Economy of the GDR), *Politická ekonomie* No. 1/1964
112. Robinson J., *An Essay on Marxist Economics*, London 1942
113. Rudolph J., "Die Ausnutzung des Gesetzes der Preisbildung im neuen ökonomischen System der Planung und Leitung der Volkswirtschaft", *Wirtschaftswissenschaft* 1963
114. Samuelson P. A., *Volkswirtschaftslehre*, Köln 1955
115. Samuelson P. A., *Foundations of Economic Analysis*, Cambridge 1963
116. *Sborník 20 let rozvoje ČSSR* (Twenty Years of Development of the ČSSR), Prague 1965
117. *Fundamentale Fragen künftiger Währungspolitik*, Basel 1965
118. *Planung in der Marktwirtschaft*, Stuttgart 1964
119. Schlessinger R., *Theorie der Geld- und Kreditwirtschaft*, Leipzig 1914
120. Schlessinger R., "Historical and Social Conditions of Planning", *Economics of Planning* No. 1–2/1965

121. Schneider E., "Über ein Problem der Preistheorie", *Weltwirtschaftliches Archiv* 1963

122. Schumpeter J. A., "Das Sozialprodukt und die Rechenpfennige. Glossen und Beiträge zur Geldtheorie von heute", *Aufsätze zur ökonomischen Theorie*, Tübingen 1952

123. Sorokin G., *Socialistické plánování – zákon rozvoje sovětské ekonomiky* (Socialist Planning—the Law of Development of the Soviet Economy), Prague 1951

124. Sorokin G., *Planirovaniye narodnogo khoziaistva SSSR*, Moscow 1961

125. Stalin J. V., *Otázky leninismu* (Problems of Leninism), Prague 1954

126. Stalin J. V., *Spisy* (Writings), 1 – 13, Prague

127. Stalin J. V., *Ekonomické problémy socialismu v SSSR* (Economic Problems of Socialism in the USSR), Prague 1952

128. *Statistické informace* (Statistical Information), ÚKLKS, No. 152, Prague 1962

129. *Statistické přehledy Státního úřadu statistického* (Statistical Surveys of the State Statistical Office), Prague 1964

130. *Statistické ročenky* (Statistical Yearbooks), 1955 – 1965, Prague

131. *Statistický obzor* (Statistical Horizon), No. 6/1961, Prague

132. Strumilin S., *Planirovaniye v SSSR*, Moscow 1957

133. Strumilin S., *Otázky socialismu a komunismu v SSSR* (Problems of Socialism and Communism in the USSR), Prague 1963

134. Sweezy P. M., "Economic Planning", *Monthly Review*, May 1960

135. Šik O., *Ekonomika, zájmy, politika* (Economics, Interests, Politics), Prague 1962

136. Taylor F. M., "The Guidance of Production in a Socialist State", *American Economic Review*, March 1929

137. Tinbergen J., *Central Planning*, New Haven 1964

138. Tureckiyi Sh. J., *Planirovaniye i problem balantsa narodnokhoziaistva*, Moscow 1961

139. Turek O., "Jak tedy centrálně plánovat" (How to Plan Centrally), *Hospodářské noviny* No. 15/1964

140. Ulbricht W., *Das neue ökonomische System der Planung und Leitung der Volkswirtschaft in der Praxis*, Berlin 1963

141. Vejvoda J., "K diskusi o zbožní výrobě za socialismu" (Discussions on Commodity Production under Socialism), *Plánované hospodářství* No. 9/1958

142. Vejvoda J., "Zákonitosti tvorby cen ve státním socialistickém sektoru" (The Laws of Price Formation in the State Socialist Sector), *Politická ekonomie* No. 4/1959

143. Vejvoda J., *Zbožní výroba ve státním socialistickém sektoru* (Commodity Production in the State Socialist Sector), Prague 1960

144. Villard H. H., *Monetary Theory*, Homewood 1964

145. Wicksell K., *Geldzins und Güterpreise*, 1898

146. Wunderlich W., "Probleme der Preisplanung", *Deutsche Finanzwirtschaft* No. 12/1965

GLOSSARY

Capital, constant. Equipment and materials employed in production. May refer to either capital stocks or flows, in either real terms or value terms (in Marx's notation – c). When seen as flows denotes physical-term inputs, or cost-component of materials and fixed-capital stock used up in production.

Capital, variable. Wage-bill, or wage-cost component (Marx's – v).

Capital accumulation. Net capital formation: invested part of surplus value ("accumulation fund"), the remainder forming part of the "consumption fund". The rate of capital accumulation broadly corresponds to the rate of net investment.

Commodity-money relations. Market relations. System of exchange economy. Under it goods become commodities.

Costs, reproduction. Production costs on a continuing basis, that is: labour and material inputs, plus cost of inventories, depreciation, and cost of incompleted investments.

Depreciation of fixed capital-stock, physical and moral. Moral denotes depreciation through obsolescence.

Funds, basic. Fixed assets.

Funds, circulating. Capital invested in raw materials, finished and semifinished goods, cash, and costs of power, but not wages.

Funds, production, or production assets. Fixed assets plus inventories.

Funds, wage and bonus. Total employee compensation = the wage fund (wages and salaries paid according to centrally set wages and bonus scales) plus fund for bonuses (based on enterprise gross profits).

Income, national. Net material product (net of depreciation of capital stock) generated in what is treated as the productive sphere of an economy. Main difference between this concept and that corresponding to Western conventions is the exclusion from the former of services defined as non-productive.

371

Income, sales = total cash receipts, income from sales and possibly from subsidies.

Income, gross. Net value added by production or total cash receipts minus material costs and amortization.

Income, enterprise. Gross income minus taxes.

Labour, living. Direct input of labour (labour-time) in production, labour power.

Labour, materialized. "Stored-up", "congealed", "past labour", labour embodied in all previous stages of production especially in means of production.

Labour, socially necessary. Labour necessary to produce a commodity under normal conditions of production, i.e. with technology and skills prevailing in the given society.

Product, social. Aggregate of all material use values produced in a given period, including intermediate products, but excluding most services like health and education.

Production, material. Production of commodities and productive services (trade, transport).

Profits, gross. Net income before taxes = gross income minus basic wage funds.

Profits, net. Gross profits after taxes.

Reproduction, simple. Stationary economy: one characterized by full replacement of inputs and zero capital formation.

Reproduction, expanded. Economic growth: a system in which output of capital goods and materials exceeds their consumption in production.

Taxes. Enterprise payments to the State = all Corporate taxes, including:
  Payments based on production assets, that is on fixed assets and on inventories;
  Basic payment, assessed on gross income after payment of production assets tax;
  Payment based on wages, assessed on increases in average wages and employment.

Value, use. A good's intrinsic property of satisfying needs.

Value. Exchange value conceived as created in the system of social production: it is an "objective category" corresponding to socially necessary labour embodied in a commodity.

INDEX

For Product Safety Concerns and Information please contact our EU
representative GPSR@taylorandfrancis.com
Taylor & Francis Verlag GmbH, Kaufingerstraße 24, 80331 München, Germany

www.ingramcontent.com/pod-product-compliance
Ingram Content Group UK Ltd.
Pitfield, Milton Keynes, MK11 3LW, UK
UKHW020936180425
457613UK00019B/416